THE UNIVERSAL DECLARATION OF HUMAN RIGHTS: FIFTY YEARS AND BEYOND

Edited by

Yael Danieli

Elsa Stamatopoulou

Clarence J. Dias

Foreword by

Kofi A. Annan
Secretary-General of the United Nations

Epilogue by

Mary Robinson
United Nations High Commissioner for Human Rights

Published for and on behalf of the United Nations

BAYWOOD PUBLISHING COMPANY, INC.
AMITYVILLE, NEW YORK

Published for and on behalf of the United Nations by Baywood Publishing Company, Inc., Amityville, New York.

The views expressed in this book are those of the authors and do not necessarily reflect the views of the United Nations.

Cover designed by Alfredo Jaar, incorporating detail of *Waiting*, 1998 from The Rwanda Project 1994-1998

Library of Congress Catalog Number: 98-39685

ISBN: 0-89503-192-2 (cloth)

Library of Congress Cataloging-in-Publication Data

The Universal Declaration of Human Rights : fifty years and beyond /
    edited by Yael Danieli, Elsa Stamatopoulou, Clarence J. Dias ;
    foreword by Kofi A. Annan ; epilogue by Mary Robinson.
        p.   cm.
    Includes bibliographical references.
    ISBN 0-89503-192-2 (cloth)
    1. Human rights.   2. United Nations.   General Assembly.   Universal
Declaration of Human Rights.   I. Danieli, Yael.   II. Stamatopoulou,
Elsa, 1951-   .   III. Dias, C. J. (Clarence J.)
    K3240.6.U56   1998
    341.4′81 - - dc21   98-39685
                                                                                 CIP

To the victim/survivors of human rights violations
and to the defenders of human rights.

Foreword

Kofi A. Annan

Secretary-General of the United Nations

The Universal Declaration of Human Rights is the product of the untiring efforts and resolute will of men and women from all parts of the world. Today, the principles enshrined in the Declaration are the yardstick by which we measure human progress. They lie at the heart of all that the United Nations aspires to achieve in its global mission of peace and development.

All people share a desire to live free from the horrors of violence, famine, disease, torture, and discrimination. Human rights are foreign to no culture and intrinsic to all nations. They belong not to a chosen few, but to all people. It is this universality that endows human rights with the power to cross any border and defy any force. Human rights are also indivisible; one cannot pick and choose among them, ignoring some while insisting on others. Only as rights equally applied can they be rights universally accepted.

Since its adoption in 1948, the Universal Declaration has extended its reach far and wide. It has served as a model for national constitutions and laws. Its provisions have supplied countless guidelines for national courts, parliaments, governments, lawyers and other professionals, and non-governmental organizations throughout the world. Still, there remains a gap between laws on the books and facts on the ground. Every day, hundreds of millions of people experience some serious violation of their human rights.

Therein lies our challenge. We cannot afford indifference, individually or collectively. If we do not speak out and act, today and every day when our conscience is challenged by inhumanity and intolerance, we will not have done our duty to ourselves or to succeeding generations. Half a century after the adoption of the Universal Declaration, it is time to embark on a new stage in our journey to bring its enduring message to life for all people, as this book aims to do.

Reflections by Nobel Laureates on the Occasion of the Fiftieth Anniversary of the Universal Declaration of Human Rights

The following four statements were contributed by Nobel Laureates at the invitation of Kofi A. Annan Secretary-General of the United Nations on the occasion of the fiftieth anniversary of the Universal Declaration of Human Rights.

Nadine Gordimer
Nobel Laureate in Literature (1991)

Everyone who ponders the Universal Declaration of Human Rights inevitably will give particular attention to those Articles that pertain to circumstances with which he or she is personally involved. As a writer, Article 19 has a special significance for me. Freedom of expression is the oxygen of writers' creativity. But this is not a professional privilege that seeks exclusive protection: literature is one of the most enduring means by which ideas cross frontiers and become universal, but freedom of expression, to impart and receive information 'through any media' is the first condition of freedom in civilized governance. Suppression by censorship, banning, imprisonment, and even edicts of death continue to exist in many countries, imposed by both secular and religious authorities. Article 19 established incontrovertably these means as a primary contravention of everyone's birthright to read, to listen, to regard, and speak out.

Article 26 is fundamental to Article 19; its Clauses 1 and 2, "Everyone has the right to education," "Education shall be directed to the full development of the human personality." Freedom of expression is an empty phrase unless education equips every individual with freedom of the word, the ability to read and write. No other form of expression, oral or visual, can compensate for deprivation of these basic skills in human intercourse, understanding, and the development of the intellect. Although the right to literacy surely is implied in Article 26, it is not specifically named. I believe it ought to be. This Article brings the hope of justice to the millions excluded—by ignorance which is no fault of their own—from participation and benefit in the making of our world.

For me, the most important Article of the Universal Declaration of Human Rights has no number, is not an Article at all. It is a paragraph of the Preamble. "Whereas it is essential, if man is not to be compelled to have recourse, as a last resort, to *rebellion against tyranny and oppression,* that human rights should be protected by the rule of law." (My italics.)

I have lived through a time in my own country, South Africa, when this "last resort" compelled the majority of the people to turn to rebellion, first in the form of civil disobedience and passive resistance and finally in the form of armed struggle, against tyranny and oppression that denied them human rights. I have seen how to be compelled to take this last resort not only brings tragic self-sacrifice and suffering to those who assume the burden, even though freedom is finally achieved as a result, but has long-term consequences which threaten the democracy so attained.

When people are deprived over years of any recourse to the provisions of civil society as a means of seeking redress for their material and spiritual deprivations, they *lose the faculty* of using the law when, at last, such recourse is open to them. The result of this conditioning now is fashionably called "the culture of violence"; an oxymoron, for culture implies enlightenment, an aim toward attaining the fullness of life, not its destruction. The tactics of a desperate liberation struggle are all that many people know how to employ. In my country, students dissatisfied with the performance of their teachers retaliated by destroying the equipment of their own schools. Taxi-bus owners, in dispute over transport routes each considers his exclusively, attack one another at gun-point. Workers forcibly occupy managers' offices and destroy plant as protest against unsatisfactory working conditions and low pay. It takes time and education in and understanding of, the protection of human rights, for a formerly oppressed people to learn to use this protection through the means provided, in civil societies, by the law. Students had no structures to deal with their grievances before. The means of settling disputes by forming a code for the transport industry was not open to, offered no peaceful resolution to those who had no civil rights of any kind. The denial of the right to form trade unions, over many years, meant that workers' violent reactions to their problems were the only ones that brought results in the political liberation struggle. The paths by which people have the right to be protected by the rule of law, not persecuted by its wrongful application, have to be learned. It is in this that the Universal Declaration of Human Rights is, and shall remain, the essential document, the touchstone, the creed of humanity that surely sums up all other creeds directing human behavior, if we are to occupy this world together now and in the 21st century.

M F Perutz
Nobel Laureate in Chemistry (1962)

This Declaration and the enshrinement of its essential rights international law is one of the great achievements of our civilization. In a large part, we owe their formulation to the great jurist Hersch Lauterpacht, professor of international law in the University of Cambridge from 1937 to 1954. In 1945 he published a seminal book, *An International Bill of the Rights of Man,* which became the basis of much that is in the United Nations Declaration and the Conventions that followed it.

According to him,

> The idea of the inherent rights of man, ultimately superior to the state itself, is the continuous thread in the historical pattern of legal and political thought. In antiquity, their substance has been a denial of the absoluteness of the State and its unconditional claim to obedience; the assertion of the value and freedom of the individual as against the State; the view that the power of the State and of its ruler is derived ultimately from the assent of those who compose the political community; the insistence that there are limits to the power of the State to interfere with man; the right to do what he considers his duty [1].

Certain governments justify their infringements of Human Rights by describing such notions as expressions of Western European culture, foreign and inapplicable to their own countries, but the subjects of these governments do not share that view, because, as Lauterpacht pointed out, the Rights are inherent to men *and women* everywhere, regardless of tradition or creed.

Article 1 of the UN Declaration states that "All human beings are born free and equal in dignity and rights," but in only a small part of the world does this apply to women.

In 1868 the English philosopher, John Stuart Mill, anticipated the Declaration when he wrote in an essay "On the Subjection of Women":

> A person should be free to do as he likes in his own concerns but he ought not to be free to do so as he likes in acting for another, under the pretext that the affairs of the other are his own affairs. This obligation is almost entirely disregarded in the case of the family relations, a case, in its direct influence on human happiness, more important than all others taken together. The almost despotic power of husbands over wives needs not be enlarged upon here, because nothing more is needed for the complete removal of the evil, than that wives should have the same rights, and should receive the protection of law in the same manner, as all other persons; and because, on this subject, the defenders of established injustice do not avail themselves of the plea of liberty, but stand forth openly as the champions of power [2].

Yet women are still subject to "the despotic power of husbands" and deprived of any rights in most of the world today.

The most glaring violations of the Declaration concern Article 5 which states that "no one shall be subject to torture or to cruel, inhuman or degrading treatment." Yet torture is still practiced in thirty-nine countries, covering most of the world's population, including thirteen countries which signed the Convention Against Torture of 1984. Far too few speak out against that barbaric practice which is a blot on our civilization.

What is needed in the next century above all is the will to put the UN Declaration of Human Rights into practice, not in just a few countries, but throughout the world, to make it truly universal.

REFERENCES

1. H. Lauterpacht, *International Law and Human Rights*, Stevens and Son Ltd., London, p. 80, 1950.
2. J. S. Mill, *On Liberty and other Writings*, Cambridge University Press, Cambridge, p. 105, 1989.

John Polanyi
Nobel Laureate in Chemistry (1986)

The Universal Declaration of Human Rights, adopted by the General Assembly of the United Nations on December 10th, 1948, will endure as one of the great documents of human history. The Declaration makes sweeping claims for the rights of each individual, and makes them, for the first time, on behalf of all humanity.

Sensing the historic nature of the occasion, the General Assembly adopted the Declaration without dissent. No nation wished to place itself in opposition to the tide of history, though many may have said, with St. Augustine, "God make us good, but not yet." Nonetheless, such is the moral force of this Declaration that it is in the process of changing the world.

The Declaration begins by spelling out the fundamental trinity of rights: that to life, which is paramount; that to liberty, which gives life meaning; and that to security, which permits the enjoyment of life. The recognition of these rights is not new. They have been in the process of definition for centuries. What makes the Universal Declaration an epochal document, exceeding in importance, for example, the Magna Carta of 1215, is first of all its global impetus, and secondly the breadth of its claims.

What we have here is a commitment to a new Social Contract, binding on all the governments of the world. Through its thirty "articles" all nations commit themselves to observe equality before the law, to submit to the rule of law, to foster freedom of speech and assembly, to validate their own authority through free elections with universal franchise, and (strikingly) to recognize the right of all to adequate food, shelter, health care, education, and employment.

These thirty articles, having been written by human beings at a particular juncture in history, will, eventually, prove to be incomplete. But they will stand forever as a declaration of principle that is both civilized and visionary.

In order to understand the origins of this Declaration we must look back at least to the start of the century. This was to be the century of science. Science, it seemed, held the key to an age of ease and plenty. And for many that proved to be the case. But for still more, it did not. That is because technology does not guarantee equity nor even elementary decency.

On the contrary, the absence of respect for human rights science and its offspring technology have been used in this century as brutal instruments for oppression. It was precisely in order to prevent a repetition of these horrors that the Universal Declaration was born. "We must beware," Winston Churchill warned, "lest the Stone Age return upon the gleaming wings of science."

However, such warnings overlook a vital element of hope that lies at the heart of modern science. The respect for human rights, essential if we are to use technology wisely, is not something alien that must be grafted onto science. On the contrary, it is integral to science, as also to scholarship in general.

Political movements that have denied this, donning the mantle of science in order to legitimize their fanatical aims, have found that they quickly killed science. For science must breathe the oxygen of freedom. This is because the scientific orthodoxy of today arises from the heterodoxy of yesterday. Science exists moreover, only as a journey toward truth. Stifle dissent, and you end that journey.

The scientific and scholarly community is marked by the belief that the truth is to be found in all; none can claim it as their monopoly. It is no surprise, therefore, that from Linus Pauling to Andrei Sakharov, from Albert Einstein to Fang Lizhi, and from Bertrand Russell to Vaclav Havel, the most notable champions of human rights over the past half-century have included scientists and scholars. But for them, the Universal Declaration might have become, rather than a symbol of hope, an object of mockery.

But this offers no ground for complacency. There should be far more scientists and scholars standing in opposition to tyranny. My community belongs to what, today, we call the "NGOs": the Non-Governmental Organizations. The power and hence the responsibility of NGOs is today apparent. Scientists and scholars should constitute themselves as an international NGO of exceptional authority.

For scholarship, if it is to be scholarship, requires, in addition to liberty, that the truth take precedence over all sectarian interests—including self-interest. The moral authority that derives from this circumstance is a precious asset. It should be used to support the movement on which all our hopes for the future depend; the movement toward peace based on respect for the individual, whose manifesto is the Universal Declaration of Human Rights.

The progress made toward the realization of the principles of the Universal Declaration, while falling tragically short of the stated objectives, far exceeds what the most optimistic of its signatories would have thought possible. In nation after nation democracy has taken the place of autocracy. A new sense of shared international responsibility is unmistakable in the voices of the United Nations and its agencies, as well as in the civil society of thousands of supra national NGOs.

In challenging my own NGO, the community of scientists, to a greater degree of awareness and activism, I am heeding a passage in the Universal Declaration which I believe must figure more largely in the half-century to come. I refer to the phrase in Article 29 that, following a long litany of rights, refers to the individual's obligation to act in support of those rights. The time has come to underscore the fact that our and others' rights are contingent on our willingness to assert and defend them.

Archbishop Desmond Tutu
Nobel Peace Laureate (1984)

I have, like many other black South Africans, come out of a period of the most awful repression and injustice when we suffered under the pernicious system of apartheid which has been rightly condemned as a crime against humanity. In all that period of apartheid's ghastly oppression we were made to suffer for something we could do nothing about—our race. Apartheid claimed that what imbued anyone with worth was actually a biological irrelevance—the color of one's skin and, since by definition, not all possessed this prized attribute as it was not a universal phenomenon, there were those, the elite, the select, who would enjoy all sorts of rights and privileges and all others would be consigned to the outer darkness.

During this awful time struggling against apartheid we were inspired by the noble sentiments contained in the Universal Declaration of Human Rights. In many ways the Declaration became a subversive instrument available to overturn injustice, oppression, racism and unfair discrimination. It told us what our oppressors were at great pains to deny that we had fundamental, inalienable rights that were not in the gift of some benevolent early ruler who could grant or withhold them as the whim moved him. No, these rights were God-given, there simply and solely because we were human beings. They were universal—everyone, just everyone whoever they might be, whether rich or poor, learned or ignorant, beautiful or ugly, black or white, man or woman by the fact of being a human being had these rights. As a Christian I would add that each person was of infinite value because everyone had been created in the image of God. Each one was a God carrier and to treat any such person as if they were less than this was blasphemous, a spitting in the face of God.

I know we were inspired in our fight against apartheid to struggle for a dispensation that would see the Universal Declaration of Human Rights come into its own, when human rights would be cultivated, upheld, and revered. And that has come in the new democratic dispensation that has seen a Nelson Mandela installed as South Africa's first democratically elected President. The Declaration has been an inspiration that has helped to subvert injustice and oppression. It has helped to open our eyes to the intrinsic and infinite worth of every single person.

But it has also served as a bearer of ideals, a setter of standards according to which governments can be judged. It has established ideals after which we must forever be straining and against which emerging and long established regimes can be measured, and when they fall short as they alas so frequently do, then the Declaration can be held up before them to inspire them to greater efforts, urging them to become more caring, more gentle, more compassionate, more people friendly.

We who have suffered under injustice where the most fundamental rights were flagrantly violated give thanks for the existence of this Universal Declaration of

Human Rights for serving to inspire us, to be subversive of that injustice and oppression. We must all, everywhere, commit ourselves to work for an ordering of society where the contents of the Declaration are embodied and also to remain forever vigilant against a violation of those rights.

May the day come when people everywhere will enjoy the rights enshrined in the Declaration when war will be no more and universal peace and justice will prevail. When the lion will lie with the lamb and we will have beaten our swords into ploughshares and hunger, poverty and ignorance will have been eradicated and children can play safely and happily again.

Is this just Utopia? No, the Universal Declaration of Human Rights says it is attainable and, after all, the world defeated apartheid and now South Africa is a democracy.

Acknowledgments

First and foremost, we thank the contributors who brought to the book broad expertise and rich experience, and those who rendered their personal experiences and wisdom through their voices.

We are deeply honored that Kofi Annan, Secretary-General of the United Nations, contributed the Foreword, and Mary Robinson, United Nations High Commissioner for Human Rights, contributed the Epilogue.

Alfredo Jaar generously designed the cover of the book.

Joe Sills reviewed and commented on the entire book and provided constant support throughout the process. Vladimir Lubomudrov of the External Publications Unit of the UN's Department of Public Information helped navigate the bureaucratic shoals.

We thank John Lee, Chairman of the Washington Coalition for Comfort Women Issues, for interviewing, collating, and translating Kim, Yoon Shim's statement; the Consulate of Croatia in New York City for translating Biba Metikos's statement; and Jo Becker, Advocacy Director, Children Rights Division of Human Rights Watch for providing the voices of child soldiers.

We recognize Stuart Cohen for once again taking on the challenge, and the staff of Baywood Publishing Company, especially our superb editor, Bobbi Olszewski. We greatly appreciate the friendship of all those who participated in this labor of love which is a tribute to the Universal Declaration of Human Rights and its progeny on its Fiftieth Anniversary.

Table of Contents

PART III. HUMAN RIGHTS OF SPECIFIC GROUPS: CONCEPTUAL AND INSTITUTIONAL DEVELOPMENT

PART IV. CREATING A CULTURE OF HUMAN RIGHTS

PART V.   INTERFACE BETWEEN GLOBAL AND REGIONAL PROTECTION AND PROMOTION OF HUMAN RIGHTS

PART VI.   THE TRAUMA OF HUMAN RIGHTS DENIAL AND VIOLATION

PART VII.   MAINSTREAMING HUMAN RIGHTS

Part I

Introduction

Voices

A Tribute to Human Rights

Elie Wiesel

The defense of human rights has, in the last fifty years, become a kind of worldwide secular religion. It has attracted millions of members and sympathizers. It is often non-political, although the context of its endeavors is. Its mission is to defend victims of injustice and despair, and in the field of therapy to heal those whose mind and soul have been mutilated, wherever they exist and whoever they are. Young and old, white or black, well-established citizens or recently arrived refugees: let their rights as human beings be violated, and there will always be a person, a group who will rise to their defense.

Why so late? Were there no political prisoners, oppressed men and women of conscience, persecuted ethnic or religious communities anywhere before 1948? Granted, here and there small groups of intellectuals and political activists did their best to alert public opinion to large-scale human disasters, but their scope was limited as was their concrete impact on decision makers.

Today, things have changed. Thanks to the quick pace of the information flow, people's awareness has been heightened. Today the concern for human rights is part of government policy in many lands, in ours above all. Statesmen, high officials, and diplomats serve as moral watchmen, each in his or her specific area of responsibility. They make it their business to know and let other people know each time an opposition member is punished, a journalist stifled, a prisoner tortured. Social or political persecution is no longer shrouded in mystery. Crimes against humanity are part of the public domain. Protests are then being issued, sanctions envisaged.

But even if the protests bear no fruit, they are not useless; they serve as a message to the victims: you will not be abandoned, you have not been forgotten. For the prisoner, nothing is more important. Faced with the tormentor's power to intimidate, blackmail, and terrorize, the prisoner is afraid only of being repudiated by his or her friends, given up by society.

In this respect, the battle must continue. Read reports by our own government and by Amnesty International, Helsinki Watch, or the various Lawyer's committees, and you will ascertain—not without sadness—that there are still prisoners of conscience in the world, and that torture is still being used in many places.

And so—the victims still need allies and friends such as the editors and authors whose writings are to be found in this volume. In defending them, we declare that human rights include not only the right to freedom and dignity, but the right to solidarity.

Introduction

In the fifty years since the adoption of the Universal Declaration of Human Rights, international action has moved from human rights standard-setting and promotion to the protection of human rights through the development of a nexus of global, regional, and national mechanisms. Clear connections have been made between human rights and correlative duties to respect, protect, promote, and fulfill human rights. The interrelatedness, interdependence, and indivisibility of civil, cultural, economic, political, and social rights has been recognized. The challenge is now to enter what United Nations Secretary-General Kofi Annan has called "an age of prevention,"[1] including prevention of human rights violations that, in many cases, spur violent conflicts and tragic devastation.

Although the focus of the international human rights machinery has been the human person, states have been slow and often reluctant to address the plight of those directly affected, namely the victim/survivors of human rights violations. Seen in historical perspective, the late recognition of the possibility of direct access of the victim to international bodies in order "to bring the state to trial," should be viewed in the context of decades of Cold War geopolitics and reticence by governments to allow UN mechanisms of control to come into effect [1]. Overpoliticization of human rights debates has often resulted, not only in inaction or ineffective action, but even when taken, such action has mainly focused on condemning culprit governments, and has barely extended to issues of reparation, including restitution, compensation, and assistance to and rehabilitation of those who have suffered. De-facing the "human" out of "human rights" has often been a convenient way of bluntly absorbing this agenda under ultimate political expediencies of governments. Although the UN has prepared studies and adopted relevant standards, still missing from the international human rights agenda is concern with remediation addressed in and of its own right.

---

[1] United Nations Secretary-General's address to the UN Commission on Human Rights, at its 54th session, on the occasion of the commemoration of the Fiftieth Anniversary of the Universal Declaration of Human rights, 9 March 1998, Geneva, Switzerland.

Effective remediation would serve as a deterrent as well, also insofar as sanctions against and punishment of violators are integral elements of remediation, thus contributing considerably to both prevention and protection. Impunity for perpetrators and lack of remedial measures for victims/survivors are two sides of the same coin. Justice must include both a formal and fair judicial process for all concerned and the implementation of relevant court decisions as well as reparation in *all* its dimensions, including the moral, to victims by governments and society as a whole. The attainment of justice through the accountability of the perpetrators and the process of redress are all critical to healing for victims [2].

It is undeniable that the human rights protection efforts by the United Nations and other intergovernmental organizations have achieved results, saved lives, and averted abuses, even if the number of successes has been extremely modest by comparison to all those in need of help. There are many whose cases have not been brought before the international human rights bodies, due to lack of information about available human rights mechanisms, or, even worse, because of the sheer impossibility of people's trapped voices to reach the outside world.

The global communications revolution has certainly helped strengthen international solidarity campaigns and urgent action appeals against human rights violations. It has, however, also prompted a culture of greed, over-consumption, and, through the Internet and otherwise, a culture that turns people, especially women, children, and migrant workers, into commodities.

An earlier volume, "International Responses to Traumatic Stress," [3] commemorating the 50th anniversary of the United Nations, broadly outlined how the UN system as a whole, and related NGOs, have responded to grave and widespread traumatizing events. This volume concentrates specifically on the international human rights system and evaluates this system critically from the point of view of whether it has reached the people by protecting individual human beings or averting their victimization.

The focus on victims or potential victims, implicit or explicit, in the chapters of the book, does not imply viewing as passive those who have suffered from human rights violations. As stated by the High Commissioner for Human Rights, Mary Robinson, in the Epilogue to this volume, the language of human rights is empowering. For example, while in the past the term "vulnerable groups" was common, the World Conference on Human Rights in 1993 developed the term "groups rendered vulnerable" and, today, even the latter term is used with discomfort, lest it convey a sense of passivity.

Since the adoption of the Universal Declaration of Human Rights, the issue of special rights for special groups continues to be raised. The norms of the Declaration are clearly universally applicable, but the particular problems faced by women, children, indigenous peoples, the disabled—to mention but a few—have prompted governments and, often concerned groups themselves, to promote the adoption of specialized standards and the establishment of specialized mechanisms. This has occasionally resulted in a certain, even if unwanted, marginalization of such groups instead of bringing them into the mainstream of the human rights regime. Women's human rights are a case in point. Historic developments over the past fifty years have allowed us to observe a full circle, both conceptual and institutional, on women's rights. Women's rights were originally incorporated in the mandate of the UN Commission on Human Rights; a specialized Commission on the Status of Women was then created; this subsequently resulted in the marginalization of women's human rights issues; and, finally, through extraordinary non-governmental and governmental action at the Global Conferences in Vienna and Beijing, in 1993 and 1995, the circle was successfully completed: women's human rights were mainstreamed within the human rights structures and the specialized bodies dealing with women, and the Commission on the Status of Women and the Committee on the Elimination of Discrimination against Women—were strengthened; the United Nations Development Fund for Women (UNIFEM) was created. This unique example of a circle completed and a balance achieved between mainstreaming and specialization could be usefully analyzed by other groups with special human rights concerns.

A review of fifty years of international human rights action reveals clearly that there is a need for participatory, people-centered approaches to all aspects of human rights promotion and protection to supplement professional elite and state-centered approaches. The positive impact of the participation of indigenous peoples and of women at UN fora provide very useful examples.

At the national level, people-centered approaches to human rights are gradually emerging from the grassroots where people themselves are struggling to become determining players in human rights standard-setting, monitoring, and enforcement [4]. Mounting frustration of communities over government inaction in implementing human rights has led to popular mobilization around the adoption of national laws or international human rights standards. Communities affected by intense economic deprivation, often resulting from environmental degradation, have joined forces with non-governmental organizations to monitor their governments' implementation of human rights. "Alternative law groups," "Peoples Tribunals," and letter petitions to courts have been some of the means used. The result has often been increasing and officially recognized participation, through state institutions, of communities in deciding on their own economic, political, and social development.

Challenges to human rights posed by globalization and non-state actors must be met. These are created by intergovernmental institutions of finance, trade and development, transnational and national corporations, and fundamentalist civil society. The traditional concept of human rights as defining the relation between the individual and the state needs to be expanded further. The participation of women's movements in the global conferences of the past decade has already resulted in the recognition that the violation of human dignity, not only in the public, but also in the private sphere, constitutes a violation of human rights.

Non-state actors in the globalized economy must be brought into line with the international human rights standards developed over the past fifty years. Crippling external debt obliges developing countries to adopt the International Monetary Fund's structural adjustment programs with devastating effects on economic, social, and cultural rights. An avalanche of privatization and deregulation has created unprecedented global lawlessness with corporations being largely accountable to no one as regards human rights [5]. In the present environment of weakening state powers and increasing power of the global economy, it would be short-sighted to ignore the impact of these non-state actors on the human rights of millions. Creative ways must be found to address this issue. The current challenges faced by the International Labour Organization (ILO) in the implementation of international labor standards, as well as the recent efforts to draft a Multilateral Agreement on Investments within the framework of the Organization for European Cooperation and Development, are eloquent examples in this respect.

International human rights activism has resulted in an awareness that human rights must be incorporated into an increasing number of areas of international work. The challenge is now to move from this awareness to the effective integration of human rights, in a way that human rights analysis, based on established international human rights standards, will be included in the political, peace, development, environment, social, and other areas of international activity. This need makes particularly relevant the development of expertise in professions other than law and political science, the traditional "carriers" of human rights. As awareness of human rights increases, the interdisciplinary, integrative cooperation among a variety of professions [2, Introduction, pp. 1-17] in fact, advances the promotion and protection of human rights. This very book is the outcome of the editors' convictions of the necessity for a multidisciplinary approach to human rights. The chapters on the trauma of human rights violation and denial demonstrate eloquently the important and innovative role of health, including mental health, professionals and the extraordinarily rich practice and research in this field.

The purpose of this book is to evaluate fifty years of international action in the field of human rights following the adoption of the Universal Declaration, and to address future challenges. The ultimate yardstick that the authors were asked to keep in mind is the extent to which the different aims of the international human rights system have reached the victims of human rights violations and have prevented victimization, rather than merely focusing on the institutional development of the system itself. Thus, the aspiration of the book has been to portray the dialogue and the interrelationship of the system with the lives of people. The contributors are prominent specialists from around the world associated with non-governmental and intergovernmental organizations, the academy, or, in the case of the "voices" that appear among the chapters, they are individuals whose personal stories add a particular dimension to the understanding of human rights.

The book thus discusses the whole spectrum of international human rights action. The first substantive part of the volume is an overview of the international human rights standards and mechanisms within the UN system developed by the UN, ILO, and the United Nations Educational, Scientific and Cultural Organization (UNESCO), and includes an evaluation of UN human rights field operations and of the efforts to create an International Criminal Court. The second part focuses on the human rights struggles of specific groups: women, children, indigenous peoples, minorities, refugees, migrants, the homeless, the disabled, the mentally ill, the elderly, and those discriminated against on the basis of sexual orientation. The third part discusses international efforts to promote a culture of human rights through institution-building and human rights education. The fourth part evaluates regional human rights action in Africa, the Americas, Asia and the Pacific, Western Europe, and East and Central Europe. The fifth part provides an overview of the specialized contribution of the health professions to the field of trauma of human rights denial and violation. The sixth part focuses on recent efforts to integrate human rights into other major areas of international action, in particular peace and security, development, including extreme poverty, the environment and challenges posed to human rights by non-state actors.

The inclusion, in 1945, of human rights in the UN Charter as one of the basic goals of the Organization and the adoption of the Universal Declaration of Human Rights in 1948 are landmarks in the history of millions of victims seeking moral justification. This extraordinary revolution in international relations and law, brought about by the internationalization of human rights, has always had a human face, in spite of the politicization of the issue. The "voices" interspersed among the chapters of this book bring to life this dimension of passion, pain, creativity, inspiration, and hope that human rights are all about.

This book is, to a large extent, about the unfinished human rights agenda of the Universal Declaration of Human Rights. The Declaration carries and will continue to carry the vision of dignity and rights of its ghost drafters and ultimate depositaries: the people of the world.

This volume is dedicated to the victim/survivors of human rights violations and denial, and to the defenders of human rights.[2]

REFERENCES

1. E. Stamatopoulou, Violations of Human Rights: UN Action from the Victim's Perspective, in *International Responses to Traumatic Stress: Humanitarian, Human Rights, Justice, Peace and Development Contributions, Collaborative Actions and Future*

---

[2] After thirteen years of drafting by the Commission on Human Rights, the General Assembly is expected to adopt, in December 1998, the "Declaration on Human Rights Defenders" (Declaration on the Right and Responsibility of Individuals, Groups and Organs of Society to Promote and Protect Universally Recognized Human Rights and Fundamental Freedoms).

Initiatives, Y. Danieli, N. S. Rodley, and L. Weisæth (eds.), Baywood Publishing Company, Amityville, New York, p. 105, pp. 101-129, 1996.

2. Y. Danieli, Conclusions and Future Directions, in *International Handbook of Multigenerational Legacies of Trauma*, Y. Danieli (ed.), Plenum Press, New York, pp. 669-689, 1998.

3. Y. Danieli, N. S. Rodley, and L. Weisæth (eds.), *International Responses to Traumatic Stress: Humanitarian, Human Rights, Justice, Peace and Development Contributions, Collaborative Actions and Future Initiatives*, Baywood Publishing Company, Amityville, New York, 1996.

4. C. Dias, A People-Centered Approach to Human Rights, in *Human Rights Dialogue*, Vol. 9, Carnegie Council on Ethics and International Affairs, New York, p. 3, June 1997.

5. C. Dias, The Unfinished Work, in *Informal: South Asian Solidarity*, Informal Sector Service Centre, INSEC, Nepal, p. 22, April 1988.

Elsa Stamatopoulou*
Yael Danieli
Clarence J. Dias

**Elsa Stamatopoulou participates in this book in her personal capacity. The views expressed do not necessarily represent those of the United Nations.

Part II

The United Nations Human Rights System

Chapter 1

The Perspective of the Victim

Theo van Boven

THE VICTIM AS A SUBJECT OF CONCERN

In its more than fifty years, the United Nations has paid only limited attention to the cause of victims. Rapporteurs and Working Groups entrusted with a mandate from the United Nations Commission on Human Rights to examine practices or situations involving gross and consistent patterns of violations of human rights mainly concentrated their activities and recommendations on policies and on facts, but paid little attention to the persons behind these policies or facts, irrespective of whether such persons were perpetrators or victims. It was rather in the area of crime prevention and criminal justice that victims became an important subject of attention. The *Declaration of Basic Principles of Justice for Victims of Crime and Abuse of Power* was finally adopted by the United Nations General Assembly in resolution 40/34 of 29 November 1985. According to the first paragraph of this Declaration, victims of crime are described as "persons who, individually or collectively, have suffered harm, including physical or mental injury, emotional suffering, economic loss or substantial impairment of their fundamental rights, through acts or omissions that are in violation of criminal laws operative in Member States, including those laws proscribing criminal abuse of power."

Recent years have seen a certain convergence between crime prevention, international criminal law, and human rights. No responsible authority or organization examining gross and massive violations of human rights or humanitarian law can remain oblivious to the sufferings of victims. Solidarity and pressure groups generated energetic efforts to provide help and relief to the survivors of rape in armed conflicts. Human rights organizations and groups spearhead the campaign to establish an effective permanent International Criminal Court. Some of these organizations have recommended that the prospective International Criminal Court help to afford appropriate forms of reparation to victims. International petition procedures providing *locus standi* to persons claiming to be victims of violations of human rights before international judicial or quasi-judicial bodies are gaining importance in reach and relevance, both under treaties functioning in the framework of the United Nations and under regional instruments that form part of the structures of the Council of Europe, the Organisation of American States, and the Organisation of African Unity. Against this background of growing emphasis on the rights and interests of victims, a United Nations study was carried out on the right of victims to restitution, compensation, and rehabilitation.[1] The UN Commission on Human Rights is now considering a set of *basic principles and guidelines on the right to reparation for victims of gross violations of human rights and international humanitarian law.*[2] These basic principles and guidelines await further decision-making by the Commission in the light of comments to be received from governments. All these developments contribute to enhancing the normative framework as well as existing and prospective accountability mechanisms [1].

A CASE FOR REPARATION; DIFFERENT MODALITIES OF REPARATION

Reparation is first and foremost the rendering of justice to individual persons and groups whose rights have been violated and who are therefore entitled to remedy and redress. It is obvious that in instances of gross violations and breaches of human rights and international humanitarian law, committed in a widespread manner, reparations often do not stand in any proportional relationship to the grave injury inflicted upon the victims. Nevertheless, it is an imperative norm of justice that the responsibility of the perpetrators be clearly established and that the rights of the victims be realized to the fullest possible extent.

In addition, when a society has been passing through a period of serious conflict and violence or when a society has been victimized by brutal forces of tyranny and oppression, reparation is a means to foster a process of healing, not only for the sake of morality but also to build a lasting peace. In this regard reparation serves a collective purpose, namely, to enhance the welfare and the vitality of the society. While it would appear that the fundamental cause for reparation is basically the same in domestic and international contexts, the factor

---

[1] *Study concerning the right to restitution, compensation and rehabilitation for victims of gross violations of human rights and fundamental freedoms.* Final report submitted by Mr. Theo van Boven, Special Rapporteur (UN doc. E/CN.4/Sub.2/1993/8).

[2] UN doc. E/CN.4/1998/34, Annex. See also International Centre for Human Rights and Democratic Development, *Campaign Against Impunity: Portrait and Plan of Action,* Montreal, 1997, pp. 263-266.

of national sovereignty and sentiments of national pride generate an additional dimension of sensitivity. Reparation implies the acknowledgment that serious wrongs were done to another party. States are, generally speaking, not inclined to acknowledge their wrongs unless forced to do so or in cases where a government wishes to disassociate itself clearly from its predecessor.

Reparations are often assessed in terms of paying compensation. While compensation is indeed an important means to indemnify damage suffered, other forms of reparation, including those which are not economically assessable, should not be overlooked. An elementary catalogue of various forms of reparation is contained in the draft articles on State responsibility provisionally adopted by the International Law Commission on first reading.[3] The relevant provisions were drawn up as part of a system of inter-state relations under the heading of "rights of the injured State and obligations of the State which has committed an internationally wrongful act" (chapter II), but the catalogue lends itself equally well to the listing of various forms of reparation at other than inter-state levels. The draft articles distinguish the following forms of reparation:

- *restitution* in kind, that is, the re-establishment of the situation which existed before the wrongful act was committed (article 43).
- *compensation* for the damage caused by the wrongful act, if and to the extent that the damage is not made good by restitution in kind (article 44).
- *satisfaction* for the damage, in particular moral damage caused by the wrongful act. Satisfaction may take the form of (a) an apology; (b) nominal damages; (c) in cases of gross infringements of rights, damages reflecting the gravity of the infringement; (d) in cases of serious misconduct of officials or criminal conduct of officials or private parties, disciplinary action against, or punishment of, those responsible (article 45).
- *assurances and guarantees of non-repetition* of the wrongful act (article 46).

Relating the above-mentioned forms of reparation to victims of violations of human rights and international humanitarian law means, in terms of the basic principles and guidelines now before the UN Commission on Human Rights (see note 2), that:

- *restitution* may require, as the case may be, the restoration of liberty, family life, citizenship, return to one's place of residence, and restoration of employment or property;
- *compensation* may be provided for any economically assessable damage resulting from physical or mental harm, lost opportunities, material

---

[3] *Draft articles on State responsibility,* Report of the International Law Commission on the work of its forty-eighth session (6 May-26 July 1996), UN doc. A/51/10, chapter III, articles 42-46.

damages and loss of earnings, harm to reputation or dignity, and costs required for legal or expert assistance, medicines, and medical services;
- *satisfaction* may be given by means of (a) cessation of continuing violations; (b) verification of the facts and full public disclosure of the truth; (c) official declaration or a judicial decision affirming or restoring the dignity, reputation, and legal rights of the victim; (d) apology, including public acknowledgment of the facts and acceptance of responsibility; (e) judicial or administrative sanctions against persons responsible for violations; (f) commemorations and paying tribute to the victims [2]; and (g) inclusion in training and in history or school books of an accurate account of the wrongs committed;
- *assurances and guarantees of non-repetition* should entail measures aiming at the prevention of the recurrence of violations by such means as (a) ensuring effective civilian control over military and security forces; (b) restricting the jurisdiction of military tribunals only to specifically military offenses committed by members of the armed forces; (c) strengthening the independence of the judiciary; (d) protecting persons in the legal profession and human rights defenders; and (e) conducting and strengthening human rights training in all sectors of society, in particular military and security forces and law enforcement officials.

In devising strategies of justice it must be borne in mind that *lack of reparation* for victims and *impunity* of perpetrators are two sides of the same coin. In many situations where impunity has been sanctioned by law or where *de facto* impunity prevails with regard to the perpetrators, the victims are effectively barred from seeking redress and reparations. Where State authorities fail to investigate the facts and establish criminal responsibility, it becomes very difficult for victims (or their relatives) to carry on effective legal proceedings aimed at obtaining just and adequate reparation.[4] Therefore, all efforts and strategies aimed at strengthening the normative framework in the quest for peace and justice must reveal the clear nexus that exists between impunity of perpetrators and the failure to provide just and adequate reparation for the victims.

REPARATION AND STATE RESPONSIBILITY

The international promotion and protection of human rights is to a large extent based on the concept of *State responsibility.* The UN Commission on Human Rights developed a whole series of devices and mechanisms to examine gross and massive violations of human rights. States are held accountable and are

---

[4] See in particular the study in note 1, chapter VII on the issue of impunity in relation to the right to reparation for victims of gross violations of human rights.

expected to respond before political fora of the United Nations. Such procedures, which function as part of a political process in connection with consistent and gross violations of human rights, are not necessarily conditioned by the consent of the States immediately involved inasmuch as these procedures apply in principle to the whole membership of the UN and find their legal basis in the responsibility of States under general international law.

A somewhat different picture presents itself where States are parties to human rights treaties and where they have explicitly agreed to subject themselves to the scrutiny of international supervisory bodies. Here the responsibility of States flows from the express acceptance of specific treaty obligations. A good number of universal and regional human rights instruments contain special provisions concerning the right of every individual to an "effective remedy" by competent national tribunals for acts violating human rights. And insofar as persons claiming to be victims of human rights violations fail to receive redress at the national level, several human rights treaties open up avenues to seek redress and satisfaction at the international level where (quasi-) judicial bodies examine their cases. It must again be emphasized that this human rights system is based on State responsibility and that the claims of victims are civil as distinct from criminal claims.

The classical doctrine of State responsibility in international law pertains to inter-state relations, that is, between injured States and wrong-doing States. The International Law Commission, in drawing up the draft articles on State responsibility, largely operated within the parameters of the classical doctrine.

It should be noted as a matter of great interest that the International Law Commission, while essentially limiting itself to the traditional confines of the doctrine of State responsibility, nevertheless made some significant openings so as to take into account new developments in international law, for instance by including in the draft articles special provisions for the protection of collective rights and interests and for the vindication of *erga omnes* obligations (i.e., obligations toward the international community as a whole). Thus, the notion of "injured State" was so phrased as to include any State party to a multilateral treaty or bound by a rule of international law if it is established that "the right has been created or is established for the protection of human rights and fundamental freedoms."[5] Here the International Law Commission clearly echoes the famous *obiter dictum* of the International Court of Justice in its *Barcelona Traction* Judgment where the court declared that all States have the right to vindicate *erga omnes* obligations. The Court stated:

> . . . an essential distinction should be drawn between obligations of a State
> towards the international community as a whole, and those arising vis-à-vis

[5] Note 3, article 40, para. 2(e) (iii).

another State in the field of diplomatic protection. By their very nature the former are the concern of all States. In view of the importance of the rights involved; they are obligations *erga omnes*. Such obligations derive, for example, in contemporary international law, from the outlawing of acts of aggression, and of genocide, and also from the principles and rules concerning the basic rights of the human person, including protection from slavery and racial discrimination. Some of the corresponding rights of protection have entered into the body of general international law; others are conferred by international instruments of a universal or quasi-universal character.[6]

Therefore, when a State breaches an obligation *erga omnes,* it injures the international legal and public order as a whole and consequently every State may have a right and an interest to bring an action against the offending State. The same notion is the underlying motive for the formulation of common Article 1 of the four Red Cross Geneva Conventions (1949) and of Additional Protocol 1 thereto (1977) to the effect that the High Contracting Parties not only undertake to respect but also to *ensure* respect for these legal instruments "in all circumstances."

Returning to the position of victims under international law, it must be assumed that the obligations resulting from State responsibility for breaches of international human rights and humanitarian law entail corresponding rights on the part of individual persons and groups of persons who are under the jurisdiction of the offending State and who are victims of those breaches. The principal right these victims are entitled to under international law is the right to effective remedy and just reparation. It should therefore be concluded that the right to reparation for victims of gross violations of human rights and humanitarian law finds a logical basis in present-day understanding of State responsibility.

REPARATIONS IN RECENT HUMAN RIGHTS PRACTICE; THE IMPORTANCE OF FOLLOW-UP CONTROL

The United Nations study mentioned earlier[7] reviewed the relevant existing norms on the right to reparation included in international instruments and discussed in detail decisions and views of international human rights organs. This chapter will review some recent developments in order to illustrate the practice of one important quasi-judicial treaty body; the Human Rights Committee which functions under the International Covenant on Civil and Political Rights and the first Optional Protocol thereto. On the basis of this Protocol, the Human Rights Committee concludes its consideration of a case by forwarding its "Views" to the

---

[6] *Case concerning the Barcelona Traction Light and Power Company, Ltd* (Second Phase, Belgium v. Spain), ICJ Reports 1970, p. 32.

[7] See note 1.

State party concerned and to the applicant. Such "Views" are not legally binding like judgments of human rights courts under the European and American conventions, but in view of the standing of the Human Rights Committee and the follow-up action which the Committee expects the State party to take, the Committee's "Views" carry more weight than mere recommendations. From the perspective of the victim it should be recalled that the Optional Protocol to the International Covenant limits the right of petition to persons "who claim to be victims of a violation of any of the rights set forth in the Covenant" (Article 1, Optional Protocol).

The Human Rights Committee, after establishing that a violation of one or more provisions of the Covenant had occurred and after recommending an appropriate remedy, developed a consistent practice of concluding its Views with the following statement:

> Bearing in mind that, by becoming a party to the Optional Protocol, the State party has recognized the competence of the Committee to determine whether there has been a violation of the Covenant or not and that, pursuant to article 2 of the Covenant, the State party has undertaken to ensure to all individuals within its territory and subject to its jurisdiction the rights recognized in the Covenant and to provide an effective and enforceable remedy in case a violation has been established, the Committee wishes to receive from the State party, within 90 days, information about the measures taken to give effect to the Committee's Views.[8]

An illustration of the Committee's case law is found in a series of "Views" expressed in cases originating from Jamaica where the alleged victim was sentenced to death. While according to the terms of the International Covenant capital punishment *per se* is not a violation of article 6 on the right to life, the Committee has consistently held that in capital punishment cases violation of fair trial provisions contained in articles 9 and 14 of the Covenant has the consequential effect of a violation of article 6 of the Covenant. Thus, in case No. 702/1996 (*McLawrence v. Jamaica*)[9] it was established that the arrested person who was later sentenced to death was apprised of the charges for his arrest only some three weeks after the arrest, that there was a delay of one week in bringing him before a judge or other judicial officer, and that there was a delay of thirty-one months between conviction and appeal. The Committee thereupon ruled that the facts disclosed a violation of articles 9, paras. 2 and 3, and 14, para. 3(c) and consequently of article 6 of the Covenant. The Committee expressed the

---

[8] Report of the Human Rights Committee to the fifty-second session of the General Assembly, UN doc. A/52/40, Vol. I, para. 517.

[9] Communication No. 702/1996 (*McLawrence v. Jamaica*), Views dated 18 July 1997, UN doc. CCPR/C/60/D/702/1996.

view that the author of the complaint was entitled, under article 2, para. 3(a), of the Covenant to an effective remedy, *entailing commutation of the death sentence.*

In a case of the murdered indigenous leaders in Colombia,[10] the Committee noted that the entitlement to an effective remedy included compensation for the victims' family members, stressed the State party's responsibility to expedite criminal proceedings against the perpetrators, and the State party's obligation to ensure that similar events do not recur. In terms of the various modalities of reparation this means that the victim's right to compensation was to be accompanied by the following measures of satisfaction: investigation of facts, sanctions against persons responsible for violations, and by assurances and guarantees of non-repetition. On the other hand, in the case involving capital punishment in Jamaica, the only, albeit very important, remedy explicitly mentioned by the Committee was the commutation of the death sentence.[11] The two types of cases, while having in common that the most fundamental human right the right to life was at stake, are very different with regard to the victimized persons and the circumstances under which violations took place. Therefore, they call for different modalities of reparation.

It is one thing for the Committee to state what remedies and reparations victims are entitled to—the Committee can only express "Views" and not render binding judgments—it is quite another matter to see what follow-up the State parties concerned actually give to these "Views." This crucial matter of follow-up control has in recent years become of major interest to the Committee. For this purpose the Committee established in 1990 a follow-up procedure and instituted a Special Rapporteur for the Follow-Up on Views whose task is to ascertain the measures taken by States parties to give effect to the Committee's Views. The Special Rapporteur is empowered to make contacts and take action as appropriate for the performance of the follow-up mandate and to make necessary recommendations for further action by the Committee (rule 95 of the rules of procedure of the Committee).[12]

As regards the effectiveness of this follow-up control, the most recent annual report of the Human Rights Committee notes that roughly 30 percent of the replies received could be considered satisfactory in that they display the State party's willingness to implement the Committee's Views or to offer the applicant an appropriate remedy. It further notes that many replies simply indicate that the

---

[10]Communication No. 612/1995 (*Arhuacos v. Colombia*), Views dated 29 July 1997, UN doc. CCPR/C/60/D/612/1995.

[11]It is disturbing that on 23 October 1997 Jamaica withdrew from the Optional Protocol, with effect on 23 January 1998. Consequently, the Human Rights Committee no longer has competence to deal with new capital punishment cases relating to Jamaica.

[12]Rules of procedure of the Human Rights Committee, UN doc. CCPR/C/3/Rev.5.

victim has failed to file a claim for compensation within statutory deadlines and that, therefore, no compensation can be paid to the victim.[13]

Using again the above-mentioned cases pertaining to Colombia and Jamaica as illustrations, it is interesting to note that Colombia enacted in 1996 enabling legislation which gives legal effect to the Committee's Views and that, in all cases in which the Committee recommended the payment of compensation to victims, the competent ministerial committee had issued favorable recommendations.[14] On the other hand, Jamaica's implementation record presents a different picture. Insofar as follow-up replies were received, they indicate that the State party is not giving effect to the Committee's recommendations, although one reply stated that a death sentence had been commuted.

VICTIMS AND THE
INTERNATIONAL CRIMINAL JUSTICE SYSTEM

While not every violation of human rights is a criminal offense, certain gross violations of human rights and humanitarian law that belong to the categories of crimes defined in the draft Code of Crimes against the Peace and Security of Mankind drawn up by the International Law Commission,[15] entail individual criminal responsibility. This is also confirmed in the Statutes of the International Criminal Tribunals for the former Yugoslavia and for Rwanda. As a victim of gross and serious violations of human rights and humanitarian law, the person is entitled to make civil claims for obtaining reparation. However, as a general rule the victim does not possess the right to pursue a criminal claim and to seek to bring the perpetrator(s) to justice. Such a right, which may even be a duty, falls within the domain of the competent prosecuting authorities. However, in many domestic legal systems the victim may become involved in the criminal procedure as *partie civile* to the criminal case and claim damages as a civil complainant. Such a course of action is commendable for various reasons. First, it makes the criminal offender more aware that not only was a wrong committed against public order and public welfare but, in addition, an injury was inflicted on one or more human beings. Second, it establishes a link between punitive measures and measures of reparation. Third, it tends to facilitate and expedite the process of obtaining civil damages.

No provision on reparation to victims is included in the Statute of the International Criminal Tribunal for the Former Yugoslavia, but the rules of

---

[13]Note 8, para. 522.

[14]Note 8, paras. 533-534.

[15]Articles on the draft *Code of Crimes against the Peace and Security of Mankind,* Report of the International Law Commission on the work of its forty-eighth session (6 May-26 July 1996), UN doc. A/51/10, paras. 30-50.

procedure and evidence of the Tribunal do establish some link between the criminal sentence of the convicted person and the right of the victim to obtain compensation. In fact, the Registrar of the Tribunal must transmit to the competent authorities of the State concerned the judgment finding the accused guilty of a crime which has caused injury to a victim, so that he or she may bring, in accordance with national legislation, an action in a national court or other competent body to obtain compensation.[16]

When the International Law Commission held a general debate on international criminal jurisdiction and the terms of a proposed International Criminal Court, the views of those members who had strong reservations about the possibility of "intermingling strictly criminal proceedings against individuals and civil claims for damages"[17] prevailed. They raised the practical objection of the potentially large numbers of victims that could be involved and they expressed doubt that compensation for injuries suffered as a result of crimes referred to the court was within the scope of their mandate. Since the basic function of a criminal court should be the rendering of criminal justice, a suggested alternative solution would be that the question of compensation be managed quasi-judicially by a commission acting as a sub-organ of the court system.[18] Consequently, the draft statute for an international criminal court submitted in 1994 by the International Law Commission to the UN General Assembly contained only a very remote reference to the question of reparation for victims. Article 47 on applicable penalties stated in subparagraphs 3(b) and (c) that fines may be transferred to a State the nationals of which were victims of the crime or to a trust fund established by the UN Secretary-General for the benefit of victims of crime. The commentary explained that these subparagraphs are not intended in any way to substitute for reparation or to prevent any action that victims may take to obtain reparation through other courts or other international means.[19] By and large the International Law Commission felt that issues of reparation, including restitution of property, were best left to national jurisdictions and to international judicial cooperation agreements.

In the further process of negotiations on the terms of reference and the establishment of a permanent International Criminal Court, which have not come to a conclusion at the time of the writing of this chapter, proposals were made to strengthen the rights and interests of victims of crime. As an example, one of the

---

[16]International Criminal Tribunal for the former Yugoslavia, Rules of Procedure and Evidence, Rule 106, Basic Documents ICTY, 1995, p. 121.

[17]Report of the International Law Commission on the work of its forty-fourth session (4 May-24 July 1992), UN doc. A/47/10, para. 89.

[18]Note 17, para. 90.

[19]*Draft Statute for an International Criminal Court,* Report of the International Law Commission on the work of its forty-sixth session (2 May-22 July 1994), UN doc. A/49/10, chapter II, Article 47 and commentary.

concerned non-governmental organizations, *Redress,* whose aim is to seek reparation for torture survivors suggested the following to the negotiations:

(a) that the Court, in imposing possible sentences on a person convicted of a crime under the Statute of the Court, may demand "without prejudice to the obligation on every State to provide reparation in respect of conduct engaging the responsibility of the State, other appropriate forms of reparation";[20]

(b) with regard to determining an appropriate sentence, that not only the gravity of the crime and the individual circumstances of the convicted person be taken into account, as is proposed in the original ILC Draft Statute, but also the impact of the crime on the victims and that attention also be paid to "the efforts made to afford reparation to the victims"; and

(c) in order to take account of the need to implement awards to the victim, that the article on the recognition of judgments of the Court be made more precise so as to cover also the obligation of States parties "to carry out the judgments of the Court."

Incorporating such proposals into the Statute of the permanent International Criminal Court would bring the victim's perspective and interests within closer reach of the international criminal justice system and would be in line with developments that can be discerned in domestic legal systems.

COMPLEXITIES

Nationally and internationally, the principle of awarding reparations is recognized, but differences of view still prevail with regard to scope, content, and modalities. More lacking is the actual implementation and enforcement of the right to reparation. Numerous victims remain unattended, uncared for, unrecognized and unresponded to. Therefore, there is need for widely accepted principles and guidelines as part of the normative framework. Some issues remain to be clarified.

First, the question of *beneficiaries* and *duty-bearers*: should beneficiaries of reparation be individual persons or both individuals and collectivities? While several legal systems assume that claims can only be made by individuals, there are no reasons of a policy nature to exclude collectivities. The Declaration of Basic Principles of Justice for Victims of Crime and Abuse of Power, referred to earlier, defines "victims" as persons who, individually or *collectively* have suffered harm. As regards duty-bearers, the *human rights system* holds the State

---

[20]Redress, *Promoting the right to reparation for survivors of torture: What role for a permanent international criminal court?* London, 1997, Chapter VII Recommendations, pp. 42-44.

responsible to make reparations. It is on the basis of this principle that, for instance, Korean "comfort women" refused to accept compensation from a private fund in Japan, arguing that the public authorities representing the State of Japan were liable to pay compensation.[21] In the *criminal law system* the duty-bearer may also be the offender. Thus, reparations may be claimed by the victims through the criminal courts, either as punitive damages and/or by way of *partie civile*. In such a system the offender is not only criminally responsible but also bears civil liability.

A second complex issue is the *passage of time*. It is illustrated by claims to reparations by Afro-Americans as descendants of the victims of the slave trade. Equally, indigenous peoples whose ancestors were forcibly deprived of their lands are claiming restitution or compensation. Verbal expressions of apology and regret, though significant in themselves, are not considered good enough by descendants who continue to suffer from neglect and discrimination. And what does the passage of time mean to victims of war crimes and crimes against humanity, crimes which, according to a relevant but not widely ratified 1968 Convention, are not subject to statutory limitations.[22] It must be realized that for many victims of gross violations of human rights and of international humanitarian law, as well as for their children and even for their grandchildren, the passage of time may have no attenuating effect and over the years there may even be an increase in post-traumatic stress [3]. Their claims for rehabilitation and for medical, psychological, social, and material assistance cannot be made dependent on time limitations.[23]

A third issue relates to *resources*. Funds are often scarce but critically needed for purposes of compensation or for policies of affirmative action in areas such as employment, housing, education, and health care on behalf of entire groups who over the years have been victimized and marginalized by neglect and discrimination. At the same time, emphasis must be given to non-financial means of reparation in the form of satisfaction and of preventive guarantees and action. As stated earlier, reparations should not only be assessed in financial terms.

Another issue requiring further consideration is that of *mechanisms for implementation*. Here, one has to rely mainly on facilities and institutions at the national level. Regrettably, few nations have as yet taken any effective action. A challenging and in many respects innovative implementation mechanism is the Truth and Reconciliation Commission [4, 5]. In South Africa, for instance, the

---

[21]International Commission of Jurists, *Comfort Women, and Unfinished Ordeal* (Report of a Mission by Ustinia Dolgopol and Snehal Paranjape), Geneva, 1994. See also the statement by Kim, Yoon Shim, in this volume, pp. 127-128.

[22]Convention on the Non-Applicability of Statutory Limitations to War Crimes and Crimes against Humanity, adopted by General Assembly resolution 2391 (XXIII) of 26 November 1968 and ratified as per 31 December 1997, by 43 States.

[23]Note 1, para. 135.

Commission is perceived and intended as a crucial device to repair the society from some of the worst effects of the evils of apartheid. In the absence of models and standard solutions, the South African experience may well provide more insight and better answers than most of the other national mechanisms developed so far. The international community may be in a position to encourage and assist national developments but, essentially, mechanisms for reconciliation should essentially be part of a national process. It would appear that only in special circumstances should reparation mechanisms be created at the international level. Examples include the UN Fund for Torture Victims, which has been operational for many years [6]; the United Nations Compensation Commission established by Security Council resolution 687 (1991) to indemnify for losses, damages, and injuries as a result of the invasion and illegal occupation of Kuwait by Iraq [7]; and the proposals to include in the draft Statute for a permanent International Criminal Court provisions for awarding civil damages to victims.

CONCLUDING NOTE

Both the present and previous UN Secretaries-General have placed great emphasis on post-conflict peace-building.[24]

Reparation to victims in its various modalities including restitution, compensation, rehabilitation, satisfaction, and guarantees of non-recurrence is an indispensable ingredient of the process of peace-building. Reconstruction of a society does not have an effective and durable basis unless human rights are respected and promoted and the rights of victims are duly and fairly met. This cause must essentially be realized within every national society. However, international assistance and international cooperation are important supplementary means for achieving justice, both as a pressing matter of right for individual persons and groups as well as for the sake of fostering a lasting peace at national and international levels.

REFERENCES

1. M. C. Bassiouni, Considerations on Peace and Justice and the Imperative of Accountability for Crimes and Consistent and Widespread Violations of Fundamental Human Rights, in *Accountability for International Crimes,* M. C. Bassiouni and M. H. Morris (eds.), 59 Law and Contemporary Problems, Nr 4, pp. 6-25, Autumn 1996.
2. Y. Danieli, Preliminary Reflections from a Psychological Perspective, in *Report of Seminar on the Right to Restitution, Compensation and Rehabilitation for Victims of Gross Violations of Human Rights and Fundamental Freedoms,* T. van Boven,

---

[24]*An Agenda for Peace* etc; see also Report of the Secretary-General on the work of the organization, UN doc. A/52/1, dated 3 September 1997, para. 121.

C. Flinterman, F. Grünfeld, and I. Westendorp (eds.), SIM Special No. 12, Utrecht, pp. 196-213, 1992.

3. Y. Danieli, *International Handbook of Multigeneration Legacies of Trauma,* Plenum Press, New York, 1998.

4. D. Bronkhorst, *Truth and Reconciliation; Obstacles and Opportunities for Human Rights,* Amnesty International Dutch Section, Amsterdam, 1995.

5. S. Landsman, Alternative Responses to Serious Human Rights Abuses: of Prosecution and Truth Commissions, in *Accountability for International Crimes,* 59 Law and Contemporary Problems, Nr 4, pp. 75-86, Autumn 1996.

6. D. Prémont, Voluntary Fund, UN Support to Victims of Torture, in *Human Rights, A Quarterly Review of the UN High Commissioner for Human Rights, 1,* pp. 23-25, Winter 1997-1998.

7. L. Gabriel, Victims of Gross Violations of Human Rights and Fundamental Freedoms Arising from the Illegal Invasion and Occupation of Kuwait by Iraq, in *Report of Seminar on the Right to Restitution, Compensation and Rehabilitation for Victims of Gross Violations of Human Rights and Fundamental Freedoms,* T. van Boven, C. Flinterman, F. Grünfeld, and I. Westendorp (eds.), SIM Special No. 12, Utrecht, pp. 29-39, 1992.

Chapter 2

A Victims' Perspective on the International Human Rights Treaty Regime

B. G. Ramcharan

A victims' perspective on the international human rights treaty regime[1] needs to proceed from an understanding of the quest of the international system for the promotion and protection of human rights, to prevent gross human rights violations and to bring the perpetrators of such violations to justice. This system is, alas, still in its infancy, operating in a world of rampant—and often oppressive— sovereignty and trying to expand the sphere of the culture of human rights and the rule of law step-by-step. There is no magic wand for human rights protection. It is a mission of sacred commitment, firm resolve, and progressive development toward the desired goal of a world in which the human rights of all would be respected and upheld.

The imagery of an expanding circle is helpful when considering the challenge of human rights protection: from a center of commitment grounded in the United Nations Charter and the Universal Declaration of Human Rights, the human rights movement seeks to push outward an inner circle of achievement grounded in the international norms on human rights elaborated since 1945. International human rights treaties take pride of place among these norms. Beyond the inner circle of achievement lies a wider circle of opportunity—the ground still to be covered to make our world one of universal respect and vindication of human rights.

---

[1] This chapter deals with treaties in force. Non-treaty normative instruments that address victims' issues directly are examined in Chapters 1 and 4 of this volume.

The plight of the victims of human rights violations was the driving force behind the international system for the promotion and the protection of human rights established by the United Nations in 1945. The founders of the United Nations were determined to prevent the recurrence of the atrocities that had led to, and had continued during, the Second World War. Their determination to save succeeding generations from the scourge of war was simultaneously to reaffirm faith in fundamental human rights, in the dignity and worth of the human person, and in the equal rights of men and women. The very year the United Nations General Assembly adopted the Universal Declaration of Human Rights it also adopted the Convention on the Prevention and Punishment of the Crime of Genocide.

Almost from the moment it adopted the Universal Declaration, the United Nations began a historic struggle to combat racism and racial discrimination, particularly as practiced during the period of *apartheid* in South Africa. Throughout its history ever since, even in the face of severe political difficulties, there would be a resolute quest to move the Organization forward from the promotion of human rights to their protection and to denounce gross violations of human rights.

The plethora of human rights fact-finding bodies, the establishment of the Office of United Nations High Commissioner for Human Rights, the partnership between the United Nations and non-governmental organizations, the denunciation of impunity, and the establishment of international tribunals to deal with the perpetrators of international crimes, all attest to the contemporary thrust of the United Nations human rights system to prevent human rights violations if possible, and to bring their perpetrators to justice.

At the heart of this enterprise are the international human rights treaties, whose unique feature is that they lay down in binding legal form the obligations of States to uphold human rights and to prevent their violations. The international human rights treaty regime seeks to prevent people from becoming victims. It is an ambitious project that is still far from realization; but it is at the core of the human rights movement.

I. THE STRATEGIES OF INTERNATIONAL HUMAN RIGHTS TREATIES FROM THE PERSPECTIVES OF VICTIMS

International human rights treaties seek to prevent violations of human rights by:

- Highlighting the plight of victims and devising strategies for alleviating their suffering.
- Proscribing crimes against humanity and working to bring about the punishment of the perpetrators of such crimes.

- Establishing legal regimes and working progressively for their universal implementation.
- Contributing to a growing network of national, regional, and international protection aiming at anticipating and preventing human rights violations, mitigating and stopping those violations, and according remedies and compensation to the extent possible. The entrenchment and strengthening of a system of protection of human rights is the *raison d'etre* of the international and regional human rights treaty systems.

One can see these strategies at work in a variety of international human rights treaties as well as in human rights treaties at the regional level:

(a) United Nations Charter (1945) as Amplified by the Universal Declaration of Human Rights (1948)

The victims' perspective leaps out of the Charter and the Universal Declaration. The central purpose of the United Nations is to help bring about a world of peace and justice grounded in respect for human rights and fundamental freedoms. That was why the United Nations Charter gave such a pivotal place to the promotion and protection of human rights. The Universal Declaration of Human Rights further elaborated upon the human rights provisions of the Charter and recognized that disregard and contempt for human rights had resulted in barbarous acts that had outraged the conscience of humankind. The advent of a world in which human beings shall enjoy freedom of speech and belief and freedom from fear and want was proclaimed by the Universal Declaration as the highest aspiration of the common people.

(b) Convention on the Prevention and Punishment of the Crime of Genocide (1948)

The victims' perspective is prominent here also. The Contracting Parties to the Genocide Convention confirm that genocide, whether committed in time of peace or in time of war, is a crime under international law, which they undertake to prevent and to punish. Under the Convention on the Non-Applicability of Statutory Limitations to War Crimes and Crimes Against Humanity (1968) no statutory limitations shall apply to such crimes, irrespective of the date on which they were committed.

(c) Declaration and Convention on the Rights of the Child (1959 and 1989)

The victimization of children is at the heart of the concern that led to the Convention on the Rights of the Child. The United Nations Declaration on the Rights of the Child (1959) proclaimed, in its second Principle, that the child shall enjoy special protection and shall be given opportunities and facilities, by law and by other means, to enable him or her to develop physically, mentally, morally, spiritually, and socially in a healthy and normal manner and in conditions of freedom and dignity. In the enactment of laws for this purpose, the best interests of the child shall be the paramount consideration.

The Convention on the Rights of the Child (1989) recalls the provisions of the Declaration that the child, by reason of his or her physical and mental immaturity, needs special safeguards and care, including appropriate legal protection, before as well as after birth. It particularly recognizes that "in all countries in the world, there are children living in exceptionally difficult conditions, and that such children need special consideration."

(d) Convention on the Elimination of Discrimination Against Women (1979)

The evaluation and elimination of systemic and personal discrimination and violence against women is the mission of this Convention. In adopting the Convention, the States Parties were concerned that extensive discrimination against women continues to exist; that in situations of poverty women have the least access to food, health, education, training, and opportunities for employment and other needs. The States Parties condemn discrimination against women in all its forms and agree to pursue by all appropriate means and without delay a policy of eliminating discrimination against women. States Parties pledge to take in all fields, in particular the political, social, economic, and cultural spheres, all appropriate measures, including legislation, to ensure the full development and advancement of women, for the purpose of guaranteeing them the exercise and enjoyment of human rights and fundamental freedoms on a basis of equality with men. States Parties also undertake to take all appropriate measures to modify the social and cultural patterns of conduct of men and women, with a view to achieving the elimination of prejudice and customary and all other practices that are based on the idea of the inferiority or the superiority of either of the sexes or on stereotyped roles for men and women.

(e) Convention on the Elimination of Racial Discrimination (1965)

Racial discrimination victimizes millions of people. The States Parties to the Convention therefore expressed their conviction that the existence of racial barriers is repugnant to the ideals of any human society. They were alarmed by manifestations of racial discrimination still in evidence and by governmental policies based on racial superiority or hatred. They, therefore, resolved to adopt all necessary measures for speedily eliminating racial discrimination in all its forms and manifestations, and to prevent and combat racist doctrines and practices in order to promote understanding between races and to build an international community free from all forms of racial segregation and racial discrimination. States Parties condemn racial discrimination and undertake to pursue by all appropriate means and without delay a policy of eliminating racial discrimination in all its forms and promoting understanding among all races.

(f) Convention Against Torture (1984)

Torture, alas, continues to be practiced against millions around the world. The States Parties to the Convention against Torture therefore laid down that any act of torture or other cruel, inhuman, or degrading treatment or punishment is an offense to human dignity and shall be condemned as a denial of the purposes of the Charter of the United Nations and as a violation of the human rights and fundamental freedoms proclaimed in the Universal Declaration of Human Rights. No state may permit or tolerate torture or other cruel, inhuman, or degrading treatment or punishment. Each State Party shall ensure that all acts of torture are offenses under its criminal law. The same shall apply to an attempt to commit torture and to an act by any person which constitutes complicity or participation in torture. Each State Party shall make these offenses punishable by appropriate penalties which take into account their grave nature.

(g) International Covenants on Human Rights (1966)

The elimination of state or systemic violence is the goal of the International Covenants. The States Parties recognize that, in accordance with the Universal Declaration of Human Rights, the ideal of free human beings enjoying freedom from fear and want can only be achieved if conditions are created whereby everyone may enjoy his or her economic, social, and cultural rights, as well as his or her civil and political rights. Each State undertakes to take steps individually and through international assistance and cooperation, especially economic and technical, to the maximum of its available resources, with a view to achieving progressively the full realization of the rights recognized in the Covenant on Economic, Social and Cultural Rights by all appropriate means, including particularly the adoption of legislative measures. Each State Party to the Civil and Political Covenant undertakes to respect and ensure to all individuals within its territory and subject to its jurisdiction the rights recognized in the Covenant, without distinction of any kind, such as race, color, sex, religion, political or other opinion, national or social origin, property or other status.

(h) The 1949 Geneva Conventions and the 1977 Protocols on International Humanitarian Law

The Geneva Conventions and Protocols on international humanitarian law are inspired by respect for human personality and dignity; together, they establish the principle of disinterested aid to all victims of war without discrimination—to all those who, whether through injury, capture, or shipwreck, are no longer enemies but merely suffering and defenseless human beings. They also impose penal sanctions for breaches, particularly for "grave breaches" of the Conventions and Protocols.

(i) An International Criminal Court

The treaty establishing an International Criminal Court will add significantly to the prevention of gross violations of human rights, and to the punishment of the perpetrators of such violations and, as such, will be a major addition to the treaty edifice for the protection for human rights.

II. ASPECTS OF THE EVOLVING PRACTICE UNDER INTERNATIONAL HUMAN RIGHTS TREATIES THAT ARE OF PARTICULAR IMPORTANCE FOR VICTIMS

The implementation of international human rights treaties gives rise to many problems in practice. Despite many obstacles, we prefer to retain the imagery of the expanding circle of international protection in which gradual progress is achieved toward the goals of making protection more effective and providing justice to victims. From this point of view, the following developments within international treaty bodies hold particular promise from the perspective of victims: (a) the increasing emphasis on early warning and prevention; (b) the increasing resort to interim measures of protection; (c) the growing insistence on remedies and compensation; (d) the use of follow-up procedures; (e) the use of concluding observations after the consideration of States reports; and (f) growing acceptance of petitions procedures such as those under the Optional Protocol to the International Covenant on Civil and Political Rights.

(a) Early Warning and Prevention

The Committee on the Elimination of Racial Discrimination has pioneered a procedure of considering situations that, in its view, need to be addressed from the point of view of early warning and prevention of violations of human rights. During its sessions the Committee gives specific consideration to situations of concern that, in its view, should be given urgent attention. At its spring session in

1998, for example, the Committee discussed several situations in depth and called upon the State Parties concerned to take urgent corrective measures.

A related practice is that of the Human Rights Committee, which calls for special reports from States Parties in situations of emergency or concern.

Procedures such as these are intended to place the international spotlight on a situation with a view to drawing attention to the possibility of excesses being committed and hopefully arresting them before they happen. In the event that the situation is one where violence has already broken out, the aim is to bring it to an end and, in the process, minimize human suffering.

(b) Interim Measures

The Human Rights Committee and similar bodies, in processing petitions complaining of violations of human rights, are resorting more and more to ordering interim measures of protection which are respected by States Parties. Out of 200 interim measures so far ordered by the Human Rights Committee, only two were not observed.[2] This is a significant development in the implementation of international human rights treaties that is particularly significant for victims.

(c) Remedies and Compensation

When individual petitions procedures under international human rights treaties were established in the mid 1960s, they were grudgingly accepted by many States. As a result, bodies such as the Human Rights Committee were given vague and general competence in considering such petitions. Article 5, paragraph 4 of the Optional Protocol to the International Covenant on Civil and Political Rights, for example, states rather blandly that the Human Rights Committee, after considering petitions, "shall forward its views to the State Party concerned and to the individual."

As is the hallmark of the human rights movement, however, this bland provision would be given teeth by the Human Rights Committee through the development of practice over time. One thus finds at the conclusion of views handed down by the Human Rights Committee these days orders such as the following:

> Bearing in mind that in becoming a State Party to the Optional Protocol the State Party has recognized the competence of the Committee to determine whether there has been a violation of the Covenant or not and that, pursuant to Article 2 of the Covenant, the State Party has undertaken to ensure to all individuals within its territory and subject to its jurisdiction the rights recognized in the Covenant and to provide an effective and enforceable remedy in

[2] Case 703/1996, Rockliffe Ross (Trinidad and Tobago); Case 580/1994, Glen Ashby (Guyana).

case a violation has been established, the Committee wishes to receive from the State Party, within 90 days, information about any measures taken to give effect to the Committee's views.[3]

(d) The Use of Follow-Up Procedures

More and more treaty bodies such as the Human Rights Committee are not content with merely handing down decisions on individual petitions. They increasingly resort to follow-up procedures designed to ensure that their decisions are implemented by States Parties.

(e) The Use of Concluding Observations After the Consideration of States Reports

All the treaty bodies, such as the Human Rights Committee and the Committee on the Rights of the Child, have now established the practice of drawing up concluding observations after they have considered reports from States Parties. These reports sometimes draw attention to vulnerable or victimized parts of the population for whom urgent measures are necessary to correct or redress their situation.

(f) Growing Acceptance of Petitions Procedures

The battle for the establishment of petitions procedures under international human rights treaties were fiercely contested in 1965 when the International Convention on the Elimination of All Forms of Racial Discrimination gave the first break-through, and again in 1966, when the Optional Protocol to the International Covenant on Civil and Political Rights was adopted. For years the number of ratifications to the Optional Protocol was paltry. Today, however, it is heartening to note that of 140 ratifications or accessions to the International Covenant on Civil and Political Rights, there are 93 ratifications of the Protocol. The case law developed under the Optional Protocol will prove to have been one of the enduring legacies of the second half of the twentieth century. Protection for victims has been the hallmark of that case law.

CONCLUSION

In this brief presentation we have sought to bring out the strategies of international human rights treaties in trying to prevent people from becoming

---

[3] See the views of the Human Rights Committee in the case of Yassin and Thomas. Spring session of the Human Rights Committee, 1998.

victims of violations of human rights and to highlight some aspects of the emerging practice of treaty bodies that are of particular relevance to victims, particularly the emergence of urgent action procedures and the increasing stress on remedies and compensation. We do not claim that international human rights treaty bodies are operating as effectively as they could, or that all is well with them. What we do say, however, is that the development of an effective international system for the protection of human rights is an incremental process and that, from this perspective, there is a great deal in the international human rights treaty regime to be hopeful about.

Chapter 3

International Labour Organization (ILO) Standards and Human Rights

Lee Swepston

The standards adopted by the International Labour Organization, and the way in which they are supervised and implemented, are a vital part of the UN system's efforts to promote human rights, and represent the ILO's way of implementing relevant aspects of the Universal Declaration of Human Rights. While ILO standards deal with many different aspects of human rights, there are seven Conventions generally held to be its "core" human rights standards. These cover the subjects of freedom of association and protection of the right to organize, and protection against forced labor, child labor, and discrimination in relation to work.[1] They develop in more depth many of the concepts found in the Universal Declaration of Human Rights, and in the two International Covenants on human rights. These Conventions are very widely ratified, and their ratification brings countries under the ILO's highly-developed supervisory system.

TRIPARTISM

A basic factor that sets the ILO apart from all other intergovernmental organizations is that it is not exclusively intergovernmental. All decisions in the ILO are made on a "tripartite" basis. Each delegation to the ILO's annual

---

[1] All ILO standards can be accessed from the ILO web site at *www.ilo.org,* under "International Labour Standards and Human Rights." Look for the ILOLEX database. Copies may also be obtained from the International Labour Office in Geneva.

Conference must include representatives of national employers and workers as well as of governments. The ILO's Governing Body is composed of 50 percent government representatives, with 25 percent each being workers and employers. In both instances, therefore, governments have only 50 percent of the voting strength. As will be seen below, the "social partners," as they are called, also have a very significant role to play in ILO standard setting and supervision. Tripartism means that the decision-making process in the ILO is very different from that in organizations where governments have all the votes.

SUPERVISORY SYSTEM

The ILO's supervisory system can seem rather complex, but in fact is simple in conception. It relies on the principle that all parts of the supervisory system must be mutually supportive, and that all the concerned parties have their role to play in assuring the implementation of standards. Its purpose is to examine whether States are implementing standards fully, and for the ILO and member States to work together to ensure this happens. To this end, all ILO technical assistance is geared to the implementation of standards, and all suggestions by its supervisory bodies for improvements in national situations are backed up by offers of assistance to help in doing so. This offer is supported, in turn, by the presence of multidisciplinary teams in sixteen developing regions around the world, most including specialists in standards and related subjects.

Regular Supervision

Almost all ILO supervision is based on periodic reports from governments, comments from employers' and workers' organizations, and discussions in the Conference. It thus is not usually an adversarial procedure, and certainly does not rely principally on complaints. When a Convention has been ratified, the government is required by article 22 of the ILO Constitution to send periodic reports at intervals of one to five years depending on the Convention and the situation. Governments must send copies of their reports to the most representative organizations of employers and of workers in the country, which have the right to make their own comments on these reports. Present reporting volume is about 1,500 government reports a year, with about 250 supplementary comments by employers' and workers' organizations. Governments' reports and the supplementary information available are examined by the *Committee of Experts on the Application of Conventions and Recommendations,* a body of twenty independent experts drawn from all economic and social systems. They issue an annual report containing a general report and a large number of *observations,* or published comments. These are supplemented by a much larger number of *direct requests,* which are not published but are sent directly to governments.[2] These comments contain questions, requests for changes in national law and practice, and a great deal of information on the situation in each country.

The Committee's report containing the observations is submitted to the International Labour Conference, where it is discussed by a tripartite *Conference Committee on the Application of Conventions and Recommendations.* This Committee invites some governments to appear before it to discuss their situation, and these discussions can be very difficult. The discussions with governments take place in public sessions, and a detailed account of the discussion is published in the Committee's report before the end of the Conference session, in three languages.[3]

COMPLAINTS PROCEDURES

The ILO Constitution also allows for two kinds of complaints procedures. Under article 24 of the Constitution, organizations of employers and of workers may make *representations* that a government has not taken measures to ensure the satisfactory observance of a Convention it has ratified. This leads to an examination by a tripartite committee of the Governing Body, and the eventual issuance of a report detailing any problems in observance and recommendations for improvement. The results of representations are followed up by the Committee of Experts.

Article 26 of the Constitution allows *complaints* to be filed by governments of other countries that have ratified the same Convention, by delegates to the Conference, and by the Governing Body itself. The Governing Body may do so to follow up a representation, or on its own initiative. A complaint is examined by a special Commission of Inquiry, composed of eminent independent persons. It usually holds hearings in Geneva, and visits the country concerned for an on-the-spot investigation. At the conclusion of its work, it adopts a report which is submitted to the Governing Body for information. The Commission's conclusions are then followed up by the Committee of Experts. Recent Commissions of Inquiry include Myanmar on forced labor (completed in mid-1998) and Nigeria (established in March 1998 concerning freedom of association).

---

[2] Though not published separately, direct requests are available on the ILOLEX database, along with observations, the texts of Conventions and Recommendations and of the Constitution, reports of the Committee on Freedom of Association (see below), and other supervisory materials. ILOLEX is available on CD-ROM and on the Internet.

[3] See *Provisional Record* containing the report of the Conference Committee, submitted to the plenary of the Conference for adoption on one of the last two days of the session. This is then incorporated in the *Record of Proceedings* of each session. Like the other elements of the supervisory procedure referred to here, it is included in the ILOLEX database.

Special procedures for freedom of association were established by agreement with the United Nations Economic and Social Council in 1950. Under this procedure, the tripartite Governing Body *Committee on Freedom of Association* (CFA) examines complaints of violations of constitutional principles of freedom of association and the right to collective bargaining from workers' and employers' organizations and—theoretically, at least—from governments. This is unique among ILO procedures as its does not depend on the ratification of the related ILO Conventions. The CFA has developed an extensive set of principles which may be found in a *Digest of Decisions and Principles of the Freedom of Association Committee of the Governing Body of the ILO.*[4] A *Fact-Finding and Conciliation Commission on Freedom of Association* can also be created. It is the equivalent of a Commission of Inquiry, except that the government's consent is required. It can examine even complaints against non-Members of the ILO, when complaints are referred to it by the Economic and Social Council of the United Nations.

Reports under article 19 of the ILO Constitution. A remarkable provision added to the Constitution in 1946, article 19 has proven extremely flexible in permitting the examination of situations even when the Conventions concerned have not been ratified. It has no equivalent in other organizations, and its use is evolving as its possibilities are better understood. Until recently, it has been used mostly as the basis for *General Surveys* carried out by the Committee of Experts, which review the way in which Conventions and Recommendations are applied by ratifying States, and draw conclusions on the general trends in connection with them, including whether to consider their revision. These Surveys are published as Report III (Part 1B) of the Committee of Experts' report to the Conference, and are excellent reference material. In recent years they have dealt, for example, with freedom of association (1994), equality of opportunity and treatment (1996), labor administration (1997), and others. They are also discussed in the Conference Committee.

Article 19 allows for other uses as well. In its 1998 Conference Session, the ILO adopted a "Declaration of Fundamental Principles and Rights at Work," which declares that certain principles are binding on all Members even in the absence of ratification of the corresponding Conventions. Article 19 is one of the key building blocks in a procedure now being put into place under this Declaration. Its follow-up procedure will allow the ILO to use article 19 to consider the consequences of non-ratification of the ILO's fundamental Conventions by Member States, and will mandate it to reorient its technical assistance as a result of its examination. The details of this procedure will be resolved at the Governing Body in November 1998.

This panoply of supervisory procedures has been highly effective, especially compared to other supervisory bodies in the international system. A high rate of

---

[4] Fourth (revised) edition, ILO, 1996. It can also be found on the ILOLEX database.

reporting,[5] acceptance by almost all States invited to appear before the Conference Committee, and a large number of complaints examined by the Committee on Freedom of Association attest to a general respect for the procedure. It is also effective in securing modifications of law and practice in members States in a large number of countries, and is generally well respected. The ILO reinforces its supervisory activity by ensuring that its technical cooperation is closely based on its standards, and that no technical assistance is given which would be contrary to those standards.

THE FUTURE OF ILO STANDARDS

The ILO system has stood the test of time extremely well. It is now more than seventy years since the Committee of Experts and the Application of Standards Committee of the Conference were established, and the Committee on Freedom of Association approaches its 50th anniversary. Ratifications of ILO Conventions have increased steadily. There are significant challenges, however, to which the ILO is adapting with more or less speed. Some of them are outlined here.

Changes in the Nature of ILO's Constituents

In the ILO's earlier years, it was simple to identify all the players. There was a relatively small number of member States, and the trade unions and employers' organizations from each country could be presumed to speak for most of the national economy. Now, States have banded together to form economic blocks, and regional organizations often set labor legislation. States can still ratify Conventions, but the European Union and the Common Market of the Southern Cone (MERCOSUR) cannot. There is a long-standing discussion between the ILO and the EU over the present nature of the "competent authority" for the submission of new ILO standards, as competence for the adoption of laws and regulations has been passed to the Union bodies, but only States may ratify Conventions.

The ILO's non-governmental partners have also changed in character. A long decline in union membership in developed countries has undermined the authority with which trade unions speak.[6] The trend was accelerated—perhaps artificially and only temporarily—by the fall of the Berlin Wall and the consequent end of compulsory trade union membership in a number of countries,

---

[5] The ILO currently receives some 65 percent of reports due by the time of the annual meeting of the Committee of Experts, rising to some 85 percent by the annual Conference. At the same time, the Committee notes in each annual report cases where governments have persistently failed to meet their reporting obligations on time.

[6] This is developed at some length in ILO: *World Labour Report* 1997, ILO, Geneva.

allowing membership rates to move toward a more "natural" level. This has now gone into reverse in some countries, and unions' membership is growing there. In addition, unions remain a very significant voice in social policy in many countries. At the same time, however, voices such as that of the World Bank[7] challenge unions as insider organizations that protect the privileged who have jobs, against the many who do not. This in turn reflects, in part, the unemployment crisis in Europe and elsewhere, with rates of unemployment that once would have been considered a recipe for revolution going on for years with no solutions in sight.

Employers also are not what they were. When national employers could presume to speak for the "capital" side of the national economy, discussions were simpler. Now, many companies report to home offices not found within the national territory. Multinational enterprises in developing countries sometimes have budgets as large as the nations within which they operate. Globalization affects workers, but it also affects the ability of managers to make their own decisions—and thus to discuss standards and rules with international organizations such as the ILO.

New Actors in International Policy-Setting

When the ILO was created, there were only two international organizations—itself and the League of Nations. That changed after World War II with the creation of the United Nations system, but the lines of authority remained relatively clear for many years. Today, however, there has been a tremendous change with the end of the Cold War and the onset of economic globalization. Labor standards and workers' rights have become a major concern, and globalization has added complexity as it brings new actors onto the scene.

Although not a new actor, the United States has for many years been setting conditions in its own trade laws for workers' rights to be observed before the privilege of trading freely with the United States could be achieved. This legislation has not been vigorously or consistently enforced, but its focus was made more intense with the adoption of the North American Free Trade Agreement (NAFTA), requiring the United States, Canada, and—the true target—Mexico to apply their own labor laws. It has sometimes been overlooked that ratified ILO Conventions form part of national law in various ways, and their application could thus be extended through NAFTA.

There are also new institutional actors. The World Trade Organization has had to consider the relation between labor standards and international trade, under pressure from the United States and the international trade union movement. While fiercely resisted by developing countries (see, e.g., the 1996 Singapore

[7] World Bank: *World Development Report 1996.*

Declaration[8]), it has dominated significant parts of the discussion concluding and following up the Uruguay Round and the creation of the World Trade Organization. The World Bank and the Organization of Economic Cooperation and Development,[9] *inter alia,* have examined the effect of labor standards on development and on national economies. While none of these studies concludes that labor standards are damaging to development and that basic standards at least should not be observed, they do bring an econometric aspect to the question which had barely been there before. This is of course by no means a bad thing—assumptions need to be re-examined and challenged periodically to ensure that they remain valid in the light of changing circumstances. It has, however, made agreement more difficult to secure on questions that the ILO once could decide alone.

It is also requiring the ILO to argue on the terrain of other organizations, and forcing it to push them to argue in its area. The ILO has always used essentially moral arguments to demonstrate the desirability of respect for basic human rights—freedom from forced and child labor, and from discrimination, and respect for freedom of association—as well as for policy questions such as minimum wages and safety and health at work. Now, organizations such as the World Bank challenge even such basic assumptions as the drive to eliminate child labor, arguing that it is often inevitable and even, in some circumstances, economically desirable. The ILO is thus adding economic analysis of the benefits of respect for human rights to its traditional moral arguments. Happily, its decades-old instincts remain fundamentally unchallenged: it is good business to protect workers and to give them a voice in making the decisions that affect them.

Another aspect may need to be brought into the equation before long. The ILO has traditionally taken the stance that its standards lay down options and descriptions of best practice that, at least in the case of the "technical" standards, are entirely optional and can be taken up in accordance with national practice. Thus, a national system which imposes requirements on termination of workers' employment contracts that virtually prevent employers from exercising either financial or disciplinary discretion, can be as compatible with the ILO Convention on the subject as one that leaves very wide discretion while still providing protection against discriminatory treatment. The ILO may have to start dealing with the reality that its standards can be applied in ways that call the very idea of standards into question for some and lead to a feeling that deregulation—rather than re-examination of draconian regulation—is the answer to achieving the necessary degree of flexibility.

---

[8] World Trade Organization, *Singapore Ministerial Declaration,* adopted on 13 December 1996, published on http://www.wto.org/wto/archives/wtodec.htm.

[9] See, e.g., Maskus, Keith, *Should Core Labour Standards be Imposed through International Trade Policy?* World Bank Working Paper No. 1817, August 1997, published on http://www.worldbank.org/html/iecit/wp1817.html; and OECD, *Trade Employment and Labour Standards: A Study of Core Workers' Rights and International Trade,* 1996.

In this connection, the ILO has undertaken a three-year examination of all its standards with a view to deciding whether they remain fully valid, whether some require revision and updating, and even whether some are out of date and should be abrogated. This has proven a productive exercise, with some 25 percent of the standards adopted since 1919 scheduled for revision or abrogation.

None of this calls into question the need for labor standards, and there have been no serious proposals to alter the way in which the ILO works or to challenge the need to harmonize labor standards around the world. The ILO's standard-setting and supervisory systems work, and are likely to continue to be seen as essential far into the future.

Chapter 4

The United Nations Educational, Scientific and Cultural Organization (UNESCO) and the Promotion and Protection of Human Rights

Janusz Symonides

THE OBLIGATION TO PROMOTE AND PROTECT HUMAN RIGHTS

This obligation is formulated in Article I of the United Nations Educational, Scientific, and Cultural Organization (UNESCO) Constitution which states that "The purpose of the Organization is to contribute to peace and security by promoting collaboration among the nations through education, science and culture in order to further universal respect for justice, for the rule of law and for human rights and fundamental freedoms."

To further universal respect for human rights, the Organization, through education, information, and documentation, as well as research and reflection, promotes human rights and makes them known and better understood. It also undertakes various actions aimed at the protection of human rights and the elimination of all forms of discrimination related to the rights that are linked with UNESCO's fields of competence, namely cultural rights such as the right to education, to take part in cultural life, to benefit from scientific progress, and to freedom of information and expression. To strengthen the protection of cultural rights, the Organization has elaborated more than thirty standard-setting instruments—conventions, declarations, and recommendations.[1] Nevertheless, these rights may still be qualified as a neglected (underdeveloped) category of human rights.

---

[1] *UNESCO and Human Rights. Standard-Setting Instruments, Major Meetings, Publications,* UNESCO, Paris, 1996.

UNESCO's activities for the implementation and observance of cultural rights are by no means limited to the preparation of normative instruments. The Organization undertakes numerous activities and operational programs to fight against illiteracy, to ensure education, to promote access and creative participation in culture and science, to encourage the free flow of ideas and information, freedom of the press, pluralism and media independence, and to help victims of violations of cultural rights.

EDUCATION FOR HUMAN RIGHTS

Education for human rights has always been among the priorities of the Organization, which follows the assumption that human rights are respected and implemented where they are known.

The day after the adoption of the Universal Declaration of Human Rights on December 10, 1948, the UNESCO General Conference voted a resolution proclaiming the importance of the Universal Declaration for all UNESCO activities, in particular for those dealing with education and international understanding.[2]

For nearly fifty years since the adoption of the Universal Declaration, UNESCO has undertaken numerous activities aimed at its dissemination and introduction into schools. The first teaching aid, *The Universal Declaration of Human Rights: A Guide for Teachers,* was published by UNESCO as early as 1951 and translated into eight languages. In 1953, UNESCO launched the Associated Schools Project, now embracing 5,000 schools and colleges in 155 countries, which became an important instrument for the promotion of human rights. Similarly, UNESCO Chairs for Human Rights, Democracy, Peace and Tolerance have been established in twenty-four countries.

In 1974, the General Conference of UNESCO adopted a Recommendation Concerning Education for International Understanding, Co-operation and Peace and Education Relating to Human Rights and Fundamental Freedoms. It calls upon Member States to take steps to ensure that the principles of the Universal Declaration of Human Rights and of the International Convention on the Elimination of All Forms of Racial Discrimination become an integral part of the developing personality of each child, young person, or adult.[3]

---

[2] As early as 1950, ECOSOC invited UNESCO to encourage and facilitate teaching about the Universal Declaration in schools and adult education programs and through the media—press, television, radio, and films. The International Conference on Human Rights (Tehran, 1968) called for the development of programs aimed at the promotion of human rights education, particularly in institutions of higher learning, where future cadres are training.

[3] In 1985, the General Conference adopted a permanent system of reporting on steps taken by Member States to apply the 1974 Recommendation.

Since 1978, the UNESCO Prize for Human Rights Education has been awarded to teaching institutions, organizations, and persons having made a particularly efficient, exemplary, and genuine contribution to the development of education for human rights.

To give an impetus to human rights education, UNESCO organized a series of international congresses on this subject: in Vienna, Austria (1978), Malta (1987), and Montreal, Canada (1993). The Montreal International Congress on Education for Human Rights and Democracy adopted the World Plan of Action for Education on Human Rights and Democracy based on the assumption that education on human rights is itself a human right and is a prerequisite for the full realization of the ideals of democracy, social justice, peace, development, and human rights, which are universal and indivisible. The Plan presents a framework of action to be tailored and executed by States, intergovernmental, and non-governmental organizations and other social actors.

UNESCO is actively involved in the implementation of the Plan of Action for the United Nations Decade for Human Rights Education (1995-2004). The Organization is now working to encourage the preparation and adoption of national plans for developing human rights education; to support the elaboration of manuals, textbooks, and teaching aids and to reinforce networks of institutions active in education for peace, human rights, and democracy. These questions are discussed at regional meetings on human rights education convened by UNESCO.

The long-term goal of UNESCO is the creation of a culture of human rights by the establishment of a comprehensive system of education and training for peace, human rights, and democracy for all groups of people that embrace all levels of education, whether formal or non-formal.

THE STRUGGLE AGAINST ALL FORMS
OF DISCRIMINATION

UNESCO attaches great importance to the elimination of all forms of discrimination. Its stand against racism was already determined by its Constitution which declares: ". . . the great and terrible war which has now ended, was a war made possible . . . by the propagation, . . . through ignorance and prejudice, of the doctrine of inequality of man and races."

In 1948, ECOSOC urged UNESCO to adopt a program for disseminating scientific facts designed to remove racial prejudice. In response to this appeal, a broad program of research on the scientific facts of race was prepared. In a series of statements adopted in the 1950s and 1960s, experts underlined that race is not so much a biological phenomenon as a "social myth." For this reason, it would be better, when speaking of human races, to drop the term "race" altogether and speak of ethnic groups. In 1978, the General Conference adopted by acclamation the Declaration on Race and Racial Prejudice. It states that all human beings belong to a single species and are descended from a common stock. The Declaration proclaims the right of all individuals and groups to be different. However, diversity of lifestyles and the right to be different may not, in any circumstances, serve as a pretext for racial prejudice.

Since the adoption of the Declaration, the Director-General has submitted five reports on its implementation to the General Conference, the sixth will be presented in 1999. During more than fifty years of activity aimed at the elimination of racism and racial discrimination, UNESCO has organized numerous meetings and published a number of studies dealing with various aspects of this question.

The position taken by UNESCO on racial problems has been unequivocal and brought about the decision of the Government of the Union of South Africa to withdraw from the Organization on December 31, 1956. Ten years later, in 1966, UNESCO produced its report on apartheid and its effects on education, science, culture, and information. In the same year, the General Conference requested the Director-General not to invite the Republic of South Africa to attend conferences or take part in other UNESCO activities until such time as the government of that country had abandoned its policy of racial discrimination.

Since its early years, UNESCO has been very active in combating all forms of inequalities based on gender within its fields of competence. Apart from incorporating into standard-setting instruments numerous provisions aimed at the elimination of discrimination in education, professional, and public life, the Organization has promoted research yielding fuller knowledge of the situation of women throughout the world and better understanding of the nature of existing inequalities. All its activities are based on the assumption that international organizations can contribute to the emancipation of women and girls through research, information, education, and training. Bearing in mind that, with very few exceptions, illiteracy rates are higher for women than for men, UNESCO has launched a number of operational activities known as literacy, functional literacy, legal literacy, and civic education for women. UNESCO participated actively in the Beijing Conference on Women and has undertaken a program to implement the Beijing Declaration and Platform of Action.

Discrimination and intolerance, as underlined by the UNESCO Medium-Term Strategy 1996-2001, often go hand in hand. The Organization has taken steps to organize a "crusade" against intolerance within the United Nations system. The General Assembly, at UNESCO's initiative, proclaimed 1995 the United Nations Year for Tolerance and invited it to assume the role of lead organization.

Tolerance is one of the great challenges of our time, as in principle most societies are pluralistic, diverse, and diversified and many of them are multicultural and multireligious. The Declaration of Principles on Tolerance was adopted by the General Conference of UNESCO at its 28th session in 1995.[4]

VIOLATIONS OF CULTURAL RIGHTS

In 1978, the Executive Board of UNESCO by its decision 104 EX/3.3 instituted a special procedure for examination of cases and questions submitted to UNESCO concerning the exercise of human rights. In exercising its competence, UNESCO is called upon to examine: (a) cases concerning violations of human rights that are individual and specific and (b) questions of massive, systematic, or flagrant violations of human rights and fundamental freedoms that result either from a policy contrary to human rights applied *de jure* or *de facto* by a State or from an accumulation of individual cases forming a consistent pattern. Individual cases are examined in private meetings of the Committee on Conventions and Recommendations (CR), one of the permanent subsidiary bodies of the Executive Board that is composed of thirty representatives of Member States (5 from each region of the world). Questions of massive, systematic, or flagrant violations of human rights which should be examined by the Executive Board and the General Conference in public meetings have not been examined to date. A complaint may be directed at any Member State and UNESCO's competence to examine individual communications alleging violations of human rights has been gradually recognized by all members.[5]

The following rights are within UNESCO's competence: the right to education; the right to share in scientific advancement; the right to participate freely in cultural life; and the right to information, including freedom of opinion and expression. These rights may imply the exercise of others, the most noteworthy of which are: the right to freedom of thought, conscience, and religion; the right to

---

[4] The Plan of Action for the follow-up to the United Nations Year for Tolerance, also adopted by the General Conference, presents the causes and factors contributing to manifestations of intolerance around the world. The aim of the Plan is to transpose the most successful components of the United Nations Year for Tolerance into more enduring strategies and structures by which promotion and sensitization of tolerance may be improved in every region of the world.

[5] To be considered admissible, a communication has to meet a number of conditions set up in paragraph 14 of the decision 104 EX/3.3: it must not be anonymous, must originate from a person or a group of persons who can be reasonably presumed to be victims, or a person or group of persons or organization having reliable knowledge of an alleged violation of human rights falling within UNESCO's fields of competence.

seek, receive, and impart information and ideas through the media regardless of frontiers; the right to the protection of the moral and material interests resulting from any scientific, literary, or artistic production; and the right to freedom of assembly and association for the purposes of activities connected with education, science, culture, and information.[6]

Having declared a communication to be admissible, the Committee continues to examine it with a view to bringing about a solution designed to advance the promotion of human rights. When the work of the CR is concluded, it adopts a confidential report containing its recommendations and all information arising from the examination of the communication. Subsequently, the Executive Board may take whatever action it considers appropriate, including endorsing a report and appealing to the government concerned to take measures to restore the necessary safeguards of human rights. The UNESCO procedure has two specific characteristics in comparison with similar procedures in other organizations of the United Nations system: it is strictly confidential and it relates to cultural rights. In fact, it is the only communication procedure which applies exclusively to cultural rights. Though the number of complaints presented to UNESCO is relatively small, nevertheless the procedure is effective as it has led in the years between 1978 and 1997 to the settlement of 277 cases. In recent years the Commission on Conventions and Recommendations has taken special efforts to make this procedure better known and therefore more effective in the protection of cultural rights.

ACTIONS AIMED AT THE PROTECTION OF SPECIAL PROFESSIONAL GROUPS

UNESCO cannot remain indifferent to the wave of hatred and violence sweeping over certain communities of educators, journalists, writers, or artists, whose most fundamental rights, including the right to life, are being systematically denied.[7] It therefore has undertaken, in accordance with its ethical mission, to alert public opinion to flagrant violations of the rights of intellectuals and to

---

[6] Any communication that at first sight appears to be covered by decision 104 EX/3.3 is dealt with in the following way: the Secretariat sends a letter to the author of the communication asking him or her to fill in a form and sign a declaration agreeing to the examination of the communication, which is then sent to the government concerned informing it that any reply it may wish to make will be brought to the notice of the Committee. The government may attend meetings of the Committee in order to provide additional information or answer questions.

[7] *Medium Term Strategy 1996-2001*, 28C/4 Approved *UNESCO*, Paris, 1996, p. 41.

attacks on their lives, dignity, and freedom of expression, of research,[8] and of creation. To this end, UNESCO has been collecting information and preparing background studies, declarations and reports aimed at raising public awareness and public condemnation of especially serious cases of violations of cultural rights.

Prior to this, the Sector of Communication, Information and Informatics has been monitoring freedom of the press and reacting to attacks on the independence and security of media and journalists. The UNESCO-supported International Freedom of Expression Exchange Network mobilizes international public opinion, non-governmental organizations, and professional associations against violations of journalists' rights.

The Director-General, in a series of special communiqués and declarations, has drawn the attention of the international community to barbarous acts of terrorism (in particular, Algeria). On a number of occasions, he has made statements condemning acts of terrorism designed to impede especially intellectuals' freedom of expression. He has also denounced situations in which their life is in jeopardy.

THE COMMEMORATION OF THE FIFTIETH ANNIVERSARY OF THE UNIVERSAL DECLARATION OF HUMAN RIGHTS

The fiftieth anniversary of the Universal Declaration of Human Rights provides an excellent opportunity to reinforce the promotion and protection of human rights. UNESCO, in close cooperation with the High Commissioner for Human Rights, has prepared a Plan of Action for the commemoration which was adopted by the Executive Board and the General Conference. Its main objectives

---

[8] In 1974, the General Conference of UNESCO adopted the "Recommendation on the Status of Scientific Researchers" which contains several provisions relating to the freedom of research and freedom to disseminate research findings. An International Conference on Academic Freedom and University Autonomy, organized by UNESCO, in Sinaia, Romania, in May 1992, adopted the Sinaia Statement in which participants urged UNESCO "to give the matter of academic freedom and university autonomy its utmost attention and to prepare an international instrument for the protection and promotion of these values." The International Congress on Education for Human Rights and Democracy (Montreal, March 1993) confirmed the importance of adopting an international instrument on academic freedom and decided to bring to the attention of the Director-General of UNESCO the document called "Contributions to the preparation of a declaration on academic freedom." This document enumerates the following rights enjoyed by members of the academic community: (a) the right to become, without discrimination of any kind, member of the academic community; (b) the right to freely determine the subject and methods of their research; (c) the right to freely determine, within the framework established by the institution of higher education, the content and methods of instruction; (d) the right of students to study, to choose the field of study, and receive official recognition of the knowledge and experience acquired; (e) the right to seek, receive, obtain, and impart information and ideas of all kinds and in all forms; and (f) the right of all members of the academic community to co-operate freely with their counterparts.

are: to disseminate as widely as possible the message of the Universal Declaration, in particular among youth; to give a new impetus to human rights education, stemming from the assumption that the right to human rights education is itself a human right and that it is an obligation of States; to assess the state of implementation of those human rights that are considered a priority by UNESCO and to reflect on practical ways and means to strengthen their implementation and universal observance; to reflect on problems and challenges in the field of human rights, in particular those linked to scientific and technological progress, the information revolution and globalization; to underline the universality; indivisibility, interdependence, and interrelation of all human rights—civil, cultural, economic, political, and social—and to promote worldwide recognition of the fact that peace, democracy, development, and respect for human rights and fundamental freedoms are interdependent and mutually reinforcing.

The Organization has encouraged the planning and coordination of special activities related to the fiftieth anniversary through National Commissions, Associated Schools, UNESCO Chairs, UNESCO Clubs, Centers and Associations, national human rights institutions, non-governmental organizations, both national and international, and training and research institutes in the field of human rights. In fact, this commemoration has led to a broad movement for human rights.

Chapter 5

The United Nations Declaration of Basic Principles of Justice for Victims of Crime and Abuse of Power

Irene Melup

The United Nations Declaration of Basic Principles of Justice for Victims of Crime and Abuse of Power has been called a Magna Carta for victims. The Declaration, adopted by the General Assembly on December 27, 1985 on the recommendation of the Seventh UN Congress on the Prevention of Crime and the Treatment of Offenders (Milan, August 26-September 6, 1985), is indeed a milestone in the treatment and protection of victims. It stipulates that they should be shown compassion and respect for their dignity, given access to the mechanisms of justice, and afforded prompt redress for the harm they have suffered, including restitution, compensation, and appropriate assistance. General Assembly resolution 40/34, adopting the Declaration, complemented it by recommending measures to be taken at the national, regional, and international levels to stem victimization and alleviate the plight of victims, which had all too often been neglected. The tragic events of recent years and the human cost of civil strife have underlined the price of inaction and the need for incisive steps to forestall future human tragedies. By including both individual and collective victims, the Declaration offers a comprehensive approach to mass victimization. Its full implementation is a priority need and a challenge facing countries, civil society, and the international community as a whole.

BREAKING NEW GROUND

The victim Declaration broke new ground in a number of other ways. While the situation of crime victims in a number of countries has improved since the early sixties, with the adoption, in some States (e.g., New Zealand), of measures for the compensation of victims of violent crimes—a movement which has gathered momentum, with the promulgation of victims' bills of rights in a number of jurisdictions (especially in the United States, where a constitutional amendment has also been proposed), effective international action has been lagging. Admittedly, the Universal Declaration of Human Rights, the International Covenants (on civil and political rights and on economic, social, and cultural rights, respectively), the Geneva Conventions on the protection of civilians in armed conflict, and various other United Nations instruments,[1] treaty mechanisms and procedures seek to curtail victimization and protect the victims of international crimes such as genocide, torture and slavery, of racial and sex discrimination, and of exploitative practices, especially those involving children, minorities, and migrant workers.

Other United Nations provisions, such as the Declaration on the Protection of all Persons from Enforced Disappearance, the Declaration on the Elimination of Violence against Women, and measures for the protection of the elderly, disabled, and mentally ill, all seek to reduce likely victimization. So does the work of the Subcommission (of the Commission on Human Rights) on Prevention of Discrimination and Protection of Minorities, and of different working groups (e.g., on contemporary forms of slavery, on indigenous populations, on minorities, etc.) and of special rapporteurs (e.g., on arbitrary and summary executions, on torture, on children in armed conflict, on the traffic in women and children). These are described elsewhere in this book, as are the complaint procedures under the international human rights treaties and mechanisms involving the Commission on Human Rights and the various human rights treaty bodies.

By seeking to promote the observance of human rights and to protect especially vulnerable members of society and population groups, these efforts have endeavored to curtail the prevalence and impact of different kinds of victimization, and to provide some avenues of recourse. UN humanitarian assistance, peacekeeping and peacebuilding, development programs, and other initiatives have also sought to alleviate the human cost of man-made disasters and inequities as a prime United Nations mission. However, due to the variety of mandates,

---

[1] They include the Convention on the Prevention and Punishment of the Crime of Genocide, the Convention Against Torture and Other Cruel or Degrading Treatment or Punishment (which grew out of the Declaration Against Torture adopted by the Fifth UN Crime Congress), the International Convention on the Elimination of all Forms of Racial Discrimination, the Convention and Supplementary Convention on the Abolition of Slavery, the Slave Trade and Practices Similar to Slavery, the Convention and Protocol relating to the Status of Refugees, the Convention on the Rights of the Child, and the Convention on the Elimination of all Forms of Discrimination Against Women.

frequent compartmentalization of efforts and other constraints, their benefits for victims and potential victims have often been limited and their role circumscribed.

In this context, the UN Declaration on victims acquires added potential. Its comprehensive scope and multilevel approach make it a suitable counterpart to the Universal Declaration of Human Rights and a complement to the UN human rights instruments and procedures. It should also be taken into account in other facets of United Nations work whose aim is to reduce suffering and to promote justice and well-being.

The United Nations Crime Prevention and Criminal Justice Programme, under which the victim Declaration was developed, has sought to formulate a series of norms and guidelines designed to foster more humane and enlightened national policies and more effective international cooperation in this field. The Declaration is a significant achievement, pioneering in its scope, which encompasses different categories of victims, and in its approach, which deems fair, sensitive, and appropriate treatment of victims, access to services and the provision of means of recourse and redress a matter of basic justice. While psychosocial assistance to victims is an essential aspect in their welfare and protection, it is seen as a basic entitlement rather than a matter of benevolence. In expanding the non-discrimination provisions of the Human Rights Declaration to include also age and disability, the victim Declaration seeks to assure equity for especially vulnerable targets and thus to further enhance justice and a better life for all.

The leitmotif of justice runs through the Declaration, beginning with its preambular part, in which the General Assembly declared that it is "cognizant that millions of people throughout the world suffer harm as a result of crime and the abuse of power and that the rights of these victims have not been adequately recognized"; "that the victims of crime and the victims of abuse of power, and also frequently their families, witnesses and others who aid them are unjustly subjected to loss, damage, or injury, and that they may, in addition, suffer hardship when assisting in the prosecution of offenders." For that reason, the General Assembly affirmed the necessity of implementing (without prejudice to the rights of suspects or offenders)[2] national and international measures in order to secure the universal and effective recognition of, and respect for, the rights of victims of crime and abuse of power, adopting the Declaration designed to assist Governments and the international community in their efforts to secure justice and assistance for such victims.

The outcome largely of an NGO initiative, the Declaration represents the fruitful result of collaboration between interested governments and civil society.

---

[2] The congruence rather than conflict between victims' and offenders' rights is an important tenet all too often ignored by those emphasizing one at the expense of the other; it is also a cardinal principle of "restorative justice" long practiced in traditional settings (e.g., in Africa) and now gaining prominence in other regions. See also [1, 2].

An international meeting of experts, which preceded the Seventh Congress debate on this subject, developed a working draft, which contained more detailed provisions, some of which had to be sacrificed to achieve consensus at the Congress. The pioneering nature of the document is further reflected in the new mind-set it required in viewing victims in a unified perspective conducive to concerted action.

In fact, the original text of the draft Declaration was a unitary document, which derived largely from the work carried out in the preceding biennium on victims of abuse of power (typologies, patterns, legislative provisions, and counterstrategies), a follow-up of the Sixth Congress recommendations on crime and the abuse of (public and economic) power. In determining the agenda of the Seventh Congress, the Committee on Crime Prevention and Control also included prominently victims of conventional crime, which received more detailed attention in the final Congress and General Assembly resolutions. A legalistic approach prevented some countries, fearful of possible politicization and the financial ramifications, from approving equivalent provisions for victims of abuse of power, a lacuna that has been deplored. It also led to the bifurcation of the Declaration into two parts: part A concerned with victims of crime and a brief part B on victims of abuse of power.

Even so, the results are impressive, for example, in the very concept of victims derived from a nuanced appreciation of the harm—including non-material harm—inflicted: "persons who, individually or collectively, have suffered harm, including physical or mental injury, emotional suffering, economic loss or substantial impairment of their fundamental rights, through acts or omissions that are in violation of criminal laws operative within Member States, including those laws proscribing criminal abuse of power." The term "victim" was deemed applicable whether or not the perpetrator was identified, apprehended, prosecuted, or convicted, and regardless of the familial relationship between perpetrator and victim (important for cases of domestic violence). The immediate family or dependents of the direct victim, and persons who suffered harm in intervening to assist victims in distress or to prevent victimization, were also to be included in the term.

SOME HURDLES

Probably the most innovative feature of the Declaration, which gave rise to extensive debate and delicate negotiations, was the inclusion of victims of abuses of power where criminal prohibitions were not (yet) in place—a situation of special concern to the inhabitants of many developing countries suffering from political and economic abuses inflicted not only nationally but also transnationally. Their victims are defined in the Declaration in terms of the harm suffered in the same way as their counterparts of part A, but the acts or omissions causing it are specified as those "that do not yet constitute violations of national criminal laws but of internationally recognized norms relating to human rights." States are urged to incorporate into national law norms proscribing abuses of power and providing remedies to the victims, including restitution and/or compensation, and the necessary material, medical, psychological, and social assistance and support. States are also urged to review periodically their existing legislation and practices to ensure their responsiveness to changing circumstances, and to enact and enforce, if necessary, legislation proscribing acts constituting serious abuses of political or economic power, as well as promoting policies and mechanisms for their prevention and appropriate rights and remedies for their victims. States are further urged to consider negotiating multilateral international treaties relating to such victims.

Some brief comments on these clauses are, perhaps, in order, especially in retrospect. The sacrifice of a more extensive treatment of part B is regrettable, especially in the light of the dire subsequent events which have claimed so many victims. They have also added particular urgency to the full implementation of the recommendations contained in General Assembly resolution 40/34 and in subsequent resolutions calling for all appropriate measures to be taken at the national, regional, and international levels to curtail victimization and alleviate the plight of victims, including "the development of ways and means of providing recourse to victims where national channels may be insufficient," as a continuing priority task.

The definition of victimizing abuses of power by reference to their violation of internationally recognized norms relating to human rights, while apposite to the subject matter of this volume, has been questioned as not fully covering the spectrum of abuses of power, especially economic and environmental abuses, the latter highlighted in a suggested remedy involving the repair ("restoration") of environmental damage inflicted on a community. It may, of course, be argued that such abuses also contravene a fundamental human right to a safe environment, but it is also true that the complexities involved and time constraints contributed to this short-cut and somewhat unilateral emphasis. It was hoped at the time that a more detailed instrument, such as a convention, might later be elaborated for the treatment of victims, or for specific aspects thereof, such as compensation and restitution (on which a set of guidelines had been prepared and submitted to the Committee on Crime Prevention and Control before the Seventh Congress).

It would, therefore, be rewarding to be able to claim that subsequent initiatives arose from this intent. Unfortunately, however, the Crime Prevention and Criminal Justice Branch lacked the resources, in the face of competing priorities, to pursue this task, although it sought to promote the implementation of the Declaration in various ways. But, while it was included both in the Compendium of UN crime prevention and criminal justice standards and norms[3] and in the UN

---

[3] United Nations. Compendium of Standards and Norms in Crime Prevention and Criminal Justice, 1992. UN Sales No. E.92.IV.I.

Compilation of Human Rights Instruments,[4] General Assembly resolution 40/34 and the annexed Declaration did not receive the publicity which they rightfully deserved, due also to the rather low visibility of this United Nations program.

However, victim-related needs persisted, leading to the designation in 1990 of a Special Rapporteur of the Sub-Commission on Prevention of Discrimination and Protection of Minorities, with the mandate to carry out a major "study concerning the right to restitution, compensation and rehabilitation for victims of gross violations of human rights and fundamental freedoms." It was clear when this initiative was taken (from the relevant resolutions and actions) that it was oblivious of the UN Declaration on victims and previous work done in this area on which to build.[5] The compartmentalization of efforts undertaken by different parts of the UN system has tended to create such situations, especially when the bodies and offices concerned have had different degrees of leverage. It underlines the need for continuous information-sharing and close collaboration on matters of mutual interest, across bureaucratic and other lines. In fact, General Assembly resolution 40/34 had called for United Nations bodies and other entities, as well as other intergovernmental and non-governmental organizations and the public to cooperate in the implementation of the provisions of the Declaration, and to assist Member States, where necessary, in improving the ways and means of protecting victims at the national level and through international cooperation. It is to be hoped that the final text and its follow-up can profit from a further partnership between the entities and programs concerned.

FURTHER DEVELOPMENTS

Because of the summary style of the Declaration and its level of generality, especially in part B, it was soon felt that more precise indications or guidelines would help the implementation process. A Meeting of a Committee of Experts was, therefore, held in May 1986 at the International Institute of Higher Studies in Criminal Sciences at Siracusa, Italy, in cooperation with the United Nations. It produced a commentary and set of recommendations to serve as measures for the implementation of the victim Declaration [3].

The Economic and Social Council, in resolution 1986/10, adopted at the recommendation of the Committee on Crime Prevention and Control, urged that continued attention be given to the implementation of the Declaration at various levels, promoting integrated action in cooperation with governments, intergovernmental and non-governmental organization, and the public. It also

---

[4] United Nations. Human Rights: a Compilation, 1998.

[5] In spite, also, of a specific ECOSOC request that in the study on the subject takes into account the relevant work and recommendations of the Committee on Crime Prevention and Control (ECOSOC resolution 1990/22 paragraph 8). It is to the Special Rapporteur's credit that, when alerted, he sought to do so.

requested the Secretary-General to submit to the Committee progress reports on measures taken to implement the Declaration, on the basis of reports received from Member States.[6] The Council, on the Committee's recommendation, in its resolution 1989/57, also called for the preparation, publication, and dissemination of a guide for criminal justice practitioners and others concerned on the application of the Declaration, taking into account the proposed procedures developed by the Siracusa meeting of experts and other relevant input.

The Economic and Social Council, in its resolution 1990/22, echoed this call and requested the Secretary-General to continue to devote attention to policy and research on the situation of victims and the effective implementation of the victim Declaration, to meet the full range of needs and circumstances of different countries. It also recognized the need to look beyond national measures in some instances, especially where victims of transnational crimes and abuse of power were concerned. The Council requested the Secretary-General, together with all the entities of the United Nations system and other appropriate organizations, to undertake and coordinate the necessary action, with a humanitarian objective, to prevent and curtail severe victimization where national means of recourse are insufficient, and to 1) monitor the situation; 2) develop and institute means of conflict resolution and mediation; 3) promote access to justice and redress for victims; and 4) assist in providing material, medical, and psychosocial assistance to victims and their families. The UN funding agencies were invited to support technical cooperation programs for the establishment of services for victims; training for personnel working with victims was to be provided, and information exchange and coordination strengthened. The Secretary-General was requested to develop further international means of recourse and redress for victims where national channels may be insufficient, and report to the Crime Committee on the subject.

The Eighth UN Crime Congress (Havana, August 27-September 7, 1990), to which the Guide on the Implementation of the Declaration was submitted,[7] adopted a resolution on the Protection of the human rights of victims of crime and abuse of power. It urged States to take into account the provisions of the Declaration on victims in their national legislation; to provide public and social support services for victims and culturally appropriate programs for victim assistance, information, and compensation; to prepare training programs based on the Declaration, as well as other kinds of technical assistance and information exchange.[8] The establishment of a United Nations fund for victims of transnational crimes was also to be explored.[9]

---

[6] See e.g. E/AC.57/1988/3 and E/AC.57/1990/3.

[7] A/CONF.144/20.

[8] A/CONF.144/17.

[9] The establishment of such a fund or expansion of the Voluntary Fund for Victims of Torture has been previously suggested, as was the designation of a special year for victims (1999 is to be devoted to victims of torture, but does not include victims who have lost their lives and/or their families).

Unfortunately, the lack of resources impeded full implementation of these recommendations, though some attempts in this direction were made with extra-budgetary means. Thus, for example, in pursuance of General Assembly resolution 40/36 and of ECOSOC resolution 1989/67, and of a report on domestic violence submitted to the Eighth Congress, containing detailed recommendations,[10] a Resource Manual on Strategies for Confronting Domestic Violence was developed, with special emphasis on violence against women.[11] The United Nations institutes have cooperated in these initiatives, for instance the European Institute (HEUNI) in the development of this Manual and by convening a meeting on victim policy in Europe. UNAFRI—the African Institute—organized a Training Seminar on Victims of Crime and the Prevention of Victimization in Africa (Kampala, 1992), which stressed the need for criminal justice reforms to return to an approach more responsive to the needs of victims and of social harmony—a traditional African concern (rather than an adversarial stance)—which is also being fostered in the calls voiced elsewhere for "restorative justice" and practices of mediation and alternative dispute resolution [1, 2].

The International Scientific and Professional Advisory Council (ISPAC) of the UN Crime Prevention and Criminal Justice Programme, established in 1991 to channel to it the contributions of non-governmental organizations and the scholarly community, set up inter alia a resource committee on the protection of, and assistance to, victims. ISPAC, in cooperation with the UN Crime Prevention and Criminal Justice Branch and the Basque authorities, organized in May 1993, at the International Institute for the Sociology of Law, in Oñati, Spain, an International Workshop on the Prevention of Victimization, Protection and Assistance for Victims, and Conflict Resolution. The Meeting stressed the need for more vigorous implementation of the UN victim Declaration, although significant progress was achieved in a number of jurisdictions (starting with South Australia, which promptly incorporated the main provisions of the Declaration in its legislation and institutional framework). While other links to the Declaration could not always be confirmed, the references to it in various reforms attest to its impact at the national level. However, it was agreed that, especially at the international level, implementation had to be reinforced, fostering integrated action by all the entities concerned. The Workshop adopted a comprehensive set of recommendations for follow-up action.[12]

The Ninth UN Congress on the Prevention of Crime and the Treatment of Offenders (Cairo, April 29-May 8, 1995) had as one of the items on its agenda the topic "Crime prevention strategies, in particular as related to crime in urban areas and juvenile and violent criminality, including the question of victims:

---

[10] A/CONF.121/17.

[11] ST/CSDHA/20.

[12] ISPAC. *Victim Issues*. Milan, 1994.

assessment and new perspectives." In its recommendations on that subject, the Congress expressed its concern about the plight of crime victims; urged the full use and application of the UN victim Declaration and intensified action for the protection of, and assistance to, victims at the national and international levels, including training, action-oriented research, ongoing information exchange, and other means of cooperation in this field.

In December 1995, as part of the regular work program in crime control, which had been restructured for greater effectiveness by the General Assembly in resolution 46/152, a Meeting of Experts, convened to consider "Victims of crime and abuse of power in the international setting," made a number of far-reaching recommendations, such as a comprehensive plan of action for the implementation of the Declaration, a model project on the establishment of victim services, and emergency assistance. The Meeting also considered the first draft of a possible training manual for the implementation of the Declaration.[13]

The intergovernmental Commission on Crime Prevention and Criminal Justice, that replaced the Committee on Crime Prevention and Control in the restructuring of the program, considered the recommendations of the expert meeting, as well as the results of a survey on the application of the Declaration (based on replies of governments to a quantifiable questionnaire, developed as part of a phased assessment of the implementation of the UN norms and standards).[14] It was agreed that priority should be given to training initiatives, especially the development of appropriate training materials, such as the proposed manuals and database that would help to upgrade victim-related practices.

With this aim in view, several working groups were convened during the next two years, with the support of interested governments and organizations. They included expert meetings hosted by the Office of Victims of Crime of the US Department of Justice and the National Organization for Victim Assistance (NOVA), in Tulsa, Oklahoma (August 1996), and in Washington, D.C. (February 1998), to develop further the Handbook on the application of the victim Declaration as a comprehensive training manual for practitioners. A counterpart initiative, also taken in cooperation with the United Nations, was the meeting of experts hosted by the Ministry of Justice of the Netherlands at the Hague in March 1997. It sought to finalize a Guide for policy makers on the application of the Declaration, to be translated into various languages and widely distributed. The Ninth International Symposium on Victimology, held in Amsterdam in August 1997, provided another occasion for discussion of the training materials prepared. It also reviewed the methodology and results of the pioneering international victimization surveys conducted by the Dutch Ministry of Justice in

---

[13]CN.15/1996/3/Add.5.
[14]CN.15/1996/3/Add.1.

cooperation with the United Nations Interregional Crime and Justice Institute (UNICRI).[15]

The Commission on Crime Prevention and Criminal Justice, at its sixth session, in 1997, noted the progress achieved and approved a draft resolution (formulated at the Hague Expert Meeting), adopted by ECOSOC as resolution 1997/31 which inter alia invited the comments and suggestions of governments and other entities concerned on the Guide for policy makers and Handbook for practitioners, as well as proposals for an international plan of action for the implementation of the victim Declaration and improvement of the situation of victims.[16]

At its Seventh session, in April 1998, the Commission approved a draft resolution, adopted by ECOSOC as resolution 1998/21, on Victims of crime and abuse of power, which stressed the importance of the 1985 Declaration as a landmark in the treatment of victims, and expressed concern about the "continuing victimization by crime, especially organized crime, violence, terrorism and abuses of power, particularly of vulnerable groups and individuals, which exacts a vast human cost and impairs the quality of life in many parts of the world." The resolution welcomed the guide for policy makers and the handbook on justice for victims in promoting the use and application of the Declaration, and urges their translation and wide dissemination, through various means, including electronically. It also recommended the continued development of a database on practical national experiences, relevant case law and legislation, taking into account different systems and traditions, and its use in guidelines to assist States in drafting appropriate laws on victims. The feasibility of establishing an international fund for victims of crime and abuse of power is to be ascertained, to help support technical assistance projects, victim services and organizations, as well as specific projects and activities, awareness campaigns on victims rights and crime prevention, and eligible victim claims resulting from international and transnational crime where national avenues of recourse and/or redress are unavailable or insufficient. A working group of interested governments is to be convened on this matter, to be hosted by the Netherlands, which will also operate the database for an initial three-year period.

Technical cooperation is to be strengthened, using where possible a multipartner approach, including the United Nations, Member States, intergovernmental and non-governmental organizations, to incorporate victim assistance modules in relevant projects and assist countries, on request, in applying the

[15]UNICRI. *Experiences of Crime and Crime Control,* Rome, 1992 (publication no. 49) and *Criminal Victimization in the Developing World,* Rome, 1995 (publication no. 55).

[16]The Commission has also dealt with specific kinds of victims, developing Guidelines for the elimination of violence against women, as well as Guidelines for action on children in the criminal justice system, and resolutions on children as victims and perpetrators, on trafficking in children, etc., adopted as ECOSOC resolutions 1997/24 and 1997/30, respectively.

guide for policy makers and handbook on justice for victims. A multifaceted training program is to be instituted to help apply the Declaration, including training courses, seminars, study tours, fellowships and advisory services, with the help of interested governments, such as the Office for Victims of Crime of the US Department of Justice. The resolution further calls for the launching of pilot or demonstration projects for the expansion of victim services and other operational activities, as well as the development of measures for special victim groups, such as victims of terrorism, victims and witnesses of organized crime, victims of hate or bias crimes, female and child victims of violence, and disabled victims.

To ensure concerted action, a coordination panel or other mechanism would be established, with an appropriate division of labor among UN entities and other parties concerned, in order to promote the implementation of the Declaration. A comprehensive plan of action for the implementation of the victim Declaration is annexed to the Council's resolution, on which the views of governments are to be sought. It includes proposed strategies for capacity-building in this sphere, for information-gathering, information exchange and research, and for the prevention of victimization, as well as for further action to be taken at the regional and international levels, and for the coordination of relevant initiatives. A report on the progress achieved in the implementation of the resolution is to be submitted to the Commission on Crime Prevention and Criminal Justice at its eighth session, in 1999.

The situation of crime victims will also be considered by the Tenth UN Congress on the Prevention of Crime and the Treatment of Offenders (Vienna, April 10-17, 2000) under an agenda item dealing with "Offenders and victims: accountability and fairness in the justice process." The promotion of the principles of "restorative justice" is expected to figure prominently in the discussion on this subject at the Congress itself and at the regional preparatory meetings to be held prior to it. Among the aspects likely to be highlighted is the viability of such an approach, which would balance the rights of victims, offenders and society, and the use of conciliation and other conflict resolution methods. Attention will be focused on ways of increasing the fairness and accountability of criminal justice systems, and of developing and applying restorative justice measures in the context of development, democratization, and post-conflict reconstruction. Emphasis will also be placed on the further development of international means of recourse and redress where national channels may be insufficient, particularly in cases of transnational crime and abuse of power.

The international criminal tribunals and envisaged International Criminal Court are breakthroughs in this regard, reflecting the international community's growing intolerance of impunity for perpetrators and solidarity with victims— though there is still a long way to go. The UN Declaration on victims and related input have played their part. The Oñati Meeting, for example, made a number of proposals on the role of victims in the Tribunal for the former Yugoslavia, including strengthening the witness-victim unit as an autonomous entity, and provisions for restitution and/or compensation to the victims. The Registrar of the International Criminal Tribunal for Rwanda has issued a "Note on a Victim-Oriented Approach to Justice," [4] urging a restorative (or "restitutive") approach to the victims, in line with the UN Declaration (attached to the Note), and specifically, its stipulation that "victims should receive the necessary material, medical, psychological and social assistance through governmental and voluntary means," and that "States should provide remedies to such victims, including restitution and compensation" as an inherent part of dispensing justice. This innovative paper contains an impressive analysis justifying this approach, and a cogent proposal to utilize some of the voluntary contributions made available to the Tribunal by donors in providing assistance to the victims in the specific ways contemplated by the Tribunal's program (including self-help efforts) in the context of development.

Reparation was among the issues pursued in the finalization of the Statute of the proposed International Criminal Court at the Plenipotentiary Conference in Rome (June 15-July 17, 1998), along with certain other victim-related issues, especially those connected with paragraphs 68 and 73 of the draft Statute. The Hague Meeting of Experts, Crime Commission (sixth session) and ECOSOC, in its resolution 1987/31, called for proper attention to be given to justice for the victims in the Court's work. Other expert meetings, including NGO-sponsored ones, have also advocated reparation to the victims as pivotal. It is to be hoped that these calls will be heeded. It is also to be hoped that United Nations funds and foundations will give favorable consideration to project proposals designed to assist victims,[17] and that the positive steps taken by some governments will be replicated, with the UN system fully involved in a joint and long overdue undertaking.

The Statute of the International Criminal Court contains several references to the UN Declaration on victims. Adequate attention to their needs is an indispensable complement to the pursuit of offenders and the principle of restorative justice. While potential offenders should be deterred by the prospect of punishment for wrongful acts, the existence of international means of recourse would enhance the sense of security and belief in justice of those who are particularly vulnerable.

The Universal Declaration of Human Rights provides a global frame of reference in terms of which acceptable (and unacceptable) conduct is to be judged and basic protections afforded. If the UN Declaration of Basic Principles of Justice for Victims of Crime and Abuse of Power is, indeed, to be a Magna Carta

---

[17]An example is a proposal by an Argentine professional association to assess the impact of abuses of power against "disappeared" persons and their children in generating asocial behavior in some youths, as a guide to preventive measures. CODESEDH. "Promoción comunitaria y adolescentes en conflicto con la ley." Buenos Aires, 1998.

for victims, then it must come to be more generally known and properly applied. This aim should be advanced by the wide dissemination of the Declaration to policy makers, practitioners, victims and the population at large, especially those at greatest risk, from among whom prospective victims are likely to come, so that they can fully utilize it. The training manuals prepared for the use of policy makers and practitioners should help in the effective implementation of the provisions of the Declaration. But to make the Declaration more accessible to victims and potential victims, an international handbook to facilitate its use by them might well be prepared. Such an initiative had been proposed in the past, and could draw on national precedents with handbooks for victims. A practical guide of this kind would serve as a reference tool and source of solace to those in need.

As we approach a new century and the next millennium, issues of human security and fulfillment are taking center stage. The regeneration of traumatized societies, restoration of faith in justice and mobilization of people's solidarity demand no less—to reclaim human beings and prevent others from falling prey to malefactors is the major challenge we must face now and in the years to come.

REFERENCES

1. M. Groenhuijsen, *Conflicts of Victims' Interests and Offenders' Rights in the Criminal Justice System—A European Perspective,* Catholic University of Brabant, Belgium, 1994.
2. P. McCold, *Restorative Justice, An Annotated Bibliography,* Alliance of NGOs on Crime Prevention and Criminal Justice, Working Party on Criminal Justice, 1997; and Restorative Justice, in *Corrections Today, 59*:7, December 1997.
3. M. C. Bassiouni (ed.), *International Protection of Victims,* Nouvelles Etudes Pénales, Eràs, Paris, AIDP, 1988.
4. A. U. Okali, *Rwanda Genocide: Towards Victim-Oriented Justice—The Case for an ICTR Assistance to Victims Programme,* Office of the Registrar of the International Tribunal for Rwanda, Arusha, December 5, 1997.

Chapter 6

Thematic Mechanisms and the Protection of Human Rights

Bacre Waly Ndiaye*

ORIGINS

The UN's thematic mechanisms on human rights are crucial to the global protection of the human rights contained in the international human rights instruments the United Nations has so proudly pioneered over the past fifty years. The thematic mechanisms are perhaps the most victim-focused component of the UN's human rights machinery. After all, they only came into existence as a result of international recognition that a practice exists which causes serious human rights violations in more than a single country. Their creation represents an expression of international will to address the plight of the victims of processes that violate human rights.

It is indeed ironic, therefore, that the thematic mechanisms came into existence as a compromise and as a result of the efforts of one country to evade its accountability to human rights standards. In the 1970s a large number of disappearances were taking place during Argentina's "dirty war." It was impossible to pretend that a serious human rights situation did not exist. But, nevertheless, it was difficult to mobilize sufficient political support within the United Nations to adopt effective measures in response. Governments were ambivalent about pointing a finger at Argentina for reasons ranging from indifference, fear that they might be next in line for scrutiny or because of trade interests. Representatives of the military junta then in control of Argentina were skilled in the arts of international diplomacy. The compromise reached by the United Nations to overcome these difficulties, while avoiding a country-specific inquiry, was to establish the

---

*This chapter was written by the author at the time that he was still Special Rapporteur on Extrajudicial, Summary or Arbitrary Executions of the UN Commission on Human Rights.

67

first "thematic" mechanism—the Working Group on Disappearances created by the UN Human Rights Commission in 1980 in response to mounting pressure from NGOs, notably Amnesty International. The Group, based upon a proposal drawn up by Iraq with help from Cuba, was adopted without vote, reflecting a shaky consensus in which individual states were required not to vote for or against the proposal. The Working Group was created for one year only and was authorized to "examine questions relevant to enforced or involuntary disappearances of persons" responding only to specific "cases" or to urgent "situations."[1] The Working Group was invited "in establishing its working methods, to bear in mind the need to be able to respond effectively to information that comes before it," "from Governments, intergovernmental organizations, humanitarian organizations and other reliable sources," "and to carry out its work with discretion." The mandate of this Working Group was created in 1980 and was renewed every year until 1992. Since then it has been renewed every three years.

Since 1980, the Working Group on Disappearances has served as a model for the creation of a growing range of "thematic" mechanisms termed Working Groups or Special Rapporteurs. In 1998, the year of the 50th anniversary of the Universal Declaration of Human Rights, "thematic" mechanisms exist on (listed in chronological order of establishment of each mandate by the Commission on Human Rights):

- Disappearances—1980
- Arbitrary executions—1982
- Arbitrary detention—1985
- Torture—1985
- Religious intolerance—1985
- Freedom of opinion—1987
- Mercenaries—1987
- Sale of children—1990
- Internally displaced persons—1992
- Extreme poverty—1992
- Right to development—1993
- Racism—1993
- Violence against women—1994
- Independence of judges and lawyers—1994
- Foreign debt and economic, social, and cultural rights—1994
- Toxic wastes—1995
- Structural adjustment and economic, social, and cultural rights—1996
- Right to education—1997
- Children in armed conflict—1997

---

[1] Commission on Human Rights resolution 20 (XXXVI) of 1980.

The thematic mechanisms, striving always for greater effectiveness, have developed several techniques and working methods that include: requests to governments for information on specific cases; an urgent action procedure requesting that a government take immediate action to rectify or clarify a case; and on-site visits in a wide variety of countries for a more intensive and enduring examination of a series of cases. It has to be noted that rights cannot take place without a government's consent. The manner in which these techniques and methods are used vary considerably from mechanism to mechanism. But, in general, these mechanisms seek to explore the conceptual aspects of the issues, develop the applicable normative human rights framework and appropriate working methods, pressure individual governments to clarify or rectify situations, and inform other UN human rights bodies with a view to taking appropriate, timely, and effective actions. This chapter provides insights into the workings of one such mechanism—the Special Rapporteur on extrajudicial, summary or arbitrary executions which came into existence on May 7, 1982.[2]

MANDATES

It is inevitable that there are far more "thematics" that deserve creation of mechanisms than there are mechanisms. In a sense, the process of creating a thematic mechanism does involve selectivity but it is a selectivity that is principled—that is rooted in human rights principles. Failure to create a mechanism to address a clearly needed theme may indeed occur as a result of political expediency or compromise. But non-creation of a thematic mechanism in no way constitutes condoning of the abusive practice involved. Indeed, the existing thematic mechanisms consciously address this problem in two ways.

First, on the basis of work on their own mandate, Special Rapporteurs do not hesitate to recommend the creation of new mechanisms. Thus, for example, as a result of work on executions, the Special Rapporteur involved has suggested the creation of a Special Rapporteur on prisons because of the high incidence of deaths taking place while in custody and because of the allegations that many such deaths occurred as a result of torture or of life-threatening prison conditions. The African Commission on Human and Peoples Rights has indeed created such a Special Rapporteur on Prisons and Prison Conditions. It has also been recommended together with the Special Rapporteur on Torture that a Special Rapporteur on Colombia be established for similar reasons.

Second, Special Rapporteurs are also conscious of the need to creatively interpret their mandate to cover new and emerging issues and to respond to the lack of protection of victims. Thus, for example, it has been important not to

---

[2] The mandate of the Special Rapporteur was established by resolution 1982/35 of the Economic and Social Council.

define too specifically the term "extrajudicial, summary or arbitrary executions." This has made it possible to address "life-threatening" conditions and situations and act preventively rather than only reactively after death has taken place. Similarly, it has been possible to address situations of private lynching by holding the state responsible for its failure to protect. Lack of prevention, lack of compensation, impunity *de jure* or *de facto* all help establish government responsibility regarding practices of private lynching which are tantamount to public executions without trial with a justified sense of total impunity. Foreigners or minorities, the socially or economically backward, the poor are all more likely to be the victims of private violence and therefore require a higher standard of protection by the state. Patterns of violation of the right to life can be considered as falling within the mandate as, for example, is the case of state *failure* to protect the victims from private violence. Failure to rescue one whose life is in danger constitutes a criminal offense for individuals in many jurisdictions. Clearly, such behavior on the part of the state would also be a violation of the duty to protect when it becomes a pattern and when state agents are generally not punished. Refugees forcibly repatriated to situations where their lives are in danger have been accepted as falling under the mandate of the Special Rapporteur on extrajudicial, summary, or arbitrary executions. The same is true in the case of forced relocation of internally displaced persons into areas not yet cleared of land mines. Such careful, interpretative extension of the mandate is firmly rooted in and justified by human rights principles and subjected to the Commission on Human Rights' approval. Thus, Special Rapporteurs view their mandate in functional terms requiring effective response to an area of concern expressed by the international community in creating the mandate. Moreover, since the mandate is thematic (rather than relating to a specific country) there is greater room for consistency and non selectivity.

WORKING METHODS

The basic response of a Special Rapporteur is to call for information from the government concerned. Inaction on the part of the government could frustrate the effectiveness of the rapporteur. According, for example, the Special Rapporteur on Executions has drawn up a questionnaire for eliciting information. Upon receipt of allegations concerning extrajudicial, summary, or arbitrary executions in a country, the Rapporteur sends to the government, in summary form, a reproduction of the allegations with the following request:

"In order to clarify the substance of these allegations, it would be useful if your government could reply to the following questions:

1. Are the facts alleged in the summary of the case accurate? If not, please provide details of the inquiries carried out to refute these allegations.
2. What is the cause of death as indicated in the death certificate?
3. Was an autopsy conducted? If so, by whom? What are the results of the autopsy? (Please provide a copy of the complete autopsy report.)
4. Has a complaint, formal or informal, been made on behalf of the victim? If so, who made the complaint and what is their relation to the victim? To whom was the complaint made? What action was undertaken upon receipt of the complaint and by whom?
5. Which is the authority responsible for investigating the allegations? Which is the authority responsible for prosecuting the perpetrators?
6. Are any inquiries, judicial or other procedures in connection with the case under way? If so, please provide details of their progress to date, and the timetable envisaged for their conclusion. If such inquiries or procedures have been completed, please provide details of the conclusions reached. (Please attach copies of any relevant documents.) Are these conclusions definitive?
7. Has the person alleged to have carried out the extrajudicial, summary or arbitrary execution been identified? To which unit or branch of the police, security forces, armed forces, or groups cooperating with them does he/she belong?
8. Have penal or disciplinary sanctions been imposed on the alleged perpetrators? If so, please provide details of the procedures followed to ascertain the penal or disciplinary responsibility of the perpetrators before imposing such penalties. If no such sanctions have been imposed, why not?
9. If no inquiries have been undertaken, why not? If the inquiries which were undertaken were inconclusive, why so?
10. Has any compensation been provided to the family of the victim? If so, please provide details including the type and the amount of the compensation involved. If no compensation has been provided, why not?
11. Please provide such other information or observation concerning the present case as you consider relevant.

Please include in your correspondence, the relevant incident and case number as well as the name(s) of the person(s) you are referring."

Such a detailed questionnaire precludes responses which are so broad and vague as to be meaningless. Special Rapporteurs do not have an investigative machinery and must make judgments based largely on the information received by them regarding the allegations and the information received in response from the government. The process could easily deteriorate into an ineffective round of allegations and denials. Hence, it is important for the Special Rapporteur to elicit the most detailed response possible. The value of a detailed formulation (such as that contained in the above questionnaire) is that it then becomes possible for the Special Rapporteur to draw inferences, both from the responses and from the lack of responses.

The Special Rapporteur can also rely on personal observation. But, obviously, no Special Rapporteur will have the capacity to go everywhere and, moreover, access to a country may be denied and access within a country may be impeded. In order to overcome such problems, Special Rapporteurs have developed the technique of observation by analysis of patterns of events or behavior. A Special Rapporteur can place a country under scrutiny (and keep such country under scrutiny) even though denied access to the country, by exercising personal judgment based on analysis of patterns of events.

Rapporteurs evolve their own methods, appropriate to individual mandate, but with the objective of making effective recommendations to the government concerned with a view to seeking and securing the fullest cooperation possible from such government. The ultimate aim of each Rapporteur is to seek the best possible protection for victims or potential victims by undertaking an analysis from human rights perspectives regarding the mandate theme. The methods of work are dictated by such analysis.

PROBLEMS ENCOUNTERED

Most Rapporteurs have to overcome a cruel lack of resources. At best, they are each allotted just one full-time assistant. They have often, therefore, relied on information from NGOs and, sometimes, assistance, but must take care not to let this affect their impartiality, credibility, or integrity. The same applies to Governments who may provide earmarked funds or staff to specific mandates. The Special Rapporteurs are usually pressed for time needed for follow-up and time needed to take up new cases by going over lengthy documentation, such as tribunal judgments, sent by governments or reports from NGOs. They lack verification mechanisms and often do not have the forensic support they might need. They serve as Special Rapporteur on a part-time and voluntary basis while continuing with their regular professional work. Proposals have been made for full-time, permanent Rapporteurs, but there is the worry that such a move might make the mechanisms more bureaucratic and possibly less impartial. Suggestions have been made to apply to Rapporteurs conditions comparable to members of international jurisdictions. Periodic renewal of the mandates has not proved to be a problem. The practice has evolved that the Commission can only decide whether to renew a mandate or not. It cannot remove a specific Rapporteur unless it abolishes the mechanism itself. This helps secure the independence of the Rapporteur and, generally, the system has safeguarded the independence of the Rapporteur. But, recently, there have been attempts to obstruct the work of a

Rapporteur, to delete a portion of the report of one of the Rapporteurs and to recall a Rapporteur from a country while in the midst of his inquiry in the country or to disregard immunities Special Rapporteurs have when on duty (e.g., the Special Rapporteur Param Cumaraswamy). The Commission, or its Chairman, can request a Rapporteur to undertake a specific investigation (e.g., in connection with the Dili killings in East Timor or the massacres and possible genocide in Eastern Zaïre (Kiru)). There have also been attempts to play some mechanisms against others (e.g., Thematic Rapporteurs and Country Rapporteurs or the High Commissioner or the Secretary-General, on the grounds of divide and rule).

A dilemma that Special Rapporteurs may face relates to confidentiality. Having the obligation to report publicly to the Commission on Human Rights indeed protects the Special Rapporteur's impartiality and independence and the victims have also benefitted from the publicity. Sometimes they may receive very sensitive information, the premature disclosure of which may result in destruction of evidence or, even worse, putting at risk witnesses or parties.

LOOKING TO THE FUTURE

There has been increasing cooperation between the different Special Rapporteurs, Special Representatives, Independent Experts, and Working Groups. The Special Rapporteurs meet annually and address cross-mandate thematic stress (such as terrorism and the difficulty to address human rights abuses by non-governmental entities) as well as administrative issues. But not much time is spent on discussing methods of work. That exchange takes place mostly through reading reports and through exchanges between assistants. Joint recommendations have been made by more than one Rapporteur and Thematic Rapporteurs and Country Rapporteurs have cooperated with one another on specific actions and on visits. There have also been joint efforts involving, for example, the Special Rapporteur on Torture and the Special Rapporteur on Executions and the Working Group on Arbitrary Detention.

The thematic mechanisms have made undoubted contributions to both protecting victims and preventing violations. But the preventive impact could be considerably enhanced if there were a proper forum to discuss their reports. Current procedures leave the Rapporteurs ten to fifteen minutes to present their report and there is no systematic discussion of the reports, either formal or informal, at the Commission on Human Rights. There is not yet a role for even the UN High Commissioner for Human Rights to formally present the report (or highlights) to the Security Council as a contribution to an effective early-warning system and human rights approach to peace and security issues. As a result, too much is left to the manner in which the government reacts. More often than is desirable, the Commission has left their questions unanswered or their recommendations forgotten.

The Special Rapporteurs are accessible to victims, especially those that have the resources to make contact or have NGOs to make the contact. Awareness of the existence and work of a Rapporteur can also produce increased access. In Pakistan, for example, allegations of summary or arbitrary killings referred to the Special Rapporteur on Executions went up from around twenty to hundreds over a one-year period. Yet dissemination of Special Rapporteurs' reports is not systematic and their language not always user friendly. There has been consideration of creating Regional-Thematic Rapporteurs, and regional approach to some human rights violations, e.g., on trafficking in women. But, so far, there has been little exploration of the creation of a thematic Rapporteur at the national level in addition to mechanisms such as ombudspersons. This option would have been more flexible and perhaps more effective than a national Human Rights Commission covering a variety of human rights problems. The thematic mechanisms do have much to contribute to the future as is evident from the expansion of the number of such mechanisms. But such expansion of numbers has not been accompanied by a corresponding expansion in resources. The thematic mechanisms need to be reinforced, strengthened, and linked to adequate resources if they are to continue to make their significant contribution to the protection of victims, the prevention of victimization, and the compensation of victims. There is a problem in addressing the responsibility of non-governmental entities and of more gender specific or children oriented action. There is also a need to find an effective international mechanism against impunity for gross human rights violations.

The Commission on Human Rights' decisions to appoint thematic Rapporteurs on economic, social, or environmental themes clearly indicate the mechanisms potential for successful monitoring and reporting, and for enhancing the enforcement of human rights standards and accountability. But we are very far from a strong, well resourced system, which would allow for a global coverage of the world's most burning human rights problems. Such a system, involving experts from many different cultural and geographical backgrounds, with due consideration to gender and linguistic balance, would certainly raise the credibility of the United Nations and the significance of the Universal Declaration of Human Rights for ordinary men, women, and children from around the world.

Chapter 7

The Country Mechanisms of the United Nations Commission on Human Rights

Mel James

When the Commission on Human Rights was created in 1946, its parent body, the UN Economic and Social Council (ECOSOC), gave it a broad mandate to make proposals, recommendations, and reports on any matter concerning human rights.[1] However, the Commission at its first meeting in January 1947 decided that "it had no power to take action in regard to any complaints concerning human rights,"[2] thus denying itself the authority to take up individuals' complaints, let alone tackle patterns of systematic violations attributable to any particular government. Instead, the Commission turned its attention to the first task in its mandate, the drafting of the Universal Declaration of Human Rights.

This decision caused considerable problems for the Commission's Secretariat. In 1950, it received over 9,000 complaints; between April 1951 and May 1952 the number rose to over 25,000. Even allowing for orchestrated efforts to submit the same complaint, the Commission's refusal to act had led the Secretariat to comment in 1949 that this was "bound to lower the prestige and authority not only of the Commission of Human Rights but of the United Nations. . . . This irritates the general public and brings disappointment and disillusionment to thousands of persons all over the world" [1]. Other UN bodies were not so reticent. At its first session in 1945, the UN General Assembly, for example, had debated allegations of human rights violations against individuals

---

[1] ECOSOC Resolution 5(I), 1946.
[2] UN Document E/259, 1947, paragraph 22.

in Hungary, Bulgaria, the Soviet Union, Spain, and Greece, and in 1946 it had taken up the issue of racial discrimination in South Africa.

It was the UN Special Committee on Decolonization (also known as the Committee of 24) that in 1965 asked the Commission to respond to the petitions that the Committee was receiving about human rights violations in southern Africa. ECOSOC encouraged a constructive response.[3] In 1967 the Commission established an *Ad Hoc* Working Group of Experts on Human Rights in Southern Africa and added an item to its agenda on the question of violation of human rights.[4] These initiatives were consolidated the following June by ECOSOC Resolution 1235 (XLII) that authorized the Commission and its suborgan, the Sub-Commission on Prevention of Discrimination and Protection of Minorities, to "examine information relevant to gross violations of human rights and fundamental freedoms" and, subject to certain constraints, "make a thorough study of situations which reveal a consistent pattern of violations of human rights." To both these paragraphs was added reference to apartheid and racial discrimination in southern Africa, thus indicating that the Commission should focus on colonial and racist violations of human rights. Three years later, the Council established a second, confidential procedure under resolution 1503 (XLVIII) which sought to identify consistent patterns of "gross and reliably attested violations of human rights" without any guidance as to the nature of states that might be the subject of communications under this procedure. Unlike the 1235 procedure, that established under resolution 1503 was to be activated by an individual victim or group of victims, or by non-governmental organizations (NGOs) with direct and reliable knowledge of the situation.

The resolutions adopted between 1966 and 1970 established the basis of both the public and confidential country mechanisms. Their provisions still broadly govern the UN country mechanisms, although there has been considerable development particularly in the public procedure. Throughout the Commission's history, one of its major tensions and greatest controversies has been its attempts to deal with country situations. On one level this is not surprising. The UN is an association of governments, represented by diplomats whose first task is to protect their country's interests. Human rights are seen all too often as an issue of national prestige and a means of scoring points over political adversaries and, even where there is concern about violations in a particular country, it usually takes second place to perceived economic and security interests.

A factor in the change of direction in the mid-1960s was the enlargement of the Commission from twenty-one to thirty-two states with twenty seats being allocated to the African, Asian, and Latin American groups.[5] Particularly for the

[3] ECOSOC Resolution 1102 (XL).

[4] Commission Resolutions 2 (XXIII) and 8 (XXIII), 1967.

[5] Commission membership comprised eighteen states in 1947. It was extended to twenty-one states in 1962; thirty-two in 1967; forty-two in 1980; and fifty-three in 1992.

new African and Asian members, the priority was racism and self-determination from colonial rule. Later, their enthusiasm for the new procedures waned as the protection of civil and political rights emerged as the priority consideration and many of them became the targets for the Commission's new mandate. However, criticism cannot be confined to any regional group of countries. The states that are most negative about the Commission's activities in examining situations of human rights violations are those who are being subjected to scrutiny, or fear they may shortly be in that position.

It follows that the victims of human rights violations are not at the forefront of the Commission's agenda. Rather, as Philip Alston has commented on the 1503 procedure which can, in theory, be triggered by an individual victim

> it is not properly called a "petition-redress" procedure since it offers no solace, or redress, to individual victims. It is better characterized as a "petition-information" system because its objective is to use complaints as a means by which to assist the Commission in identifying situations involving "a consistent pattern of gross and reliably attested violations." In that sense, an individual victim is but a piece of evidence whose case might, if accompanied by a sufficient number of related cases, spur the United Nations to action of some kind [2, p. 146].

The other group of actors in the Commission, the NGOs, mostly have the victims and the defenders of human rights as their focus. In the early days of the Commission, their participation was limited to a small number of international NGOs, but the numbers attending have increased rapidly in recent years, particularly since the 1993 UN World Conference on Human Rights which brought the UN's human rights activities to a much wider NGO audience. Through affiliation to organizations in consultative status with ECOSOC, a prerequisite for accreditation to the Commission, and the efforts of many organizations to include activists from the South, the numbers of local human rights defenders is increasing, although some countries, including some whose human rights practice is often raised at the Commission, allow no independent NGOs.

NGOs, of course, have no formal role in the Commission's proceedings apart from contributing written and short oral statements [3]. Their oral interventions, in particular, have attracted criticism from governments for many years, the gist of the complaints being that they speak too often, for too long, and are too political. On occasion this criticism is justified although it has to be said that governments are very poor role models in this respect. Most NGOs aim to provide accurate and impartial information and remind governments that action, albeit displeasing to some of their number, is the necessary route to stopping human rights violations. NGOs are also the main source of information for both country and thematic mechanisms and play a major role in disseminating the outcome of UN human rights bodies to a wider audience.

The 1503 procedure initially seemed the more attractive to NGOs since this was initiated by NGO allegations. However, complaints, known as communications, take about a year from their submission to the Secretariat until the Commission decides what action, if any, it will take [1]. The Commission, meeting in closed session but with the government of the country concerned present, has various options at its disposal. It can cease consideration or keep the situation under review. Its more pro-active possibilities are to appoint a rapporteur or independent expert to study the situation more thoroughly, request the UN Secretary-General to establish direct contacts with the government, ask the government for further information, or for the file to be made public. These days, the Commission Chairperson announces the names of the countries that have been discussed, those that have dropped from consideration, and any that are to be transferred to the Commission's public agenda.

Recorded criticisms of the 1503 procedure by NGOs have been revealing. Amnesty International condemned an early failure by the Commission as "an ignominious abdication of the Commission's responsibility to promote respect for and protection of human rights and individual freedoms. . . . The present rules of confidentiality are an undisguised stratagem for using the UN, not as an instrument for promoting and protecting and exposing large-scale violations of human rights, but rather for concealing their occurrence" [4, p. 66]. More recently the procedure has been described as "a screen behind which gross violators dance a long, slow, diplomatic minuet without ceasing to torture and kill" [5, p. 282].

It seems anachronistic in the 1990s for a UN human rights procedure to rely on NGOs for its information, but allow the governments that are the subjects of the allegations to participate in discussions about the outcome. It touches on the absurd in the appointment of a rapporteur or expert, the implementation of whose mandate depends at least in part on access to information from NGOs—who are not supposed to know about his or her existence. Governments, on the other hand, do not necessarily respect the procedure's confidentiality, although not often as spectacularly as in 1989 when the Government of Zaire took a paid advertisement in the *New York Times* reproducing the Commission's decision to cease consideration of their case [6, p. 38].

The paucity of information makes evaluation almost impossible. For example, Brunei was kept under review in 1988 and 1989 but dropped in February 1990. Was this connected to the release in Brunei in January 1990 of seven prisoners of conscience, four of whom had been held without charge or trial for twenty-seven years? On the positive side, the 1503 procedure has increased the number of countries under consideration[6] by the Commission, both within the

---

[6] Between 1984 and 1997, the Commission had under consideration for one year or more: Armenia, Albania, Azerbaijan, Bahrain, Benin, Brunei, Chad, Gambia, Haiti, Honduras, Indonesia (East Timor), Krygyzstan, Myanmar, Paraguay, Philippines, Rwanda, Saudi Arabia, Sierra Leone, Somalia, Sudan, Turkey, Uruguay, and Zaire.

procedure and by transfer to the public agenda. Equatorial Guinea was the first example in 1979. Haiti followed in 1987; Albania in 1988; Myanmar (Burma) in 1992; and Somalia, Sudan, and Zaire in 1993. Special rapporteurs or independent experts had been appointed under the confidential procedure for Haiti, Myanmar (Burma), Somalia, Sudan, and Zaire.

As stated above, the Commission's early identification of country situations that warranted public scrutiny—southern Africa in 1967 and the Arab Occupied Territories in 1968—followed the focus on racism and colonialism. The scope was widened by the appointment in 1975 of a Working Group on Chile, with the encouragement of the Sub-Commission on Prevention of Discrimination and Protection of Minorities and the General Assembly.

Southern Africa, the Arab Occupied Territories, and Chile were seen as the exceptions and each had its own agenda item. It was only in the late 1970s that the Commission began to adopt resolutions on countries under its agenda item termed "Question of the violation of human rights and fundamental freedoms in any part of the world, with particular reference to colonial and other dependent countries and territories" (the "violations" item). In 1979, in an unprecedented rush of enthusiasm, the Commission transferred Equatorial Guinea from the 1503 procedure, adopted a resolution on Nicaragua, and mandated a Sub-Commission member to undertake a review of the available information on Democratic Kampuchea. In 1981, it took up El Salvador and Bolivia; in 1982, Guatemala and Poland; and in 1984, Afghanistan and Iran. In 1987, Haiti was transferred from the 1503 procedure.

From naught to thirteen countries on the Commission's agenda in twenty years appears to be progress. However, there were other well-documented situations of human rights violations which the Commission ignored, such as Argentina, the Central African Republic, Democratic Kampuchea (no action was taken on the study mentioned above), East Timor, Greece, Uganda, and Uruguay. Argentina, nonetheless, unintentionally played a major role in the development of the Commission's mechanisms. Its military rulers were determined to avoid investigation, particularly into the systematic disappearances that characterized its "dirty war." Sustained campaigning by relatives of the victims, survivors, NGOs, and some parts of the UN system led to the creation of the first of the thematic mechanisms, the Working Group on Enforced and Involuntary Disappearances (this story is graphically told in [7]). The development of the thematic mechanisms ensured that a wider range of countries was raised in the Commission's debates which, in turn, facilitated a relaxation in the rules that had previously restricted NGO oral interventions to countries named on the Commission's agenda.

By the 1980s the Commission had established a model for the consideration of countries on its public agenda—a special rapporteur, or representative mandated under the item on human rights violations in any part of the world to examine the situation in a particular country, report back to the Commission at its next session and in some cases, also to the intervening session of the General Assembly. Under the "violations" item, the Commission adopts resolutions on individual countries without appointing a special rapporteur. Albeit a weaker response, this type of resolution often includes a request to the UN Secretary-General to prepare a report for the next session, thus keeping the country on the Commission's agenda for the following year.

There are limitations to the system of special rapporteurs: the mandates are vague and variously interpreted. The attention given, for example, to economic and social rights, the impact of human rights violations on women or minorities is inconsistent. Additionally they are unpaid and meagerly supported by an under-resourced Secretariat. But for the NGOs, the appointment of a special rapporteur is invariably regarded as a major step forward. Here is a recognized individual who can receive information, make urgent appeals to the government, carry out investigations in the country itself (providing the government concerned permits entry), discuss with the government and report to the Commission on the current state of human rights violations and what might be done to stop them.

Governments, particularly those who are the subject of such scrutiny, take quite a different view. The usual response to reports of human rights viola-tions, however well-attested, is invariably denial, characterized by Stanley Cohen as *"literal denial* (nothing happened); *interpretive denial* (what happened is really something else); and *implicatory denial* (what happened is justified)" [8]. Each session of the Commission offers plentiful examples of each of these responses.

Largely because of such governmental sensitivities, the Commission started to use the advisory services agenda item, as well as the "violations" item, for discussion of country situations. Advisory services (now known as advisory services and technical assistance) had been established in 1955 under General Assembly resolution 926 (X) to provide seminars, expert assistance, fellowships, and from 1967, regional seminars. It was intended as a transfer of expertise, rather than resources, to be provided only at the request of governments. The Commission began to prescribe it as a solution to human rights violations for Equatorial Guinea in 1980, Guatemala and Haiti in 1987. In 1983, Uganda introduced a resolution calling for such assistance for itself.

By the late 1980s, NGOs were becoming seriously concerned about the Commission's use of advisory services. They felt that it was being offered to governments on the Commission's agenda prematurely, as a way of keeping them in the public eye, but avoiding the criticism associated with the "violations" agenda item. The concern was not about assistance to governments in itself—although many NGOs were highly sceptical about the value of the program—but that the assistance mandated by the Commission was so bland as effectively to avoid any analysis of the situation and thus made it highly unlikely that it would relate to, let alone tackle, the violations in question. In the early 1990s, the question of the agenda item "violations" or advisory services, for countries such as El Salvador and Guatemala, became an annual battle between NGOs and governments.

First the thawing and then the end of the Cold War in the late 1980s and early 1990s could have opened the way to a major resurgence of the UN's human rights programs, including the country mechanisms. Indeed, this was a major assumption behind the General Assembly's decision to convene a World Conference on Human Rights, held in Vienna in 1993. To their complaints that the Commission was "selective" in its choice for the public procedure, implying that some countries or regions were the particular targets for attention, some governments added a challenge to the universality and indivisibility of all human rights. Into the 1990s, this debate has shifted toward "cooperation" as opposed to the supposed "confrontation" of the country procedures. This idea has gained considerable support in recent years, even from governments who traditionally have supported country resolutions.

The NGOs' response to this has been that the Commission has adequate means at its disposal to identify the most serious violators of human rights and the responsibility, as the main UN human rights body, to act on those situations. Governments, working through bodies such as the Commission, have developed international human rights standards. These have been adopted by all UN members at the General Assembly and should serve as benchmarks against which the behavior of any government may be measured. Other UN bodies, including those established to monitor compliance with human rights treaties and the Commission's own thematic mechanisms, as well as regional intergovernmental organizations, regularly provide information on human rights violations. Not only should this information, combined with that presented by NGOs, provide an objective basis for the Commission to take action but it might be used to identify situations where prompt action could save lives.

Rwanda was one such example. The Commission had kept it under review under the 1503 procedure in 1993 and 1994. More telling still, the Commission's thematic rapporteur on extrajudicial, summary, and arbitrary executions had visited the country in 1993 and recommended to the 1994 session that structures be set up to protect civilians from massacres in which "it has been shown time and time again that government officials were involved."[7] A matter of weeks before the massacres of April 1994 began, the Commission failed to heed of his warnings or take action on his recommendations.

The Commission's scope for action has increased considerably during the 1990s. Since 1990 it has been able to hold intersessional meetings to consider emergency situations, a procedure it has invoked three times: in August and November/December 1992 on the former Yugoslavia, and in May 1994 on Rwanda. Although the Commission was only a small part of the UN's response to

---

[7] UN Document E/CN.4/1994/7/Add.1.

these crises, these emergency sessions did enable it to appoint special rapporteurs and send representatives to investigate human rights violations on-site sooner than the annual session would have allowed.

The appointment of a High Commissioner for Human Rights, one of the more positive results of the World Conference on Human Rights, effective from April 1994, has led to other developments. Through a field presence and preventative technical assistance projects, the Commission's work has begun to reach out much further into other areas of UN work. Indeed, during the 1990s, a substantial number of the countries on the Commission's agenda—Cambodia, Burundi, El Salvador, Guatemala, Haiti, Rwanda, Somalia, the former Yugoslavia, and Zaire (now the Democratic Republic of the Congo)—have been also the subject of UN peace-keeping and field operations.

Meanwhile, the lottery continued in Geneva and some states responsible for systematic and gross human rights violations made it onto the Commission's agenda while others escaped. Between 1984 and 1991 only Romania (in 1989) was added to the "violations" agenda item. After a single-minded campaign by the United States, a special rapporteur on Cuba was appointed in 1991. Two other mandates were established that session, on Iraq and Occupied Kuwait. The former Yugoslavia and Myanmar (Burma) were added in 1992; Sudan and Zaire in 1993; Rwanda in 1994; Burundi in 1995; and Nigeria in 1997. The mechanisms were ended on Chile (1990), Romania (1993), El Salvador (1995), South Africa (1995), Guatemala (1997), and Cuba (1998). Resolutions were adopted, without appointing a special rapporteur, on Albania (1989-93), Western Sahara (1992), Bougainville (1993-95), Togo (1993-94), Angola (1994), southern Lebanon (1994-95), and southern Lebanon and Western Bakaa (from 1996).

To the advisory services item were added Cambodia, with a Secretary-General's special representative and a field office, and Somalia with an independent expert in 1993. Resolutions were adopted on Georgia (1993-94), Albania (1994), and Togo (1995-96). The distinction between the "violations" and the advisory services agenda items has decreased as the Commission has introduced elements of both scrutiny and assistance into its resolutions.

It is sometimes assumed that the Commission's appointment of a special rapporteur on Iraq, as Iraqi troops were withdrawing from Kuwait, was yet another front for the Gulf War. In fact, NGOs had been raising Iraq as a matter of priority in the Commission for some years and the group of West European and Other states had tabled resolutions in 1989 and 1990. On both occasions, discussion had been stopped by Iraq successfully proposing and gathering votes in favor of a motion to take no action on the draft resolutions. In 1991 it was noticeable that the Asian group which, with the exception of Japan, had previously supported the no-action motion, abstained. Possibly the fact that Asian migrant workers in Kuwait at the time of the invasion had been among the victims influenced their decision. Another factor was the considerable pressure on China following the widespread and highly publicized human rights violations that had occurred there in 1989.

China, Colombia, Indonesia, Turkey, and more recently Algeria, have been the most prominent examples of countries that escaped the Commission's scrutiny during the 1990s despite well-documented evidence of flagrant human rights violations. Initiatives by the Sub-Commission and some members of the Commission resulted in the tabling of resolutions of China, although most of these were worded very mildly. They were all, however, defeated by motions to take no action with the exception of 1995 when the substantive resolution was defeated by one vote. In 1997, public disagreement among members of the European Union, with France, Germany, Italy, and Spain reluctant to support a resolution, followed by the US decision in 1998 not to seek a resolution, effectively ended any potential for Commission action on China.

Human rights violations in Colombia were repeatedly brought to the Commission's attention, but to limited effect. In 1995, after immense pressure from NGOs supported by some governments, the Chairperson read out a letter from the government asking some of the thematic mechanisms to "regularize their visits" and promising some reforms. Since then, Colombia has featured annually in Chairperson's statements. Despite the reservations of many NGOs to this device—they are seen as evading a resolution and, since they are written in consultation with the government concerned, not reflecting the reality of the human rights situation—those on Colombia have been stronger than others.[8] The opening of an office of the High Commissioner for Human Rights in Bogota in 1997 has kept Colombia in the Commissioner's eye, although the persistence of human rights violations, including the killing of human rights defenders, demands that more be done.

Another example of half-hearted action by the Commission is East Timor. NGOs have raised continuing and widespread violations by the Indonesian government in both Indonesia and East Timor. Only East Timor has been the subject of resolutions, but without the appointment of a special rapporteur, in 1993 and 1997. In other years, the Commission has been content with extremely weak Chairperson's statements which usually ignore outstanding requests from the Commission, for example, to allow thematic mechanisms to visit.

The Commission has still to take any action on Turkey and Algeria.

In April 1998, one of the final decisions of the Commission's 54th session was to adopt by consensus resolution 1998/81 on enhancement of international cooperation in the field of human rights. This calls for "constructive dialogue and consultation for the enhancement of understanding and the promotion and

---

[8] Other Chairperson's statements have been on: Lithuania and Latvia (1991); Sri Lanka (1992-95), East Timor (1992, 1995, 1998); Latvia and Estonia (1993); Tadjikistan (1993); Romania (1994); Chechnya (1995-96); Colombia (1996-98); Liberia (1996-97); Peru (1997).

protection of human rights" between states and the UN, by its human rights mechanisms and even by NGOs.

During this session, human rights defender Eduardo Umaña Mendoza was shot dead at his home in Bogota, Colombia. The Commission, which he had often attended, held a minute's silence. His death occurred shortly after the Commission adopted, after thirteen years' debate, the Declaration on Human Rights Defenders. As the Chairperson pointed out, the simple adoption of the declaration was not sufficient to bring about change for the protection of human rights defenders.

This demonstrates the challenge that faces the Commission and the future of its country mechanisms. "Constructive dialogue and consultation" could be an improvement if, and only if, it takes place within the framework of international human rights standards and uses information from UN human rights mechanisms and well-documented accounts of human rights violations raised by NGOs. On the other hand, such proposals may confirm the Commission as merely another forum for governments' political and economic negotiations. That would be a sorry reflection on the UN's main human rights body, and the one that fifty years ago drafted the Universal Declaration of Human Rights as "a common standard of achievement for all peoples and all nations."

REFERENCES

1. H. Tolley, Jr., *The UN Commission on Human Rights,* Westview Press, Boulder, Colorado, 1987.
2. P. Alston, The Commission on Human Rights, in *The United Nations and Human Rights: A Critical Appraisal,* P. Alston (ed.), Clarendon Press, Oxford, United Kingdom, 1992.
3. R. Brett, The Role and Limits of Human Rights NGOs at the United Nations, *Political Studies, XLIII,* pp. 96-110, 1995.
4. W. Shawcross, *The Quality of Mercy, Cambodia, Holocaust and Modern Conscience,* André Deutsch, United Kingdom, 1984.
5. T. J. Farer and F. Gaer, The UN and Human Rights, in *United Nations, Divided World,* A. Roberts and B. Kingsbury (eds.), Oxford, United Kingdom, 1993.
6. International Service for Human Rights, *Human Rights Monitor, 4,* May 1989.
7. I. Guest, *Behind the Disappearances: Argentina's Dirty War Against Human Rights and the United Nations,* University of Pennsylvania Press, Philadelphia, 1990.
8. S. Cohen, Government Responses to Human Rights Reports: Claims, Denials and Counterclaims, in *Human Rights Quarterly, 18:3,* August 1996, emphasis in original.

Chapter 8

Closer to the Victim: United Nations Human Rights Field Operations

Ian Martin

THE DEVELOPMENT OF HUMAN RIGHTS FIELD OPERATIONS

For the international lawyer, the developments of the five decades after the adoption of the Universal Declaration were an impressively rapid evolution of international human rights standards and mechanisms for their implementation. But for the victim, the human rights work of the United Nations and other international organizations was remote: it might reduce the number of victims in the future, or occasionally bring belated redress to the victims of the past, but it rarely intervened quickly or effectively enough for the victims of the present.

For when this work moved beyond standard-setting into implementation, it still took place mostly in the committee rooms of the United Nations and regional organizations. Country rapporteurs and experts and the thematic procedures of the UN Commission on Human Rights, as well as the Inter-American Commission on Human Rights, began to make short visits to allow for in-country fact-finding and a more direct dialogue with the government concerned. These have become of increasing frequency, and occasionally the UN treaty bodies too have made their own country visits. But it is only in the last six years that human rights has moved to the field—and thus closer to the victim—in a radically different manner, as substantial human rights field operations have been established in a number of countries, by the UN, by the UN jointly with a regional organization, or by a regional organization alone.

The pioneering operation was in El Salvador where UN-brokered peace negotiations led to commitments by both government and armed opposition to respect human rights and invite UN verification of their observance; in July 1991, the human rights division of ONUSAL was established with an international staff of 101 including forty-two human rights observers. The huge UN Transitional Administration in Cambodia, established in February 1992, had one human rights officer in each province and a substantial headquarters and training staff, although the Human Rights Component remained a relatively small one. The Organization of American States established a small International Civilian Mission under military rule in Haiti in September 1992; from February 1993 this was absorbed into a large joint UN/OAS human rights mission (MICIVIH). At its peak before its first evacuation in October 1993, the number of MICIVIH observers reached around 200, the largest human rights presence in any single country up to that time. This was exceeded in Guatemala, where peace negotiations led to a human rights verification mission (MINUGUA) being established from November 1994, with an authorized strength of 245 international staff, including ten military liaison officers and sixty civilian police observers.

These four human rights field presences had their origins in attempts to negotiate and oversee political transitions: they were part of a new generation of UN peace operations. They were conceptualized and mounted by the UN's political departments in New York, in virtual isolation from its human rights mechanisms and supporting staff in the Centre for Human Rights in Geneva.

The advantages of a field presence were quickly apparent, however, to the Geneva human rights milieu. The Special Rapporteur on former Yugoslavia was provided with field staff based in the territory of his mandate from March 1993. It rapidly became *de rigueur* for special country rapporteurs to recommend that they be similarly supported by in-country monitoring.

By the time the proposal to create the post of UN High Commissioner for Human Rights was debated ahead of the 1993 World Conference on Human Rights, the disconnection between the New York initiatives and the Geneva-based system was well-recognized.

The General Assembly resolution establishing the post of High Commissioner for Human Rights made no explicit reference to peace-keeping and human rights field operations, but gave the High Commissioner the responsibility "to coordinate the human rights promotion and protection activities throughout the UN system," and "to rationalize, adapt, strengthen and streamline the UN machinery in the field of human rights with a view to improving its efficiency and effectiveness."

The first High Commissioner, José Ayala-Lasso, took up his post on April 5, 1994. The next day, genocide was unleashed in Rwanda. The High Commissioner visited Rwanda and called for a special session of the Commission on Human Rights. This mandated a special rapporteur on Rwanda and requested the High Commissioner "to make the necessary arrangements for the Special Rapporteur to be assisted by a team of human rights field officers." Initially a small team was envisaged, but during a second visit to Rwanda in late August the High

Commissioner agreed with the government that as many as 147 officers would be deployed, corresponding to the 147 communes of the country. The dependence of this Human Rights Field Operation in Rwanda (HRFOR) on voluntary funding (rather than the UN regular or peace-keeping budgets, from which the New York-run operations were funded), combined with the lack of Geneva-based systems or experience for mounting a large field operation, resulted in the deployment being painfully slow. The figure of 147 was never reached; by February 1995 there were eighty-five officers, and later that year the operation reached a peak of about 130 international staff.

HRFOR was the first large human rights field operation responsible to the High Commissioner in Geneva, rather than to the political or peace-keeping departments in New York. The High Commissioner became personally convinced that the future of human rights lay in the field, noting in February 1997 (shortly before his resignation):

> A human rights field presence, established with the consent of the authorities of the State concerned, is one of the major innovations introduced under the mandate of the High Commissioner for Human Rights in the implementation of the United Nations human rights programme. Experience has proved that the effective implementation of human rights is greatly facilitated by activities *in situ*. . . . In 1992 there were no human rights field activities; the High Commissioner/Centre for Human Rights now has offices in 11 countries in all regions.[1]

The office in Cambodia is the only field presence whose funding has been fully incorporated in the regular budget of the Office of the High Commissioner for Human Rights (OHCHR—as the Centre for Human Rights was renamed in 1997). The Human Rights Component of UNTAC lobbied for the continuation of its work beyond UNTAC's withdrawal, and this passed to the Centre—after a hiatus, since the Centre had had no involvement during the peace-keeping operation. As of mid-1997, it had an international staff of seventeen, including those engaged in a judicial mentor program.

The office of the HCHR in Burundi is intended to be the largest of the Geneva-run field presences after Rwanda. It began as a technical cooperation effort, intended as "preventive action," but in June 1995 the government agreed to the deployment of thirty-five human rights monitors. Due to funding delays, this deployment began only in April 1996; by mid-1997, fifteen observers had been deployed, with the intention of further expansion toward the agreed thirty-five.

---

[1] Report of the High Commissioner for Human Rights to the Commission on Human Rights, "Building a partnership for human rights," E/CN.4/1997/98, 24 February 1997. The countries were: Bosnia and Herzegovina, Croatia, Federal Republic of Yugoslavia and the former Yugoslav Republic of Macedonia (managed together as the Human Rights Field Operation in the former Yugoslavia, HRFOY); Abkhazia (Georgia), Burundi, Cambodia, Colombia, Gaza (Palestine), Rwanda, and Zaire.

The government of Zaire finally signed an agreement in August 1996 accepting a two-person human rights office, the functions of which include monitoring, technical cooperation, and training, both for governmental institutions and NGOs; this had been recommended by the Special Rapporteur on Zaire and supported by the Commission on Human Rights. It continues to function in the Democratic Republic of Congo.

The November 1996 agreement on the Colombia office followed a statement by the Chairman of the Commission on Human Rights in April 1996, requesting the High Commissioner to proceed "upon the initiative of the Government of Colombia" to establish an office in Colombia. This was widely seen as an alternative to the imposition of a special country rapporteur. It provides for the office "to observe the human rights situation with a view to advising the Colombian authorities on the formulation and implementation of policies, programmes and measures to promote and protect human rights . . . and to enable the High Commissioner to make analytical reports to the Commission on Human Rights," as well as to advise NGOs and individuals. It was initially staffed by a Director funded and nominated by the Spanish government, and five human rights professionals funded by the European Commission through the International Commission of Jurists.

Following the Dayton Agreement, the main human rights monitoring mandate for Bosnia and Herzegovina was bestowed upon the OSCE, leaving the High Commissioner to define for himself a threefold contribution: conducting human rights training for international personnel, making available human rights experts to the High Representative, and supporting the work of the Special Rapporteur and the Expert on Missing Persons. Small offices have also been maintained in Croatia and the Federal Republic of Yugoslavia (Serbia and Montenegro), to support the work of the Special Rapporteur, whose mandate continues to cover all three countries.

The office in Abkhazia, Georgia, consists of a single UN professional, working in tandem with a single OSCE official, but set an important structural precedent when it was decided that the office would report to the High Commissioner through the Head of the UN Mission, UNOMIG.

Each of these field operations or offices has a dual mandate, including both monitoring and technical cooperation functions. Elsewhere, the OHCHR has established small offices with the exclusive function of implementing technical cooperation projects.

Meanwhile the case for the more consistent incorporation of human rights components in multi-dimensional UN peace operations was being pressed.[2] Other such operations, including UNAVEM III in Angola, UNOMIL in Liberia, and UNTAES in Eastern Slavonia (Croatia), had human rights officers included in their staffing. Their functions varied widely: the Angola unit placed its emphasis

---

[2] See Amnesty International, *Peace-Keeping and Human Rights,* January 1994; and Alice Henkin (ed.), *Honoring Human Rights and Keeping the Peace: Lessons from El Salvador, Cambodia and Haiti,* Aspen Institute, 1995.

on promotional activities with little effective investigation or monitoring over a vast territory; the human rights unit in Eastern Slavonia monitored closely the situation of a small population subjected to discriminatory administrative procedures; while the officers in Liberia worked with NGOs but were politically powerless to address the human rights violations of African peace-keepers. Elsewhere, the mandate for human rights monitoring was given to a regional organization; in addition to OAS participation in the joint OAS/UN mission in Haiti, the OSCE became responsible for human rights monitoring in Bosnia and Herzegovina and Croatia, and assumed joint responsibility with the UN in Abkhazia, Georgia.

Other UN operations have not been designated as human rights operations and have not operated within a human rights framework, but have carried out activities that had much in common with human rights field work. This applies to civilian operations paving the way for multi-party elections in Namibia and South Africa. UN civilian police have a crucial human rights role to play wherever they are deployed, and UN human rights components have benefited from working alongside them, usually with difficulty on both sides in defining their respective roles and reconciling their organizational cultures, but with much to be gained from cooperation and joint action. UN civilian police operations have played major human rights roles in Mozambique and Bosnia and Herzegovina, where there were no or few UN human rights staff. MINUGUA in Guatemala is unique in incorporating police and military officers fully under the civilian direction of a human rights mission.

TOWARD AN EVALUATION OF HUMAN RIGHTS FIELD OPERATIONS

It is too early to reach any definitive or overall evaluation of even the first generation of human rights field operations when only El Salvador and Cambodia are concluded. But it is certainly not too early to point to the absence of ongoing evaluation within the UN system that would enable some clear lessons to be learned and applied in later phases or operations.[3] An interim evaluation can currently be informed by comparative assessments made outside the UN, writings by those who have participated in such operations and external studies by NGOs.[4]

---

[3] The Lessons Learned Unit in DPKO undertakes evaluations of DPKO-managed peace-keeping operations only. The European Commission commissioned two evaluations of the European Union participation in HRFOR.

[4] Alice Henkin (ed.), *Honoring Human Rights and Keeping the Peace: Lessons from El Salvador, Cambodia and Haiti,* Aspen Institute, 1995, is the outcome of a comparative assessment which had the participation of UN human rights directors from the three country operations. The papers from a second round of assessment including experience from Guatemala, Rwanda, and Bosnia, as well as later experience from El Salvador, Cambodia, and Haiti, will be published by the Aspen Institute in 1998. A full set of references to the literature can be found in [1].

Most of the existing literature is focused on the early phases of operations and, thus, already somewhat outdated.

Despite a difficult beginning and some criticisms of its functioning, there appears to be a consensus that ONUSAL in El Salvador was a success as well as a pioneer, although its longer-term impact remains to be evaluated. It was part of an overall political strategy and operated within a clear framework, not only of international human rights law, but of an agreement negotiated between parties. Its deployment ahead of a ceasefire and comprehensive peace agreement, while not originally envisaged by the UN negotiators, contributed to an improvement in the human rights situation, which in turn helped create a positive climate for overall agreement. Its legacy in the development of the judicial system, the Human Rights Ombudsman and the National Civilian Police seems also to have been significant. The same political rationale was explicitly followed in Guatemala, where the deployment of MINUGUA from November 1994 similarly is seen to have contributed to the climate in which an overall peace agreement was concluded in December 1996. The success of MINUGUA in the period since, during which its verification responsibilities have extended into new areas, remains to be seen.

The human rights component within UNTAC—subsequently characterized by its director as the "poor cousin" of the operation in both staffing and administrative support[5]—was much less central to the overall UN operation in Cambodia, and had a less clear mandate under the Paris Peace Agreements than the verification mandates of ONUSAL and MINUGUA. As well as its monitoring during pre-election violence, attention to detention conditions, and extensive human rights training and education, it played an innovative role in encouraging the growth of national human rights NGOs where none had existed, involving Asian and Western human rights NGOs in this task. It secured support for UN human rights work to continue beyond the peace-keeping mandate.

When the UN joined the OAS in deploying the International Civilian Mission in Haiti (MICIVIH), it hoped that here too an amelioration of the human rights situation would contribute to the success of negotiations for a return to constitutional government. But these broke down, and the mission was twice evacuated before the Security Council authorized military intervention to force the restoration of President Aristide.[6] In its first phase, in 1993, MICIVIH was able to achieve three things: without its presence, human rights abuse would have been worse than it was; many individual victims were aided as a result of its intervention; and where it could not check human rights violations, it drew them to international attention. But its evacuation put its contacts at risk, and when it

---

[5] Dennis McNamara, *UN Human Rights Activities in Cambodia: An Evaluation,* in Alice Henkin (ed.), note 2, p. 62.

[6] Ian Martin, Paper versus Steel: The First Phase of the International Civilian Mission in Haiti, in Alice Henkin (ed.), note 2; and Haiti: Mangled Multilateralism, *Foreign Policy, 95,* Summer 1994.

was sent back in early 1994, the *de facto* authorities gave it no cooperation and it could do little beyond speaking out publicly; nevertheless, its findings were well-publicized internationally and played an important role in the US and UN debates which preceded a tougher policy to oust the military regime. Its third phase under restored constitutional government, still continuing, has focused on monitoring the human rights conditions for successive elections, support for institution-building (the civilian police force, justice system and prisons), and human rights education.

The High Commissioner's first Human Rights Field Operation in Rwanda was much criticized for the inadequacy of its response to an urgent situation. Much of its early focus was on investigating the genocide, but it was not well equipped for this task. Once the International Criminal Tribunal for Rwanda was established in November 1994, information collected by HRFOR was handed over to it, and the Prosecutor made clear that future investigation for the purposes of prosecution should be done by the Tribunal's investigators.

The mandate of HRFOR was extremely broad: to investigate the genocide and violations which had already occurred; to monitor the ongoing human rights situation and maintain a preventive presence; to help reestablish confidence, the return of refugees and displaced persons, and the rebuilding of civic society; to implement programs of technical cooperation, particularly in the administration of justice; and to report to the High Commissioner and through him to the Special Rapporteur. The positive effects of HRFOR's presence were offset by the worsening security situation, as Hutu insurgency penetrated further into Rwanda from the camps in Zaire, with killings of Tutsi civilians and local officials, and killings of unarmed Hutu civilians in the army's counter-insurgency response. Similarly, progress in the creation of a judicial system and some limited amelioration of indescribable prison conditions were overwhelmed by the tens of thousands of persons accused of involvement in the genocide, especially after mass returns of Hutus at the end of 1996. However, an evaluation commissioned by the European Commission at the end of 1996 found that the large majority of its interlocutors in the Government of Rwanda, human rights NGOs, and international agencies were positive about HRFOR's impact.[7] Its presence outside the capital became severely restricted after five of its staff were murdered in the course of duty in February 1997. Its continuing reporting on killings by an army that was facing a growing genocidal insurgency became most unwelcome to the Government, which in late 1997 began to move toward terminating its monitoring role.

The OHCHR presence in Burundi raises even starker questions regarding the role of a human rights presence in a situation of acute armed conflict. Its technical cooperation activities appear naive in the absence of a political context in which

---

[7] Ingrid Kircher and Paul LaRose-Edwards, *Evaluation of the European Union Contingent to the UN Human Rights Field Operation in Rwanda,* for DG VIII Development (External Relations and ACP Unit) of the European Commission, January 1997.

respect for human rights could be institutionalized. When a substantial monitoring presence was first agreed to in 1995, it could have been deployed outside the capital and played some role at least in providing reliable information on the killings of civilians by both sides to the conflict, but the moment was lost due to funding constraints, and the security situation had so deteriorated by the time monitors were deployed that their role could only be a severely limited one.

Notwithstanding the strong stated commitment in the Dayton Agreement to human rights observance in Bosnia and Herzegovina, a central weakness in the implementation of its civilian aspects has been the failure to give a strong human rights monitoring mandate, together with the necessary resources, to a single international organization able to implement it. While the International Police Task Force (IPTF) was deployed by the UN, the main human rights monitoring role was allocated to the OSCE; two closely-related functions were thus placed under different international organizations. The OSCE's staffing resources were inadequate, and it initially subordinated its human rights responsibility to its electoral functions. Meanwhile the UN civilian police of the IPTF, with a strong human rights mandate, operated largely without professional human rights guidance until a Human Rights Unit was established in mid-1997. The human rights activities of these and many other actors are coordinated through a Human Rights Coordination Center established within the Office of the High Representative. But the consequence of these arrangements has been substantial duplication of first-order reporting of human rights incidents, while further investigation remains weak, as does follow-up with the authorities and public reporting.

In Angola, the UN was asked to monitor the Angolan national police, but not explicitly to verify the parties' human rights commitments. The Security Council, however, welcomed the intention expressed by the Secretary-General to include human rights specialists in the political component of UNAVEM III, and this became the starting point for a human rights unit which by early 1997 had fourteen officers. It emphasized promotional activities in collaboration with the Government and UNITA, while taking an extremely cautious approach in relation to the investigation of human rights violations. In Eastern Slavonia (Croatia), the UN Transitional Administration (UNTAES) created at the beginning of 1996 had a strong human rights mandate and human rights officers were included in its budget, but no human rights unit was established until mid-1997. Both operations were managed by the Department of Peace-Keeping Operations (DPKO), with little or no human rights professionalism. The OHCHR became involved only in early 1997, when it was agreed that it should give professional direction and support to these human rights units.

From the experience of these missions, three main sets of factors can be seen as relevant to the performance of human rights field operations: the clarity of their mandates, the quality of implementation, and the funding arrangements.

MANDATES

The most obviously successful human rights field operations have been those in El Salvador and Guatemala, where the mandate established for each mission was clearest and was related to a feasible political strategy on the part of the international community. Conversely, the lack of definition of the mandate of HRFOR in Rwanda, and the proliferation of human rights mandates of weakly-coordinated international organizations in Bosnia and Herzegovina, have contributed to their difficulties.

This should not, however, be taken to imply that human rights field operations should be attempted only in the most favorable of conditions. In Haiti, the mandate was clear, but the political strategy initially failed, which is not to say that it should not have been attempted. The acceptance of a human rights field presence and its mandate depends upon the government or the parties to a conflict: in Angola, the attitude of the government may have precluded a clear human rights mandate, and it may thus have been necessary to proceed from a modest beginning.

The mandates of previous operations can usefully inform negotiators, and all mandates should be founded upon relevant international human rights standards, especially those by which the state is bound. But each mandate must be formulated according to the specific country situation: in Rwanda, the genocide and scale of internal and external displacement; in Guatemala, the situation of indigenous people. In Haiti, it was right to exclude technical assistance until such time as constitutional government was restored.

Optimally, human rights field operations should be conceived as integrating preventive, monitoring (verification), and assistance (technical cooperation, institution- or capacity-building) functions. They have played an important role in developing justice systems; there is a complementarity between UNDP's long-term project management capability, the criminal justice expertise of the UN Crime Prevention and Criminal Justice Division (now the Centre for International Crime Prevention), and the capacity of a human rights field operation to make available professional human rights expertise, and to utilize its unique outreach to identify needs and be supportive at the local level. In an integrated operation, the monitoring identifies needs for training and resources, the technical cooperation ensures that those needs can be addressed, and the monitoring again provides feedback on the effectiveness of technical cooperation projects in improving aspects of the human rights situation to which they are directed. Certainly in a situation where institutions have been destroyed or have never existed, such as post-genocide Rwanda, to point to human rights violations while offering no linkage to assistance is to invite dismissal, and to pursue technical cooperation while ignoring serious ongoing violations is naive and unacceptable.

Human rights field operations of international organizations will and should always have a limited life. Developing institutions for the protection and promotion of human rights is a long-term task, in which the role of civil society as well as government is crucial. Such operations must consciously seek to avoid displacing indigenous human rights activity, and do all they can to support and encourage it. The extent to which non-governmental organizations can be directly associated with their work will vary according to the political and security context, and to different areas of activity. Human rights promotion is best done by local actors, with international operations playing only a supporting role; while the international and local actors should normally maintain the autonomy of their respective monitoring and investigation. The international operation should plan for the sustainability of human rights protection beyond its own withdrawal. This will be facilitated if a UN human rights presence is not completely withdrawn at the end of a peace-keeping operation: a limited human rights presence can be sustained under the mandate of the High Commissioner.

IMPLEMENTATION AND FUNDING

The three human rights field operations launched by the Department of Political Affairs (DPA)—El Salvador, Haiti, and Guatemala—were each preceded by planning missions, involving human rights professionals from outside the Secretariat. These contributed significantly to the conceptualizing, planning, and budgeting for the operations, and could usefully become standard practice where such an operation is envisaged.

Both the speed and quality of recruitment of staff for the operations have been criticized, to different degrees but in all cases. To some extent this was related to the novelty of the type of operation. The cumulative experience of five major UN operations has now developed a cadre of human rights field officers, able to transfer what they have learned from one operation to another. However, neither New York nor Geneva have adequate procedures to evaluate the human rights credentials and field orientation of large numbers of recruits.

The training arrangements for human rights field officers have also been justifiably criticized. Inseparable from the clarity of the mandate of the operation and the development of country-specific guidance, training is not simply a matter of familiarization with international human rights standards. Each operation has been left to develop its own field guidance, often too long after its deployment. Building on the cross-fertilization across the efforts of different operations, the OHCHR has belatedly developed generic training materials for human rights field monitoring.

The serious administrative and logistical difficulties which have impaired the functioning of human rights field operations cannot be separated from the issue of funding. There are four current methods of funding UN human rights field operations: within a peace-keeping operation mandated by the Security Council (e.g., Angola); as a civilian mission mandated by the General Assembly from the regular budget (e.g., Haiti and Guatemala); from the regular budget of the OHCHR (Cambodia); or from voluntary contributions (e.g., Rwanda, Burundi, Colombia).

Difficulties are associated with each of these. Funding within a peace-keeping operation encounters the resistance of some members of the Security Council to any human rights (as distinct from humanitarian law) mandate, which may run counter to the appropriate mandate or to involvement of the High Commissioner. Funding from the regular budget is most appropriate to a substantial civilian human rights operation, but has become difficult in view of the determination of member states to maintain an absolute ceiling on the regular budget, without a substantial contingency from which one or more sizeable operations can be funded.

By far the greatest difficulties are associated with trying to mount and sustain a large human rights field operation on voluntary funding. Under UN financial procedures, commitments can only be entered into once funds to cover them have actually been received. Contracts in HRFOR and elsewhere were often issued only from month to month, and the consequences for morale, efficient management, and recruitment of much-needed professionals were obvious.

In 1996, the High Commissioner proposed to the Commission on Human Rights that a human rights fund for field activities be established to ensure that his Office could conduct its work in those countries where such initiatives and cooperation were necessary and welcome, based on a predictable source of funding that allowed for proper planning and management of the operation. A few governments have now made major contributions which are not earmarked for a particular operation.

STRUCTURES

Different organizational structures have applied to UN human rights field operations or components. Some (El Salvador, Haiti, Guatemala) have primarily been managed by DPA in New York; others (Cambodia, Angola) have been fully part of a peace-keeping operation; while in Rwanda the High Commissioner mounted a human rights field operation alongside, but completely outside, an already-established peace-keeping operation. In October 1996, the Security Council authorized and funded a human rights office in Abkhazia, Georgia, which reports to the High Commissioner through the Head of Mission of UNOMIG. Similar arrangements were agreed for the follow-up operation to UNAVEM III in Angola, MONUA, and for the human rights unit within UNTAES in Eastern Slavonia.

Where the UN has a political mandate, and especially where there is a UN peace operation or political office in the country, the organizational arrangements for human rights operations or components need to meet a number of criteria:

1. a UN human rights field presence must be part of the overall UN strategy for building peace and accomplishing a political transition;
2. the integrity of UN human rights monitoring and reporting must be seen as independent of political pressures;
3. UN activities in-country must be effectively coordinated, and close working relationships established between the human rights field presence and others with closely connected mandates, who may be inside (e.g., CIVPOL) or outside (e.g., UNDP, UNHCR) the peace-keeping operation;
4. a UN human rights field presence must receive professional human rights guidance and support, benefit from the experience of similar operations elsewhere, and be coordinated with the UN human rights system;
5. administrative and logistical support to UN operations in the field must be provided in the most efficient and cost-effective manner, with a human rights presence receiving equal priority to other components.

Consistent with the mandate of the High Commissioner, it is increasingly recognized that she should have substantive reporting responsibility and give professional direction to any human rights presence in the field, whether it stands independently of or is within a peace-keeping operation. The current lack of capacity and experience in OHCHR in Geneva to support this role must be addressed: the central recommendation of the Aspen Institute's 1995 study, that there must be a specialized unit supporting human rights field work, remains valid more than three years after it was formulated.[8] At the same time, human rights activities should not be pursued in isolation from wider UN strategies, as has tended to be the case with the first High Commissioner's own initiatives, in Rwanda and elsewhere. The High Commissioner should be the link between human rights operations and mechanisms and overall UN political, peace-keeping, humanitarian, and development activities.

CONCLUSION

Notwithstanding the difficulties experienced by the early operations, they are in most cases outweighed by their positive contributions; human rights work in the field is indeed the frontier of effective human rights protection and promotion today, and the work which is closest to the victim. The appointment of the second High Commissioner for Human Rights, and a new Secretary-General's commitment to UN reform based on better integration of the work of the UN system, offer a moment when more effective arrangements can and must be made to carry this work forward.

---

[8] See Alice Henkin (ed.), note 2, pp. 28-29, where the essential functions are spelled out.

The first High Commissioner for Human Rights placed the development of human rights work in the field at the center of his objectives for the UN human rights system. It falls to his successor to learn the lessons of the early operations and to develop a capacity to carry on such work according to the highest professional standards, in a manner which will not fail the victims or potential victims.

REFERENCE

1. I. Martin, A New Frontier: The Early Experience and Future of International Human Rights Field Operations, *Netherlands Quarterly of Human Rights, 16*:2, pp. 121-139, 1998.

Chapter 9

Toward an International Criminal Court

Roger S. Clark and David Tolbert

The standards established by the Universal Declaration of Human Rights and its progeny have limited effects unless there are means to enforce them. While in the fifty years since the adoption of the Declaration a number of organizations and institutions have been created on both the international and regional levels to "ensure that states comply," to monitor states' compliance with their human rights obligations, the individuals who have committed systematic abuses of human rights have largely escaped punishment, leaving their victims without justice and without redress. Thus, one of the most significant developments in the last fifty years in the human rights field is the movement to establish an International Criminal Court (ICC) which would have jurisdiction to bring to justice the perpetrators of the most serious breaches of human rights and humanitarian law. For victims, the establishment of the ICC would mean the acknowledgment of the crimes, the punishment of the perpetrators, and the redress, if only symbolic, of victims' injuries—in short, the vindication of the victim. The advent of the ICC thus creates real hope for victims that the promises of the Universal Declaration will be fulfilled and that justice will actually be done.

As this book goes to press, representatives of most of the countries of the World, spurred on by several hundred Non-Governmental Organizations (NGOs), are making final preparations to meet in a Diplomatic Conference in Rome. There they are expected to adopt a treaty setting out the Statute for an International Criminal Court (ICC). A draft Statute has been produced by the Preparatory Committee on the Establishment of an International Criminal Court ("the

PrepCom") which was created by the United Nations General Assembly in December 1995.[1] The ICC will likely have jurisdiction over genocide, crimes against humanity and serious war crimes, where national jurisdictions are unable or unwilling to bring the individuals who are responsible to justice.

The idea is not new, but the political will is. Efforts to create permanent structures following the precedents set by the trials after World War II in Nuremberg and Tokyo floundered in the Cold War. With the end of that preoccupation, the Security Council found it possible in the early 1990s to create *ad hoc* Tribunals to try those responsible for serious breaches of humanitarian law in Former Yugoslavia (ICTY) and Rwanda (ICTR). As we move to the end of the century, it seems likely that there will soon be in place a permanent structure which builds on the *ad hoc* lessons of Nuremberg, Tokyo, Former Yugoslavia, and Rwanda.

The rationale expressed by the Security Council in approving the creation of the Tribunal for Former Yugoslavia had a distinctly victim-oriented perspective. In its Resolution 827 creating the Tribunal, the Council expressed its "grave alarm" at "continuing reports of widespread and flagrant violations of international humanitarian law occurring within the territory of former Yugoslavia . . . including reports of mass killing, organized and systematic detention and rape of women and the continuance of the practice of 'ethnic cleansing,' including for the acquisition and holding of territory." The Council spoke of bringing those responsible "to justice" and of its belief that their prosecution before an international tribunal "would contribute to the restoration and maintenance of peace" and "will contribute to ensuring that such violations are halted and effectively redressed." Similar sentiments were included in the resolution adopting the Statute for the Rwanda Tribunal and have been expressed by delegations and NGOs throughout the drafting of the Statute for the proposed ICC. Perhaps the best articulated expression of the point is in a paragraph proposed for the preamble to the ICC Statute by an NGO group, the Faith-Based Caucus on the ICC. It reads:

> Desirous that the quest for justice includes retributive justice whose purpose is the prosecution and punishment of offenders while insuring the rights of the accused to fair trials, restorative justice whose purpose is that of reparation, restitution and rehabilitation for the victims, and redemptive justice which must be seen as the enablement of communities and peoples to deal with the truths of the past in ways which will allow and

[1] Our discussion is based on the text in U.N. Doc. A/CONF.183/2/Add. 1, Draft Statute for the International Criminal Court (14 April 1998).

enable social reconstruction and reconciliation, and the ending of cycles of violence.[2]

Included among the multiple rationales expressed here are a commitment to the ending of impunity for at least some of those who perpetrate atrocities and a desire to vindicate the interests of the victims. The achievement of such goals carries with it the imperative that the Court be an effective one. A Statute which contains all kinds of progressive materials on victims but which is incapable of obtaining convictions would be a mockery of these lofty ideals.

VICTIMS AND THE INTERNATIONAL CRIMINAL COURT

If an effective ICC is to be established, what relationship will victims have to that court? To what extent will the court be empowered to attempt to redress the real injuries victims have suffered as individuals or as groups?

There are two distinct ways in which a victim may be involved in the proceedings of the ICC. One is to serve as a witness, whereby the victim testifies about his or her personal knowledge of the crimes alleged against a particular accused. This aspect of the victim's involvement in the proceedings raises a number of important issues relating to the treatment and protection of, as well as the assistance given to, victims in the course of inquiries and investigations and, if they become witnesses (victims as witnesses), during their travel to, and appearance before, the court. In some instances, there is the further question of what happens to the victim/witness *after* the trial. The second manner in which the victim may be involved with the court and its proceedings is as a victim: the victim *qua* victim. This raises the question: Does the victim have a role in the proceedings other than as a witness? If so, what should be the nature of the relationship with the court? Closely connected is the issue of whether the court should itself provide, or facilitate some other body to provide, financial and other

---

[2] *Draft preamble,* Faith-Based Caucus on the ICC (not dated but circulated at March 1998 PrepCom meeting). See also, *Suggestions Regarding the Victim's Role in the ICC,* submitted by the International Society for Traumatic Stress Studies and the International League for Human Rights to the August 1997 PrepCom; *Promoting the Right to Reparation of Survivors of Torture: What Role for a Permanent International Criminal Court?* Redress Trust, London, 1997; German Women Lawyers Association, *Reparation for Victims of Crime* (circulated at March 1998 PrepCom); European Law Students Association, Working Group on International Justice, *The Right of Victims of Serious Violations of Human Rights and International Crimes to Participate in Proceedings: a Standard for International Jurisdictions?* (1997); Women's Caucus for Gender Justice in the International Criminal Court, *Recommendations and Commentary on Penalties and Reparations,* circulated to the PrepCom in December 1997; *Human Rights Watch Commentary for the December 1997 Preparatory Committee Meeting on the Establishment of an International Criminal Court* 69-72.

redress for the injuries suffered. If so, what kind of mechanism would be appropriate to achieve that end?

We will explore questions such as these in a later section when we offer some comments on proposals contained in the draft to be considered in Rome. They are not, however, issues which can be approached with an entirely clean slate. At the conceptual level, there have been efforts to address them in two very significant United Nations instruments, the 1985 General Assembly Declaration of Basic Principles of Justice for Victims of Crime and Abuse of Power ("Victims Declaration")[3] and the Basic Principles and Guidelines on the Right to Reparation for Victims of Gross Violations of Human Rights and Humanitarian Law ("van Boven Principles")[4] that are discussed more fully in other Chapters of this volume. At the practical level, the issues have been dealt with in the context of the *ad hoc* Tribunals for Former Yugoslavia and Rwanda. We turn first to the conceptual endeavors and then to the operational experience.

THE 1985 GENERAL ASSEMBLY DECLARATION ON VICTIMS, THE VAN BOVEN PRINCIPLES, AND THEIR INFLUENCE ON THE AD HOC TRIBUNALS

The United Nations Declaration of Basic Principles of Justice for Victims of Crime and Abuse of Power has been discussed thoroughly in Chapter 5 in this volume. It is necessary here merely to recall some of the basic concepts therein, particularly those that have been stressed by participants in the drafting of the Statute of the proposed ICC. We have noticed considerable confusion during the drafting, brought about by lack of familiarity with the nomenclature used in the Declaration and in the van Boven Principles, and we shall try to dispel some of that.

The Basic Principles contained in the Declaration are addressed to states generally. They should apply no less to the collective legal person that will be the International Criminal Court.

The Victims Declaration lays down four categories of claim that victims might make on the State, and on the criminal justice system in particular: access to justice and fair treatment, restitution, compensation, and assistance. Access to justice and to fair treatment includes being treated with compassion and respect

---

[3] G. A. Res. 40/34 (1985). On the Declaration in general, see Chapter 7 of Roger S. Clark, *The United Nations Crime Prevention and Criminal Justice Program: Development of Standards and Efforts at Their Implementation*, University of Pennsylvania Press, Philadelphia, 1994.

[4] The material primarily considered by the PrepCom on this was Sub-Commission on Prevention of Discrimination and Protection of Minorities, Revised set of basic principles and guidelines on the right to reparation for victims of gross violations of human rights and humanitarian law prepared by Mr. Theo van Boven pursuant to Sub-Commission decision 1995/117, U.N. Doc. E/CN.4/Sub.2/1996/17 (1996). See also van Boven et al., Treatment and Compensation of Victims, in *Transitional Justice: How Emerging Democracies Reckon with Former Regimes*, 500, N. Kritz (ed.), United States Institute for Peace, Washington, D.C., 1995.

for dignity. The system should act promptly and adequate information should be provided to victims about their role and the scope, timing, and progress of proceedings. An opportunity should be provided, where appropriate, to have the views and concerns of the victims presented and considered. "Restitution" is based on the premise that offenders or third parties (including possibly States) responsible for their behavior should, where appropriate, make fair restitution to victims, their families, or dependents. "Compensation" is the term chosen in the Declaration to refer to recompense made by the State even though it has no "responsibility" under international or national law to do so since the criminal was acting in a purely individual capacity and not as an agent of the state. Thus, when (as is commonly the case) recompense is not available from the individual perpetrators, states are exhorted to make financial compensation available for the direct victims and family members who have suffered bodily injury or impairment of physical or mental health as a result of serious crimes. "Assistance" proceeds from the insight that some victims need more than money to make them whole. A support system must be in place. There is no single "right" way to do this; it may be organized through governmental, non-governmental, indigenous, or other means, but a system should be in place, and victims must be made aware of its availability.

Professor van Boven has discussed his study on The Right to Reparation for Victims of Gross Violations of Human Rights and Humanitarian Law in Chapter 1 in this volume. The comments that follow are based on the statement of principles he did for the Sub-Commission on Prevention of Discrimination and Protection of Minorities in 1996 ("van Boven Principles"). In the van Boven Principles, the term "reparation" (which does not appear in the Victims Declaration) is used as a general term to describe all forms of redress. The emphasis for van Boven is on state, rather than individual, responsibility, so that the focus can be slightly different from that in the case of the Victims Declaration where the emphasis in respect of restitution was on individual responsibility. The various forms of reparation that are mentioned in the van Boven Principles, in a list that is described as non-exhaustive, are restitution, compensation, and rehabilitation. "Restitution" is here aimed at re-establishing the situation that existed prior to the violations of human rights and humanitarian law. Examples given include the restoration of liberty or of family life and return to one's place of residence. "Compensation" is a concept which is close to the sense of the word "restitution" as that term is used in the Victims Declaration. It refers here to the payment of economically assessable damages flowing from violations, including physical and mental harm, lost opportunities including education, loss of earnings and earning potential, harms to the dignity and the costs of legal or expert assistance. "Rehabilitation" refers to medical and psychological care as well as legal and social services.

A United Nations Expert Meeting on Victims Issues took place while the report of the Secretary-General setting out the draft Statute for the International

Tribunal for the Former Yugoslavia was before the Security Council. The group had before it the 1985 Declaration and various follow-up material, as well as the preliminary efforts of Professor van Boven. While the draft Statute for the ICTY already made a general reference in three of its Articles to the question of victims, the expert group believed that more should be said and, in particular, that specific provision should be made for the care, privacy, and safety of victim witnesses and for limiting the questioning of both children and rape victims. A number of specific recommendations along these lines were forwarded to the Security Council.[5] In light of a tacit decision by the Security Council to make no amendments to the draft Statute, for fear of unravelling the whole enterprise, the suggestions were then pressed in the context of drafting the Tribunal's Rules of Procedure and Evidence ("the Rules"). The thrust of the Experts' suggestions found their way into the Rules which were, as foreshadowed in the Statute, drafted by the judges as a first order of business.[6] We turn, therefore, to the Tribunal experience to see how the treatment of victims has worked out in practice.

VICTIMS AND THE AD HOC TRIBUNALS

The Statutes of the Tribunals address the subject of victims in three separate provisions, each of which contemplates further development in the Rules. Article 15 of the ICTY Statute (Article 14 of the ICTR Statute) instructs the judges of the Tribunal to adopt rules of procedure and evidence, *inter alia,* for "the protection of victims and witnesses." Article 20 (1) of the Statute for Former Yugoslavia (Article 19 (1) of ICTR) provides that trials are to be conducted "with full respect for the rights of the accused and due regard for the protection of victims and witnesses." Article 22 of the ICTY Statute (Article 21 of ICTR) states that the Tribunal's Rules should provide for "the protection of victims and witnesses," and that such protection measures "shall include, but not be limited to, the conduct of *in camera* proceedings and the protection of the victim's identity." These provisions all clearly relate to victims as witnesses. Significantly the Statutes further provide that an accused's right to a public hearing *is subject to such protection measures.*[7] This is an important statement of principle; the

---

[5] International Scientific and Professional Advisory Council of the United Nations Crime Prevention and Criminal Justice Programme, *Prevention of Victimization, Protection and Assistance for Victims, and Conflict Resolution, Report of the Workshop held at Onati, Spain, 13-16 May 1993,* at 48-50.

[6] D. Nsereko, Rules of Procedure and Evidence of the International Tribunal for the Former Yugoslavia, in *The Prosecution of International Crimes: A Critical Study of the Tribunal for Former Yugoslavia,* R. Clark and M. Sann (eds.), Transaction, New Brunswick, New Jersey, p. 293, 1996.

[7] ICTY Statute Article 21(2) and ICTR Statute Article 20(2) provide: ". . . the accused shall be entitled to a fair and public hearing, subject to article 22 [ICTR 21] of the [ICTY] Statute." See also, Decision on the prosecutor's Motion Requesting Protective Measures for Victims and Witnesses, 10 August 1995, reproduced in 7 *Criminal Law Forum* 139, 156: ". . . the Statute . . . *does* provide that the protection of victims and witnesses is an acceptable reason to limit the accused's right to a public trial." (Emphasis in original.)

Security Council has taken into account the unique difficulties faced by victims who testify before an international tribunal on serious violations of international humanitarian law. Apart from a brief reference to restitution in the penalties Article, to which reference will be made shortly, the Statutes are otherwise silent on victims' issues.

The Tribunals' Rules do, however, build on these rather limited references in the Statutes and contain a number of provisions which relate to victims, primarily victims as witnesses. Under Rule 34, a Victims and Witnesses Unit ("VWU") is established under the authority of the Registrar, with a mandate to recommend protection measures for victims/witnesses in accordance with the Statute and to provide "counseling and support for them, in particular in cases of rape and sexual assault." The ICTR has further provided that its VWU "develop short and long term plans for the protection of witnesses who have testified before the Tribunal and who fear a threat to their life, property or family."

Rules 69 and 75 establish the procedural and substantive framework for providing protective measures for victims as witnesses. These Rules provide that in cases where the victim/witness "may be in danger or at risk," measures may be taken to prevent the disclosure of the identity or location of the witness or of persons associated with that witness. These measures include: non-disclosure of a witness's identity in court documents, providing image/voice alteration during testimony, assignment of a pseudonym and closed, non-public court sessions during a witness's testimony. Of particular importance in cases of sexual abuse, the Rules provide for the facilitation of testimony of vulnerable witnesses by means "such as one-way closed circuit television," which would allow a victim/ witness to avoid seeing the accused who may have perpetrated crimes against him or her. Finally, a Trial Chamber "shall, whenever necessary, control the manner of questioning to avoid harassment or intimidation" of a victim/witness.

The Tribunals now have some jurisprudence relating to these Rules as well as considerable practical experience in dealing with victims as witnesses. In several decisions, the ICTY has wrestled with the difficult issue of to what extent a victim/witness's entitlement to anonymity can override the accused's right to know the identity of his/her accuser. These decisions have held that the identity of a witness may be withheld even from an accused where clearly defined criteria have been met; these include, *inter alia:* real fear for the safety of witnesses or their families; the importance of the witness to the prosecutor's case; the prima facie trustworthiness of the witness; and full cross-examination of the witness on non-identity issues. The difficulties with withholding a victim's identity from the accused were evident in the *Tadic* case when the identity of a witness was withheld, but it emerged that the witness had serious credibility problems requiring withdrawal of anonymity. On the other hand, in another case, where partial protection measures were employed, but the identity was not completely withheld, the names of certain protected witnesses appeared in the press.

The Rules also provide special roles for the VWU. The VWU has standing to request that a Chamber or Judge issue protection measures for a particular victim/witness. Moreover, a Trial Chamber may consult with the VWU on which protection measures should be granted. Decisions by ICTY Trial Chambers have also provided that in those cases where testimony has been obtained in closed session, the VWU will review the transcripts with a view to redacting evidence which might put a victim/witness in danger. While these are important roles for the VWU to play in protecting victims as witnesses, the VWUs' day-to-day work involves providing logistical support to witnesses, with assistance for travel, accommodation, translation, and counseling before and after testifying. These responsibilities have led to the development of various policies relating to reimbursement for travel expenses and compensation for loss of employment, etc. The VWUs have also been active in seeking to establish witness relocation arrangements for witnesses who, as a result of their appearance before the Tribunal, cannot return to their homes due to concerns for their safety. In sum, the VWUs have been entrusted with the responsibility of providing assistance to, and ensuring the rights of, victims—at least to the extent they are witnesses.

The Tribunals' relationship with victims has been limited, thus far at least, to victims as witnesses. As the above discussion indicates, the Tribunals have developed a number of mechanisms to protect victims as witnesses which the ICC will need to emulate. The practical experience gained from the work of the Tribunals, and, in particular, the experience gained by the VWUs should be invaluable to the ICC.

The remaining issues regarding reparations and compensation for victims have not been addressed by the Tribunals thus far. Article 24 (3) of the ICTY Statute (Article 23 (3) of ICTR) provides that: "In addition to imprisonment, the Trial Chambers may order the return of any property and proceeds acquired by criminal conduct, including by means of duress, to their rightful owners." The Rules provide for the restitution of property in certain cases (Rule 105) and for the communication to "the States concerned the judgment finding the accused guilty of a crime which caused injury to a victim" (Rule 106). However, these provisions have not been interpreted or applied by either Tribunal, and their scope and efficacy will have to await further developments. In any event, these rules fall well short of providing reparations or establishing a compensation scheme. As the Tribunals' Statutes and Rules are otherwise silent, there have been no developments which would be of assistance in testing the proposals made in respect of the ICC for reparations or compensation.

It should be noted, however, that the Registry in Rwanda is examining the idea of using its Trust Fund to provide financial support to programs, primarily operated by non-governmental organizations and other institutions, which would assist victims. This assistance would encompass programs that would contribute to medical and psychological care of victims and provide legal assistance and related support. The Tribunals' Trust Funds have been established to provide extra-budgetary support to the respective Tribunals. States and other actors have made voluntary contributions to these Trust Funds, usually for the purpose of funding specific projects which support the Tribunals' work.

The argument put forward for using Trust Fund monies for such a victims' assistance program is that even though there is no express provision in the Statutes or Rules for such a program, it is inherent in the Tribunal's mandate that it must do justice, including restitutive justice. A number of issues arise with relation to this proposal, both as to the feasibility of using the funds for these purposes under applicable United Nations rules and procedures and as to how such a program would be administered, e.g., the criteria applied in making financial payments or providing material or other assistance. Moreover, the available resources in the Trust Fund are relatively small and the number of victims quite large. It is believed, however, that some governments would be prepared to make contributions to the Fund specifically for this purpose. It is not yet clear how these issues might be resolved, but developments regarding this proposal may well prove to be instructive on how the ICC might approach issues related to compensation and reparations.

THE ICC DRAFT STATUTE

All of the types of claims of victims contained (and variously described) in the Victims Declaration and in the van Boven Principles have received attention in the course of the drafting of the Statute of the ICC. Since these words are being written in May of 1998 (see Postscript, p. 111), on the very eve of the Diplomatic Conference to finalize the Statute, none of the material is yet set in stone. Much of the material on victims in the Draft Statute going into Rome is highly bracketed and rife with alternative formulations. Moreover, not everything will need to be addressed in the Statute; some material on the subject will ultimately find its way into the practice of the organs of the Court and, as has been the case with the Tribunals for Former Yugoslavia and Rwanda, into the Rules of Procedure and Evidence. Indeed, some items will depend in substantial part on ongoing choices to be made about the provision of resources.

Given the variety of issues involved, it is apparent that some questions will need to be dealt with by the Court itself, both in its relations with victims (and witnesses) and in its bi-lateral relations with States. Other issues will involve actions that will need to be taken by States Parties. Others will be matters that can fairly be cast as involving the actions (and assets) of defendants. We turn to an examination of the ways in which discussions in the Preparatory Committee, and tentative formulations in the draft Statute, suggest that matters might be approached.

At the very threshold of inquiry is the question of the treatment of victims and (if they are not the same persons) witnesses by the Prosecutor's office. This is the basic dignity value discussed in the Victims Declaration. Thus, a (bracketed) provision in the Draft insists that the prosecutor shall take appropriate measures to ensure the effective investigation and prosecution of crimes within the jurisdiction of the Court. In so doing, the Prosecutor is required to respect the interests and personal circumstances of victims and witnesses, including age, gender, and health, and to take into account the nature of the crime, in particular, but not limited to, where it involves sexual or gender violence or violence against children. A very close linkage is made, it will be noticed, between effective investigation and prosecution on the one hand, and sensitivity to victims on the other.

It is axiomatic, as has been noted above, that some victims will appear as witnesses in proceedings in the ICC. Victims are, in a real sense, *the* witnesses in such proceedings, as often only they can establish the identities of their tormentors. Although documents, experts, and other witnesses will provide important evidence in certain cases, victims will provide critical testimony in establishing the occurrence of events as well as those involved. Thus, victims will necessarily have to enter courtrooms physically, generally in an unfamiliar country, and "face" those who have committed crimes which are of the most heinous nature, against themselves and their families. Those who have been sexually assaulted will find themselves re-living a nightmare. Moreover, some victims will find that by testifying publicly they will have put themselves at risk and that they cannot return to their homes because of fear of retaliation for testifying.

Accordingly, it is clear that the ICC's Statute and Rules will need to make specific provisions for the protection and proper treatment of victims who are witnesses. In extreme cases, such witnesses will have to be afforded entry into witness protection programs in countries that have such programs or, if the situation allows, simply relocated to another country. Relocation in itself can serve as a protection measure, even without a witness protection program. In other cases, it may be sufficient for the court to take measures to protect the witness during the course of his or her testimony. Such measures could include protecting the witness's identity during the course of testimony by using a pseudonym and closed sessions of the court. Moreover, in cases of sexual assault, further steps to safeguard and protect the victim who is testifying may be justified. Such measures are, of course, subject to the accused's rights to a fair trial, and the court will have to weigh carefully the appropriateness of such measures in the individual circumstances of each case; nonetheless, it is critical for victims that the court have these mechanisms and that it use them appropriately and effectively.

While the protection of victims as witnesses is important, it should be recognized that specific protection measures will have to be undertaken only in certain cases and that the need for relocation of witnesses will happen only rarely. Perhaps more important is that the victims who are testifying in a strange land in a courtroom that is unfamiliar, if not terrifying, are treated with dignity and provided with the necessary assistance, so that they avoid being re-traumatized or having their dignity again trampled upon. This is particularly true since many of them will be subject to rigorous cross-examination. It is also important that the victims/witnesses have the proceedings and their rights explained to them by a neutral party, rather than the prosecution or defense, who are after all combatants in the proceedings and have an interest in victims' testimony. In the ICTY and ICTR, the role of informing and protecting the victim/witness is entrusted to the Victims and Witnesses Unit which is located in the Registry, thus ensuring that the victims are the responsibility of a non-combatant in the proceedings. Finally, for victims to testify they must have logistical support, such as travel, accommodation, translators, and assistance, as well as emotional support, including counseling for them and their families, during the time they spend at the situs of the court; support in some cases will also include the victims being accompanied by a family member or friend. This requires a financial commitment to ensure that the necessary resources are available.

While the treatment of victims as witnesses is not without its difficulties, it is relatively straightforward compared with the issues raised by the other ways in which victims might participate in the proceedings. Proposals made during the debates on the ICC fall roughly into two categories. One relates to reparation issues, the term being used in van Boven's broad sense. The other category involves the participation of victims in the proceedings of the court, either as a party to the proceedings or in an advisory capacity.

Reparation proposals emphasize "restitutive" or "restorative" justice. Those who will be prosecuted before the ICC for war crimes, genocide and crimes against humanity which will be the mainstay of the Court's jurisdiction, will for the most part be individuals who nevertheless were acting on behalf of a state or quasi-state entry. Some of them may have resources (plundered, perhaps) that might be used for restitution/reparation/compensation, although this is likely to be the exception rather than the rule. There has, consequently and not surprisingly, been some tension in the debate between attributing responsibility to make reparation solely to those individual actors and, alternatively, also attributing responsibility for redress to their masters, the state. Bear in mind that the *criminal* responsibility of the state will not be an issue before the ICC. While the state is not being "prosecuted," it might nonetheless be thought expedient in the criminal proceedings to find some way to deal with its responsibility for reparation in the van Boven sense, or to encourage it, or the international community, to provide compensation and assistance in the sense of the Victims Declaration. Highly controversial, in short, was the extent to which the Court, in its work in general, could develop principles relating to reparation, and in a particular case could make an appropriate penalty order directly against a particular individual. Such an order would presumably be part of a set of available sentencing options. Even more divisive was the possibility that the Court could recommend, or even order that appropriate forms of reparations might be made by the state on behalf of which the accused was acting at the time of the offense. Many participants thought that this was a hopeless confusion of criminal and compensatory principles. Others believed that a Court created to do justice must have the power to go in such directions. Less controversial was the notion, derived from the 1985 Declaration, that there be an international fund available when defendants' ill-gotten gains and national sources are inadequate. Such a fund, by its very nature, would rely primarily on voluntary contributions from states and other donors. There was, however, a proposal before the Diplomatic Conference that fines and assets collected by the Court from convicted persons would be transferred to such a fund for the benefit of victims generally, in priority to being used for defraying the costs of trial.

One of the proposals put forward for participation by victims was based on the civil law concept of *partie civile,* which allows a victim to join criminal proceedings as a civil complainant and to claim damage, thus avoiding the additional step of civil litigation. Another was for creating a victim's group that would have standing, or at least consultative rights, to draw the court's, or the prosecutor's, attention to matters concerning victims. Other proposals would require that the court take into account the views of victims prior to imposing sentence or provide the victims who might otherwise not be witnesses with a right to testify during the proceedings.

CONCLUSION

The ICC, if it is established as an effective institution, represents perhaps the most significant development in the enforcement of humanitarian law and human rights standards of our time. An effective ICC would provide the first genuine opportunity for the international community to bring, on a systematic basis, the perpetrators of serious violations of international humanitarian law to justice, thereby vindicating the rights of their victims. Such a development would, by itself, constitute a very significant achievement for the rights of victims, but the ICC has the potential to do much more. Indeed, the ICC's treatment of victims in the conduct of its proceedings, as witnesses and, potentially, as participants, will be an important measure of its effectiveness as an instrument of enforcing humanitarian law and as an institution devoted to addressing the breaches of that law.

In many ways, victims have been the silent partners in the legal process, with little role other than as witnesses, and at the mercy of litigants. The Victims Declaration and the van Boven Principles attempt to remedy this anomaly, and the two *ad hoc* Tribunals have taken steps to address most of the protection and assistance issues faced by victims as witnesses. In many respects the fact that there is now little disagreement on these particular issues demonstrates how far the debate has moved on. Thus, it is now generally accepted that victims as witnesses are entitled to protection, sometimes even if this means that their identity is withheld from the accused. VWUs, which are non-combatants in the proceedings and which have a duty to provide assistance, are entrusted with responsibility for the interests of victims who are witnesses. The ICC has a sound theoretical basis, as well as a reservoir of practical experience, on which to build appropriate mechanisms for the protection of victims/witnesses and provide assistance to them during the sometimes difficult appearances they will make before the ICC.

It is clear that, as a result of the Victims Declaration, the van Boven Principles and the energetic work of NGOs, the terms of the debate have been changed and the position of victims has moved from the margins to a central part of the ICC discussion.

Postscript

As adopted in Rome on 17 July 1998, the Statute for the International Criminal Court contains strong provisions concerning the interests of victims.

The tone is set in the preamble to the Statute which notes that "during this century millions of children, women and men have been victims of unimaginable atrocities that deeply shock the conscience of humanity." It calls for an end to the impunity of perpetrators of crimes of concern to the international community. As was envisaged in the draft, the Registrar of the Court will be obliged to set up a Victims and Witnesses Unit within the Registry. That Unit is to include staff with expertise in dealing with trauma, including trauma related to crimes of sexual violence. Measures for the protection of victims and witnesses and the participation of victims in the process have been included, along the lines discussed above. The modalities by which the views and concerns of the victims are to be presented to the Court will be further spelled out in the Rules of Procedure and Evidence. These Rules will be drafted by the Preparatory Commission whose task is to make arrangements for bringing the Statute into force. A lengthy provision in the Statute incorporates the thrust of the 1985 Victims Declaration and the van Boven Principles. It provides for the making of orders for reparation that may include restitution, compensation and rehabilitation. The provisions dealing with state responsibility did not survive the Diplomatic Conference. Nor did proposals which were hotly debated at the Conference to include provisions for the criminal responsibility of corporate entities which are complicit in crimes within the jurisdiction of the Court. This might, in some instances, have provided further sources of reparation for victims. Nonetheless, the Statute makes it clear that individual perpetrators with means may be required to pay. Moreover, a Trust Fund is to be established to receive contributions for the benefit of victims and their families. Where appropriate, the International Criminal Court may order that money and other property collected through fines or forfeiture be transferred to the Fund.

In short, the Statute of the Court represents a strong merger of the lessons of Nuremberg, of the Universal Declaration of Human Rights and of the ad hoc tribunals. The rights of victims find their expression in the context of individual criminal responsibility.

Part III

Human Rights of Specific Groups: Conceptual and Institutional Development

Chapter 10

Recognizing and Realizing Women's Human Rights

Maria Suarez Toro
Shanthi Dairiam

Part I: Sexual Politics and Human Rights

Maria Suarez Toro

In 1948 Eleanor Roosevelt, together with other women delegates of United Nations Member States from Africa, Latin America, and the Caribbean, lobbied the United Nations to get the word "sex" to be part of the types of discrimination mentioned in the then draft Universal Declaration of Human Rights (UDHR).

Little could they have known at the time that a single word would unleash the further development of a powerful global movement of women which fifty years later would challenge the United Nations to end sexism in the overall human rights framework. They could not have imagined that this movement would be able to break through the resistance to recognize the harmful laws and practices of discrimination on the basis of sex and finally lead the world to call violations of women's rights an international human rights issue. Or perhaps those female delegates that struggled so tenaciously fifty years ago at the United

Nations did know the power of language. They might have realized how the inclusion of a single word could legitimize the historical continuity of the struggle for women's human rights during the second half of the twentieth century, despite the ongoing resistance to bridging the gender gap in human rights.

Today, as the United Nations celebrates the Fiftieth Anniversary of the Universal Declaration of Human Rights (UDHR), it is clear that women have come a long way in the struggle for formal and legal recognition by the international community that women's rights are human rights.

On the conceptual level, non-discrimination on the basis of sex was part of the human rights framework long before the existence of the United Nations and the Universal Declaration itself. According to Linda Poole, former Executive Secretary of the Interamerican Commission on Women (CIM):

> The first international treaty dealing with women's human rights issues was the Interamerican Convention on the Nationality of Women and was created in the [Latin American] region in 1933 [by the Organization of American States]. That was the instrument that spurred a debate on how the region of Latin America was, in fact, developing a body of law that would deal with human rights. There was no governmental body dealing with women's human rights before CIM was created, way back in 1928.[1]

The United Nations began the inclusion of women's rights in the Charter and the UDHR. Both documents prohibit discrimination on the basis of sex. Women around the world have come a long way since then, toward including their rights in the human rights conceptual framework. In a comprehensive account of related international instruments, Elsa Stamatopoulou, UN official with the then Center for Human Rights, wrote:

> The principle [of non-discrimination on the basis of sex] found its way into the two main International Covenants: the International Covenant on Economic, Social and Cultural Rights, and the International Covenant on Civil and Political Rights. In addition to non-discrimination, a number of other provisions of great importance to women are also contained in these instruments. The Universal Declaration of Human Rights calls for equal rights in marriage, which, it stipulates, "shall be entered into only with the free and full consent of the intending spouses." It also calls for "equal pay for equal work" and for the protection of motherhood. The Covenant on Economic, Social and Cultural Rights states that all workers must be provided with "fair wages and equal remuneration for work of equal value without discrimination of any kind, in particular women being guaranteed conditions of work not inferior to those enjoyed by men, with equal pay for equal work." It also provides for the protection of motherhood, and calls for

---

[1] Interview for FIRE, September 14th, 1992.

paid maternity leave or leave with adequate social security benefits. The Covenant on Civil and Political Rights prohibits the use of the death sentence on pregnant women, provides for equality between men and women during marriage and at its dissolution, and for the right to participate in public life without discrimination, while declaring, finally, that equality before the law and the principle of nondiscrimination are enforceable rights [1].

A number of other international treaties are devoted to issues affecting specific aspects of women's lives. These include: the Discrimination (Employment and Occupation) Convention, the Convention against Discrimination in Education, the Equal Remuneration Convention, the Slavery Conventions, the Convention on the Suppression of the Traffic in Persons and the Exploitation of the Prostitution of Others, the Convention on the Nationality of Married Women, the Convention on the Political Rights of Women, the Declaration on the Protection of Women and Children in Emergency Armed Conflict, and the Convention on the Rights of Migrant Workers and Members of their Families [1].

The UN Decade of Women in the 1970s resulted in the adoption, in 1979, of a very strong Convention for the protection of women against discrimination, so much so, that the Convention on the Elimination of All Forms of Discrimination Against Women (CEDAW) is better known as "the Women's Convention." Although the concept of discrimination on the basis of sex has been expanded to include ever more issues between 1948 and the decade of the 1990s, violence against women has become the new cornerstone for the recognition that women's rights are human rights. The issue bridges the gap between the public and the private in human rights conceptualization with regards to gender.

Margaret Bruce, formerly with the UN Secretariat, reminds us that "the issue of violence against women was not even on the international agendas. It was the women of the Third World, especially in Latin America, who put it on the agenda for the Decade (the UN Decade of Women, 1975-1985)."[2]

The strongest drive to put women's rights on the UN's human rights agenda took place in 1992, when the Committee on the Elimination of All Forms of Discrimination Against Women, which is the body that supervises the CEDAW Convention, adopted a "General Comment" interpretative of the Convention at their 11th session held in January of that year. Recommendation No. 19 states that States parties

in reviewing their laws and policies, and in reporting under the Convention, . . . should pay regard to the following comments of the Committee concerning gender-based violence: -Gender based violence is discrimination . . . -Gender based violence violates human rights . . . -The Convention covers public and private acts . . . and that the States parties should take appropriate

[2] Interview for Feminist International Radio Endeavor (FIRE), January 15, 1992.

and effective measures to overcome all forms of gender based violence, whether by public or private act" [2].

The UNIFEM perspective that presented violence against women as an obstacle to development was also instrumental in advancing the struggle of the women's movement to include violence against women in the international agenda. In 1993, at the United Nations Second World Conference on Human Rights in Vienna and at the parallel Non-Governmental Organizations Forum, an unprecedented global women's movement demanded that women's rights be recognized as human rights, especially violence against women. Women came to Vienna representing thousands who had taken part in local and regional satellite meetings to draft their demands for the UN Conference. They came representing the almost one million people who had signed the historic petition to the UN demanding that women's rights be recognized as human rights; thirty-three of them came from their respective countries to testify at the Global Tribunal on Violations of Women's Human Rights held in the NGO Forum. They came to pay tribute to the millions of girls and women assassinated because of lack of respect to even the basic human right to life. Convened by a coalition of women's organizations from around the globe, the Global Tribunal on Violations of Women's Human Rights held in Vienna on that occasion was part of a historic campaign undertaken by women since the origins of the UDHR itself to get the UN to recognize that women's rights are human rights; to recognize that women are human in their own right, and that historically, it was about time that the issues and experiences that stem from that fact be placed on the international human rights agenda. Among many questions, the Global Tribunal heard the appeal of witnesses that sex discrimination should not wait until the serious life or death issues of war, peace, and justice be resolved, since sexism is a life and death issue for the female half of the world. "Sexism kills" read a press release in Vienna during the World Conference. "In childhood, some of the forms it takes are female infanticide and the neglect to feed and provide health care to girls. In adulthood, some of the forms it takes are complications due to genital mutilation, lack of services for safe abortions, the beatings, the rapes, the dowry deaths, and the 'honor killings,' and in old age, some forms are abandonment, poverty and neglect."[3] The Tribunal issued a statement containing a series of recommendations that were taken into consideration by the Plenary of the official Conference. Violence against women as a human rights issue and proposals for specific human rights instruments and mechanisms for the protection of women against these wrongs were among them.

As an unprecedented event at that kind of formal UN setting, the moment when the findings and recommendations of the Global Tribunal were presented to

---

[3] Fact Sheet, *Vienna 1993*, source: C.W.G.L.

the Conference, women walked into the official meeting hall pulling carts full of petitions signed, during the previous two-year-long grassroots campaign, by almost half a million women. The signed petitions of the "Women's Rights are Human Rights" campaign were deposited in front of the podium at the Plenary of the World Conference.

Yet another highlight of the actions undertaken by the women's movement to ensure that their demands were heard and taken into account was when African activist Mary Casunga addressed the Plenary session of the World Conference on behalf of the women's caucus. Instead of using her three-minute time to speak, she asked the delegates to stand up for a minute of silence, to honor the women who had died as a result of violations of their rights.

The Vienna Declaration and Programme of Action, adopted by consensus, finally recognized that violence against women is a violation of human rights, whether perpetrated in the public or in the private sphere. It also called for the appointment of a Special Rapporteur on Violence Against Women, a measure that was implemented in March 1994 when the Commission on Human Rights appointed Radhika Coomaraswamy, a lawyer from Sri Lanka, to the position. Ever since, on an annual basis, the Special Rapporteur has issued reports based on studies about violence against women. The Vienna Declaration also called for the adoption of a UN Declaration on Violence Against Women which was officially adopted by the UN General Assembly in December 1993. Further, the Vienna Declaration stated that the human rights of women and the girl child are an inalienable and indivisible part of universal human rights. The statement also recognizes that the human rights of women should form an integral part of UN human rights activities, including the promotion of all human rights instruments relating to women.

The adoption of an Optional Protocol to the CEDAW Convention was also recommended by the World Conference. The Protocol will give teeth to the Convention that up to today has no mechanisms for the presentation of individual complaints or class actions to the Committee, based on violations of CEDAW.

At the regional level, the Organization of American States (OAS) adopted the Interamerican Convention on the Prevention, Punishment and Eradication of Violence Against Women in June of 1994. Contrary to the CEDAW, the OAS Convention contains mechanisms for the presentation of cases of violations of articles of the Convention. According to Rhonda Copelon, one of the experts, "this groundbreaking Convention was the result of the work of the Interamerican Women's Commission (CIM), since the recommendation for such a Convention was made by CIM at an expert group meeting in Caracas, in 1991, but it was finally adopted by the OAS mainly as a result of the mobilization of Latin American and Caribbean women."[4]

---

[4] Interview for FIRE, June 2, 1995.

The fourth World Conference on Women held in Beijing in 1995 affirmed the recommendations of the World Conference on Human Rights regarding the human rights of women. Indeed, women have come a long way in getting the world to recognize that women's rights are human rights. But it seems that the road for practical respect, implementation, and accountability to international human rights standards in the protection of women's human rights remains full of obstacles.

The use of the "rights" language appears to be one of the main obstacles to the respect for women's rights worldwide. Perhaps one of the characteristics of the end of this century is the realization of the power of language in politics. This relates to the incredible ability of states to use the argument of the "ambiguity" of language they approved themselves in international instruments to evade the obligations that stem from the agreements they concluded in UN Conferences regarding women's rights. But even when the text of a human rights law is clear, there is a structural obstacle in implementation: the interpretation of the law usually falls into the traditional androcentric framework. As Alda Facio has said, "the language of the law is usually interpreted in male terms, because the law stands within an androcentric 'rights' framework" [3]. Another language barrier is the exclusion in human rights law of the ordinary language that stems from women's own experiences and perspectives. This has become one of the most serious obstacles for women themselves in using the UN instruments. The resistance of the UN to incorporating in its official documents language other than that of formal law has forced the women's movement to re-phrase, in human rights legal terminology, the day-to-day experiences of women in naming rights and the violation of those rights. In the long run, the majority of women find it difficult to identify what the human rights instruments are all about because the language is so foreign to their experience. As Elizabeth Friedman commented about the inclusion of women's recommendations in the Vienna Declaration and Programme of Action: "there were . . . significant omissions . . . Appropriately gendered language was not found throughout the document" [4]. The same remains true of the Platform for Action of the fourth World Conference on Women in Beijing.

Part II: Equality and the Structures of Discrimination

Shanthi Dairiam

It is clear that the women's campaign on human rights has brought about con-siderable recognition that women too are human and hence the recipients of human rights, but obstacles still remain with regard to the realization of rights. Sunila Abeyesekera points out that the gains made in Vienna through the women's campaign have not necessarily advanced the agenda [5, p. 5]. She cites examples from documents of the 1994 meeting of the Sub-Commission on Prevention of Discrimination and Protection of Minorities that continue to exclude violations of women's rights. She refers to a 1994 proposal for the prevention of discrimination and protection of minorities that makes no mention of women as being particularly vulnerable to discrimination and to two other documents: one spelling out the relationship between human rights and income distribution, the other a report on human rights and poverty, both of which make no reference to the gendered power differentials that affect income distribution or the specific ways in which women have become the poorest of the poor. At that meeting, violations of women's rights were only mentioned with regard to their bodies, in the context of traditional practices affecting the health of women and children, and trafficking, prostitution, and in the context of the link between debt bondage and the sexual enslavement of women. The problems of early marriage and military sexual slavery were also considered [5, p. 8].

WOMEN'S RIGHTS AS HUMAN RIGHTS, THE EQUALITY DIMENSION

While the struggle for the recognition of the human rights of women has to continue, it must move from taking into account violations and abuses particu-larly affecting women to including the struggle for equality. This requires clarity with regard to the concept of equality and to the structural nature of discrimina-tion against women.

First, in many contexts, formal notions of equality premised on the assump-tions of sameness between people situated in similar circumstances have not benefitted disadvantaged groups. Therefore, the discourse has to move toward a substantive definition of equality, which takes into account diversity, difference, disadvantage, and discrimination. It has been clear that "equal treatment" of women and men is not sufficient to transform the situation of women. Neutrality does not allow for sensitivity to disadvantages that may prevent some people from benefiting from equal treatment. Hence the focus must move to an emphasis to "equal outcomes" or "equal benefits."

For example, labor legislation in many countries has provisions for equal pay. However, in most countries, women are confined to traditional low paying jobs, most women work inside and outside the home and at the same time face the risk of physical insecurity within their home, at the work site and in other public places, hampering their mobility. Their lack of exposure, at times limited skills, the absence of male responsibility for family care, the lack of family support services, and the possible lack of autonomy at the personal level may prevent women from accessing opportunities for upward mobility. Under these conditions, the clause of equal pay for equal work does not really benefit women. This is not to underestimate the importance of equal pay for equal work, but to remind ourselves that it is not enough.

What is needed are pro-active, pro-women policies and practices, mechanisms that will not only ask whether there are laws that guarantee equal pay for equal work but will also ask whether there are programmatic measures to free women from family support services, that make special provisions to secure personal security. We need mechanisms that guarantee affirmative action for training opportunities, long-term measures that attempt to change cultural patterns of conduct that place women and men in stereotypical roles that disadvantage women, and measures that ensure that structures are not male dominated.

Gender analysis has to unpackage the systemic nature of discrimination and reveal the complex processes by which social norms practiced on the private and community level, underpin the manner in which institutions reproduce discrimination through law and policy. We need to expose the linkages between discrimination against women and the structural basis of inequality through examining the way social rules operate in different institutions of society. For example, the social expectation that men are responsible for the economic provisioning of the family (even if this is not always so in reality) and that women are homemakers underpins the phenomenon of occupational segregation of women in low paying jobs. It is also the basis of discrimination in inheritance or citizenship laws, or of laws that view fathers as natural guardians of their children. As Naila Kabeer points out, these are important issues to consider because gender relations are present in all these institutions, and they are fundamentally interlinked [6, pp. 61, 308]. Institutions do not function as isolated units of society, but instead draw on the rules structured within the household. Assumptions that the household, community institutions, the market, and the state are all independent of each other, mask the extent to which gender differences get constructed and reproduced.

Kabeer states that looking at inter-institutional relationships which determine the reproduction of inequalities between women and men will also enable us to consider the nature of relationships that will need to be addressed [6, pp. 299, 308]. We cannot only speak about rights in the context of the individual and the state, but we need to look at the way relationships can be regulated across all these institutions.

STATE RESPONSIBILITY
FOR WOMEN'S HUMAN RIGHTS

State responsibility for the defense of women's human rights has also evolved toward understanding the pervasive and structural nature of discrimination against women. Rebecca Cook has pointed out that there are three overlapping and interacting developments [7, p. 5]. During the first phase of development, states focused on the promotion of specific legal rights of particular concern to women through accession to specialized conventions relating to employment, maternity, trafficking in persons, nationality, civil and political rights, marriage, education, and violence against women. During the second stage of development, states have succeeded in including sex as prohibited grounds of discrimination in such instruments as the Universal Declaration of Human Rights and the two International Covenants and the regional human rights agreements, although many states have yet to implement them fully. The third stage of development addresses the pervasive and structural nature of violations of women's human rights, through the Convention on the Elimination of All Forms of Discrimination Against Women.

Although many states have placed reservations on critical articles of the Convention and do not report to the Committee on the Elimination of Discrimination Against Women in a timely manner, nevertheless, by acceding to the Convention, the implication is that states are acknowledging the following:

- They recognize the need to take measures against discrimination and inequality.
- They recognize the need for state action.
- They commit themselves to do certain things and not do certain things.
- They are willing to be held accountable at state and international levels.

THE INVOLVEMENT OF WOMEN IN THE REALIZATION
OF THEIR RIGHTS

Women need to participate in the definition of rights, in the interpretation of needs, identification of obstacles, and actions to be taken by the state in the establishment of criteria for success and in documenting the impact of state action. This is not merely a technical task, but one that is deeply political. While rights may be recognized and norms and standards set through the treaties, this situation does not automatically confer rights on women. Rights have to be claimed by women, both individually and collectively. Many factors contribute toward women's capacity to claim rights. First of all, laws, policies, and the relevant infrastructure at the national level through which women claim their rights have to absorb the norms and standards of the human rights treaties. Second, support services for women have to be provided through which women's awareness of rights can be created. When women make a decision to claim their rights, they often put themselves at risk of community censure and, hence, they need strong support to withstand family and community pressure. A culture of compliance with human rights standards has to be created requiring sensitizing of law enforcers and implementers, and awareness raising of society at large.

Realizing women's rights requires the political will of governments. The emergence of the requisite political will is influenced by a dynamic relationship between the state and its citizenry that will put pressure on the state to fulfill its obligations to women.

Women must, therefore, be organized and vigilant, engage in sustained constructive dialogue with the state, and present themselves as a political constituency that the state cannot afford to neglect. They have to consistently monitor the obstacles to the realization of their rights, spell out state obligations in specific contexts, monitor state compliance, advocate for change in concrete rather than in rhetorical terms, and facilitate the development of jurisprudence on equality and non-discrimination by making claims through the court system.

THE LINK BETWEEN THE LOCAL AND
THE INTERNATIONAL

At the international level, the human rights treaties have their own monitoring system, and the monitoring and advocacy by women at the local level is essential to enhance the effectiveness of the international processes. It helps to bring back the effects of international advocacy to strengthen local advocacy and vice versa. For example, the fact that there are 161 ratifications or accessions to the Women's Convention provides a powerful mandate for the principles of equality and non-discrimination. The international system not only monitors state compliance, it also interprets the scope of the application of the Convention. The participation of women in the international process through the presentation of "shadow" reports to the Committee Against the Discrimination of Women, their presence at the review of State Party reports, and their contribution to the formulation of general recommendations facilitates the inclusion of local realities into the international process. The treaty then truly becomes a living instrument relevant to the lives of women.

Abeyesekera states that the women's campaign that was so successful at the time of the World Conference on Human Rights in 1993 has not organized itself after the Conference as to what strategies and methodologies should be adopted in order to continue to work collectively on women's human rights issues [5, pp. 8-9]. A more consistent strategy to influence the international community and to create gendered mechanisms for claiming rights at the local level needs to form the next phase of the women's campaign. Needless to say, the development of the capacity of women to claim their rights must be a critical component.

REFERENCES

1. E. Stamatopoulou, Women's Rights and the United Nations, in *Women's Rights, Human Rights,* J. Peters and A. Wolper (eds.), Routledge, pp. 37-38, 1995.
2. *WIN News,* 8:2, Spring 1992.
3. A. Facio, *Cuardo El Genero Suena, Piedras Trae: Metodologia para el Analisis de Genero del Fenomeno Legal,* I.L.A.N.U.D. (UN Latin American Institute for the Prevention of Delinquency), San Jose, 1992.
4. E. Friedman, Women's Human Rights: The Emergence of a Movement, in *Women's Rights, Human Rights,* J. Peters and A. Wolper (eds.), Routledge, 1995.
5. S. Abeyesekera, Consolidating Our Gains at the World Conference on Human Rights: A Personal Reflection, *Canadian Women's Studies, 15*:2&3, 1995.
6. N. Kabeer, *Reversed Realities—Gender Hierarchies in Development Thought,* Verso Press, London and New York, 1995.
7. R. Cook, The Elimination of Sexual Apartheid: Prospects for the Fourth World Conference on Women, *ASIL,* 1995.

Voices

Lessening the Suffering After Wartime Sexual Slavery

Kim, Yoon Shim[1]

In 1943, when I was fourteen years old, growing up in a rural village in Korea, a Japanese military truck picked me up and drove away to a harbor. A policeman and a military person guarded me and other girls whom they had also rounded up. When I attempted to escape, they tied my legs and hands with a rope. Finally, they shipped us to a camp in Manchuria to serve as military sexual slaves. There, day and night, the Japanese military raped us repeatedly. When any one of us became ill, the Japanese military buried her alive. At the end of the War, I was able to return to my homeland.[2]

It took me a long time before I came forward to report that I was a sex slave of the Japanese army. At first, I did not think of claiming any compensation from the Japanese government. But I wanted to show the world what the Japanese did to us. Ever since then, I have been participating in the demonstrations that take place each Wednesday in front of the Japanese Embassy in Seoul.

Until I die I want to serve as a witness against the Japanese for their inhuman treatment of the sexual slaves and their atrocious war crimes. In the spring of 1997, I presented my testimony at a women's rights forum in Northern Ireland. There, I met Dutch women who had also been sex slaves of the Japanese as well

---

[1] The footnotes are provided by John Y. Lee, Attorney, Chairman of the Washington Coalition for Comfort Women Issues, a non-profit organization created to seek redress for the victims who were sexual slaves of the Japanese Army.

[2] Japanese armed forces took captive about 200,000 women for use as sexual slaves in military brothels during the Second World War.

as women who are working for the protection of women's human rights.[3] I found that I am not alone and felt tremendous comfort in meeting them. My spirit was uplifted. I felt that my belief that the Japanese must be made accountable for their crimes and that the victims must be compensated was supported by the people of the world.

I was deeply pleased to learn that the United Nations Commission on Human Rights appointed a Special Rapporteur on Violence Against Women who investigated the human rights violations of the sexual slavery practiced by the Japanese military during the Second World War. In 1996, the Special Rapporteur, Radhika Coomaraswamy, found that most of the women were kept at the comfort stations against their will, and that the Government of Japan should be held responsible for its acts. I came to believe that the world community is now paying attention to our cause, that justice may be done, and that our rights may be realized. The people of the world may be looking at us with compassion. I am sure that many countries within the United Nations will act for our cause.

My wish is that the Government of Japan admit its wrongs, apologize for its crimes, and punish the offenders. Further, the Japanese Government should record the true facts of the sex slavery in its textbooks. I wish that the United Nations would act positively in this area.[4]

I and the other victims are weak and old and will die soon. If the United Nations paid attention to our issues, our pain and suffering would be lessened. Even if we die soon, our hope will not be quashed. We are earnestly seeking the United Nations' assistance.

---

[3] The Japanese Imperial Army forced the women taken from Korea, China, Philippines, Malaysia, Indonesia, Singapore, and the Dutch East Indies to commit sexual acts with its soldiers. Often, they were beaten and tortured in addition to being raped.

[4] Despite the action of the United Nations and individual countries holding Japan responsible for violating the human rights of the comfort women, the Government of Japan still refuses to recognize its legal responsibility for crimes involving the sexual slavery system. To evade its state responsibility, Japan has established the misleadingly-named "Asia Women's Fund," a private fund to compensate the victims. Moreover, Japan is resisting full disclosure of documents and materials in its possession with regard to the comfort women system.

Voices

Work Tools:
Patience and Understanding[1]

Biba Metikos

My name is Habiba. I was born in 1942 in Visegrad. Soon after my birth, my family left Visegrad for Sarajevo for the same reasons that I and my daughter are today in Zagreb. They say, "History repeats itself," which is exactly my case. I have lived my whole life in Sarajevo. I graduated with a law degree and married Vasilij. We had a happy marriage. Our daughter Dunja was born in 1979. Our lives would have been truly beautiful had it not been for the war.

After the war broke out in Bosnia and Herzegovina in April of 1992—which now seems so far away—I embarked on my treacherous path together with my child. On a bright spring day we left our home, Sarajevo, today perhaps the most famous city in the world. The bombs were falling, people were falling, and the graves were rising. Today, in that once beautiful city, known for its multiethnicity and multiculturality, a city full of youth and life, there is more death than life. When we arrived in Zagreb we thought that the war in Bosnia could not last much longer. We thought that the ethnic differences would be resolved quickly; there were not that many families of only one ethnic background in Bosnia and Herzegovina. But the war did not stop, and my daughter and I had nothing to live on.

My world started to crumble. I thought about suicide. As a woman who was once successful, independent, a true professional, now I found myself unable to provide basic necessities for my daughter and myself.

---

[1] This statement was excerpted from B. Metikos, Work tools: patience and understanding, in Zbornik. Zenski Informativno-Dokumentacijski Centar, Centar Za Zene Zrtve Rata, pp. 98-99, Zagreb, 1994. It was suggested by Vesna Kesic, Director of B.a.B.e., Women's Human Rights Group, Zagreb, Croatia, and translated from Croatian, courtesy of the Consulate of Croatia in New York City.

Until not so long ago, the entire territory of the Former Yugoslavia was my home. Now, they say, it is no longer so. In Croatia I do not have the right to work or the right to my identity since I do not have the right nationality. I tried without success to find any work that would at least pay for our food. One day I was wandering aimlessly, looking for light in the darkness, and I found myself in an unfamiliar but pleasant place. It was a Center for the Women Victims of War.

They did not care who I was or where I came from. They only cared that I was a WOMAN who needed help and who in turn would be able to help other unhappy women. I started to want to live again and to work. I finished the training and began forming self-help groups in refugee camps. Working with women refugees is very painful since it makes me relive my own traumas. Eventually, though, it helped me overcome them. Meeting women from the camps is like meeting unhappiness face to face. One gets the feeling that these are just sick human bodies. Every inch of the diseased tissue has to be healed separately so that it can be put together again. This requires so much patience and understanding.

After a year of working on myself and with other women, I still feel pain. Sometimes, I think that the whole world comes down on me, that I will never make it. Still, with the passing of each day, the pain becomes smaller and smaller, while my hopes for a better life are getting bigger and bigger.

The whole world will be my new home.

But to hope is a human tragedy.

Chapter 11

A Vision for Children: The Convention on the Rights of the Child

Marta Santos Pais

We are confronted today with difficult challenges arising from increasing globalization in the economy, trade and communications, a growing marginalization of the poorest groups in society, and a visible weakening of solidarity at the national and international levels. These trends are combined with the movement by governments toward decentralization, which constitutes both an opportunity for the reinforcement of democracy and a challenge to achieve equity and promote human rights.

All of these conditions have a clear impact on children—often deeper than on any other group in society. Unemployment, homelessness, political violence, and economic recession are certainly not only experienced by adults. Moreover, sexual exploitation, war crimes, and human rights violations are particularly grave when committed against children. But differently from adults, children usually suffer in a hidden way. They do not vote to express disapproval and are often not reflected in tangible data to indicate the extent to which they have been affected or victimized. Children live with us in the same world but are kept invisible and unheard, as if their existence makes no difference to our global scenario or has no relevance for the way in which our policies are shaped and implemented.

The disturbing reality is that children are acknowledged in moments of distress. Unacceptable cases of child prostitution, atrocities in conflicts, or cases of abuse and ill-treatment bring them to the front pages of newspapers. The extreme nature of these cases pave the way for a movement of social outcry where societal responsibility is challenged. Children are then recognized as a problem society must face, but rarely does this result in decisive action to prevent future incidents.

At the same time, however, it continues to be rare to envisage children as positive indicators of progress or as criteria for development. It is even more rare to view them as subjects of rights, entitled to committed action by the family, society, and the state or as citizens able to participate in society.

ESTABLISHING A CULTURE OF HUMAN RIGHTS

The Convention on the Rights of the Child, adopted in November 1989, has provided us with a unique tool with which to challenge this reality. It calls on us all to take children seriously. It no longer tolerates indifference. It has led us to recognize that children must be placed at the center of the political agenda and that they constitute a distinct and priority concern in the national and international context.

Being the fruit of a political consensus, the Convention constitutes a lively illustration of the universality of human rights. In fact, it has been ratified by 191 countries around the world with the exception of only two: Somalia and the United States. No other Convention has achieved such wide acceptance. For the first time in history there is a normative consensus which States parties have freely accepted and pledged to transform into an agenda for all children. This illustrates the universality of human rights as proclaimed fifty years ago by the Universal Declaration. Furthermore, the Convention constitutes a common reference point against which progress can be assessed and results compared.

The Convention was negotiated over a long period of ten years. Initial indifference and political confrontation gave way to an environment of openness and convergence, eventually leading to the adoption of this charter on children's rights. As its Preamble recognizes, the Convention takes into account the importance of the traditions and cultural values of each people for the protection and harmonious development of the child. It reflects the principal legal systems of the world and acknowledges the specific needs of developing countries. Based on the richness of such diversity, the Convention affirms the value of the universality of human rights, a fact that undoubtedly contributed to its rapid entry into force in less than a year.

A NEW ETHICAL ATTITUDE TOWARD CHILDREN

In light of the Convention on the Rights of the Child, children are no longer envisaged as mere recipients or services or beneficiaries of protective measures. Rather, they are subjects of rights and participants in actions affecting them. They need to be respected in their individuality and in their evolving capacity to influence decisions relevant to their lives. However, in countries where democratic institutions have been established, children made us realize that the system, which was proclaimed to be based on participation and public scrutiny, has failed to listen to the voices of the most vulnerable. The system was not prepared to take into real consideration the special needs and the unique potential of children. However, in the light of the Convention, the views of children need to be respected and taken into account when policies are shaped, actions undertaken, and results assessed.

Respect for children's rights cannot be perceived as an option, as a question of favor or kindness to children, or as an expression of charity. Children's rights generate obligations and responsibilities that must be honored. They need to be perceived as an expression of solidarity and partnership, empowering children to participate actively in the improvement of their situation and in the broader process of social change.

The Convention stresses the fundamental importance of the human rights of every child. Each child has equal and inalienable rights, wherever he or she may live. While it is important to improve the situation of children as a group, it is essential to go beyond attaining good averages or a high rate of progress. It is necessary to consider the specific reality of those children who have not been affected by the wave of general progress, who have remained invisible or forgotten and who are becoming increasingly vulnerable and marginalized. Thus, it is important to fight the invisibility of the disadvantaged, to promote support to those in greater need, and to narrow prevailing social, economic, or geographic disparities. It is necessary to address children in younger age groups as well as in adolescence, girls as well as boys, children in rural and urban areas, including those living in the poor peripheral areas, children in institutions, children belonging to minority or indigenous groups, asylum seekers, and refugee children.

The Convention also stresses that it is important to consider all areas that are relevant to children's lives, including those previously neglected by researchers, data collectors or policy makers: sexual exploitation to armed conflicts; child labor to the family environment; birth registration to juvenile justice; the right to play and leisure to the right of freedom of opinion. With this purpose in mind, relevant indicators of a quantitative and qualitative nature have increasingly been identified[1] to assess trends over time, identify disparities, and to help understand the root causes of problems affecting children. These indicators must assess new ways to realize rights, for example, equity and non-discrimination in access to services or quality education.

The Convention indicates in an unequivocal manner that children's rights are human rights. They are not special rights: they are simply the fundamental rights inherent to the human dignity of every person. The rights of the child are

---

[1] See, for example, the Summary Report of the International Meeting on "Indicators for Global Monitoring of Child Rights" and the "Implementation Handbook for the Convention on the Rights of the Child" both available from the Division of Evaluation, Policy and Planning, UNICEF, New York.

indivisible and interrelated; all are important and essential to the harmonious development of the child.

ACCOUNTABILITY AND TRANSPARENCY

The Convention's spirit of consensus goes hand in hand with notions of accountability and transparency. Caring for children means having a responsibility for them and acting accordingly, consistent with the provisions and principles of the Convention.

For example, democratic governments have surprisingly discovered that their important human rights policies and structures, their long tradition of adherence to the rule of law, respect for individual freedoms, and concern for good governance were not necessarily sufficient to ensure the specific promotion and protection of children's rights. Children call for special consideration and must be visible in their distinct existence. They cannot continue to be considered simply as an accessory element of society or addressed only in a reflexive manner as non-distinct members of the family, as non-distinct actors in the school or community, or as non-identifiable victims of poverty and social exclusion.

For this reason, article 4 of the Convention sets a general obligation, of conduct and of purpose, for States parties to adopt all appropriate legislative, administrative, educational, economic, social, or other measures to ensure the implementation of children's rights and to fully harmonize national law and policy with the Convention. Thus, *no* country has the right to remain passive, even when it may believe that it has attained a sufficiently developed level of progress. In the field of human rights there is always room for improvement.

Indeed, the Convention requires that States undertake transparent self-assessment by establishing a process by which they are required to submit, periodically, reports to the Committee on the Rights of the Child[2] containing information on the process of implementation of the Convention. Reports should include information on measures adopted by the State, the results achieved and the factors and difficulties hindering further progress. These reports are intended to be self-critical and objective, giving the Committee a comprehensive understanding of the reality in the country and enabling it to make suggestions and recommendations aimed at improving the situation of children and at effectively realizing their rights.

Above all, the reports are an important political tool to promote social change. They should reflect an accurate assessment of the reality of all children, make an appraisal of policies adopted to improve their situation, provide an evaluation of the degree of success achieved, and identify areas where future priority action should be focused.

[2] See article 44 of the CRC.

THE COMMITTEE AND ITS COMPOSITION

For the purpose of monitoring the progress made by States Parties in meeting the obligations undertaken under the Convention, a Committee on the Rights of the Child has been established by the Convention. It consists of ten experts of high moral standing and recognized competence in the fields covered by the Convention. The Secretary-General convenes a meeting of States Parties in which they are elected by secret ballot from a list of persons nominated by States Parties. In this election, consideration is given to equitable geographical distribution, as well as to representation of the principal legal systems. The members of the Committee are elected for a term of four years and are eligible for re-election if they are re-nominated.

Committee members serve in a personal capacity and are in no way delegates of the State (Article 43 para. 2). In fact, the Committee stresses that members do not represent their Government, their country, or any organization to which they may belong. Their mandate derives from the principles and provisions of the Convention and they are solely accountable to the children of the world.

THE ROLE OF THE COMMITTEE

Complementing its monitoring functions, the Committee is also entrusted with important tasks in the field of promoting and protecting children's rights. Some are designed to ensure a better understanding of the principles and provisions of the Convention—as in the case of the formulation of General Recommendations and General Comments, the organization of thematic discussions on specific topics or rights of the Convention, or the request for studies on the rights of the child in the light of Article 45(c) of the Convention. Others are linked to the Committee's role as a supervisory body, wherein the Committee assesses the progress made by States Parties in implementing the Convention through a system of constructive dialogue, and assists them to identify problems and consider possible solutions. Moreover, pursuant to Article 45(a) and (b), the Committee acts as a catalyst in the area of international cooperation, encouraging a combined effort of States, United Nations bodies and other competent bodies to foster the realization of children's rights at the national level.

In reviewing the reports of States Parties, the Committee may request additional information including a progress report. Such requests are made particularly in situations where the report lacks sufficient information about the implementation of the provisions of the Convention or when the situation has evolved or changed in such a way that the information previously submitted is no longer appropriate.

The request for specific or urgent information may further contribute to preventing the deterioration or violation of children's rights. For this reason, the

Committee has developed an urgent procedure in the general framework of the reporting obligations of States Parties. On the basis of such an urgent procedure, the Committee may request a report on the implementation of specific provisions of the Convention or additional information relevant to its implementation. The Committee may also suggest a visit to the country concerned. All of these initiatives are intended to enable the State Party to provide the Committee, in the spirit of dialogue and cooperation that guides the reporting process, with a comprehensive understanding of the implementation of the Convention and in particular of those provisions where a specific concern was expressed. They may play an important role as an early warning and thus contribute to preventing the deterioration of a particularly serious situation or to limiting the scale of existing violations of children's rights.

Other important initiatives undertaken by the Committee include encouraging the Commission on Human Rights in 1994 to establish a Working Group to draft an Optional Protocol to the Convention in order to raise the minimum age of involvement in armed conflicts to eighteen years and proposing that the Secretary-General prepare a report on the impact of armed conflict on children.[3] The subsequent study, conducted by Mrs. Graça Machel, brought considerable attention to this issue and resulted in far reaching recommendations.[4] In September 1997, the Secretary-General of the United Nations appointed a Special Representative for children in armed conflict, who is mandated to focus specifically on the issues of children in conflict situations.

THE CONVENTION CREATES A SYSTEM OF INTERNATIONAL COOPERATION AND SOLIDARITY

In the spirit of the United Nations Charter,[5] the Convention promotes international cooperation and assistance to achieve the rights of the child. It recognizes that international cooperation is particularly important to implementing the economic, social, and cultural rights of children,[6] and it pays particular attention to the special needs of developing countries.[7] The Convention specifically encourages the production, exchange, and dissemination of information aimed at the promotion of the child's social, spiritual, and moral well-being and physical and mental health.[8] In relation to the rights of the child

---

[3] See Report of the Third Session, Jan. 1993, CRC/C/16, p. 4 and Annex VI, p. 58.

[4] In particular, see A/51/306, para. 240.

[5] See in particular articles 1 para. 3, 55, and 56 of the UN Charter.

[6] See article 4 of the CRC.

[7] See the last paragraph of the Preamble and the specific references made in the context of the rights of children with disabilities (article 23 para. 4), the right to health (article 24 para. 4) and the right to education (article 28 para. 4).

[8] See article 17 para. B of the CRC.

with disabilities,[9] it calls for a full and decent life in conditions that ensure dignity, promote self-reliance, and facilitate the child's active participation in the community in the context of the rights to health and education.[10]

International cooperation and assistance are an expression of the international commitment made by Member States of the United Nations to take joint and separate action "to achieve the promotion of universal respect for, and observance of, human rights and fundamental freedoms."[11] It is in this context that multilateral and bilateral cooperation are instrumental to the realization of children's rights.[12] In the absence of such cooperation, these rights remain an unfulfilled aspiration for many countries and an ignored reality for millions of children.

The Convention on the Rights of the Child associates States' accountability for the fulfillment of children's rights with international cooperation. Thus, it calls on all States, both donor and receiving countries, to give priority to children and to channel resources to the maximum extent for children's rights. It requires States to identify factors and difficulties affecting the degree of fulfillment of the obligations arising from the Convention, and it encourages them to formulate requests or indicate a need for technical advice or assistance[13] to overcome them.

In this process, the Committee on the Rights of the Child plays a catalytic role. In examining States Parties' reports, the Committee may acknowledge the relevance of their requests and encourage the international community to take them into consideration. In particular, it may forward those requests to United Nations organizations and other competent bodies[14] with a view to promoting follow-up through relevant programs of cooperation. The Convention also foresees the Committee inviting the specialized agencies, the United Nations Children's Fund and other United Nations programs to submit reports on the implementation of the Convention in areas falling within the scope of their activities and, along with NGOs, to provide it with expert advice on areas falling within their respective mandates.

These important and unique provisions of the Convention stress the need for close cooperation between the Committee, as a treaty monitoring body, and other entities competent and active in the field of children's rights. The flow and convergence of information on the implementation of the Convention arising

---

[9] See article 23 para. 4 of the CRC.

[10] See respectively articles 24 para. 4 and 28 para. 3 of the CRC.

[11] See the Preamble of the Universal Declaration, para. 6 and the Charter of the UN (including articles 55 and 56).

[12] See above section (d).

[13] See articles 44 para. 2 and 45(b) of the CRC.

[14] With this expression, the CRC addresses all international, regional, or national institutions and organizations which may be relevant to the realization of children's rights, including non-governmental organizations.

therefrom, together with an integrated consideration of the complementary measures adopted by States and those pursued by specialized agencies and other competent bodies, including NGOs, will pave the way for a deeper knowledge of the national realities and will enable the consideration of solutions that better address the prevailing difficulties.

This dynamic process has paved the way for the recognition of the Convention as a decisive reference for the work of United Nations bodies and specialized agencies. As stressed by the final document of the World Conference on Human Rights, matters relating to human rights and the situation of children should be regularly reviewed and monitored by all relevant United Nations organs and mechanisms and by the supervisory bodies of the specialized agencies in accordance with their mandates, and the rights of the child should be a priority in United Nations system-wide action on human rights. For example, UNHCR Policy on Refugee Children states that "a United Nations Convention (the Convention on the Rights of the Child) constitutes a normative frame of reference for UNHCR's action." Similarly, the Mission Statement adopted by UNICEF is an undeniable example of this approach. In this document, the organization stresses inter alia that it "is guided by the Convention on the Rights of the Child and strives to establish children's rights as enduring ethical principles and international standards of behavior towards children."

States are also required to make the implementation reports widely available to the public in the country.[15] This transparency contributes to the promotion of a national debate on children and their rights, encouraging the engagement and participation of the civil society and generally fostering a process of public scrutiny of governmental policies in this area.

This momentum will only make a real difference, however, if it is effectively experienced at national as well as local levels. And while the implementation of the Convention will certainly not put an automatic and magic end to the violation of children's rights (we continue to be confronted with the recruitment of children into armed groups; the sexual exploitation of young girls, or abuse of children as laborers), it clearly promotes a growing awareness, keeping such situations under debate, and creating a sense of social shame and refusal which will undoubtedly have a lasting and positive effect.

A PROCESS OF SOCIAL CHANGE

Around the world, a unique process of social change is taking place. Awareness and information campaigns have been launched, often specially shaped for children; training activities have been developed, including revisions of curricula to make sure that new professionals are knowledgeable and prepared to defend

---

[15] See CRC article 44 para. 6.

the human rights of children; codes of conduct are being shaped promoting an ethical intervention in the light of non-discrimination, best interests of the child and the participation of children in decisions affecting them.

Finally, it is illustrative to cite some examples of where the Convention on the Rights of the Child has led to institutional reform because of children, such as the steps taken toward a national mechanism on children's rights or an independent Commissioner for Children. And it is important to refer to the role played by national coalitions on children's rights, the participation of children as well as by national courts in ensuring respect for the provisions of the Convention on the Rights of the Child.

a) A National Mechanism on Children's Rights

To face the challenges of the Convention, a special governmental structure has been set up in different countries to deal with children's rights. Sometimes even a Ministry responsible for Children has been established, as in the case of Senegal and Bangladesh, to ensure policy coordination for children across governmental departments and to promote policy initiatives addressed to them.

It is, of course, not sufficient to have only a structure or to pretend that a single department could effectively attend to all the different areas where children's rights are at stake. But in cases where the Minister ensures a holistic approach to children's policies, promotes close institutional collaboration, assesses the impact on children of adopted policies and has high political stature, children may in fact become a political priority. This becomes even more visible when coordination with provincial and local services is ensured.

In other nations, including Ethiopia, Solomon Islands, Vanuatu, Fiji, China, and Bulgaria, an Inter-Ministerial Committee has been set up. In Denmark, this Committee aims to create consistent and coherent rules and to improve the living and upbringing conditions of children.

Elsewhere, parliaments have taken the rights of the child as a serious and prioritized area for action. Some have set up Parliamentary Committees, as in Denmark and Sweden. The importance of this is clear when we recall the role played by national parliaments in monitoring Governments' activities, as well as their main function in adopting new legislations and approving the national budget.

It is also decisively important to stress the relevance of experiences where the rights of the child are systematically considered in the overall policy decisions of the Government. Two examples might be given: a Swedish Commission systematically assesses the best interests of the child, and in the Netherlands a child-impact assessment is made in relation to all policies adopted by the Government. Mention should also be made of an annual report submitted by the Government to the Parliament on the measures adopted to promote and protect children's rights. This ensures an ongoing evaluation and monitoring of policies adopted to that effect. Such an approach has been considered by France in the context of the annual meeting between the National Convention of NGOs and relevant public authorities.

b) A Child Rights Commissioner or Ombudsperson

Various countries have established independent institutions designed to act as watchdogs of the work of public bodies and catalysts for action for children. These institutions promote respect for children's rights, identify existing violations and in some cases consider children's complaints.

Norway was the first in 1981 to establish an Ombudsperson. Today, other countries such as Iceland (1995), Sweden (1993), Belgium (1992), and Austria (1991), have followed. In Portugal and Spain, the Ombudsperson is competent to deal with children's issues as well as the rights of other individuals, thus stressing the citizenship of children as full-fledged subjects of rights. Ethiopia is also considering a proposal to establish an Ombudsperson competent to deal with children's rights.

Of course, these institutions cannot simply be symbolic political gestures. Monitoring children's rights will only be effective if the Ombudsperson-like institution is independent, acts in an impartial manner, and has adequate resources both human and material. Its activities need to be publicized, thus encouraging further respect for children's rights and having a deterrent effect on those feeling tempted to neglect them. In this regard, the solution followed by some countries to submit to Parliament an annual report of activities has proven to be of special relevance with the intent to ensure a wide and serious consideration and follow-up.

c) National Coalitions on Children's Rights

National coalitions constitute another important monitoring mechanism emerging in this field. Around the world, they mobilize a very strong social movement around children, promote advocacy for their rights, encourage children's participation and inculcate in each and every individual and group the sense of being a child's right defender. Moreover, they can decisively influence governments' action as monitors and as partners in the realization of children's rights. In addition, these coalitions on children's rights have become essential partners of the Committee on the Rights of the Child, making the principles and provisions of the Convention widely known and promoting effective follow-up to the recommendations made by the Committee upon consideration of reports.

d) Participation of Children

With the adoption of the Convention on the Rights of the Child, the world has recognized the right of children to express their views freely and to have those views taken into consideration in "all matters affecting the child." Children's views cannot be simply ignored or automatically endorsed; rather, they need to be taken into account in decisions relevant to the child.

In this spirit, we insist today on the increasing participation of children in decision-making processes: from participation in administrative and judicial proceedings, for instance when the adoption of a child has to be decided, to participation in associations, children's parliaments, school, or municipal councils. Participation is not only to defend their rights (for example, when a school needs to take a decision on the possible suspension or expulsion of a student), but also to influence solutions (for instance, when the local authorities have to consider where to build a playground or place safe zones for children to cross the street).

Moreover, children are now frequently participating in electoral processes, thus learning about democratic processes. In many countries, children have been called to vote on those rights that seem of a greater relevance for them—the right to an identity following the war in Mozambique, the right to peace in Colombia, to right to protection from abuse and ill-treatment in Ecuador, the right to education with quality in Mexico. Similarly, opinion polls have been organized for children to express views on issues of relevance for them, but also meaningful for the national political agenda. In this regard, mention could be made of the process held in Chile, where the education system became the major theme of the opinion poll. With these processes, children gain skills facilitating their active participation in decision-making processes, while at the same time they contribute to the strengthening of democratic institutions in the country.

e) National Courts

Judicial authorities are also playing an instrumental role in the protection and monitoring of children's rights. They ensure the applicability of norms dealing with the rights of the child, as those set forth in the United Nations Convention. For example, in a recent decision of the Italian Corte di Cassazione on ill-treatment and abuse of a child as a means of correction, the Court stressed that the relevant provisions of the Penal Code "had to be interpreted in a way which is in line with . . . the individualistic and pluralistic tenets of the Constitution and confirmed by the United Nations Convention"[16] on the Rights of the Child, particularly its article 19.

---

[16]See *Republic of Italy v. Cambria* (1996) Supreme Court of Cassation (6th Penal Section).

The judgment states, "the judiciary plays a decisive role in ensuring the implementation of commitments which the State has assumed. Not only is it required to directly apply all the provisions which do not require legislative intervention, but in the interpretation of pre-existing legislation it is also required to use the values and principles of the Convention as criteria on the basis of which to interpret previous provisions. . . . In this spirit, the use of violence for educational purposes can no longer be considered lawful."

In a case involving two ten-year-old boys who were convicted of the brutal murder of a two-year-old boy in the United Kingdom,[17] the House of Lords was to determine whether the Secretary of State had acted lawfully in deciding that the boys should be detained for fifteen years. The majority opinion noted that under the law (Children and Young Persons Act of 1933) courts must look to the "welfare of the child offender," a conclusion reinforced by the fact that the United Kingdom is a party to the Convention on the Rights of the Child. And although the Convention had not been incorporated into English Law, "it is legitimate to assume that Parliament has not maintained on the Statute book a power capable of being exercised in a manner inconsistent with the treaty obligations of this country." In this regard, guided by the best interests of the child and in the light of the need to promote the reintegration of the child, the decision of the Secretary of State was challenged.

Also of interest is the fact that decisions of the European Court on Human Rights are increasingly making references to the Convention on the Rights of the Child as an element of their own interpretation. In a recent case where a child had been placed for adoption by her mother, without the consent of the unmarried father, the European Court on Human Rights ruled that the State should act to ensure that family ties develop and are protected from the moment of birth, in the light of article 7 of the United Nations Convention on the Rights of the Child which states that "the child should be, as far as possible, cared for by his or her parents."[18]

In a recent Canadian judicial decision,[19] a federal deportation order against a single mother was quashed on the grounds that it violated the rights of the woman's Canadian-born children. The Convention was cited in this decision and the deportation stopped until "the Court is satisfied that the best interests of the children had been considered in the course of the deportation proceeding." In the decision, it was stressed that it is the responsibility of the Government to ensure that "a child should not be separated from his or her parents against their will,

---

[17]See *Rv. Secretary of State for the Home Department, exparte Venables; Rv. Secretary of State for the Home Department, exparte Thompson*, 3 W.L.R. 23 (App. Cas. 1997) (H.L.).

[18]See *Keegan* vs. *Ireland*, (ECHR/466/1994/290).

[19]See *Baker* vs. *Canada (Minister of Citizenship and Immigration)*, (Nov. 29, 1996) DOC. A-441-95 (fed. C.A.).

except where competent authorities subject to judicial review determine . . . that such separation is in the best interests of the child."

Even in the United States, where the Convention has not been ratified, the treaty's universal nature is influencing court decisions already. In *Batista* vs. *Batista*,[20] the Court cited article 12 of the Convention in support of its decision that a fifteen-year-old girl's views and concerns should be heard in a custody case.

CONCLUSION

This brief overview makes clear that the Convention on the Rights of the Child has had an undeniable impact on the way children are perceived and on the way actions are increasingly being taken on their behalf. The process of implementation has just begun and much remains to be done. Progress achieved is a strong motive to feel enthusiastic, determined to be demanding, and tireless. Prevailing imperfection is the reason to continue; it gives meaning to what we do and sets the agenda for our work. We must not miss this opportunity.

[20]See *Batista* vs. *Batista* 1992, W.I. 156171, 6 (Conn. Super.).

Voices

JOHN, AN AUSTRALIAN ABORIGINAL CHILD*

John was removed from his family as an infant in the 1940s. He spent his first years in Bomaderry Children's Home at Nowra. At ten he was transferred to Kinchela.

We didn't have a clue where we came from. We thought the Sisters were our parents. They didn't tell anybody—any of the kids—where they came from. Babies were coming in nearly every day. Some kids came in at two, three, four days old—not months—but days. They were just placed in the home and it was run by Christian women and all the kids thought it was one big family. We didn't know what it meant by "parents" cause we didn't have parents and we thought those women were our mothers.

I was definitely not told that I was Aboriginal. What the Sisters told us was that we had to be white. It was drummed into our heads that we were white. It didn't matter what shade you were. We thought we were white. They said you can't talk to any of them coloured people because you're white.

I can't remember anyone from the welfare coming there. If they did I can't remember . . . We hardly saw any visitors whatsoever. None of the other kids had visits from their parents. No visits from family. The worst part is, we didn't know we had a family.

When you got to a certain age—like I got to ten years old . . . they just told us we were going on a train trip . . . We all lined up with our little ports [school cases] with a bible inside. That's all that was in the ports, see. We really treasured that—we thought it was a good thing that we had something . . . the old man from La Perouse took us from Sydney—well actually from Bomaderry to Kinchela Boys' Home. That's when our problems really started—you know!

This is where we learned that we weren't white. First of all they took you in through these iron gates and took our little ports [suitcases] off us. Stick it in the fire with your little bible inside. They took us around to a room and shaved

*Used by permission of the Human Rights and Equal Opportunity Commission, Commonwealth of Australia. Excerpted from "Bringing Them Home," the report of the National Inquiry into the Separation of Aboriginal and Torres Strait Islander Children From Their Families, pp. 166-167, 1997.

our hair off . . . They gave you your clothes and stamped a number on them . . . They never called you by your name; they called you by your number. That number was stamped on everything.

If we answered an attendant back we were "sent up the line." Now I don't know if you can imagine, seventy-nine boys punching the hell out of you—just knuckling you. Even your brother, your cousin.

They had to—if they didn't do it, they were sent up the line. When the boys who had broken ribs or broken noses—they'd have to pick you up and carry you right through to the last bloke. Now that didn't happen once—that happened every day.

Before I went to Kinchela, they used to use the cat-o'-nine-tails on the boys instead of being sent up the line. This was in the 30s and early 40s.

Kinchela was a place where they thought you were animals. You know it was like a place where they go around and kick us like a dog . . . It was just like a prison. Truthfully, there were boys having sex with boys . . . But these other dirty mongrels didn't care. We had a manager who was sent to prison because he was doing it to a lot of the boys, sexual abuse. Nothing was done. There was a pommie bloke that was doing it. These attendants—if the boys told them, they wouldn't even listen. It just happened . . . I don't like talking about it.

We never went into town . . . the school was in the home . . . all we did was work, work, work. Every six months you were dressed up. Oh mate! You were done up beautiful—white shirt. The welfare used to come up from Bridge St. the main bloke, the superintendent to check the home out—every six months.

We were prisoners from when we were born . . . The girls who went to Cootamundra and the boys who went to Kinchela—we were all prisoners. Even today they have our file number so we're still prisoners you know. And we'll always be prisoners while our files are in archives.

Voices

Former Child Soldiers

ALFREDO, ABDUCTED BY RENAMO IN MOZAMBIQUE[1]

When RENAMO . . . abducted Alfredo, they tied his hands behind his back, put a 50 kilo bag of stolen food on his head, and forced him to march like that for two days to the RENAMO base camp . . . "The bandits killed my mother. And my brothers too. They took me to their base camp. Yes, I was with the bandits. I had a gun. The chief taught me to use it. He beat me up. I had a gun to kill. I killed people and soldiers. I didn't like it. I killed. I killed.

SUSAN, 16, ABDUCTED BY THE LORD'S RESISTANCE ARMY IN UGANDA[2]

One boy tried to escape, but he was caught. They made him eat a mouthful of red pepper, and five people were beating him. His hands were tied, and then they made us, the other new captives, kill him with a stick. I felt sick. I knew this boy from before. We were from the same village. I refused to kill him and they told me they would shoot me. They pointed a gun at me, so I had to do it. The boy was asking me, "Why are you doing this?" I said I had no choice. After we killed him, they made us smear his blood on our arms. I felt dizzy. There was another dead body nearby, and I could smell the body. I felt so sick. They said we had to do this so we would not fear death and so we would not try to escape.

I feel so bad about the things that I did. . . . It disturbs me so much—that I inflicted death on other people. . . . When I go home I must do some traditional rites because I have killed. I must perform these rites and cleanse myself. I still dream about the boy from my village who I killed. I see him in my dreams, and he is talking to me and saying I killed him for nothing, and I am crying?

---

[1] As described in Neil Boothby, Living in the War Zone, in US Committee for Refugees, *Work Refugee Survey—1989 in Review*, pp. 40-41.

[2] Human Rights Watch interview, Gulu, Uganda, May 1997.

Chapter 12

Indigenous Peoples and Their Demands within the Modern Human Rights Movement

S. James Anaya

Change is as certain as the passage of time. But in the dynamics of human history certain changes have been brought on by parts of humanity at the expense of others, with disastrous, widespread, and lasting effects. The international human rights program meets perhaps its most formidable challenge in the face of such oppressive change and its legacies.

Half a millennium ago, people living on the continents now called North and South America began to experience change of a kind they had not experienced before. Europeans arrived and began to lay claim to their lands, overpowering their political institutions and disrupting the integrity of their economies and cultures. The European encroachments frequently were accompanied by the slaughter of children, women, and men who stood in the way. For many of the people who survived, the Europeans brought disease and slavery. Similar patterns of empire and conquest extended to other parts of the globe, resulting in human suffering and turmoil on a massive scale.

As empire building and colonial settlement proceeded from the sixteenth century onward, those already inhabiting the encroached upon lands, and that were subjected to oppressive forces, became known as indigenous, native, or aboriginal. Such designations have continued to apply to people by virtue of their place and condition within the phenomena of life-altering human encounter set in motion by colonialism. Today, the term indigenous refers broadly to the living descendants of pre-invasion inhabitants of lands now dominated by others. Indigenous peoples, nations, or communities are culturally distinctive groups that are engulfed by settler societies born of the forces of empire and conquest. The diverse surviving Indian communities and nations of the Western Hemisphere, the Inuit and Aleut of the Arctic region, the Aboriginal peoples of Australia, the Maori of New Zealand, tribal communities of Asia, and other such groups are among those generally regarded as indigenous. They are *indigenous* because their ancestral roots are imbedded in the lands in which they live, or would like to live, much more deeply than the roots of more powerful sectors of society living on the same lands or in close proximity. Furthermore, they are *peoples* to the extent they comprise distinct communities with a continuity of existence or identity linking them to the communities, tribes, or nations of their ancestral past.

In the contemporary world, indigenous peoples characteristically exist under conditions of severe disadvantage relative to others within the states constructed around them. Historical phenomena grounded upon racially discriminatory attitudes are not just blemishes of the past, but rather translate into current inequities. Indigenous peoples have been deprived of vast landholdings and access to life-sustaining resources, and have otherwise suffered historical forces that actively suppressed their political and cultural institutions. As a result, indigenous peoples have been crippled economically and socially, their cohesiveness as communities has been damaged or threatened, and the integrity of their cultures has been undermined. In both industrial and less developed countries in which indigenous people live, they almost invariably are at the lowest rung of the socioeconomic ladder, and they exist at the margins of the reins of power.

If the weight of historical oppression were not enough, indigenous peoples worldwide continue to face adverse forces that threaten their survival. Indigenous peoples in forested areas in many parts of the world find their lands invaded by multinational logging companies that operate with the acquiescence, and often active encouragement, of governments. In numerous places mining enterprises, oil developers, and government military operations are disrupting indigenous subsistence patterns and in many cases wreaking havoc on indigenous environments. Today, even the most isolated indigenous groups are threatened by encroaching commercial, governmental, or other interests motivated by prospects of accumulating wealth from the natural resources of indigenous lands. History is repeating or threatening to repeat itself in the name of modernization, development, and security.

In the face of tremendous adversity, indigenous peoples have long sought to flourish as distinct communities on their ancestral lands, and they have endeavored to roll back inequities lingering as the result of historical patterns of colonization. Armed resistance, diplomacy, and law have been tools in this quest for survival. Over the last several years especially, in conjunction with efforts through domestic or municipal arenas of decision making, indigenous peoples have appealed to the international community and its promise of human rights as a means to advance their cause. Through the language and institutions of human rights, indigenous peoples have been increasingly successful in drawing international attention to their demands and in forging a body of international norms that is responsive to those demands.

HUMAN RIGHTS, DECOLONIZATION, AND THE MID-TWENTIETH-CENTURY ASSIMILATION MODEL

Among the founding principles of the United Nations and other major international organizations are ethical and moral precepts that undergird the modern international human rights movement. The Universal Declaration of Human Rights built upon the ethical precepts of the UN Charter and became the cornerstone of a regime of norms and accompanying oversight procedures that are concerned directly with the welfare of human begins. A burgeoning human rights regime of norms and procedures exists that engages states as well as non-state actors in scrutiny of human conditions and also challenges state claims of absolute sovereignty or exclusive jurisdiction over such conditions.

The normative and operational elements of the modern international human rights regime, however, have evolved along with changes in prevailing philosophical perspectives about human rights. While the human rights regime has been the conduit for developing international concern for indigenous peoples, human rights concepts prevailing in the mid-twentieth century were at odds with the demands of group identity and survival promoted by indigenous peoples themselves.

A prominent feature of the international human rights program, in its early post-UN Charter development, was its concern for those segments of humanity that had experienced histories of colonization and continued to suffer the legacies of those histories. Despite the divergence of mid-twentieth-century political theory that fueled the polarization of geopolitical forces until the late 1980s, there was agreement on human rights precepts upon which the international community viewed colonialism and its legacies as oppressive. Accordingly, the international system instituted at the close of World War II, with the UN Charter and its human rights provisions, promoted the demise of colonialism where it continued to exist in its classical form and the building of self-government in its place.

The normative nexus that promoted the emancipation of colonial territories during the middle part of this century, however, simultaneously promoted the assimilation of members of culturally distinctive indigenous groups into the dominant political and social orders that engulfed them. Assimilation and rights of full citizenship were means of bringing into the fold of self-government indigenous groups living in independent and newly independent states. Precepts of self-government and human rights largely remained conditioned by the theoretical ideal of a culturally homogenous nation-state. Nation-building was a corresponding policy of breaking down competing ethnic or cultural bonds, a policy engaged in by even, or perhaps especially, newly independent states. To the extent that the international community valued cultural diversity, it was largely the diversity existing *among* the different states and colonial territories but not the diversity that might exist wholly *within* them.

The major embodiment of the mid-twentieth-century international human rights program for indigenous populations as such was International Labour Organisation (ILO) Convention No. 107 of 1957.[1] The ILO, a specialized agency pre-dating but now affiliated with the UN, developed Convention No. 107 and its accompanying Recommendation 104 following a series of studies and expert meetings signalling the particular vulnerability of indigenous workers. Although representing elements of non-state influence within the international system, these studies and expert meetings proceeded with no apparent participation on the part of the indigenous peoples' own designated representatives. While identifying members of indigenous groups as in need of special measures for the protection of their human rights, the Convention reflected the premise of assimilation operative among dominant political elements in national and international circles at the time of its adoption. The thrust of Convention No. 107 of 1957 was to promote improved social and economic conditions for indigenous populations generally, but within a perceptual scheme that did not envisage a place for robust, politically significant cultural and associational patterns of indigenous groups.

ILO Convention No. 107 and other programs developed within the international human rights frame of the middle part of this century in regarding indigenous peoples have become much maligned for their assimilationist or integrationist elements. Nonetheless, these programs established foothold in the international system, through the conceptual and institutional medium of human rights, for people identified by their indigenousness vis-à-vis majority or dominant populations. That foothold would prove to be the basis for a much enhanced international concern for indigenous peoples and a reformed normative regime regarding them.

THE INDIGENOUS RIGHTS MOVEMENT

The international system's contemporary treatment of indigenous peoples has been shaped substantially by activity over the last three decades that has involved, and in large part been driven by, indigenous peoples themselves. They have ceased to be mere objects of the discussion of their rights and have become

---

[1] Convention (No. 107) Concerning the Protection and Integration of Indigenous and other Tribal and Semi-Tribal Populations in Independent Countries, June 26, 1957, 328 U.N.T.S. 247 (entered into force June 2, 1959).

real participants in an extensive multilateral dialogue that also has engaged states, non-governmental organizations, and independent experts, a dialogue facilitated by human rights organs of international institutions.

During the 1960s, armed with a new generation of men and women educated in the ways of the societies that had encroached upon them, indigenous peoples articulated and promoted a vision of themselves different from that previously advanced and acted upon by dominant sectors. They began drawing increased attention to demands for their continued survival as distinct communities with historically-based cultures, political institutions, and entitlements to land. A transnational identity of interests among diverse indigenous groups was forged as indigenous peoples extended their efforts through a series of international conferences and direct appeals to international intergovernmental institutions. These efforts coalesced into a veritable campaign, aided by concerned international non-governmental organizations (NGOs) and an increase of supportive scholarly and popular writings from moral and sociological, as well as juridical, perspectives.

The 1980s and 90s have seen indigenous peoples' representatives appearing before UN human rights bodies in increasing numbers and with increasing frequency, and grounding their demands in generally applicable human rights principles. They have enhanced their access to these bodies as several organizations representative of indigenous groups have obtained consultative status with the UN Economic and Social Council, the parent body of the UN human rights machinery. Indigenous peoples also have invoked procedures within the Organization of American States, particularly its Inter-American Commission on Human Rights.

Indigenous peoples' contemporary efforts internationally build on the initiative of the Council of the Iroquois Confederacy in the 1920s. Deskaheh, the Speaker of the Council, led an attempt to have the League of Nations consider the Iroquois' long-standing dispute with Canada. Although Deskaheh found support among some League members, the League ultimately closed its door to the Iroquois, yielding to the position that the Iroquois grievances were a domestic concern of Canada and hence outside the League's competence. In more recent years, however, benefitting from an international system in which assertions of domestic jurisdiction are less and less a barrier to international concern over issues of human rights, indigenous peoples have successfully attracted an unprecedented amount of attention to their demands at the international level.

As a result of indigenous peoples' efforts, their demands have been addressed continuously in one way or another over the last two and a half decades within the United Nations and other important international venues. A watershed in relevant United Nations activity was the 1971 resolution of the UN Economic and Social Council authorizing the Sub-Commission on Prevention of Discrimination and Protection of Minorities to conduct a study on the "Problem of Discrimination against Indigenous Populations." The resulting multi-volume work by Special Rapporteur Jose Martinez Cobo compiled extensive data on indigenous peoples worldwide and made a series of findings and recommendations generally supportive of indigenous peoples' demands.[2] The Martinez Cobo study became a standard reference for discussion of the subject of indigenous peoples within the United Nations system. Moreover, it initiated a pattern of further information gathering and evaluative work within the UN and other international organizations.

Upon the recommendation of the Martinez Cobo study and representatives of indigenous groups, the UN Commission on Human Rights and the Economic and Social Council approved in 1982 the establishment of the UN Working Group on Indigenous Populations. An organ of the Sub-Commission on Prevention of Discrimination and Protection of Minorities, the Working Group has met annually since its creation in one or two week sessions with a mandate to review developments concerning indigenous peoples and to work toward the development of corresponding international standards.

The Working Group is itself composed of five rotating members of the Sub-Commission who act in the capacity of individual experts rather than government representatives. Through its policy of open participation in its annual sessions, however, the Working Group has become probably the most important platform for indigenous peoples in the international arena. Literally hundreds of indigenous representatives can be seen in attendance at the Working Groups sessions, along with expert observers and the representatives of numerous UN members states, including most states in the Western Hemisphere and other states in which indigenous peoples live.

The UN Working Group has been a catalyst for generating heightened international concern for indigenous peoples. This international concern was highlighted and further promoted by the UN General Assembly's designation of 1993 as "The International Year for the World's Indigenous People" followed by the proclaiming of an "International Decade" on the same theme. With this heightened concern has come a reformulated understanding of the contours of generally applicable human rights principles and their implications for indigenous peoples. And grounded upon this reformulated understanding, there is a developing new generation of international norms specifically concerned with indigenous peoples.

---

[2] See U.N. Sub-Comm'n on the Prevention of Discrimination and Protection of Minorities, *Study on the Problem of Discrimination Against Indigenous Populations,* U.N. Doc. E/Cn.4/Sub.2/1986/7 & Adds. 1-4 (1986) (Jose Martinez Cobo, Special Rapporteur). The study originally was issued as a series of partial reports from 1981 to 1983. The original documents comprising the study are, in order of publication: U.N. Docs. E/CN.4/Sub.2/476/Adds. 1-6 (1981); E/CN.4/Sub.2/1982/2/Adds. 1-7 (1982); and E/CN.4/Sub.2/1983/21/Adds. 1-7 (1983).

THE DEVELOPMENT OF A UN DECLARATION
ON INDIGENOUS RIGHTS

The most groundbreaking work of the UN Working Group on Indigenous Populations has been pursuant to its standard-setting mandate. In 1985 the Sub-Commission approved the Working Group's decision to draft a declaration on the rights of indigenous peoples for adoption by the UN General Assembly. In 1993 the Working Group completed its Draft United Nations Declaration on the Rights of Indigenous Peoples.[3] In 1994 the Sub-Commission adopted the Working Group draft and submitted it to the UN Commission on Human Rights for its consideration.

Through the process of drafting the declaration, the Working Group engaged states and others in an extended multilateral dialogue with indigenous peoples on the specific content of their rights. By welcoming commentary and proposals by indigenous peoples for over a decade, the Working Group provided an important means for indigenous peoples to develop and promote within the international system their own conceptions about their rights.

The draft UN declaration developed by the Working Group is comprehensive in scope and coverage of the range of issues raised by indigenous peoples in international forums. It includes bold statements affirming rights of self-determination, lands and resources, cultural integrity, and political autonomy. Produced by five independent human rights experts, and adopted by the full body of twenty-six experts that make up the Sub-Commission, the draft declaration stands in its own right as an authoritative statement of norms concerning indigenous peoples on the basis of generally applicable human rights principles. The extensive deliberations leading to the draft declaration, in which indigenous peoples themselves played a leading role, enhance the authoritativeness and legitimacy of the draft.

Further, the draft UN declaration is a manifestation of the movement toward a nexus of common opinion on the subject. It is clear that not *all* are satisfied with *all* aspects of the draft. Some indigenous peoples' representatives have criticized the draft for not going far enough, while governments typically have held that it goes too far. In ongoing discussions about the declaration within the UN Human Rights Commission, controversy has arisen as indigenous representatives persistently have resisted efforts of states to articulate limits on the meaning of self-determination and other rights expressed in the draft. Nonetheless, there is a discernible new generation of common ground of opinion among experts, indigenous peoples, and governments about indigenous peoples' rights, and that

---

[3] U.N. Doc. E/CN.4/Sub./1993/29, Annex 1 (1993). See also *Technical Review of the Draft United Nations Declaration on the Rights of Indigenous Peoples,* U.N. Doc. E/Cn.4/Sub.2/1994/2 (1994).

widening common ground is in some measures reflected in the Working Group draft and in the continuing discussions about it.

ILO CONVENTION NO. 169

A tacit assumption in ongoing discussions at the United Nations is that the declaration on indigenous rights that is ultimately proclaimed by the UN General Assembly will include greater affirmations of rights than those in already-adopted international instruments, in particular International Labour Organisation Convention No. 169 on Indigenous and Tribal Peoples.[4] Building upon the standard-setting discussion on indigenous rights that had taken place within the United Nations since the early 1980s, the ILO developed and adopted in 1989 its Convention No. 169 as a revision of its earlier Convention No. 107. An international treaty that already has entered into force and been ratified by several states, the 1989 ILO Convention No. 169 is the most concrete manifestation in international law of the growing responsiveness to indigenous peoples' demands. The newer convention, while far less ambitious than the draft UN declaration currently under consideration, represents a marked departure from the philosophy of integration or assimilation underlying the earlier ILO convention.

By the mid 1980s, with indigenous peoples increasingly taking charge of the international human rights agenda concerning them, the earlier 1957 Convention No. 107 came to be regarded as anachronistic. In 1986, the ILO convened a "Meeting of Experts" which included representatives of the World Council of Indigenous Peoples, a loose confederation of indigenous groups from throughout the world. The Meeting recommended the revision of Convention No. 107, concluding that "the integrationist language of Convention No. 107 is outdated, and that the application of the principle is destructive in the modern world."

The discussion on the revision of the convention proceeded at the 1988 and 1989 sessions of the International Labour Conference, the highest decision-making body of the ILO. Special arrangements were made to allow representatives of indigenous groups limited participation in the deliberations of the Conference Committee designated for the revision. At the close of the 1989 session, the full Labour Conference adopted by an overwhelming majority the new Convention No. 169 and its shift from the prior philosophical stand. The Convention came into force in 1991 with ratifications by Norway and Mexico.

The basic theme of Convention No. 169 is indicated by the Convention's preamble, which recognizes "the aspirations of [indigenous] peoples to exercise control over their own institutions, ways of life and economic development and to maintain and develop their identities, languages and religions, within the

---

[4] Convention (No. 169) Concerning Indigenous and Tribal Peoples in Independent Countries, June 27, 1989 (entered into force September 5, 1991).

framework of the States in which they live." Upon this premise, the Convention includes provisions advancing indigenous cultural integrity, land and resource rights, and non-discrimination in social welfare spheres; and it generally enjoins states to respect indigenous peoples' aspirations in all decisions affecting them.

Upon adoption of Convention No. 169 by the International Labour Conference in 1989, several indigenous rights advocates expressed dissatisfaction with it, viewing the Convention as not sufficiently constraining of government conduct in relation to indigenous peoples' concerns. Criticism was leveled at several of the Convention's provisions that contain caveats or appear in the form of recommendations, and at the underlying assumption of state authority over indigenous peoples. Much of this criticism, however, was couched in highly legalistic terms and worst-case scenario readings of the Convention, without due regard to overall context. The overriding reason for disappointment appeared simply to be frustration over their inability to persuade delegates to adopt a Convention with terms more sweeping than those included in the final text.

Convention No. 169 can be seen as a manifestation of the simultaneous movement toward responsiveness to indigenous peoples' demands through formal international institutions and the tensions in that movement. Indigenous peoples have demanded recognition of rights that are of a collective character, rights among whose beneficiaries are historically-grounded communities rather than individuals alone. The conceptualization and articulation of such rights collides with Western individualistic conceptions of human rights that have dominated international human rights discourse. The asserted collective rights, furthermore, pose formidable challenges to notions of state sovereignty that continue as tools of state power within the international system. Such notions are especially jealous of the spheres of social and political organization that are inherent to indigenous peoples and that compete with state authority within its presumed domestic domain.

It is nonetheless evident that the normative concept underlying indigenous peoples' demands of group identity and self-determination took hold to a substantial degree in Convention No. 169. The usage of the term "peoples" to refer to the beneficiaries of the Convention, even in its qualified form, implies an affirmation of indigenous group identity and corresponding attributes of community. Whatever its shortcomings, Convention No. 169 succeeds in affirming the value of indigenous communities and cultures, and in setting forth a series of precepts that follow generally from indigenous peoples' articulated demands. The Convention, furthermore, provides grounds for the invocation of international scrutiny of the particularized concerns of indigenous groups pursuant to the ILO's fairly well-developed mechanisms for implementing the standards expressed in ILO conventions. These mechanisms include required periodic reporting by states, ILO committee review of the reports, and complaint procedures.

Since the Convention was adopted at the 1989 ILO Conference, indigenous peoples' organizations and their representatives increasingly have taken a pragmatic view and expressed support for the Convention's ratification. Indigenous peoples' organizations from Central and South America have been especially active in pressing for ratification. In certain countries that have ratified Convention No. 169, particularly Mexico and Colombia, indigenous groups already have invoked the Convention in domestic and ILO proceedings with some success in their efforts to gain redress of problem situations.

Although relatively few states have ratified the Convention, the territories of those that have comprise a substantial part of the indigenous world. The failure on the part of other states to ratify the Convention can likely be attributed more to political inertia than to a rejection of the Convention's essential terms. Even those states that have expressed difficulty with the Convention, typically have pointed out certain limited problematic aspects of the Convention while manifesting agreement with its core precepts.

OTHER DEVELOPMENTS

With the increase in international attention to the articulation of indigenous peoples' rights has come an expanding core of international opinion on the content of those rights, a core of opinion substantially shaped by indigenous peoples' contemporary demands and supported by years of official inquiry into the subject. This is reflected at least partly in the text of the Convention No. 169 and confirmed in other international developments. Since Convention No. 169 was adopted in 1989, government comments directed at developing a United Nations declaration on indigenous rights generally have affirmed the basic precepts set forth in the Convention; and indeed, despite continuing contentiousness between indigenous peoples and states over the language of the declaration, government comments indicate movement toward a consensus that even more closely accords with indigenous peoples' demands.

This movement is reflected further in government and other authoritative statements made in the context of ongoing parallel efforts within the Organization of American States to develop a declaration on indigenous peoples' rights. In 1989, the OAS General Assembly resolved to "request the Inter-American Commission on Human Rights to prepare a juridical instrument relative to the rights of indigenous peoples." Pursuant to this task, the Inter-American Commission on Human Rights—a body of eight experts that is the principal arm of the OAS in matters of human rights—collected commentary from governments and indigenous peoples from throughout the Americas on the nature and content of the rights to be included in the proposed instrument. In September of 1995 the Inter-American Commission adopted a Proposed American Declaration on the Rights of Indigenous Peoples, and in February of 1997 the Commission issued a revised version of the document.[5] The proposed OAS declaration, which is currently under review by OAS member states and indigenous groups, confirms but also goes substantially beyond the provisions of ILO Convention No. 169, while not being as far-reaching in affirming indigenous rights as the draft UN declaration.

Numerous other international initiatives, including resolutions adopted at major UN conferences over the last several years, manifest responsiveness to indigenous peoples demands and contribute to a developing international consensus on indigenous peoples' rights. Resolutions adopted at the 1992 United Nations Conference on Environment and Development include provisions on indigenous people and their communities. The Rio Declaration, and the more detailed environmental program and policy statement known as Agenda 21, reiterate precepts of indigenous peoples' rights and seek to incorporate them within the larger agenda of global environmentalism and sustainable development. The Vienna Declaration and Programme of Action, adopted by the 1993 United Nations World Conference on Human Rights, calls on states to respect the diversity of indigenous peoples and "their distinct identities, cultures and social organization," and it urges greater focus within the UN system on the concerns of indigenous peoples. Resolutions adopted at the 1994 UN Conference on Population and Development, the Fourth World Conference on Women in 1995, the 1996 World Summit for Social Development, and the Second United Nations Conference on Human Settlement in 1996 (Habitat II) similarly include relevant provisions on indigenous people and affirm prevailing normative assumptions in this regard.

EMERGING CUSTOMARY INTERNATIONAL LAW

It is evident that indigenous peoples have achieved a substantial level of international concern for their interests, and with this concern there is substantial movement toward a convergence of international opinion on the content of indigenous peoples' rights. The developments toward consensus about the content of indigenous rights simultaneously give rise to expectations that the rights will be upheld, regardless of any formal act of assent to articulated norms. The discussion of indigenous peoples and their rights promoted through international institutions and conferences has proceeded in response to demands made by indigenous groups over several years and upon an extensive record of justification. The pervasive assumption has been that the articulation of norms concerning indigenous peoples is an exercise in identifying standards of conduct that are *required* to uphold widely-shared values of human dignity. Accordingly,

---

[5] See Proposed American Declaration on the Rights of Indigenous Peoples, in *Annual Report of the Inter-American Commission on Human Rights, 1997,* OEA/Ser.L/V/II.95.doc.7, rev. 1997.

indigenous peoples' rights typically have been posited as deriving from previously accepted, generally applicable human rights principles such as non-discrimination, self-determination, and property. The multilateral processes that build a common understanding of the content of indigenous peoples' rights, therefore, also build expectations of behavior in conformity with those rights.

Under modern legal theory, these processes that generate international consensus about indigenous peoples' rights are processes that build customary international law. As a general matter, norms of customary law arise when a preponderance of states and other authoritative actors converge upon a common understanding of the norms' content and generally expect future behavior in conformity with the norms. The traditional points of reference for determining the existence and contours of customary norms are the relevant patterns of actual conduct on the part of state agencies. Today, however, actual state conduct is not the only or necessarily determinative indicia of customary norms. With the advent of modern international intergovernmental institutions and enhanced communications media, states and other relevant actors increasingly engage in prescriptive dialogue. Especially in multilateral settings, explicit communication may itself bring about a convergence of understanding and expectation about rules, establishing in those rules a pull toward compliance, even in advance of a widespread corresponding pattern of physical conduct. It is thus increasingly understood that explicit communication, of the sort that has been ongoing in United Nations and other international forums in regard to indigenous peoples' rights, is itself a form of practice that builds customary rules.

The claim here is not that each of the authoritative documents referred to above can be taken in their entirety as articulating customary law, but that collectively they represent core normative precepts that are now or are becoming widely accepted among authoritative actors and, to that extent, are indicative of emerging customary law. This is significant because customary international law, once crystallized, imposes obligations upon constituent units of the world community independently of obligations formally assumed by acts of treaty ratification or accession. Norms concerning indigenous peoples that are grounded in human rights precepts and generally accepted by the international community provide motivation for states to take initiatives to bring about conditions that are in conformity with the norms. Over the last several years, numerous states have enacted constitutional provisions or laws that more or less reflect the developing international consensus about indigenous peoples' rights. Of course, a great deal remains to be done to see these constitutional provisions and laws fully implemented, just as for many indigenous peoples the emerging international customary norms remain an ideal rather than a reality. Nonetheless, the international customary norms are tools by which indigenous peoples may appeal to authoritative actors in both domestic and international settings and hold states responsible for acts or omissions that are adverse to their interests.

The specific contours of a new generation of international customary norms concerning indigenous peoples are still evolving and remain somewhat ambiguous. Yet the core elements of the developing norms—including precepts of non-discrimination, self-determination, land and resource rights, and cultural integrity—are confirmed and reflected in the extensive multilateral dialogue and processes of decision focused on indigenous peoples and their rights.

CONCLUSION

Indigenous peoples have inserted themselves prominently into the international human rights agenda. In doing so they have created a movement that has challenged state-centered structures of power and long-standing precepts that failed to value indigenous cultures, institutions, and group identities. This movement, although fraught with tension, has resulted in a heightened international concern over indigenous peoples and a developing constellation of internationally accepted norms that are generally in line with indigenous peoples' own demands and aspirations. These norms find expression in ILO Convention No. 169 and other international instruments, and are otherwise discernible in the ongoing multilateral discussion about indigenous peoples and their rights. In essential aspects, the articulated standards concerning indigenous peoples can be seen as developing into customary international law.

The full extent of international affirmation of indigenous peoples' rights is still developing as indigenous peoples continue to press their cause. Nonetheless, commensurate with the degree of their acceptance by relevant international actors, new and emergent norms concerning indigenous peoples are grounds upon which nonconforming conduct may be subject to scrutiny within the international system's burgeoning human rights regime. For many indigenous peoples, such scrutiny may be a critical, if not determinative, factor in the quest for survival. The movement toward a new normative order concerning indigenous peoples is a dramatic manifestation of the capacities for social progress and change for the better that exist in the human rights frame of the contemporary international system.

Chapter 13

New Minority Rights for the Twenty-First Century

Hurst Hannum

In the same resolution that proclaimed the Universal Declaration of Human Rights on December 10, 1948, the General Assembly confessed its inability to agree even on general principles that would define and protect the rights of minority populations in independent countries. "It was difficult to adopt a uniform solution for this complex and delicate question [of minorities], which had special aspects in each State in which it arose."[1] While this did not mean that the United Nations ignored issues related to minorities in succeeding years, it did underscore the sensitivity with which the issue was viewed.

This sensitivity was due, in part, to abuses of the concept of minority rights by the Nazi regime in Germany, as well as to the Western-led push to recognize individual human rights for all, not just special rights for groups with powerful and interested neighbors. The United Nations and human rights advocates believed that the norms of equality and non-discrimination—combined, eventually, with the norm of self-determination in the form of decolonization—would suffice to protect the interests of groups in preserving their culture.[2] At the same time, most states (whether new or old) assumed that assimilation into the dominant culture would eventually decrease or even eliminate the need for special minority protections.

The United Nations did create a Sub-Commission on Prevention of Discrimination and Protection of Minorities, but its parent bodies soon made it clear that they preferred that the Sub-Commission focus on the first aspect of its

[1] G.A. Res. 217C (III) (1948).

[2] Articles 1(3) and 55 of the UN Charter refer, for example, to human rights "for all without distinction as to race, sex, language, or religion."

163

mandate. The Sub-Commission eventually expanded its work to the whole range of human rights issues (to the occasional displeasure of the Commission on Human Rights), but it never regained its initial focus on discrimination and minority issues.

In its early years, the United Nations also addressed several specific situations in which minority issues were at the heart of political conflicts. These included Trieste, the Italian South Tyrol, the Croat and Slovene minorities in Austria, and Eritrea.[3] However, attention to such politically sensitive situations was more reminiscent of the selective attention to minority rights paid by the League of Nations than of the "universal" human rights proclaimed by the United Nations.

Finally, the adoption of the 1948 Genocide Convention is additional evidence of the United Nation's awareness of the potentially devastating consequences of unchecked violations of minority rights.

As human rights standard-setting expanded during the 1960s, several international texts were adopted that addressed aspects of minority rights. The UNESCO Convention Against Discrimination in Education recognized, inter alia, the right of members of minorities to engage in their own educational activities, although these remained subject to the educational policy of each state.[4] The International Convention on the Elimination of All Forms of Racial Discrimination contained a broad definition of racial discrimination that incorporates discrimination against many minorities, i.e., any distinction "based on race, colour, descent, or national or ethnic origin."[5] Article 27 of the International Covenant on Civil and Political Rights addressed minority religious, linguistic, and cultural rights.[6]

In the mid-1970s, the Sub-Commission on Prevention of Discrimination and Protection of Minorities finally began to address minority issues in greater detail. In a well-received study, Special Rapporteur Francesco Capotorti outlined many of the problems facing minorities around the world and proposed what has remained perhaps the most widely accepted definition of a minority:

> [a] group numerically inferior to the rest of the population of a State, in a non-dominant position, whose members—being nationals of the State—

---

[3] For a brief discussion of these situations, see Hurst Hannum, Autonomy, Sovereignty, and Self-Determination: The Accommodation of Conflicting Rights (2d ed. 1996), at 57-58, 337-41, 400-06, 432-40.

[4] Adopted 14 Dec. 1960, entered into force 22 May 1962, 429 U.N.T.S. 93, arts. 5, 6.

[5] Adopted 21 Dec. 1965, entered into force 4 Jan. 1969, 660 U.N.T.S. 195. See generally Natan Lerner, Group Rights and Discrimination in International Law (1991), at 45-74.

[6] Adopted 16 Dec. 1996, entered into force 23 Mar. 1976, 999 U.N.T.S. 171. Article 27 reads in its entirety: "In those States in which ethnic, religious or linguistic minorities exist, persons belonging to such minorities shall not be denied the right, in community with the other members of their group, to enjoy their own culture, to profess and practise their own religion, or to use their own language."

possess ethnic, religious or linguistic characteristics differing from those of the rest of the population and show, if only implicitly, a sense of solidarity, directed towards preserving their culture, traditions, religion or language."[7]

Partially in response to the Capotorti report, in 1979 Yugoslavia introduced a draft declaration on minority rights to the UN Commission on Human Rights; thirteen years later (and, ironically, at about the same time that Yugoslavia itself disintegrated), the General Assembly finally adopted a Declaration on the Rights of Persons belonging to National or Ethnic, Religious or Linguistic Minorities ("Minorities Declaration").[8] In 1981, the General Assembly adopted a Declaration on the Elimination of All Forms of Intolerance and of Discrimination Based on Religion or Belief.[9]

None of the major regional human rights instruments adopted prior to the 1990s specifically refers to minority rights, with the exception of a rather vague reference to protecting "national minorities" that is found in the 1975 Helsinki Final Act of the Conference on Security and Cooperation in Europe.

Thus, even up to the early 1980s, minorities had received little formal recognition in international law. The minimalist rights recognized in the Civil and Political Covenant and the general non-discrimination rights in the Racial Discrimination Convention added very little to the scope of human rights applicable to all individuals, whether or not they also were members of a minority community. While the Helsinki Final Act inspired a resurgence of human rights activity in eastern Europe and the Soviet Union, little attention was paid to minority issues per se.

Of course, members of minorities were frequently the victims of violations of "ordinary" human rights, such as those related to free expression, freedom of religion, freedom of association, and the right to engage in political activities. Complaints of discrimination were raised in UN and regional fora by groups as varied as Catholics in Northern Ireland, Kurds, Tamils in Sri Lanka, Tibetans, Bretons, German-speakers in Italy, Blacks in the United States, Fijian Indians, Ugandan Asians, Roma in various European countries, and politically marginalized tribes in many countries in Africa. Well before the end of the Cold War and the contemporary preoccupation with "ethnic conflicts," violent, ethnically charged conflicts erupted in Congo-Kinshasa, Nigeria, Pakistan, India, Sri Lanka, Turkey, Iraq, Lebanon, Cyprus, and Spain, and unfulfilled demands for "minority" rights often led to the assertion of rights to self-determination and secession.

---

[7] Study on the rights of persons belonging to ethnic, religious and linguistic minorities (1979), reissued as UN Sales No. E.91.XIV.2 (1991), at 96.

[8] G.A. Res. 47/135 (1992). See discussion *infra* at 6-7.

[9] G.A. Res. 36/55 (1981).

Periodic reports submitted by states to the Human Rights Committee and the Committee on the Elimination of All Forms of Racial Discrimination tend to recite domestic legal provisions regarding minorities, but they rarely concede that members of minorities suffer any adverse consequences because of their minority status.[10]

Under the First Optional Protocol to the Civil and Political Covenant and article 14 to the Racial Discrimination Convention, individuals may file communications with the respective committees, alleging the violation of rights guaranteed under the treaties. Although the process tends to be long and relies purely on written evidence, some individuals have been able to receive redress under these procedures.

In interpreting article 27 of the Covenant, for example, the Human Rights Committee found that withdrawing the right of a woman to reside on an Indian reserve because of her marriage to a non-Indian violated her right, "in community with the other members of [her] group, to enjoy [her] own culture."[11] The Committee also has addressed whether or not various governmental acts interfere with the rights of ethnic Saami to engage in reindeer herding, an integral part of Saami culture.[12] The Committee determined that the reference in article 27 to minorities "within . . . States" does not include the English-speaking minority in the province of Quebec,[13] but a subsequent case held that freedom of expression under article 19 of the Covenant includes the right to express oneself in the language of one's choice outside the spheres of public life in which use of an official language may be required.[14]

The Committee on the Elimination of All Forms of Racial Discrimination has considered very few cases under article 14, and none of its first five cases dealt with minority rights per se.

New procedures to implement human rights norms created in the United Nations in the 1970s and 1980s largely responded to gross violations of civil and political rights rather than to the problems of vulnerable groups. The so-called "thematic mechanisms" of the Commission on Human Rights, for example,

---

[10]Surveys of some of these country reports may be found in Hannum, *supra* note 3, at 64-69; Theodor Meron, Human Rights Law-Making in the United Nations (1986), at 36-44; Sia Spiliopoulou, "Protection of Minorities under Article 27 of the International Covenant on Civil and Political Rights and the Reporting System [under] the Human Rights Committee," in Frank Horn, ed., Writings in Human and Minority Rights (1994), at 57-99; and Patrick Thornberry, International Law and the Rights of Minorities (1991), at 272-80.

[11]*Lovelace v. Canada*, Communication No. 24/1977, reported in the Human Rights Committee's Annual Report, UN Doc. A/36/40 (1981), at 166.

[12]See, e.g., *Kitok v. Sweden*, Communication No. 197/1985 (27 July 1988); *Sara et al. v. Finland*, Communication No. 431/1990 (23 Mar. 1994); *Länsman et al. v. Finland*, Communication No. 511/1992 (26 Oct. 1994); *Jouni E. Länsman et al. v. Finland*, Communication No. 671/1995 (14 Mar. 1996).

[13]*Ballantyne et al. v. Canada*, Communication No. 359/1989 (31 Mar. 1993).

[14]*Singer v. Canada*, Communication No. 455/1991 (26 July 1994).

initially addressed violations of personal security and integrity, such as disappearances, arbitrary executions and detention, and torture (although a rapporteur on religious intolerance was appointed by the Commission in 1986 and on racism and xenophobia in 1993). Nongovernmental organizations frequently voiced concerns over the situation of minorities in many states during statements to the Commission on Human Rights and Sub-Commission on Prevention of Discrimination and Protection of Minorities, but they were forced to couch their complaints in terms of traditional human rights. There was little acceptance of any affirmative obligation on the part of states to protect and promote minority cultures.[15]

Although many long-standing conflicts fueled by the East-West rivalry began to wind down in the 1980s, the political uncertainty and economic insecurity that followed the withdrawal of the Soviet Union from central and eastern Europe and, soon thereafter, the dissolution of the Soviet Union itself, brought new and widely publicized instances in which minority groups seemed to be the targets of persecution. Just as newly independent states in the 1960s often sacrificed pluralism and diversity on the altar of "nation building," those states freed from Soviet domination appeared to be more interested in consolidating their often ethnically-defined states than in tolerance.

The normative response to this new situation was surprisingly rapid. In 1990, the Copenhagen meeting of the Conference on the Human Dimension of the Conference on Security and Cooperation in Europe (CSCE) adopted a Final Document by consensus.[16] This remarkable document (which also contains detailed provisions relating to democracy, the rule of law, and other human rights issues) was drafted and agreed to in only six weeks, and it represents the first detailed articulation of minority rights by governments since the post-World War I minorities treaties. Its provisions went well beyond existing guarantees in article 27 of the Civil and Political Covenant, addressing, in particular, language use, education, and political participation.

Not to be outdone, the Council of Europe adopted and opened for ratification in 1992 a Charter on the Protection of Minority and Regional Languages.[17] Modeled after the European Social Charter, the 1992 Charter offers a wide range

---

[15]Article 2 of the Racial Discrimination Convention does require that state parties take, in appropriate circumstances, "special and concrete measures to ensure the adequate development and protection of certain racial groups or individuals belonging to them, for the purpose of guaranteeing them the full and equal enjoyment of human rights and fundamental freedoms." However, this provision does not set forth additional minority rights, per se; it merely addresses the issue of equality. In addition, the measures to be taken should be temporary, which may not be sufficient to protect legitimate minority interests in the long term.

[16]Document of the Copenhagen Meeting of the Conference on the Human Dimension of the CSCE, adopted 29 June 1990, reprinted in *United Nations, A Compilation of International Instruments,* vol. II, Regional Instruments, UN Sales No. E.97.XIV.1, at 389-405.

[17]European Charter for Regional or Minority Languages, signed 5 Nov. 1992, entered into force 1 Mar. 1998, Europ. T.S. No. 148.

of obligations from among which States may choose the provisions they are willing to accept. In the following years, the Parliamentary Assembly of the Council of Europe recommended that a protocol on minority rights be added to the European Convention on Human Rights, although that suggestion has not yet been acted upon.[18] A more ambitious Framework Convention for the Protection of National Minorities was adopted in 1995.[19]

The Declaration on the Rights of Persons belonging to National or Ethnic, Religious or Linguistic Minorities was finally completed and adopted by the UN General Assembly in 1992.[20] While it continues the individualistic orientation of article 27 of the Covenant on Civil and Political Rights by referring to "the rights of persons" belonging to minorities, the Declaration does expand on existing provisions and contains progressive language related to minority participation in the political and economic life of the State. In addition, the Preamble recognizes that protecting minority rights will "contribute to the political and social stability of States in which they live" and, in turn, "contribute to the strengthening of friendship and co-operation among peoples and States."

The UN Declaration is the only universally applicable instrument on minority rights and was adopted by the General Assembly without a dissenting vote. Among the more noteworthy provisions of this relatively short declaration are the following paragraphs:

Article 1

1. States shall protect the existence and the national or ethnic, cultural, religious and linguistic identity of minorities within their respective territories, and shall encourage conditions for the promotion of that identity.

2. States shall adopt appropriate legislative and other measures to achieve these ends.

Article 2

...

2. Persons belonging to minorities have the right to participate effectively in cultural, religious, social, economic and public life.

3. Persons belonging to minorities have the right to participate effectively in decisions on the national and, where appropriate, regional level concerning the minority to which they belong or the regions in which they live, in a manner not incompatible with national legislation. . . .

---

[18]Parliamentary Assembly of the Council of Europe, Recommendation 1201 (1993), 44th Sess., 22nd Sitting, 1 Feb. 1993.

[19]Framework Convention for the Protection of National Minorities, signed 1 Feb. 1995, entered into force 1 Feb. 1998, Europ. T.S. No. 157, reprinted in UN Compilation, *supra* note 16, at 286-95. The convention had been ratified by twenty states as of spring 1998.

[20]*Supra* note 8.

5. Persons belonging to minorities have the right to establish and maintain, without any discrimination, free and peaceful contacts with other members of their group and with persons belonging to other minorities, as well as contacts across frontiers with citizens of other States to whom they are related by national or ethnic, religious or linguistic ties. . . .

Article 4

...

2. States shall take measures to create favourable conditions to enable persons belonging to minorities to express their characteristics and to develop their culture, language, religion, traditions and customs, except where specific practices are in violation of national law and contrary to international standards.

3. States should take appropriate measures so that, wherever possible, persons belonging to minorities have adequate opportunities to learn their mother tongue or to have instruction in their mother tongue. . . .

5. States should consider appropriate measures so that persons belonging to minorities may participate fully in the economic progress and development in their country.

Article 5

1. National policies and programmes shall be planned and implemented with due regard for the legitimate interests of persons belonging to minorities.

Perhaps in an attempt to breathe more meaning into the narrow language of article 27 of the Civil and Political Covenant, the Human Rights Committee, after much debate, issued a General Comment on minority rights in 1994. The Committee observed in a cursory manner that "it is not relevant to determine the degree of permanence that the term 'exist' connotes" and then went on to express the view that article 27 applies to everyone belonging to one of the named categories of minorities and present within a country, including "migrant workers or even visitors."[21] The Committee does not refer to the relevant legislative history to support its conclusions, and the General Comment is perhaps best interpreted as representing the personal views of Committee members rather than an authoritative interpretation of the text of the Covenant.[22] At the same time, however, the

---

[21]General Comment No. 23(5), para. 5.2 (1994).

[22]Compare, for example, the Annotations on the text of the draft International Covenants on Human Rights, prepared by the Secretary-General for the General Assembly in 1955: "It was agreed that the article should cover only separate or distinct groups, well-defined and long-established on the territory of a State." UN Doc. A/2929 (1955), para. 184. Other references may be found in M. Bossuyt, Guide to the *"Travaux Préparatoires"* of the International Covenant on Civil and Political Rights, Dordrecht, Martinus Nijhoff, 1987, pp. 493-499. Citing, inter alia, the Capotorti study, *supra* note 7, a more recent commentator concluded (prior to the adoption of the Committee's General Comment) that "aliens are *prima facie* excluded" from the scope of article 27. Thornberry, *supra* note 10, at 171.

expansive reading is generally consistent with the more detailed principles set forth in the 1992 General Assembly Declaration.

Thus, by the fiftieth anniversary of the Universal Declaration, the international community had agreed on a fairly substantial set of norms concerned directly with the rights of minorities. While these norms remain largely undefined beyond the texts of the various instruments, they certainly go a considerable distance to offering the "uniform solution for this complex and delicate question" that eluded the drafters of the Universal Declaration of Human Rights in 1948.

Of course, members of minority groups who are victims of violations of either "new" minority rights defined since 1990 or the more traditional rights of non-discrimination and equality need procedures to enforce the rights that are guaranteed on paper. In addition to the activities of the Human Rights Committee and the Committee on the Elimination of All Forms of Racial Discrimination, referred to earlier in this chapter, there are two additional mechanisms specifically concerned with minority rights that deserve attention.

Two years after adopting the Copenhagen Document, the CSCE (now known as the Organization on Security and Cooperation in Europe [OSCE]) created the position of High Commissioner on National Minorities, in order to provide " 'early warning' and, as appropriate, 'early action' at the earliest possible stage in regard to tensions involving national minority issues that have the potential to develop into a conflict within the CSCE area, affecting peace, stability, or relations between participating States."[23] Although the high Commissioner's mandate is to prevent conflict rather than to protect minority rights per se, his interventions thus far appear to have contributed to both objectives.

The work of the High Commissioner is theoretically confidential, but the OSCE has authorized publication of most of his formal communications with governments. Primarily through quiet diplomacy, the High Commissioner (the position has been held by former Dutch Foreign Minister Max van der Stoel since its inception) has consulted with governments, NGOs, and others regarding the situations of, in particular, minorities in a number of newly independent states that were formerly part of the Soviet Union.[24] Although the High Commissioner cannot formally address violations of the rights of individuals, his office should certainly be viewed as a focal point to which aggrieved minorities within the geographic scope of the OSCE should appeal.

Following approval of the 1992 Minorities Declaration by the General Assembly, the UN Sub-Commission adopted a report on "the possible ways and means of facilitating the peaceful and constructive solution of problems involving

---

[23]Conference on Security and Cooperation in Europe, Helsinki Document 1992, Decisions, Sec. II, reprinted in UN Compilation, *supra* note 16 at 430, 431-37.

[24]A useful summary of the High Commissioner's work is Foundation on Inter-Ethnic Relations, The Role of the High Commissioner on National Minorities in OSCE Conflict Prevention: An Introduction (1997).

minorities."[25] It was not until 1995 that the Commission on Human Rights agreed to create a mechanism to monitor observance of the Minorities Declaration, when it authorized the Sub-Commission to establish a five-member working group to "[r]eview the promotion and practical realization" of the Declaration, "[e]xamine possible solutions to problems involving minorities . . . [and recommend] further measures, as appropriate, for the promotion and protection of the rights of persons belonging to national or ethnic, religious and linguistic minorities."[26]

This Sub-Commission working group, which meets annually in Geneva for a one-week session, usually in May, is likely to become the major forum for discussion of minority-specific issues within the UN system. Its mandate was extended indefinitely by the Commission on Human Rights in 1998, in a resolution that "[r]eaffirm[ed] the obligation of States to ensure" implementation of the rights in the Minorities Declaration.[27] As is true of the OSCE High Commissioner, the working group cannot consider individual complaints of violations. Nonetheless, it provides a means whereby minority grievances can be inserted into the UN system in an informal way. Perhaps more importantly, the working group also provides an international setting in which dialogue between minorities and governments can be initiated, to address both positive and negative aspects of minority-majority relations.

Another task of the working group will be to articulate in greater detail what is meant by the Declaration's various provisions. Phrases such as "appropriate measures," "adequate opportunities," and "participate effectively" can only be given content in the context of specific situations, and it is hoped that the working group will develop expertise in the comparative law of minorities so that it may contribute to resolving or preventing conflicts in situations in which tensions between minority and majority are increasing.

Minority rights remains a particularly sensitive issue for many governments, and international activity in this area often is made more difficult because of concerns over the rights of the majority, the political and territorial integrity of states, and the right of every people to determine its own form of government. Creating a meaningful national identity is a legitimate goal of any state, even though such an identity may be perceived by some as conflicting with pre-existing identities based on regionalism, ethnicity, or culture.

At the same time, members of minorities are concerned that they will lose their identity as an inevitable result of the social pressures of modern society and the modern state. Increasing global communication and homogenization—

---

[25]The final report, by Sub-Commission member Asbjørn Eide, is found in UN Doc. E/CN.4/Sub.2/1993/34 and Adds. 1-4 (1993).

[26]Commission on Human Rights Res. 1995/24 (3 Mar. 1995), para. 9.

[27]Commission on Human Rights Res. 1998/19 (9 Apr. 1998), para. 2. The resolution also calls upon the human rights treaty bodies, special rapporteurs, the High Commissioner for Human Rights, and others to give particular attention to issues within their competence that affect minorities.

particularly economic and social—may only reflect the timeless tension between change and the status quo, but it also has contributed to a cultural resurgence among ethnic and linguistic groups around the world that feel threatened. Economically weaker regions inhabited primarily by minorities may feel isolated from centralized decision makers, and minorities may view economic and political marginalization as resulting from discrimination rather than simply reflecting inevitable regional disparities.

Minority rights can only be understood within the broader context of international human rights law, which has developed considerably since the adoption of the Universal Declaration in 1948. Formerly, the treatment of minorities fell within the domestic jurisdiction of the state; unless there were broader geopolitical reasons to be concerned about their fate, they would be left wholly to the mercy of the majority. Today, however, members of minorities are protected by the same umbrella of human rights that protects all other persons within a state's jurisdiction.

In many cases, victims of violations of minority rights are also victims of other human rights violations, and it is with the latter violations that any attempt at redress must begin. For example, among the "minority" rights identified in the various instruments referred to in this chapter are the rights to physical integrity and existence, including protection against forced assimilation; non-discrimination; freedom of religion; the right to enjoy one's own culture; the right to establish one's own associations; and the right to use one's language. These rights are already guaranteed in international instruments and are widely accepted by states.

Of course, there are other rights more directly related to the needs of minority groups and individuals, such as the right of minorities to participate effectively in political, economic, and cultural life, including participation in decisions which directly affect them; the right to use one's language in various public ways, such as before administrative authorities or to identify local place-names; and the right to establish one's own schools and to be educated in one's mother tongue. These rights may be more difficult to articulate with precision, and their protection may require greater modification of internal constitutional structures or governmental institutions than is generally required to protect other human rights.

At the same time, it must be borne in mind that the protection of minority rights does not require the artificial conservation of every existing culture, without change. Individuals and groups should remain free to encourage either assimilation or greater distinctiveness, so long as these choices are available without undue pressure to conform—to either the minority or majority culture.

The challenge of protecting the rights of persons belonging to minorities is to balance the legitimate concerns of majority and minority communities, so that broader political and economic decisions may be reached in an atmosphere of full equality and respect for human rights. The international community has made significant strides in articulating this balance in only a few years. As with other human rights, however, the task now is to ensure that the political and legal commitments accepted by states are monitored and implemented in good faith.

Now that meaningful minority rights are becoming more widely accepted, it may be possible to prevent future victimization through preemptive dialogue about government structures, devolution, and power-sharing. Such a dialogue is possible only in a country in which human rights and the rule of law are respected. Only in such a context can the will of the majority to govern successfully accommodate the rights of the minority to exist and prosper.

Chapter 14

Searching for Human Security and Dignity: Human Rights, Refugees, and the Internally Displaced

Maria Stavropoulou*

An attempt to evaluate whether human rights doctrine and action have had any impact on safeguarding (some of) "all human rights for all" fifty years after the Universal Declaration of Human Rights was signed, seems to point to failure when one looks at the numbers of refugees and internally displaced persons that have grown rapidly over those fifty years. In theory, if all human rights were guaranteed,[1] there would be no refugees or displaced persons. Thus, if the measure of progress on the human rights front is the numbers of displaced persons, certainly progress is limited.[2]

The kinds of violations of the Universal Declaration and the resultant victimization that on many occasions cause displacement and refugee movements[3]

---

*The views expressed in this chapter do not necessarily reflect the views of the United Nations or UNHCR.

---

[1] See also, UNCHR, *The State of the World's Refugees—The Challenge of Protection*, 1993, p. 22.

[2] This would be an abstract approach, since refugee flows are also influenced by other factors not necessarily related to human rights protection, such as the changing nature of conflicts, greater population mobility and wider media coverage of conditions in other parts of the world, Note 1, p. 64.

[3] See also, *Sadruddin Aga Khan, Special Rapporteur, Study on Human Rights and Massive Exoduses,* U.N. ESCOR, Comm'n on Hum. Rts., 38th Sess., Agenda Item 12 (b), U.N. Doc. E/CN.4/1503, 1981, in which he analyzes the causes of mass exoduses within the context of the Universal Declaration.

are described elsewhere in this book. This chapter is an attempt to show the extent to which the rights of refugees and internally displaced persons have been articulated in international law and the degree to which they are being implemented, noting progress and failures on both levels.

A. DEVELOPMENTS IN INTERNATIONAL LAW

While the right to seek and enjoy asylum has not been articulated into binding international law, the right of non-refoulement (the right to be protected against return to a country where one's life and liberty might be in danger), and certain civil and socioeconomic rights of refugees have. With regard to the internally displaced, only very recently was it recognized that they may be in need of special protection, including under the terms of an international instrument.

1. The Right to Asylum

Article 14(1) of the Universal Declaration states that "everyone has the right to seek and enjoy in other countries asylum from persecution." The language of this article was not repeated later in the International Covenant on Civil and Political Rights and it appears that even at the time of the drafting of the Universal Declaration, states were not prepared to accept an individual human right to be granted asylum and to be bound by such a right.[4] While it is also clear from subsequent legal developments that the granting of asylum was always conceived of as the sovereign right of the state,[5] it is also true that in the last fifty years asylum was often given: "the humanitarian practice exists, but the sense of obligation is missing."[6]

2. Non-Refoulement and Non-Rejection at the Frontier

Even though asylum in the sense of according a lasting solution has not been codified in international law, the principle of non-refoulement, which is, after all, the cornerstone of the institution of asylum and of international protection, has. According to article 33 (1) of the 1951 Convention relating to the Status of Refugees,[7] "[n]o contracting State shall expel or return ("refouler") a refugee in

---

[4] See Guy S. Goodwin-Gill, *The Refugee in International Law* (Second Edition), 1996, p. 175.

[5] *Ibid.* pp. 174-179 (describing *inter alia* the 1967 Declaration on Territorial Asylum, the 1954 Caracas Convention on Territorial Asylum and the OAU Convention Governing the Specific Aspects of Refugee Problems in Africa).

[6] See Note 4, p. 178.

[7] 189 U.N.T.S. 2545, entered into force on April 22, 1954 [hereinafter the Refugee Convention].

any manner whatsoever to the frontiers of territories where his life or freedom would be threatened on account of his race, religion, nationality, membership of a particular social group or political opinion." This provision is today considered to be part of general international law, meaning that even states not parties to the Refugee Convention are bound by it.[8]

With regard to the personal scope of the principle of non-refoulement, this applies to refugees as defined in article 1 of the Refugee Convention, asylum seekers, at least during an initial period until their status as refugees is determined, and "to every individual who has a well-founded fear of persecution, or where there are substantial grounds for believing that he or she would be in danger of torture if returned to a particular country."[9]

Regional developments in the sphere of refugee law have, over the past fifty years, served to clarify and even extend the personal scope of the principle: The 1969 OAU Convention Governing the Specific Aspects of Refugee Problems in Africa[10] extended protection to all persons compelled to flee across national borders by reason of human-made disasters in Africa, and the 1984 Cartagena Declaration[11] closely followed this by adopting its own expanded definition of the term "refugee." In Europe, the European Convention on Human Rights,[12] which in article 3 proclaims the freedom from torture, inhuman or degrading treatment or punishment, has also been interpreted to include prohibition of return to a country where the danger of such treatment exists.[13]

Finally, the 1984 UN Convention against Torture and Other Cruel, Inhuman or Degrading Treatment or Punishment[14] adopted in 1984 provides in article 3 that "1. [n]o State Party shall expel, return ("refouler") or extradite a person to another State where there are substantial grounds for believing that he would be in danger of being subjected to torture. 2. For the purpose of determining whether there are such grounds, the competent authorities shall take into account all relevant considerations including where applicable, the existence in the State concerned of a consistent pattern of gross, flagrant or mass violations of human rights."

[8] Goodwin-Gill, *supra* note 4, p. 169.

[9] *Ibid.* p. 39.

[10] U.N.T.S. 14,691, entered into force June 20, 1974.

[11] Cartagena Declaration on Refugees, reprinted in UNHCR, *Collection of International Instruments and Other Legal Texts Concerning Refugees and Displaced Persons, Vol. II—Regional Instruments,* p. 206 (1995).

[12] European Convention for the Protection of Human Rights and Fundamental Freedoms, reprinted in ibid., p. 239.

[13] Goodwin-Gill, *supra* note 4, p. 176, note 24 and accompanying text and pp. 315-322.

[14] Reprinted in UNHCR, *supra* note 11, p. 233.

The principle of non-refoulement is today considered to have expanded so as to encompass also the principle of admission and non-rejection at the frontier. Writing in 1953, Nehemiah Robinson suggested that "[a]rticle 33 concerns refugees who have gained entry into the territory of a Contracting State, legally or illegally, but not to refugees who seek entrance into this territory . . . In other words, if a refugee has succeeded in eluding the frontier guards, he is safe; if he has not, it is his hard luck. It cannot be said that this is a satisfactory solution of the problem of asylum."[15] Writing in 1996, Goodwin-Gill suggests that "States in their practice and in their recorded views, have recognized that non-refoulement applies to the moment at which asylum seekers present themselves for entry. Certain factual elements may be necessary (such as human rights violations in the country of origin) before the principle is triggered, but the concept now encompasses both non-return and non-rejection."[16]

3. Civil and Socioeconomic Rights of Refugees

The Refugee Convention includes a number of articles concerning rights that are granted to refugees as inhabitants of the host country, including religious rights, juridical status rights, gainful employment rights, welfare rights, and protection under administrative measures. The Convention does not impair the realization of rights granted to refugees by the state by virtue of their own national legislations or other binding international instruments. Given that the entry into force of the Refugee Convention predates that of the International Covenant on Civil and Political Rights and the Covenant on Economic, Social and Cultural Rights, many of the rights as articulated in the Convention have now been clarified in the light of those more recent instruments. Furthermore, all rights pertaining to the persons who come under the jurisdiction of the state apply appropriately to refugees and asylum seekers.

4. Internally Displaced Persons

The Universal Declaration itself does not use the terms "displacement" or "internally displaced." Internally displaced persons did not become an "issue" on the international legal agenda until 1991. At that time the Commission on Human Rights requested the UN Secretary-General to appoint a Representative to prepare a study on the human rights issues pertaining to the internally displaced,[17]

---

[15]Institute of Jewish Affairs, *Convention Relating to the Status of Refugees, Its History, Contents and Interpretation, A Commentary by Nehemiah Robinson,* pp. 138-139 (republished by the Division of International Protection of UNHCR, 1997).

[16]Goodwin-Gill, *supra* note 4, pp. 123-124.

[17]*Internally displaced persons,* C.H.R. Res. 1991/25, Comm'n on Hum. Rts., 47th Sess., Supp. No. 2, at 69, U.N. Doc. E/CN.4/1991/91.

subsequent to which it renewed the mandate so as to allow him to prepare a relevant legal analysis[18] and draft a set of guiding principles to be followed in situations of internal displacement.[19]

The Guiding Principles on Internal Displacement address the specific needs of internally displaced persons and identify rights and guarantees relevant to the protection of persons from forced displacement and to their protection and assistance during displacement, as well as during return of resettlement or reintegration.

B. IMPLEMENTATION OF INTERNATIONAL OBLIGATIONS

Despite this gradual growth of international law in respect of refugees, the situation of refugees in countries of asylum is at present not encouraging. Interdiction policies and less-than-generous granting of the status of refugees have placed in question the entire system of refugee protection;[20] at the same time, they have triggered a set of other mechanisms to secure the rights of refugees.

1. Asylum Under Threat

Over the past fifty years, persons in need of international protection have more often found it than not. It is estimated that in the early 1990s there were more than eighteen million refugees worldwide—a six-fold increase within fifteen years.[21] Most of those refugees were hosted in poor countries, which makes their hospitality all the more remarkable. For instance, a million Mozambicans found asylum in Malawi, a country with few resources and an eight million population of its own.[22]

Nonetheless, at present the international principles of refugee law are often violated by both industrial and less developed countries. This backward trend started in the early 1990s with the restrictive policies being implemented by certain countries in Western Europe and North America—policies that aimed

---

[18] *Internally Displaced Persons: Report of the Representative of the Secretary-General, Mr. Francis M. Deng, Submitted Pursuant to Commission on Human Rights Resolution 1995/57: Compilation and Analysis of Legal Norms.* U.N. ESCOR, Comm'n on Hum. Rts., 51st Sess., Agenda Item 9(d), U.N. Doc. E/CN.4/1996/52/Add.2 (1995).

[19] *Report of the Representative of the Secretary-General, Guiding Principles on Internal Displacement,* U.N. ESCOR, Comm'n on Hum. Rts., 54th Sess., Agenda Item 9(d), U.N. Doc. E/CN.4/1998/53/Add.2 (1998).

[20] See James C. Hathaway and John A. Dent, *Refugee Rights, Report on a Comparative Survey,* 1995, pp. 35-43.

[21] UNHCR, *The State of the World's Refugees—A Humanitarian Agenda,* fig. 2.1, p. 54, 1997. In the past few years figures have declined with the completion of large repatriation operations in Afghanistan, Cambodia, Mozambique, and Rwanda.

[22] See note 21, p. 62.

either to deny entrance to asylum seekers or to establish interpretations of the law and procedures that effectively denied the status of refugee to many persons in need of international protection. Measures to obstruct entrance were put in place, for example, by the United States and Turkey; in 1991, the former initiated a policy of interdicting Haitian asylum seekers trying to reach the United States by boat, and the latter refused to allow Iraqi Kurds fleeing an armed offensive in North Iraq to enter its territory.[23] An example of a restrictive interpretation of the term "refugee," on the other hand, is the fact that certain European states require that persecution be based on acts of state agents only, such as the government forces or other forces or groups under governmental control.[24]

In addition, admission to a country is no longer a guarantee of safety. Especially in the past few years, refugees have found their lives threatened in their countries of refuge as well. For instance, refugee camps have been used as havens by armed groups, and consequently were targeted by both rebel factions and governmental armies; forced conscription of refugee boys and men, sexual and other forms of violence against refugee women and girls, and arbitrary detention of refugees are being reported.[25]

2. Non-Refoulement and Human Rights Bodies

Non-refoulement of refugees who have already gained access to the territory of a state remains a principle respected by most states, although exceptions do occur. In the case of developed countries, refoulement of non-recognized yet genuine refugees remains a serious challenge. Many of these states now grant subsidiary status (B status, or humanitarian status) to refugees whom they deem do not fulfill the "individualized persecution" test or who fear persecution from non-state agents. Refoulement remains the only clear principle for persons with such status; however, its unclear legal basis may result in a watering-down of the entire institution of asylum.

Gradually, the international system for monitoring the implementation of human rights is meeting this challenge to the principles of international protection of refugees. In the absence of an enforcement regime in the context of international refugee law, refugees have turned to the UN human rights treaty bodies[26] and regional bodies that have often vindicated them.

---

[23]*State of the World's Refugees, supra* note 1, pp. 42 and 34, respectively.

[24]See, e.g., *Joint Position of 4 March 1996, defined by the Council on the basis of Article K.3 of the Treaty of European Union on the harmonized application of the definition of the term "refugee" in article 1 of the Geneva Convention of 28 July 1951 relating to the status of refugees,* 96/196/JHA, Official Journal of the European Communities No. L. 63/2 (13.3.96), para. 5.1.

[25]UNHCR, *supra* note 21, p. 65.

[26]Such as the Human Rights Committee, the Committee Against Torture and the Committee on the Rights of the Child established by the respective instruments. For a description of mechanisms available to refugees see Amnesty International, *The UN and refugees' human rights—A manual on how UN human rights mechanisms can protect the rights of refugees,* 1997.

Most noteworthy in this respect are the jurisprudence of the European Court and the European Commission of Human Rights which have established that article 3 of the European Convention on Human Rights and Fundamental Freedoms, which prohibits torture, applies to persons threatened with deportation or extradition from a State Party to the Convention, including asylum seekers,[27] to countries where they risk being subjected to the proscribed treatment.

3. Employment and Social Welfare

Convention refugees, i.e., those granted asylum, enjoy in most developed countries full employment rights (articles 17 and 18 of the 1951 Convention), even though their access to the labor market may be hampered by inhospitable social conditions. In less-developed countries, governments are more hesitant to grant employment rights to refugees for fear of undermining the local labor market and hospitality, and have declared reservations to the employment provisions of the Convention.

Practice as to persons granted humanitarian status and asylum seekers varies greatly. In many countries these persons have no right to employment whatsoever; in others they do for as long as they hold the humanitarian status or until their status has been determined.

With regard to relief, public assistance and social assistance (arts. 23 and 24), the situation is again similar, with many developed countries granting full access to the social and public assistance services to refugees and asylum seekers, while others limit such benefits to emergencies, or only to recognized refugees.

In the poorer countries of the South, where social assistance schemes as those envisaged in the Convention do not exist for nationals, governments frequently cooperate with the international community, in particular UNHCR, in order to meet the basic subsistence needs of refugees. Even in such cases, however, the limited assistance which might be available is not always distributed among different groups of refugees without discrimination.[28]

4. Securing the Rights of the Internally Displaced

Intervening with national authorities to ensure that the human rights of persons who have been displaced but remain in their own country has not been easily accepted by a large segment of the international community, whose argument has been that these persons are in no need of international protection

[27]For a critical analysis, see Guy Goodwin-Gill, *supra* note 4, pp. 317-323.

[28]See, e.g., Refugee Rights, *supra* note 20 at p. 33 regarding treatment of refugees from different countries in India.

since they have not left their countries. As absolute sovereignty with regard to human rights questions has increasingly been questioned, however, the specific violations affecting the internally displaced have also been the object of increased monitoring.

Internally displaced populations frequently find themselves in difficult and dangerous circumstances, primarily because they remain under the jurisdiction of a state unable or unwilling to protect them; hence the need for international protection. Acute conditions of physical, material, legal, and psychological insecurity are experienced by the internally displaced who, in addition, are less likely than refugees to come to the attention of the international community, as recently shown again by the displacement of ethnic Albanians in Kosovo.[29]

Internally displaced persons often face threats to their security and welfare throughout the process of flight and displacement. Like refugees, they are obliged to abandon their homes on short notice and may have to flee through a conflict zone. Children may be separated from their parents and forcible conscription may be unavoidable. Camps and temporary settlements are often overcrowded and may be exposed to direct physical threats. Finally, internally displaced persons may suffer from discrimination within their own country, very much like refugees do once they reach third countries, since they often move into areas inhabited by different ethnic communities, or into urban environments, that may be hostile toward them.

Being, so far, the only international entity with a specific mandate to monitor the human rights of the internally displaced, the Representative of the Secretary-General on internally displaced persons has encouraged inter-governmental and non-governmental agencies providing assistance to these populations to become involved in their human rights matters as well,[30] to increase the protection capacity of the international community toward the internally displaced.

C. CONCLUSION

A recent publication of the United Nations High Commissioner for Refugees assessing the situation of refugees and displaced persons of concern to the humanitarian agency suggests that if forced displacement is to be averted and the growing number of displaced people are to return safely to their homes, then a diversity of economic, political, and humanitarian agendas must be followed, all of which have to be based on the principle that everyone has a right to security and freedom: security from persecution, discrimination, armed conflict and

---

[29]See also the State of the World's Refugees, *supra* note 21, p. 112.

[30]See Roberta Cohen and Francis M. Deng, *Masses in Flight*, pp. 126-212, 1998, suggesting that there is need for involvement by international and regional organizations as well as by non-governmental organizations.

poverty; and the freedom to fulfill their personal potential; to participate in the decisions which affect their lives and future, and to express their individual and collective identity. "If such rights and freedoms could be realized, then millions of people around the world could be spared the physical and emotional pain of being uprooted."[31]

Refugees and internally displaced persons are victims of human rights violations. They should, therefore, be able to find support and solidarity from the rest of humanity to resume their lives in an environment fostering and guaranteeing their security and dignity. While their present situation does not allow for euphoria, the fact that states are prepared to abide by the basic principles of international protection gives hope that, for most, an end to their displacement will not be elusive.

[31] See State of the World's Refugees, *supra* note 21, p. 8.

Chapter 15

Protection of the Rights of Migrants

Graziano Battistella

The relevance of international migration in the contemporary world needs little emphasis. United Nations estimates speak of perhaps 125 million persons living outside of their country of birth. But more than numbers, it is the issues deriving from international migration that make it relevant. The frequency with which migration appears in the newspapers testifies to the range of concerns it draws. Unfortunately, news often speaks of episodes of maltreatment and abuse against migrants.

Infringement of migrants' rights has acquired disturbing notoriety in recent times because of the interconnection of migration with other social phenomena. Specifically, migrants become victims of international criminality engaged in trafficking across international borders. Migrant women in particular begin a search for a better job abroad which ends up in activities related to sexual exploitation or in forms of employment which amount to slavery. Such forms of criminality have passed the preoccupation of individual countries and concerted action has been advocated in the recent Group of 8 (G8) Summit meeting in Birmingham.

However, abuse against migrants cannot be considered just an occasional deviance. It is instead structurally inserted in the recourse to workers who can be exploited through low salaries, substandard terms of employment, or precarious living and working conditions. This is because migrants do not simply constitute an available workforce in a situation of scarcity of labor, but a cheap and disposable workforce. The vulnerability of migrants lies in their status as aliens and as workers and it is aggravated when migrants are women and children.

Because international migration implies movement beyond the jurisdiction of the state of which one is a national, protection of migrants is dependent on the legislation of receiving countries. To overcome such narrow perspective, migrants can avail themselves of protection granted by the international community under different entitlements. Migrants, in fact, are aliens and workers in a foreign country and an extensive body of rights has been developing through the years, but particularly in the last fifty years, which can be invoked in some form or the other by migrants. This chapter will first review international protection available to migrants, and will then examine recent developments concerning migrants deriving from the international conferences organized by the United Nations in this decade. The final part of the chapter will be devoted to the growing participation of civil society in the concern for the protection of migrants.

THE INTERNATIONAL PROTECTION OF MIGRANT WORKERS

The protection of migrant workers is a complex issue because of the simultaneous belonging of migrant workers to different branches of the law. As a foreigner, the migrant falls under provisions of international law. As a worker, he is protected by labor law. As a migrant, he enjoys the rights given by specific conventions and bilateral and multilateral treaties.

INTERNATIONAL LAW

The international law of the foreigner found its origin in the attempts to protect the interest of people abroad, particularly in the matter of compensation to be given for injuries suffered by aliens. Two principles animated the evolution of this law: on one side, the international standard, supported in particular by the Western countries, implying that foreigners should be protected and compensated according to international norms and customs; on the other side, the national standard, supported in particular by the Latin American nations, implying that the foreigner should enjoy the same protection and guarantees afforded to nationals. The irreconcilable contrast between the two standards is the reason for the failure to adopt the Convention on the treatment of foreigners by the League of Nations in 1929 [1], as well as the failure by the International Law Commission to adopt the Draft Convention on the International Responsibility of States for Injuries to Aliens [2].

The troubled process found a conclusion in the adoption by the United Nations in 1985 of the Declaration on the Rights of Aliens Who Are Not Citizens of the State in Which They Live. The Declaration lists in 10 articles rights basically taken from the Universal Declaration and the Covenants. A state may introduce a differential treatment for nationals and foreigners, "however, such laws and regulations shall not be incompatible with the international legal obligations of that state, including those in the fields of human rights" (Art. 2,1). The

Declaration did not mention the rights to compensation in case of expropriation, which goes to the heart of the dispute between national and international standards; furthermore, it does not apply to foreigners illegally present on the territory of a state and it refers to human rights as the indispensable element of any successful attempt to restate the law governing the treatment of aliens.

MIGRATION LAW

International instruments specifically related to the protection of migrant workers have been prepared by the International Labor Organisation and by regional institutions.

International Labor Organization (ILO)

The protection of migrant workers is inherent to the purpose of the ILO and it is included among the objectives of the ILO statute. In addition to standards applying to all workers, migrants have been the object of specific conventions and recommendations.

The Migration for Employment Convention (Revised) (97) and Recommendation (Revised) (86) of 1949 are the most widely accepted ILO instruments concerning migrant workers. The convention grants free information (Art. 2); forbids false advertising of job opportunities (Art. 3); facilitates the departure, the travel and arrival of migrant workers (Art. 4); imposes adequate medical services (Art. 5); and equality of treatment with nationals as to employment, participation with Trade Unions, and benefits of collective agreements (Art. 6). Three addenda, which can be excluded by governments at the time of ratification, detail additional norms on recruiting and work conditions. The convention, which did not reach all its objectives, applies only to dependent migrant workers legally admitted. Recommendation 86 includes also refugees and displaced persons, revealing the ambiguity of clear distinctions among people involved in human mobility.

The Migrant Workers (Supplementary Provisions) Convention (143) was adopted in 1975. It is the ILO response to the increasing phenomenon of irregular migration. The first part of the convention, in fact, applies also to irregular migrants and invites states to take the necessary measures to suppress clandestine trafficking of workforce and employment of irregular migrants as well as to impose sanctions on employers who hire irregular migrants. The second part of the convention aims at establishing equality of opportunity and treatment between migrants and nationals. Frontier workers, professionals, and seafarers are excluded, as in convention 97. Excluded also are students and migrants tied to a temporary project.

The codification of labor standards by the ILO reveals an evolution in two aspects. While maintaining the principle of the international standard, more emphasis has been placed recently by the ILO on the principle of equality of treatment. Secondly, the ideological approach to migration has been modified. In the Declaration of Philadelphia attached to the ILO statute migration was recognized as a means to attain full employment, and Recommendation 86 explicitly encouraged such exchange of work force. Recommendation 169 of 1984 instead invites the countries of immigration "to create more employment opportunities and better conditions of work in countries of emigration so as to reduce the need to migrate to find employment" (Art. 39, par. e).

A recent evolution within international discussion is toward linking labor standards to trade agreements [3]. It is an attempt of developed economies to ensure that developing countries do not gain unfair advantage through exploitation of workers. The attempt was defeated at the WTO 1996 conference in Singapore. However, it smacks of hypocrisy that a similar linkage between exploitation of migrants and unfair advantage for developed economies is not made.

Regional Instruments

The development of regional agreements for economic, social, and political benefits of the nations involved has proliferated after World War II, with contrasting results. Within regional areas, the facilitation of movement of people has always occupied a prominent place. Migrant workers have benefited from such agreements, whose scope, however, is limited only to persons belonging to the region. The most successful experiments of regional cooperation were accomplished in Europe. European international organizations have also produced juridical instruments concerning migration. The Council of Europe is responsible for some of the most relevant of such instruments. The European Convention on Establishment, adopted in 1955, is considered the first code of a statute of the foreigner and regulates practically all aspects concerning a foreigner resident in a European nation, except for the social aspects.

The void on social concerns in the Convention on Establishment was filled by the European Social Charter, adopted in 1961. Art. 19 is specifically devoted to the protection and assistance of migrant workers and their families and it is basically taken from ILO Convention 97. Par. 4 of Art. 19 is specifically relevant because it ensures equality of treatment with nationals in regard to remuneration and working conditions, membership in trade unions, and accommodation.

The most ambitious attempt to codify the protection of migrant workers was the European Convention on the Legal Status of Migrant Workers. Adopted by the Council of Europe in 1977 and entering into force in 1983, it intended to specify the minimum requirements accepted by all states concerning the statute of migrant workers. It intended to be a framework convention, referring to national or international instruments for the regulation of details. The convention does not apply to migrants from a country not a member of the Council of Europe, to those who are not in a regular situation, to the self-employed, and to those excluded by Art. 1 (2): frontier workers, seasonal workers, seafarers, trainees, artists, and sportsmen. In other words, it does not apply to the majority of migrant workers currently in Europe. Generally speaking, the convention confirms what was already provided in bilateral agreements among European countries, without proceeding further. Even though it does not impose heavy duties on states, only five countries have ratified it. This reflects the dominant reservation toward migration in Europe, subsequent to the restrictive policies adopted in 1973.

The most successful experiment of regional integration of sovereign states is that of the European Union. With the Treaty of Rome a process was initiated to overcome for the citizens of the member states the notion of foreigner in favor of that of "communitarian citizen." Equality of treatment with nationals is the guiding criterion for non-discrimination. Yet it is to be understood as a tendency to reach a higher standard for everyone through cooperation among states. The decisive improvement toward full freedom of movement was established by the Single European Act of July 1, 1987, which redefined the internal European market as an area without frontiers in which the free movement of goods, persons, services, and capital was to be encouraged and realized before January 1, 1993. The Maastricht Treaty, however, recognized the difficulty of implementing freedom of movement for migrants, and the need to introduce coordination in regard to admission of migrants from non-European Union countries. The image of a fortress Europe was not dismantled by the Schengen Accord (1995). Of the four original freedoms established as an objective by the Treaty of Rome, freedom of movement for persons remains the one still not fully implemented, since police controls at the borders still remain [4].

HUMANITARIAN LAW

The protection of migrants as aliens in the territory of another state relies on international law which has not yet been codified, which remains entangled in the conflict between national and international standards, and which does not apply to irregular migrants. The protection afforded by labor instruments, such as those of the ILO, depends on the international adherence to those instruments, still scarce, or on bilateral and multilateral treaties, binding only the states concerned. For a wider perspective ensuring the widest protection and political agreement a foundation on a more common level is necessary: the migrant considered not as an alien or a worker but as a human person, protected as such by the humanitarian law.

The rights expressed in the International Bill of Human Rights are everyone's rights, foreigners included except when explicitly provided otherwise. The general principle which grants the rights also to foreigners is the principle of non-discrimination, which forbids discrimination on the basis of nationality. Even though nationality is not a synonym of citizenship, discrimination on the basis of citizenship must still be considered contrary to the Declaration, unless specifically provided otherwise. Foreigners are explicitly excluded from political rights and from the right to re-enter the country in which they are foreigners.

The articles of the Covenants more directly concerning migrants are Art. 12 and 13 of the International Covenant on Civil and Political Rights. Art. 12 concerns the right to leave any state and provides the foundation for the right to migrate. Restrictions to this right must be provided by law and must be necessary to protect national security, public order, public health or morals, or the rights and freedoms of others. Some of these terms maintain a degree of uncertainty in their interpretation which justifies different migration restrictive practices.

To the right to leave a state there is no correspondent right to enter another state. Thus, a restrictive immigration policy empties the right to leave of its substance. However, increasing consensus is growing on freedom of movement across borders as a long-term goal. In fact, the goal of liberal democracy is "to create a world in which movement is generally voluntary rather than enforced by adverse social and political conditions."[1] It is still utopian thinking, but not incompatible with a world divided in a plurality of states. The principle of state sovereignty, without which "a society has no control over its basic character" [5, p. 14], must be mitigated by the principle of interdependence and cooperation. Furthermore, if states are not obliged to admit particular individuals or categories of people, they do have a general duty to admit foreigners in their territory.

The right to leave, defined also as the right to vote with one's feet, is accompanied by the right to return. On the discussion whether the right to return is an individual right, humanitarian law and practice among states have led to the conclusion that "a state's duty to admit its national to its territory is not merely the corollary of each other state's right to expel aliens. . . . The duty of admission is also a reflection of the individual's right to return to his own country and reside therein" [6, p. 137].

After protection of the right to migrate and to return, a basic right concerns protection against, or in case of, expulsion. Art. 13 provides that expulsion be subsequent to a decision reached in accordance with law and that the alien be allowed to submit the reasons against his expulsion and to have his case reviewed. The innovative aspect of human rights consists in the juridical relevance that the violation of human rights acquires for all states members, which recognize that, for maintaining peace, the protection of human rights coexists with the principle of non-intervention [1].

The International Bill of Human Rights has found regional expressions in the European Convention on Human Rights (1950), the American Convention on Human Rights (1968), and the African Charter on Human Rights (1981). These

---

[1] Rainer Bauböck, *Transnational Citizenship*, 1997.

instruments find inspiration in the Universal Declaration and repeat the principle of non-discrimination and the tendency to overcome the distinction between citizens and non-citizens. This distinction remains for the right to enter a country, which is reserved only to citizens, for political rights, and for protection against expulsion. It is forbidden to expel citizens; it is not forbidden to expel aliens as long as it is done in accordance with law. Regional instruments prohibit collective expulsion (a prohibition not present in the Covenant). The African Charter, however, specifies that "mass expulsion shall be that which is aimed at national, social, ethnic, or religious groups" (Art. 12, 5). Thus, freedom of mass expulsion of migrant workers is maintained as long as they do not belong to just one specific national, racial, ethnic, or religious group.

THE UN CONVENTION ON THE RIGHTS OF MIGRANTS

The most recent and ambitious attempt by the international community to ensure the protection of migrant workers is the International Convention on the Protection of the Rights of All Migrant Workers and Members of Their Families adopted by the United Nations in December 1990. The convention finds its origin in three growing concerns in the 1970s: the spreading of irregular migration, the increase of racial discrimination and the lack of respect for human rights. Initiated in 1980, the drafting process was completed in 1990 and the convention is comprised of a Preamble and 93 articles, distributed in nine parts. From the initial concern for irregular migrants, the convention has broadened its scope to include all migrants, in a regular or irregular situation, regardless of the temporary or permanent nature of migration, and including special categories which were usually left out in previous instruments. The large scope of the convention has forced the distribution of provisions in parts which progressively limit the range of people covered by the convention.

Irregular migrants are protected by the convention insofar as the convention reaffirms their human rights which apply to everyone. Irregular migrants, in fact, are people living within a group without the group's authorization. Their protection has to come from rights that are not given because of legal status but because migrants are human beings. Human rights are precisely those that are invoked when no appeal is possible to positive rights. Normally, they are the last resource [7], but for the irregular migrants they are the only resource.

The human rights listed in the 28 articles of Part III of the Convention are basically taken from the Covenant on Civil and Political Rights, often reproducing that text verbatim, and apply also to irregular migrants. Additional rights are granted to migrants who are in a regular situation, or to special categories of migrants, such as frontier workers, seasonal workers, project-tied workers, and self-employed workers. The Convention also elaborates on specific recommendations to facilitate the promotion of sound, equitable, humane, and lawful conditions in connection with international migration. As with other UN instruments, it provides for a committee for the purpose of reviewing the application of the Convention. Twenty ratifications are needed before the Convention enters into force.

MIGRANTS IN THE RECENT CONCERNS OF THE UNITED NATIONS

Establishing standards was not the only way the international community through the United Nations approached the issue of migration. A whole effort through resolutions, declarations, and international conferences has continued to develop, particularly in this decade. Such effort, if lacking the efficacy which derives from legislation, achieves results in terms of progress in conceptualization and understanding. It is often the result of concerns and ideas expressed by the grass root movements and in turn provides support for additional action by such movement.

The World Conference on Human Rights (Vienna, 1993) where major concerns on the issue of human rights were discussed, such as the universality, indivisibility, and the international responsibility for human rights, did not devote much attention to the specific situation of migrants. In the Declaration, it is recommended that great importance be given to "the promotion and protection of the human rights of persons belonging to groups which have been rendered vulnerable, including migrant workers" (para. 24). The explicit mention of migrant workers singles them out as a particularly vulnerable category. However, the language is very general. The three paragraphs in the Program of Action (paras. 33-35) also contain general language focusing on the need for protection, for harmony and tolerance within the host society, and for the need to ratify the Migrants Workers Convention.

The Declaration adopted by the International Conference on Population and Development (Cairo, 1994) dedicated two sections to migration, which is inserted in the wider issue of development. In that regard, migrants should first of all have the option to remain in their country of origin. Such option is a real possibility, only if there is more balance in the development of economies at the international level. This opens the discussion on the controversial right to development and its relevance for migrants [8]. Certainly, migrant workers, compelled as they are to seek work abroad, are a clear indication of the lack of possibility for development in their own country. If from a neo-liberal economic perspective migration can be considered just a natural way for the system to find its own equilibrium, from the perspectives of the hardships and abuse suffered by migrants migration compelled by necessity appears a distorted way to achieve development. For documented migrants the Cairo conference recommends equality of treatment with nationals, integration and family reunification, and respect for basic human rights. For undocumented migrants it recommends is cooperation to reduce the causes of undocumented migration, sanctions against those who traffic in migrants, better information on the conditions to enter, stay and work in a foreign country, and responsibility in accepting undocumented migrants who have been repatriated.

The World Summit for Social Development (Copenhagen, 1995) considered migration in relation to full employment and social integration. The recommendations repeat those made at the conference in Cairo. In addition, there is an explicit recommendation to provide migrants with long-term residence permits, access to civil and political rights and responsibilities and to ensure the protection of undocumented migrants, particularly against racism, ethnocentrism, and xenophobia. Such recommendations do not break new ground, as some European countries already provide long-term migrants with political rights at least at the administrative level. However, what is relevant is the reaffirmation of principles which in the long run become useful to form a mentality.

The Platform for Action of the Fourth World Conference on Women (Beijing, 1995) contains extensive mention of migrant women, particularly women migrant workers. Recommendations concern the full realization of human rights, awareness of their rights, empowerment, facilitation of productive employment, access to literacy and education and recognition of skills and credentials. However, the text can be considered disappointing, as migrant women are in most cases mentioned together with other categories of vulnerable groups. The disappointment is perhaps more significant because women migrant workers have significantly increased in number in recent years and in several countries, particularly in Asia, they are the majority of migrants. Women no longer migrate simply as the spouse or relative of male migrants, but they are the migrants originating the process. In this regard, specific attention must be devoted to the protection of migrant women, not simply because they are more vulnerable, but also because of the specificity which derives from the condition of women as migrants.

Specific attention to the vulnerability of migrant women derived as a corollary of the concern on violence against women is recognized in the Declaration on the Elimination of Violence against Women (General Assembly Resolution 48/104). It received the widest attention at the UN Expert Group Meeting on violence against women migrant workers (Resolution 50/168) held in Manila, May 27-31, 1996. At the meeting it was recognized that statistics for measuring violence are not compiled comprehensively or regularly. Two occupations that increase the risk of violence are domestic service and entertainment-related services. Specifically, domestic workers are, in many instances, unprepared, unprotected, and therefore open to exploitation and violent treatment. Six areas of intervention were identified: conventions, legislation, government control of processes, supervision, preparation and empowerment of the women, and support to NGOs including self-help groups [9]. At the same time, the meeting explored the possibility of arriving at a list of indicators to measure violence in the economic, social/psychological, and physical/sexual areas [10].

The limits of United Nations action in regard to migration originate from the fact that migration implies crossing borders, and the protection of borders has been perceived as one of the most jealous prerogatives of the nation state. As a consequence, migration policies have always been recognized as pertaining to the sovereignty of the state. An international organization such as the United Nations is rather helpless when it comes to influencing migration policies. The disappointing status of the Migrant Workers Convention, only ratified by nine countries eight years after being adopted by the UN General Assembly, speaks volumes on the practical acceptance of an international regime on migration. At the same time, the strongest attack on the independence of each country in determining migration policies has originated from the recognition and importance of human rights. Because individuals are recognized as bearers of human rights, which are universal, not granted by the state, and inherent to the individual, nations do not have absolute discretion on migrants. Several commentators have indicated that a tradition of respect for human rights constitutes an obstacle to the despotic management of migration in liberal societies.[2] Migration demands an international approach and to be managed by an international regime.

THE CONCERN OF CIVIL SOCIETY FOR MIGRATION

In the presence of insufficient protection granted by the state, a variety of organizations of different nature have become involved in the issue of migration. Such organizations encompass migrant associations, particularly in receiving countries, NGOs in receiving countries or countries of origin—specifically established for migrants or with a wider interest, such as human rights or women organizations, but embracing also the concern for migrants—and people's organizations. Directories of organizations involved with migration can be voluminous and express the variety of activities they carry out. In Europe, such a directory lists more than 1,800 organizations, with primary interests in migration issues, solidarity aspects, human rights and research, or documentation on migration [11]. Issues concerning migrants have also become an occasion to discover the inter-connectiveness of problems traversing our society and the need to look at issues from a variety of perspectives. Sometimes, these organizations have reached some form of networking and multiple membership is not rare.

The relevance of the role of NGOs was recognized in the Chapter XV of the Program of Action of the Cairo conference. Direct services by NGOs to migrants cover the whole migration process, from information services before departure, to

---

[2] Wayne Cornelius, James Hollifield, and Philip Martin, *Controlling Immigration*, 1996.

services to orient and help new arrivals to settle, and to help in the reintegration process, particularly through counseling. Furthermore, "they are constructive voices in legislative and intergovernmental meetings on policies and programs concerning international migration. . . . They are well positioned to promote the ratification and implementation of international conventions" (UN Doc. E/CN.9/1997/5).

The preoccupation of NGOs for the protection of the rights of migrants is widespread. This is particularly evident among NGOs operating in areas of new immigration, such as Asia, where the need to respond to emergencies is particularly felt.[3] The combat of illegal recruiting, shelter for abused women, legal counseling, and livelihood programs are the main areas of NGO interventions. However, also in countries of traditional immigration and where basic rights are guaranteed to migrants, furthering the promotion of migrants' rights is a primary objective.

The need to promote the protection of migrants in all countries has also generated the coalescing of concerns and initiatives at the international level, to the point of establishing the International Migrants Rights Watch Committee (IMRWC). Spurred by the concern of the migration office of the World Council of Churches, IMRWC was established during the Cairo conference in 1994. It counts approximately thirty members from all over the world, with a secretariat in Geneva. A recent initiative (March 20, 1998) of IMRWC was the launching of a campaign for the ratification of the Migrant Workers Convention. A similar initiative at the regional or local level had already received attention from local NGOs. The Philippine Migrant Rights Watch (PMRW) was instrumental in lobbying for the ratification of the convention by the Philippines. Last year it joined forces with the Asian Partnership in International Migration (APIM) to launch last year December 18 (the day on which the Migrant Workers Convention was ratified) as an international day of solidarity with migrants. The initiative aims at calling attention to the problems of migrants and specifically to the need to ratify the Migrant Workers Convention as a basic instrument to ensure the protection of the rights of migrants.

The important role of NGOs in the promotion of human rights was recognized by the Vienna Declaration, appreciative of their contribution "to increasing public awareness of human rights issues, to the conduct of education, training and research in this field and to the promotion and protection of all human rights and fundamental freedoms." Unfortunately, the power of NGOs rests solely on their capacity to "mobilize shame." This objective requires the capacity to link and network, so as to increase the relevance of organizations which are mostly small and with limited means.

---

[3] SMC, Directory of NGOs for Migrants in Asia. Quezon City: Scalabrini Migration Center, 1997.

CONCLUSION

Concern for the rights of migrants comprises several aspects: furthering the establishment of standards to cover categories of migrants who are still unprotected or aspects of the migration process still neglected; to ensure the ratification of available instruments; and to ensure the effective implementation of instruments.

In terms of additional coverage to be provided to migrants, the specific situation of migrant women was highlighted [12]. The Migrant Workers Convention fails to address gender-based vulnerability and specifically violence perpetrated against migrant women. It also fails to acknowledge and address the actual differentiation existing between men's work and women's work. Specific issues concerning the second generation of migrants were also neglected in the Convention. The distinction between documented and undocumented migrants also amounted to limitation of human rights, such as the right of association, which are fully guaranteed in other instruments.

Even more important than ensuring coverage of specific categories of migrant workers, what is needed is ratification of existing instruments. In this regard, instruments concerning migrants show a disheartening history of ratification. ILO Convention 97 has been ratified by forty-nine countries, while Convention 143 has received seventeen ratifications. Furthermore, only nine countries have become members of the Migrant Workers Convention and they are only countries of origin of migration (Egypt, Morocco, Uganda, Cape Verde, Colombia, Seychelles, Sri Lanka, Philippines, and Bosnia and Herzegovina). Although migrants suffer violations of human rights also in countries of origin, it is particularly while in the receiving country that they experience abuse. The prospect of major receiving countries becoming parties to the Convention is not rosy. The most used arguments are that either they are not concerned with the Convention as they mostly receive immigrants, or that the Convention bestows too many rights on undocumented migrants. In reality, the Convention is suffering from the restrictive climate toward migrants which has been developing in the last fifteen years, with the decline of the welfare state.

Finally, even if instruments are ratified, what remains crucial for effective protection is implementation. International conventions are as effective as the monitoring system put in place to supervise their application. In this regard, while ILO monitoring mechanisms is usually praised as quite effective, the same is not said of UN instruments. The Migrant Workers Convention establishes a committee, which examines the reports submitted by the states and sends comments to the states. For the states which recognize its competence the committee also considers claims made by states or individuals on the non-application of the convention. The state and individual complaint procedures are optional and the committee can at most present an opinion. Such a mechanism is considered weak and inadequate [13].

If lacking direct effectiveness, international conventions play, nevertheless, a role as moral force which indicates the direction that protection of people and rights should take. The same role is also played by human right instruments for which attribution of a decisive contribution to international protection is increasingly recognized. International law, in fact, remains problematic because of the difficulty in ascertaining the meaning of the provisions of international treaties and because of the uncertainty as to whether a certain international treaty contains actually valid rules of international law binding upon the signatories. Humanitarian law does not improve in the fundamental aspects in which international law is deficient: "compulsory jurisdiction, hierarchy of judicial decisions and the application of the rule of *stare decisis*, at least to the decisions of the highest court" [14, p. 303]. But humanitarian law tends to be founded not "on the will of states or any other legislative measure, nor internationally, on treaty or convention in which the express or tacit consent of states constitutes the essential element, but in the conscience of mankind" [15, p. 69]. It is the same as concluding that international norms dealing with human rights have the character of *ius cogens*.

Even if far from completed, a process is evolving in which "the criterion of citizenship as a requisite for the substantial and jurisdictional protection of the rights of the person has been overcome" [1]. If human rights exist independently of and before the state, no state can freely dispose of the rights of its own nationals and aliens must not be deprived of fundamental human rights. This entails some "world law" dealing with human rights and having a universal character, which limits the sovereignty of the member states. It also implies the candid recognition of the interest of the organized international community or "Universal Common Good" [15]. Humanitarian law does not add to the rights of the migrant nor does it make him a subject in international law, since he remains the object of the norms [16]; however, it constitutes a limit to the absolute power of the state [17], and it peculiarly concerns migrant workers, whose protection requires the self- limitation of such power. Because of its moral rather than juridical force, humanitarian law relies heavily on public opinion to be effective. And even if world public opinion, from a realist point of view, is just a myth [14], it plays a powerful role in today's politics. Here is where non-governmental organizations find ample room for action; here is where practical responses must be found to the question: what can be done to protect the rights of migrant workers? The question is not only raising increasing interest not only in migrants' associations and organizations. The United Nations Commission on Human Rights has addressed it by establishing an intergovernmental working group of experts on the human rights of migrants (Resolution 1997/15). Preliminary findings by the working group have indicated that the issue is of interest for many countries, since "the number of responses (40, with more expected) to the questionnaire had been unprecedented" (UN Doc. E/CN.4/1998/76). More than one-third of the countries acknowledged the presence of problems concerning prejudice, xenophobia, or racial discrimination. Vulnerability is the common ground for all migrants and "the experts agreed that an essential element in the understanding of vulnerability was the factor of powerlessness" (UN Doc. E/CN.4/1998/76).

Nation states somehow must come to grips with the growing contradiction that is evolving in our days. While they relinquish growing portions of their power over economic matters to international organizations and quasi-governmental institutions, they maintain official control over the circulation of labor, a control increasingly eroded by irregular flows of workers and illegal activities of recruiters and traffickers. "The existence of two very different regimes for the circulation of capital and the circulation of immigrants poses problems that cannot be solved through the old rules of the game" [18]. It might be time to recognize that international migration requires a coordinated international approach, based on the recognition and protection of migrants' human rights.

REFERENCES

1. B. Nascimbene, *Il trattamento dello straniero nel diritto internazionale ed europeo,* Giuffré Editore, Milano, 1984.
2. F. V. Garcia-Amador, L. B. Sohn, and R. R. Baxter, *Recent Codification of the Law of State Responsibility for Injuries to Aliens,* Oceania Publications, New York, 1974.
3. R. Castle, C. Nyland, and D. Kelly, International Migration and Labor Regulation, *Asian Migrant, 10*:3, 1997.
4. V. Palumbo, La realizzazione della libera circolazione delle persone negli Stati parte dell'Unione Europea e la politica di asilo, *Gli Stranieri, 4*:1, 1997.
5. A. Dowty, *Closed Borders,* Yale University Press, New Haven, 1987.
6. R. Plender, *International Migration Law,* Martins Nijhoff Publishers, Dordrecht, 1988.
7. J. Donnelly, *Universal Human Rights in Theory and Practice,* Cornell University Press, Ithaca, 1989.
8. R. Cholewinski, *Migrant Workers in International Human Rights Law,* Clarendon Press, Oxford, 1997.
9. D. Cox, The Vulnerability of Asian Women Migrant Workers to a Lack of Protection and to Violence, *Asian and Pacific Migration Journal, 6*:1, 1997.
10. N. M. Shah and I. Menon, Violence Against Women Migrant Workers: Issues, Data and Partial Solutions, *Asian and Pacific Migration Journal, 6*:1, 1997.
11. CIEMI, *Répertoire des Associations Immigrées et de Solidarité dans l'Union Européenne,* CIEMI, Paris, 1994.
12. S. Hune, Migrant Women in the Context of the International Convention on the Protection of the Rights of All Migrant Workers and Members of Their Families, *International Migration Review, 25*:4, 1991.
13. V. P. Nanda, The Protection of the Rights of Migrant Workers: Unfinished Business, in *Human Rights of Migrant Workers: Agenda for NGOs,* Graziano Battistella (ed.), Scalabrini Migration Center, Quezon City, 1993.

14. H. J. Morgenthau and K. W. Thompson, *Politics Among Nations,* Alfred A. Knopf, New York, 1985.
15. Y. Saito, Humanity Transcends Sovereignty, in *Congress on International Solidarity and Humanitarian Action,* International Institute of Humanitarian Law, San Remo, 1980.
16. R. Chiroux, "Les travailleurs etrangers et le development des relations internationales," in *Societé Francaise pour le Droit International, Les travailleurs etrangers et le droit itnernational,* Editions A. Pedone, Paris, 1979.
17. B. H. Weston, Human Rights, in *Human Rights in the World Community: Issues and Action,* R. C. Claude and B. H. Weston (eds.), University of Pennsylvania Press, Philadelphia, 1989.
18. S. Sassen, *Transnational Economies and National Migration Policies,* IMES, Amsterdam, 1995.

Chapter 16

Homelessness and the Right to Adequate Housing: Confronting Exclusion, Sustaining Change

Miloon Kothari

More and more people and communities in today's world are forced to live in varying degrees of inadequate and insecure housing and living conditions. Ranging from sheer homelessness to inadequate shelter, people are forced to live on the margins, separated from natural resources, from economic opportunities, and in situations lacking the social cohesiveness essential for peaceful societies.

Many questions arise from this abysmal state of affairs. Where and in what conditions do people and communities live? What kinds of social and community relations are developed? What bases of ethnic and social conflict, violence, and distrust of governance are being created by such existence on the margins? What is the cost of such disintegration of social cohesiveness? And, most pertinently, what perspective, what type of culture and value system is necessary to tackle this enormous problem? Is such denial of a secure housing and living environment seen as a denial of people's fundamental human rights, of the inalienable right to security of home and community, of the dignity of the individual, and the collective right of the community?

Consider the overall numbers: Between a fifth and a quarter of the world's population live in absolute poverty, without adequate food, clothing, and shelter. The number of homeless people, those who have no shelter at all, is estimated at 100 million. If we include all those that are living in inadequate housing and living conditions the estimate goes up to 1 billion.[1] In the countries of the

---

[1] For a discussion on the extent of the homelessness worldwide, see *An Urbanizing World: Global Report on Human Settlements 1996,* United Nations Centre on Human Settlements (UNCHS), Oxford University Press for UNCHS. As the study points out the estimates of homelessness vary from 100 million to 1 billion depending on how homelessness is defined.

European Union it is estimated that between 2.3 million and 2.7 million people are homeless over the course of the year.[2] In the United States current estimates are that on any given night over 700,000 persons are homeless—living in public places or in emergency shelters. Over a year, some 2 million are homeless.[3]

Consider further the following types of some contemporary forms of distressed housing: cages (Hong Kong); buses and shipping containers (Israel and Occupied Palestine); pavements (India and Bangladesh); cellars, staircases, containers, and rooftops (Europe); street children (across Asia, Africa, Latin America, and Eastern Europe); and streets and cardboard boxes (United States).

The contention of this chapter is that an overarching human rights approach, as expressed in the Universal Declaration of Human Rights (UDHR), and a specific housing and land rights approach afford a valuable entry point to grapple with the crisis of deteriorating housing and living conditions being faced by dwellers in most countries of the world today. The principles of human rights and the empowering provisions contained in the various international human rights instruments offer the most promising perspective for designing interventions to comprehend and overcome the crisis.

Such a holistic perspective rooted in the dignity of the individual and the collective identity of the community is necessary because the assault that is taking place on the space and place where people live is multidimensional. This assault not only impacts on the house, the four walls, and the roof, but also through the targeting of the home, undermines life itself. It violates the basic right to a place to live and the basic right of people and communities to gain and sustain an adequate standard of living.

Such a broad perspective[4] calls for housing and land rights to be viewed within the following inviolable principles derived from international human rights instruments: the rule of law; non-discrimination and equality; self-determination; the right to information; the right to a healthy living environment; democratic participation; equality in land relations; gender equality; economic parity; the maintenance of cultural identity and skills and the democratic role of the government. In the current crisis state of housing, land, and living conditions, all of the above principles are compromised.

---

[2] This figure is based on an exhaustive survey, of the fifteen countries that made up the European Union in 1995, by the European Observatory on Homelessness as cited in, Dragana Avramov, *Homelessness in the European Union: Social Exclusion in the 1990's*, FEANTSA (European Federation of National Organizations Working with the Homeless), Brussels, 1995.

[3] See Written statement submitted by the National Law Center on Homelessness and Poverty (Washington, United States) and Habitat International Coalition to the UN Commission on Human Rights (U.N. doc. E/CN.4/1997/NGO/46).

[4] For a definition of the right to housing that flows from this understanding, see discussion under the section, "Toward a definition of the essential components of the right to housing."

This chapter also argues that the many civil society initiatives at local and national levels since the mid-eighties have spurred the enhancement of housing rights in international human rights instruments and UN bodies. In some cases UN bodies, emboldened by the spirited partnership of civil society groups, have adopted instruments and pronouncements that have directly benefitted vulnerable communities. The task that remains is to publicize these developments, to devise human rights education based on these standards and strategies and to keep up the pressure so that institutions, such as those in the UN system, can continue to play a supportive role for the defense and realization of the right to housing.

MEASURES THAT PROMOTE EXCLUSION AND VIOLENCE

The following have been identified as contributing to the housing and living conditions crisis and to the failure of state responsibility: Insecurity of home, land, and person; misuse of planning mechanisms; abuse of law; denial of essential civic services; inability to control market forces; prevalence of forced evictions; economic globalization; the loss of common property resources; ghettoization and segregation; and non-compliance with national and international legal human rights instruments.

The consequences of these phenomena include growing marginalization and alienation of the poor and the disadvantaged; the creation of ethnic conflict; the creation of landlessness and homelessness; and increase of those living in health and life-threatening conditions and the deleterious impact on women. For a description of these phenomenon and their consequences, see [1].

They point to a lack of governance and a severe default of government obligations to promote and protect housing as a human right. Cumulatively, their continued prevalence points to a failure of governance that leads to exclusion, dispossession, and violence becoming endemic to societies. This colossal failure has also led throughout the world to the institutionalization of insecure and inadequate housing and living conditions [1, p. 6].

INTERNATIONAL INSTRUMENTS AND THE RIGHT TO HOUSING

The right to housing has received detailed articulation over the past ten years by various social movements across the world. The relevant UN bodies, primarily the UN Committee on Economic, Social and Cultural Rights (CESCR), have substantiated the content of the right based both on the work done by civil society groups and on the fact that the right to housing has been firmly entrenched in international human rights instruments following the adoption of the UDHR in 1948.[5]

The Declaration in Article 25(1) states that: "Everyone has the right to a standard of living adequate for the health and well-being of himself and of his family, including food, clothing, housing and medical care and the necessary social services, and the right to security in the event of unemployment, sickness, disability, widowhood, old age or other lack of livelihood in circumstances beyond his control."

The most comprehensive article on the right to housing, evolving out of the basis established in the UDHR, is contained in Article 11(1) of the International Covenant on Economic, Social and Cultural Rights: "The States Parties to the present Covenant recognise the right of everyone to an adequate standard of living for himself and his family, including adequate food, clothing and housing and to the continuous improvement of living conditions."

International instruments also confer rights to housing on particular groups, in particular women, and children. The Convention on the Elimination of All Forms of Discrimination Against Women, Article 14(2)(h) states: "States Parties shall take all appropriate measures to eliminate discrimination against women in rural areas in order to ensure, on a basis of equality of men and women, that they participate in and behalf from rural development and, in particular, shall ensure to such women the right . . . (h) to enjoy adequate living conditions, particularly in relation to housing, sanitation, electricity and water supply, transport and communications."

The Convention on the Rights of the Child in article 27(3) urges that: "State Parties, in accordance with national conditions and within their means, shall take appropriate measures to assist parents and others responsible for the child to implement this right and shall in case of need provide material assistance and support programs, particularly with regard to nutrition, clothing and housing. Article 16(1) of the Convention is also relevant as it recognises that 'No child shall be subjected to arbitrary or unlawful interference with his or her privacy, family, home or correspondence, nor to unlawful attacks on his or her honour and reputation'."

Also valuable, in a growing climate of racial and ethnic divisions across the world, are provisions in the International Convention on the Elimination of All Forms of Racial Discrimination, especially articles 5 (c) (iii) that embody a binding agreement among states to recognize and uphold "the right of everyone . . . to equality before the law, notably in the enjoyment of the . . . right to housing" and Article 3 that places an obligation upon States to "particularly

---

[5] For a comprehensive listing of sources of legal recognition of housing rights, see Centre on Housing Rights and Evictions (COHRE), *Legal Provisions on Housing Rights: National and International Approaches,* COHRE, Netherlands, 1994, revised 1998. Also see United Nations Centre for Human Rights, Human Rights Fact Sheet no. 21, *The Human Right to Adequate Housing,* 1993.

condemn racial segregation and apartheid and undertake to prevent, prohibit and eradicate all practices of this nature in territories under their jurisdiction."

Although legally not in the same category as international human rights treaties, valuable provisions also exist regarding housing, living conditions, and land rights in numerous international declarations and recommendations.[6]

LEGAL INTERPRETATIONS OF THE RIGHT TO HOUSING BY CESCR

In December 1991 the Committee on Economic, Social and Cultural Rights adopted its General Comment No. 4 on the right to adequate housing (hereafter G.C. 4). This is the first General Comment adopted on a specific right contained in the Covenant and indicates the importance given to the right by the Committee.[7] G.C. 4 is at the international level, the single most authoritative legal interpretation of the right to housing and forms a significant advance in developing international jurisprudence on this right.

A critical dimension of the right to housing identified in G.C. 4 is the relevance of recognizing both the holistic conception of the right and the value it gains from the concept of adequacy. The Committee views the right to housing as comprising not only a roof or being viewed as a commodity but a right that should be seen as the right to live in security, peace, and dignity.[8]

The General Comment identified seven aspects of the right to housing: (a) Legal security of tenure including legal protection against forced evictions; (b) Availability of services, materials, facilities and infrastructure essential for health, security, comfort and nutrition; (c) Affordable Housing including the provision of housing subsidies for those unable to obtain affordable housing; (d) Habitable housing with adequate protection from cold, damp, heat, rain, wind, or other threats to health, structural hazards, and disease vectors; (e) Accessible housing with priority consideration for such disadvantaged groups as the elderly, children, the physically disabled, the terminally ill, HIV-positive individuals,

---

[6] Of particular relevance are the Declaration on Social Progress and Development (1969, Part I article 6 and Part II article 10(1)), the Vancouver Declaration on Human Settlements (1976, Section III (8) and Chapter II (A.3)), the Declaration on the Right to Development (1986, Article 8(1)), the Declaration on Race and Racial Prejudice (Article 9(2)), and the Istanbul Declaration and the Habitat Agenda (1996, Chapter II, Section 26 and Chapter IIIA (Section 39 and 40).

[7] UN Committee on Economic, Social and Cultural Rights, "General Comment No. 4 on the Right to Adequate Housing (Article 11 of the Covenant)," adopted on 12 December 1991 (E/1992/23, pp. 114-120).

[8] The formulation used by the Committee: "The right to housing should be interpreted as . . . 'the right to live somewhere in security and dignity' is clearly inspired by the formulation of the Indian National Campaign on Housing Rights which defined the right as: "The right of every woman, man and child to a place to live in security and dignity" [Draft Approach Paper: Towards a People's Bill of Housing Rights" (final draft), April 1990, Calcutta, India].

persons with persistent medical problems, the mentally ill, victims of natural disasters, and people living in disaster-prone areas; (f) Housing at an adequate location allowing access to employment options, health care services, schools, childcare centers, and other social facilities; (g) Culturally adequate housing assuring that expressions of cultural identity and diversity of housing are enabled.[9]

In 1996 the CESCR adopted General Comment 7 entitled "Forced Evictions" which clarified the conditions and consequences of the most dislocating and destructive of housing rights violations. In this legal interpretation, of article 11(1) of the Covenant on Economic, Social and Cultural Rights, the Committee defines the practice of forced evictions and identifies the following as suffering disproportionately from the practice of forced evictions: Women, children, youth, older persons, indigenous people, ethnic and other minorities and other vulnerable individuals and groups.[10]

THE UNITED NATIONS SUB-COMMISSION ON THE PREVENTION OF DISCRIMINATION AND PROTECTION OF MINORITIES

In August 1992 the Sub-Commission appointed Justice Rajindar Sachar from India as the UN Special Rapporteur on promoting the realization of the right to adequate housing. His working paper of 1992 identified the following root causes of the prevalence of housing crises: the failure of government policies, discrimination in the housing sphere, structural adjustment programs and debt, poverty and the deprivation of means and forced evictions.

Justice Sachar presented from 1992 to 1995 four reports to the Sub-Commission.[11] In 1993 he presented his First Progress Report focusing on the nature of governmental obligations regarding the right to housing. This report has contributed to furthering the understanding of how economic, social, and cultural rights can be realized and what actions governments are expected to undertake, and what processes they are supposed to halt, so that these rights can be gained and retained.

The Special Rapporteur's Second Progress Report, presented in 1994, included a draft convention on the right to housing. This report also discusses

[9] See note 7, article 8.

[10]UN doc. E/C.12/1997/4. General Comment 7 of the Committee on Economic, Social and Cultural Rights entitled: "The right to adequate housing (art. 11.1 of the Covenant): forced evictions."

[11]See Working Paper, First and Second Progress Reports and Final Report of the UN Special Rapporteur on the Right to Adequate Housing (UN Doc. no's: E/CN.4/Sub.2/1992/15; E/CN.4/Sub.2/1993/15; E/CN.4/Sub.2/1994/20; and E/CN.4/Sub.2/1995/12). The Final report is also available as *The Right to Adequate Housing,* UN Centre for Human Rights, Study Series #7, United Nations, New York and Geneva, 1996.

twelve misconceptions and misinterpretations to which the right to housing is subject. The final report submitted to the Sub-Commission in August 1995 contains a framework for identifying principles and indicators for the right to housing as well as recommendations for UN system-wide action on the right. In a departure from the normal practice of UN Special Rapporteurs in their final reports, Justice Sachar has also included detailed recommendations for civil society on various ways in which international legal instruments can be utilized by housing rights and anti-eviction struggles throughout the world.

The four-year work of the Special Rapporteur has made serious attempts to identify a series of elements of the right to housing that are justiciable and to project the need for sustained work on "preventive" rights so as to gain a grasp on the structural causes for the decline of housing and living conditions worldwide. The Special Rapporteur, in his final report, in a chapter devoted to the justiciability of housing rights, states that: "Based on the detailed analysis of the human right to adequate housing carried out by the Special Rapporteur since 1992, coupled with recent developments in this area, the following elements of this right must be viewed as inherently justiciable, whether in national, regional or international settings: a) Protection against arbitrary, unreasonable, punitive, or unlawful forced evictions and/or demolitions; b) Security of tenure; c) Non-discrimination and equality of access in housing; d) Housing affordability and accessibility; e) Tenants rights; f) The right to equality and equal protection and benefit of the law; g) Equality of access to land, basic civic services, building materials and amenities; h) equitable access to credit, subsidies, and financing on reasonable terms for disadvantaged groups; i) The right to special measures to ensure adequate housing for households with special needs or lacking necessary resources; j) The right to the provision of appropriate emergency housing to the poorest section of society; k) The right to participation within all aspects of the housing sphere; and l) The right to clean environment and safe and secure habitable housing."[12]

In this respect a more recent development is worth mentioning. The constitution of South Africa is the first to accord economic, social, and cultural rights, including the right to housing, justiciable status.[13] It remains to be seen whether such recognition in a national constitution will in any form empower the many grassroots groups working on housing and land rights in South Africa, particularly given the embrace by the current government of the neo-liberal economic model.

The Sub-Commission, spurred by NGO pressure to clarify further and initiate UN system-wide action on the need for the realization of housing rights of specific groups, has adopted significant resolutions on children and women's

---

[12]Final Report of the Special Rapporteur on the Right to Adequate Housing, note 11, para. 95.

[13]See Chapter 12, "Bill of Rights," Constitution of the Republic of South Africa, 1996.

rights to housing. These resolutions demonstrate the utility of the housing rights approach in addressing the basic survival and livelihood questions confronting different sectors of society. They detail, in their operative paragraphs, the role that the UN agencies and human rights mechanisms, can play in the realization of housing rights for women and children.[14]

CIVIL SOCIETY RESPONSE[15]

The past twelve years have seen the emergence of numerous national grassroots campaigns, networks, and movements on the right to housing and against forced evictions. Significant initiatives have been taken in India, the Philippines, Columbia, Hong Kong, Canada, and Great Britain. More recently such initiatives have emerged in Palestine, Israel, Panama, Dominican Republic, Nigeria Zimbabwe, and Brazil. Attention is also growing among coalitions of civil society organizations in South Africa, the United States, Italy, Peru, France, Kenya, and Mexico.

The activities of these campaigns and alliance-building initiatives have been diverse. Using as a fundamental basis the human right to adequate housing, their work has ranged from popular processes of drafting housing rights legislation (India, the Philippines), conceptual work on the content of the right to housing incorporating learning from vernacular languages and local understandings of the right (India, Palestine), launching a successful nationwide campaign to get the right to housing into national constitutions (Columbia, South Africa), forming campaigns and task forces of the urban poor to counter evictions (the Philippines, Brazil), collaboration on regional campaigns on urban land rights and against evictions (Latin America and the Caribbean and Asia), preparing through popular processes alternate development plans to counter insensitive government master plans (Israel) and preparing alternate reports for UN human rights treaty bodies (the Philippines, the Dominican Republic, Panama, Canada, Italy, Israel, Palestine, Mexico, Nigeria). All these groups have also conducted informa- tion and awareness campaigns through which they have attempted to mobilize

---

[14]For a text of the resolutions, see UN doc. no's E/CN.4/Sub.2/1997/19 entitled "Women and the right to adequate housing and to land and property" and E/CN.4/Sub.2/1994/8 entitled "Children and the right to adequate housing." For a discussion on the relevance of focussing attention on women and children, see Sachar final report, note 11, para. 45-52.

[15]For the purpose of this chapter, "civil society" is an overarching term that encompasses NGOs, community-based organizations (CBOs), and social movements such as campaigns. For clarity, the term NGO is sometimes used to connote an intermediary organization as opposed to a CBO which are organizations such as village-based or neighborhood associations or cooperatives. For a useful discussion on the range of actors involved in representing affected people and communities, see Deborah Eade, *Capacity Building: An Approach to People-Centered Development,* Oxfam (UK and Ireland), 1997.

national public opinion on the imperative of the human rights approach to tackling housing and land issues.[16]

Of particular importance is the work of the Indian National Campaign for Housing Rights (NCHR)[17] which on the basis of hundreds of meetings across the country, coordinated the drafting of the following proposed amendment to the Indian constitution:[18] "Adequate housing includes: (a) The right to reside in security and dignity; (b) The right to have the means of adequate shelter including land exclusively for the use of every family or group of families; (c) The right of equal access to any public service system or public distribution system; (d) The right to equitable distribution of common building material resources; (e) The right to be provided with necessary building materials where such building materials are not available as common natural resources; (f) The right to priority use, for personal domestic consumption, common natural resources including water, fuels and fodder; (g) The right to live in healthy, hygienic and safe living environment and (h) The right to information pertaining to adequate housing."

The process generated by the NCHR bill led to a nationwide debate on housing as a human right and brought together a diverse range of actors in civil society. Also notable as a mobilization instrument is the Jerusalem Declaration of the Palestine Housing Rights Movement (PHRM).[19] As recognized by the UN Special Rapporteur on the Right to Adequate Housing, this Declaration is a result of grassroots activism and collective effort that deserves recognition from groups across the world that are mobilizing on economic, social, and cultural rights.

INTERNATIONAL WORK

Utilizing the conceptual and practical basis of local-level and national-level housing rights work and the wide-ranging legal recognition accorded to the right to housing in international human rights law, the last decade has also seen Habitat International Coalition (HIC)[20] initiating global campaigns for housing rights and

---

[16]For information on these campaigns, write to the Habitat International Coalition—Housing Rights Committee (HIC-HRC) at 8, rue Gustave Moynier, 1202 Geneva. Tel/fax: 41.22.7388167. e-mail: <hic_hrc@iprolink.ch>. For a description of campaigning strategies, see HIC-HRC policy paper, "Campaigning for housing rights: strategies for awareness and mobilization," forthcoming, November 1998, Mexico.

[17]From the voluminous material generated by the campaign, see in particular the campaign publications on gender and housing, on the political economy of housing policy and on essential steps to be taken by the government to fulfil housing rights.

[18]National Campaign for Housing Rights, *The Housing Rights Bill,* July 1992, Bombay, India.

[19]See Palestine Housing Rights Movement, *The Jerusalem Declaration,* May 1995, Jerusalem. Reprinted in the final report of the Special Rapporteur on the right to adequate housing, note 11, annex II.

[20]HIC is a global movement of 350 civil society organizations from seventy countries. The HIC membership consists of groups working on a range of issues around human settlements, women's rights to property, land and inheritance, children's rights, land rights, environment, and evictions and displacement.

against forced evictions. The principle organ of HIC charged with coordinating and providing guidance in all areas of work related to the right to housing and forced evictions is its Housing Rights Committee (HRC).[21]

The current phase of the work of the HIC-HRC is leading toward a "national focus program,"[22] the main elements of which will be: (a) Training at local and national levels in the areas of campaigning; Women's rights and children's rights; Research and documentation; Law and legal activism; the United Nations system, Community finance; Fund-raising for NGO and CBO housing rights work; Upgrading of living conditions and use of appropriate building materials; Alternate planning strategies and strategies for regularization of land; (b) Lobbying, advocacy, and training work at the UN; (c) Regular visits to national focus countries to maintain contact with local groups and develop joint strategies for international work; (d) Fact-finding missions to highlight the situation in particular areas of a national focus country; (e) Coordination of exchange programs between activists and groups of national focus countries; (f) Solidarity work between countries to share strategies and experiences; and (g) Urgent actions on situations requiring rapid action at the international level.

Over the past eight years a number of local and national civil society groups have taken advantage, in collaboration with HIC, of the channels at the UN to publicize their causes internationally and to expose, and where possible minimize, the forces causing violations of the housing and land rights, including forced evictions, at home. These groups have utilized a number of strategies from directly testifying to preparing alternate reports for presentation at the UN.[23] The strategies developed have brought results. For a description of how the UN system can be utilized, see [2].

Based on information submitted by civil society organizations to the CESCR on the prevailing circumstance of evictions in Panama and the Dominican Republic, the Committee declared both these countries to be in violation of the Covenant on Economic, Social and Cultural Rights.[24] The subsequent exposure, combined with spirited mobilization work against the government policies in both countries by civil society groups, has led to a significant decrease in the

[21]The HIC-HRC membership consists primarily of CBOs and national level social movements, from fourteen countries.

[22]For a detailed consideration of this program, see "The Housing Rights Committee's National Focus Program" HIC-HRC, Mexico, 1997.

[23]The groups that have taken advantage of these channels are the Brazilian Movement in the Defense of Life, Brazil; COPADEBA (Committee for the Rights of the Barrio) and Ciudad Alternativa, Dominican Republic; Urban Poor Associates and the Urban Poor Task Force, Philippines; Palestinian Movement for Housing Rights, Palestine; Arab Co-ordinating Committee for Housing Rights in Israel; Unione Inquilini, Italy; Centre for Equality Rights and Accommodation, Canada; Habitat-Mexico and Casa y Ciudad, Mexico; ZWOSAG, Zambia; CONADEHUPA (National Commission of Human Rights in Panama) and CCS (Centro Capacitation Social), Panama and Shelter Rights Initiative, Nigeria.

[24]See UN Doc. no. E/C.12/1990/8 (p. 64, Dominican Republic) and E/C.12/1991/4 (p. 32 Panama), Reports of the Fifth and Sixth Sessions of the Committee on Economic, Social and Cultural Rights.

prevalence of forced evictions. The Committee continues to rebuke governments for the practice of forced evictions and to monitor the situation in the Philippines, Kenya, Panama, the Dominican Republic and Nigeria. Other countries that have received cautionary statements from the Committee, and have been dealt with firmly in the concluding observations that the Committee prepares after examining each country, are Italy, Mexico, Kenya, and Canada.

The resolutions of the Commission on Human Rights and its Sub-Commission[25] and the positions taken by the CESCR as well as the attempts made by groups such as the Habitat International Coalition and its members to disseminate these pronouncements to groups across the world have already resulted in the protection from planned evictions of at least 250,000 families, primarily in the Dominican Republic, Brazil, and Zambia.[26]

A recent development, which has led to an increase in the information being presented directly to the Committee, is the adoption at its eighth session in May 1993 of new rules of participation for NGOs. This unique procedure, which allows for direct NGO testimony to the Committee, creates the opportunity for human rights activists to participate in the Committee's work, to compile and present reports on violations of human rights and to share their experience in defending human rights, including strategies to confront forced evictions.[27]

TOWARD A DEFINITION OF THE ESSENTIAL COMPONENTS OF THE RIGHT TO HOUSING

The preceding discussion has demonstrated that the right to housing, like other human rights, is a complex and multifaceted right, given the scale of diversity that exists on how people devise their housing and living environments across the world.

It should be possible, nevertheless, to attempt a general yet comprehensive definition of the right to housing: "The right to adequate housing is the human right of every woman, man and child to gain and sustain a secure home and community in which to live in peace and dignity."[28]

Taking into account this definition and the contents of the right as put forward by civil society groups and the UN bodies that have elaborated on this right, the following content emerges: The gaining of security of tenure assuring

[25]See in particular UN Commission on Human Rights resolution 1993/77. For the text of this and other UN instruments against forced evictions, see UN Centre for Human Rights, *Forced Evictions,* Fact Sheet no. 25, United Nations, 1996.

[26]Estimate based on assessment by the groups from the Dominican Republic, Brazil, and Zambia as presented to the HIC-HRC annual meeting (1996), Valle de Bravo, Mexico.

[27]For the full text of the procedure, see "Committee on Economic, Social and Cultural Rights: Report of the Eighth Session," UN doc. E/C.12/1993/19.

[28]For a discussion of the reasoning behind this definition, see [3].

the right to reside and settle; The right not to be dispossessed from one's home and surroundings; The right to resettle for communities living in health-threatening environments; The right of equal access to civic services; The right to natural resources; The right to a healthy and safe environment; The right to required housing finance; The right to self-expression in all housing activity; The right to form local community-based organizations and the vesting of control over the production, distribution and regeneration of dwelling resources; and The right of gender equality in all dimensions of the housing process outlined above.

Such an overarching and holistic understanding of the human right to housing, as encompassing a broad range of entitlements and freedoms, resonates with a wide range of civil society groups that are struggling with the issues and imperatives around the right to a place to live.

LESSONS FOR PROMOTING AND SUSTAINING CHANGE

Following the work on the right to housing at all levels it is possible to delineate main elements and examples that have contributed to harmonious collaborative efforts among groups at local, national, regional, and international levels.

(a) The formation of campaigns on housing rights and against forced evictions: Very effective, these have been based on the trust gained through sustained work. Once the campaigns have formed, the HIC-HRC has worked alongside local groups to develop a "National Focus" program as described above. The campaigns are now self-sustaining and able to train others in the use of human rights principles, law, strategies, and forums. For example, two national campaigns have formed, the Arab Co-ordinating Committee on Housing Rights in Israel and the Palestine Housing Rights Movement in Palestine. Their activities include: grassroots human rights education; local monitoring of human rights violations; training on housing and land rights; publications, international dissemination of information on the situation in the area; and preparing reports and providing testimony for various United Nations bodies.

(b) Fact-finding missions by the HIC-HRC determine the state of housing and living conditions and report on the situation regarding forced evictions. These missions, and the coordination required from local organizations to plan the missions, have also contributed to identifying the need for "national focus" programs (The Dominican Republic, Palestine, Israel, Brazil, Turkey, and India). For example, in June 1997 a massive eviction of 8,000 to 10,000 families took place in Babrekar Nagar, Mumbai, India. The local HIC-HRC member, Youth for Unity and Voluntary Action (YUVA) immediately organized a HIC fact-finding mission. The report of the mission and the publicity generated by the mission resulted in the announcement by the city government of full resettlement for the people affected.

(c) The HIC-HRC work at the United Nations has included testifying before UN bodies and preparing alternate reports that have often involved collaborative work by various local and national groups. The network thus established has continued work at the national level in mobilizing on the right to housing and in monitoring how the respective governments are complying with their obligations on the right to housing under international human rights instruments (Mexico, Panama, and Israel).

(d) Global meetings: The annual meetings of the HIC-HRC, UN human rights sessions, and UN Conferences like Habitat II, have made clear the need for campaigning work at the national level. In some cases representatives of local groups have been influenced by exposure at these meetings to the possibilities of linking national and international work and are attempting to form coalitions and campaigns in their countries (Brazil, Peru, United States, and Nigeria).

(e) Standard setting: The work of pressuring UN bodies to adopt resolutions on housing rights and forced evictions has resulted in those instruments being used at home, for local awareness, and policy-influencing activities. For example, in August 1997 the HIC-HRC successfully advocated, at the UN Sub-Commission on the Prevention of Discrimination and Protection of Minorities, the passage of a resolution entitled: "Women and the right to adequate housing and land and property." The Women's Advancement Trust in Tanzania, a HIC-HRC member, is currently using this resolution as an educational tool to inform women about their human rights and to ensure that women's rights to land and inheritance figure prominently in the drafting process currently underway in the Tanzanian Parliament for a new land bill. This NGO has translated the resolution into Kiswahili and produced leaflets for use in a nationwide campaign on the rights of women to equal access to land and property.

(f) Preventing evictions: A number of the groups have used UN human rights sessions to publicize the threat of eviction of communities. Such first-hand testimony by local activists has resulted in some cases in the reduction of evictions. For example, the participation of leaders from local communities in Rio de Janeiro, Brazil at the 1994 session of the UN Commission on Human Rights, led to publicity being generated and a heightened sense of awareness among the slum-dwellers of their human rights. This process over a period of one year led to a reduction of planned evictions and a reevaluation by the Rio municipality of development plans that had threatened large-scale evictions.

(g) Needs assessment and training: The constant local-national-international linkages and processes have clarified the type of needs and training imperative for the work to continue effectively. The HIC-HRC is now able to develop flexible needs assessment and training modules that link human rights to practical issues such as service provision and community finance. The objective has been to create a strong link between human rights principles and law, on the one hand, and the concrete issues facing communities on the other. For example, after a series of needs assessment visits, the HIC-HRC and civil society organizations in Israel and Palestine have developed a training and training-of-trainers program that is being implemented for a two-year period beginning in January 1998.

The areas of work noted have resulted in the creation of local level expertise on the range of conceptual and practical aspects on the right to housing and the practice of creating a consistent channel between local, national, and international work, both at the UN and in other international forums. This has opened up spaces for local participation in international level decision making, in the overcoming of politics between civil society organizations within a country, and the development of strong solidarity work between countries for exchange and sharing of strategies.

LOOKING AHEAD: FUTURE CHALLENGES

The following challenges must be tackled for change to be on a firm footing.

Stress the Human Rights Approach

For groups at all levels, including governmental bodies involved in legal, policy, and mobilization work, the use, as guideposts, of the principles contained in international human rights law is imperative: non-discrimination, self-determination, the rule of law and equality. The adoption of these inviolable principles and the respect of human rights that they call for are essential for sustaining change. The respect, in turn, for the right to housing and land, is an imperative to be able to counter the industrial, speculative, and market-dominated and dictated policy directives that land and housing have become hostage to today.

It is especially critical to stress the role of human rights as a means of both empowering people and communities, of holding states accountable, and of transforming the internal structure of states through the empowering of civic society. Simultaneously, we need to stress that social policies at national levels need to be evolved that recognize the primacy of human rights and the "empowering" dimensions of human rights.

Sustain Focus on Women and Housing Rights

All the work at the United Nations and at local, national, and international levels has shown that a sustained focus is vital on women and housing rights. The need is to understand better the impact of housing rights violations on women that lead to the undermining of their capacities on the one hand and the need to create spaces for the use of women's skills and managerial capacities on the other.[29]

Use the UN System

It is critical that more and more groups are informed about the possibilities of using the UN charter and treaty body mechanisms. There is a need to encourage the preparation of alternate reports by civil society groups working at the local and national levels to provide a mechanism through which they can participate at the United Nations and to evolve a means through which local and national civil society organizations can take part in exposing and monitoring the practices of governments. In this process it is also essential that groups offer their own solutions, such as alternate development plans, to the problems they face.

The work on the right to housing has demonstrated the role that civil society organizations can play in rejuvenating the United Nations and in expanding and challenging the contexts and the platforms provided by international human rights bodies. This work also reinforces the value of using the umbrella of principles contained in international human rights instruments as a powerful basis with which to monitor the violation and the realization of human rights.

There is also a need for groups at both the local and national levels to hold their governments accountable for their obligations under the international human rights treaties they have ratified and the relevant international plans of actions they have agreed to. It is critical that violations of these rights, when possible, be internationalized and that international human rights law and principles be used as a basis for collective action and the establishment of civil society organizations that can play a role in implementing and monitoring human rights.

Deepen the Work on Housing and Land Rights

A comprehensive treatment of the right to housing and land rights is necessary to bring out the many dimensions of land and housing issues. It is only through such a detailed approach that these rights will figure in the work of a wider spectrum of individuals, communities, and institutions at local, regional, and international levels. A more direct human rights approach can provide for a sharper critique of government responsibility and provide benchmarks that can lead to needed interventions by all sectors of society, including by the empowered and the marginalized and discriminated communities themselves.

---

[29]For a powerful human rights analysis of the issues facing women at a national level, see NCHR, "The Essential Homelessness of Women," Calcutta, 1988. For a comprehensive look at the development of international standards on women and housing rights, see [4, 5].

This approach is all the more necessary as it can counter one of the main obstacles to the realization of economic, social, and cultural rights: the contention, among the powerful sections of society, that it is the poor and the marginalized that are the main perpetrators of social violence and environmental degradation. There is an urgent need to dispel this misperception and to stress that, in fact, it is the poor and the marginalized that are the greatest victims of social violence and environmental degradation.[30]

Grapple with the Phenomena of Globalization

Many local and national groups have raised questions about the impact of globalization on the issues they are seized with. It is imperative that groups at all levels attempt to comprehend the many dimensions of economic globalization and to equip themselves with sufficient data and case study material to develop strategies to counter the deleterious effect. More rigorous research is needed to draw out the many human rights implications of international trade, investment and finance regimes, and there is a need to demonstrate the impact of these phenomena on the issues that people and communities confront daily such as housing and living conditions.

Strengthen Local and International Work

Numerous benefits can accrue from local and national groups collaborating with international civil society organizations. These benefits are even more likely if campaigning and mobilizing capacities are increased at all levels. It is also important for these international civil society organizations, once trust has been gained, to play a mediating role between local and national organizations to help overcome political and ideological differences.

Training, in full collaboration with local and national groups, on all aspects of the right to housing and land rights has been particularly beneficial and continues to be in great demand in many countries.

The main underlying message that emerges through the work at the international level, including the United Nations, is the need for sustained human rights education. The standards are there; and spaces for representation and redress exist within the UN human rights system. The need of the hour is for more human rights educators at all levels. The principle task we face is to work toward the creation of a widespread temper imbued with human rights consciousness. Spread across different sectors of society, it would necessarily embrace justice and

---

[30]For moving testimony by community leaders in Rio de Janeiro in support of this contention, see [2], p. 26.

equality for every woman, man, and child and would work toward the fulfillment of all human rights. For such a formidable but unavoidable task, the principles and provisions contained in the international human rights instruments, led by the UDHR, provide a universally applicable basis for action and sustenance.

REFERENCES

1. M. Kothari, The Global Struggle for the Right to a Place to Live, *Development in Practice, 7*:1, Oxfam, Oxford (United Kingdom and Ireland), 1997.
2. M. Kothari, Tijuca Lagoon; Evictions and Human Rights in Rio de Janeiro, *Environment and Urbanization, 6*:1, International Institute of Environment and Development, London, April 1994.
3. M. Kothari, The Human Right to Adequate Housing: An Inviolable Right Not Only a Social Goal, *People's Decade for Human Rights Education,* New York, January 1996.
4. L. Farha, Is There a Woman in the House: Women and the Right to Adequate Housing, in *A Resource Guide to Women's International Human Rights,* Transnational Publishers (forthcoming, 1998).
5. M. Sanders, *Women and the Right to Adequate Housing,* doctoral thesis, University of Utrecht, The Netherlands, 1997.

Chapter 17

Other Groups in Struggles Against Discrimination

Leandro Despouy, Hugo Garcia Garcilazo,
Eugene B. Brody, Julia Tavares de Alvarez,
and Julie Dorf

Part I:
Fifty Years: Achievements and
Obstacles in the Area of Disability

Leandro Despouy and Hugo Garcia Garcilazo

This chapter reviews briefly the most important achievements of the last decades regarding human rights and their relation to the issue of disability[1] and the great challenges still pending.

The issue of disability has been given considerable attention in the United Nations, as one of a wide range of subjects comprising the human rights agenda. The group of instruments that are the core of the human rights regime, emanating from the Universal Declaration of Human Rights, provide international legal support for the rights of disabled persons. The rules and specific mechanisms for disabled persons arose out of the necessity to reinforce the principle of equality of

---

[1] In Latin America, some individuals and organizations prefer the expression "persons with different abilities" to persons with disabilities.

219

opportunities and rights. They do not confer new rights to disabled persons, but they attempt to facilitate their access to the same rights acknowledged for the general population.

Since 1971 additional instruments have been developed specifically related to disability, primarily as a result of the continuing efforts of a large number of NGOs, mainly composed of disabled persons. The actions taken by the UN General Assembly specifically related to disability include the Declaration of the Rights of Mentally Retarded Persons in 1971; Declaration on the Rights of Disabled Persons in 1975; Resolution proclaiming 1981 as the International Year of Disabled Persons in 1975; Declaration on the Rights of Deaf-Blind Persons in 1979; UN Decade of Disabled Persons and World Programme of Action Concerning Disabled Persons for the Decade 1983-1992[2] in 1982; Appointment of a Special Rapporteur to study human rights in relation to disabled persons in 1984 (report published in 1992);[3] Resolution proclaiming December 3 as The World Day of Disabled Persons in 1991; Approval of Standard Rules on the Equalization of Opportunities for Persons with Disabilities in 1993;[4] Appointment of a Special Rapporteur on the application of the Standard Rules in 1994;[5] and report of the Special Rapporteur to the General Assembly,[6] and the renewal of the mandate for three years in 1997.

In addition, the ILO (since 1955 with its initial Recommendation number 99), the WHO, UNESCO, the different commissions of ECOSOC, the Center for Social Development and Humanitarian Affairs, the Regional Economic Commissions, the UN Development Programme, and the UN High Commissioner for Human Rights have incorporated this issue into their work agendas, and are making considerable efforts on behalf of the disabled. According to the WHO, more than 500 million persons—10 percent of the world's total population—suffer from some type of disability. In a majority of countries, at least one of ten persons has a physical, mental, or sensory impairment, and at least 25 percent of the entire population is adversely affected by disabilities.[7] These figures speak eloquently of the enormous size of the problem and, in addition to its universal scope, highlight the well-known impact of this phenomenon on society as a whole. However, quantification alone is not a sufficient basis for evaluating the actual gravity of the problem, since disabled persons frequently live in deplorable

[2] World Programme of Action concerning Disabled Persons. General Assembly Resolution 37/52.

[3] Resolution 1984/31 of the Commission on Human rights; the final report, by L. Despouy, entitled, Human Rights and Disabled Persons, was published by the UN in *Human Rights Study Series* Number 6 (1993) (E.92.XIV.4 & CORR. 1).

[4] General Assembly Resolution 48/96.

[5] In March 1994, the UN Secretary-general appointed Mr. Bengt Lindqvist (Sweden) as Special Rapporteur.

[6] UN World Programme of Action concerning Disabled Persons for the Decade 1983-1992, Para. 1. General Assembly Resolution 37/52.

[7] L. Despouy, *supra* 3, para. 2.

conditions, due to physical and social barriers that prevent their integration and full participation in the community. As a result, millions of children and adults throughout the world are segregated and deprived of virtually all their rights and lead a wretched, marginal life.

The scope of the problem made apparent the need to address it. The first step was to overcome ignorance and to suppress denial about disability. Later, the concepts of mere assistance and dependence were put aside, to let in orienting principles, aims, and definitions such as "full participation." The principle of "equalization of opportunities" came from the UN World Programme of Action concerning Disabled Persons for the Decade 1983-1992 and the Standard Rules on the Equalization of Opportunities for Persons with Disabilities.[8] These formulations are present in research, surveys, recommendations, resolutions, and other instruments and papers of the UN. Memorable was the change, through the firm and convincing actions of organizations representing disabled persons, from the proposed motto of "charity and sympathy" for the International Year of Disabled Persons to "full participation and equality."

The recognition of disabled persons as the best experts on their own problems resulted in a special emphasis of the need for continuous consultation with organizations that represent them. Persons with disabilities should take an active part in all decision-making, as well as in the application, enforcement, supervision, and assessment of measures.

It is important to point out that, while joint responsibility may be the dominant concept behind the World Programme of Action, the principal obligation to remove obstacles impeding or hindering the integration and full participation of disabled persons lies with Governments. They cannot be mere onlookers; they must act, sometimes with great vigor, and especially in difficult situations, in order to prevent marginalization and to ensure that the equalization of opportunities is not just rhetoric but real and effective. The largest barriers remaining are not in the UN system, but in many of its Member States. The few positive exceptions deserving full recognition are Belgium, Canada, Finland, Norway, Sweden, and the United States. Many States that approve agreements, programs, uniform rules, and declarations postpone or hinder their ratification or implementation. And it is well known that, unfortunately, many ratifications of treaties are the result of momentary political convenience or demagogic manipulation.

It may take years to ratify agreements, and then begin the struggle to pass laws and implement those laws and turn them into programs and action. Such measures normally receive apparent support of officials, but even then few or no resources are made available to implement them. In decentralized countries, this process may be repeated in provinces, states, and municipalities. Fortunately,

---

[8] B. Lindqvist, *Final Report of the Special Rapporteur of the Commission on Social Development on the Supervision of the application of the Uniform Rules on Equalization of Opportunities for Disabled Persons,* A/52/56.

judges are paying more attention to laws that protect the rights of disabled persons.

The report submitted to the General Assembly in 1997 by Mr. Bengt Lindqvist, Special Rapporteur on the application of the Uniform Rules on Equalization of Opportunities, speaks for itself: the situation of disabled persons has not improved substantially, even in the most developed countries. It is discouraging to see how little progress has been made in such fundamental areas as education, professional development, and job opportunities.[9]

Violations of human rights that affect the majority of the population in many parts of the world continue. They include inadequate food and housing, lack of proper sanitation, poor education and medical care, unemployment, and marginalization. Under such conditions, disabled persons suffer a two- or three-fold discrimination. In addition, torture and mutilation for political or religious reasons are still the cause of disabilities in some regions.

In a developed community, the formal acceptance of general and specific rights, together with the actual denial of opportunity, can be as morally torturing as physical mistreatment in other geographic areas. The impossibility of getting a job, even when the disabled person is qualified for it, is demeaning and is a cruel violation of essential human rights. Furthermore, the number of disabled persons is increasing constantly as a result of a general rise of crime due to such factors as drug abuse and violent television programs, with their known negative impact.

It is extremely worrisome that governments and other organizations with power in different countries have neglected to foster a culture of solidarity and social development with regard to the disabled. Rather, privatization of basic services is creating problems of quality, cost, and access, thus provoking exclusion, marginalization, and of course, injustice and poverty. However, the basis for change and positive improvement is there, thanks to the efforts of the UN system, of many countries, and mainly to the intelligent pressure brought by organizations representing disabled persons.

As a result, disability is no longer a shame, as it used to be. In most countries, it is not hidden. On the contrary, it is raised as a flag of vindication and successful examples are put forward to mark the way for other disabled persons, and for the whole community. Positive measures include the mention of disabled persons in the adoption of specific laws, the establishment of special commissions, or of ombudsmen. Such measures were not present fifty years ago. At the same time, it is also true that these actions are more formal than real, and that intentions always give way to bad excuses to delay.

In conclusion, 1) the UN has contributed in a decisive way to the changes and advances experienced in the last fifty years; 2) the UN should intensify its

---

[9] See footnote 8.

effort to have all countries apply effectively the Standard Rules for Equalization of Opportunities for Disabled Persons; 3) the mechanisms, procedures of monitoring, denunciation, mediation, and judgment should be maintained, improved when needed, and properly financed; 4) actions should concentrate on governments and local groups with power over the economy, culture, education, and the media; and 5) disabled persons and the organizations representing them should intensify their efforts in order to transform their formal achievements and positive changes of attitude in the community into genuine change of behavior, which will produce real and equal chances for all. Measures like these will help create a society consistent with the spirit and ideas that inspired the founders of the United Nations and the creators of the Universal Declaration of Human Rights.

Part II:
Human Rights and the Mentally Ill:
A Global Concern

Eugene B. Brody

Maltreatment and brutal restraint or abandonment were the routine fates of mentally ill persons for most of recorded history. Perhaps the most dramatic efforts to create a new perception of these misunderstood individuals, enabling their compassionate care, came in the climate of the French Revolution with its emphasis on individual freedom and self-determination. Thus, in 1792, Philippe Pinel tried to transform the mentally ill men confined in the Bicetre asylum from chained "wild beasts" to patients with the dignity appropriate to human beings [1]. More than 100 years later, in 1908, Clifford Beers' confinement in a mental hospital led him to form the U.S. National Committee for Mental Hygiene [2]. In 1919, he founded the first international organization dedicated to the welfare and protection of mentally ill persons, the International Committee for Mental Hygiene (ICMH) [3].

The ICMH was succeeded on August 21, 1948 by the World Federation for Mental Health (WFMH) conceived after World War II with the idea that preserving world peace is the best means of promoting mental health and protecting human rights. This idea was embodied in its founding Declaration, "Mental Health and World Citizenship," which emphasized an allegiance to humankind as a whole, "free consent and respect for individual and cultural differences," and the concept of a "common humanity." The WFMH Declaration antedated by four months the Universal Declaration of Human Rights which espoused similar goals through its reference to "the human family."

The Federation's founding Declaration extended its stated mission far beyond the needs of those already mentally ill. Recognizing the range of human societies and cultures, this mission was *to promote the mental health of all of the world's peoples.* Mental health was understood as more than the absence of illness. In positive terms it referred to optimal function, legitimating attention to the social circumstances in which people were born, developed, and lived their lives. Central to this concept was the ability of different peoples to live together in harmony in their one world. Fifty years later, WFMH retains this philosophy, continuing as the oldest international, multidisciplinary, voluntary and ecumenical, non-governmental mental health organization in official status with the major agencies of the United Nations.

WFMH has been a continuous advocate for concerns bearing on the prevention of mental illness and disability and the rights of vulnerable populations. Prominent among these last have been refugees and migrants, members of sociocultural and political minorities, women, the elderly and the young, as well as persons confined in mental hospitals or at risk of involuntary confinement. While promoting world peace has not been an explicit goal, it has remained implicit in the Federation's emphasis on creating new centers of local and regional initiative through the formation of mental health associations where they have not heretofore existed and its continued efforts at international collaboration in pursuit of mental health and the preservation of human rights. These efforts have included recurrent attention to the non-violent resolution of conflict between national, ethnic, or religious adversaries.

During the past half-century, the Universal Declaration, with its specific inclusion of rights to mental and physical health, education and the benefits of science, and freedom from involuntary experimentation (a right to informed consent), has been a basic reference for the rights of mentally ill persons. Related health rights have included access to family planning services, the elimination of discrimination against women, the well-being of refugees, the rights of citizens traumatized by governments and their agents, and the right of children to be free from commercial sexual exploitation.

The right to freedom from involuntary experimentation was elaborated at the First UN Conference on Human Rights in 1968 which warned that scientific and technological advances could "endanger the rights and freedoms of individuals"[10] This concern extended to the many facets of advancing biomedical technology was explored over several years by UNESCO and the International Social

---

[10]United Nations (1968). *The Proclamation of Teheran.* International Conference on Human Rights, 13 May. Human Rights and Scientific and Technological Developments, Resolution XI. UN No. E.68.XIV.2, United Nations: New York.

Science Council (ISSC) resulting in a volume published under joint UNESCO, ISSC, and WFMH auspices [4].

Meanwhile WFMH continued its focus on involuntary detention in mental hospitals. In 1971, it had been the first international non-governmental organization to issue a resolution condemning the Soviet hospitalization of political dissidents. This was followed by a series of actions and resolutions over several years. In 1989, it adopted a *Declaration of Human Rights and Mental Health* which was widely disseminated.[11] A *Declaration of Principles and Guarantees for the Protection of Mentally Ill Persons and for the Improvement of Mental Health Care*, drafted by the UN Commission on Human Rights with the participation of WHO, WFMH, and other NGOs was adopted by the UN General Assembly in December 1991.[12] To date, however, despite occasional inspections ordered by national governments or regional organizations, such as the European Union, there has been no systematic UN effort to monitor compliance with the Declaration's standards. The work of elaborating and adjusting its provisions to the socioeconomic and cultural contexts of the world's regions remains to be done, as does the translation of its general principles into national legislation.

The ubiquitous conflict between universal standards and local customs and values continues to impede full access to health services by all sectors of the world's population. The challenge continues to be the promotion of awareness of the nature and treatability of mental illness and a decrease in its associated stigma. Vigorous efforts in this direction should contribute to a political and social climate supportive of the rights of those vulnerable to disabling emotional distress as well as those defined as mentally ill.

REFERENCES

1. D. Weiner, "Le geste de Pinel": The history of a Psychiatric Myth, in *Discovering the History of Psychiatry*, M. S. Micale and R. Porter (eds.), Oxford University Press, Oxford, New York, pp. 232-247, 1994.
2. C. W. Beers, *A Mind that Found Itself*, Longmans, Green, New York, 1908.
3. E. B. Brody, *The Search for Mental Health: A History and Memoir of WFMH, 1948-1997*, Williams & Wilkins Co., Baltimore, 1998.
4. E. B. Brody, *Biomedical Technology and Human Rights*, Dartmouth Publishing, Hants, England; Ashcroft Press, Brookfield, Vermont. Published under the auspices of UNESCO, ISSC, WFMH, 1993.

[11]World Federation for Mental Health (1989). *Declaration of Human Rights and Mental Health.* Baltimore: Office of the WFMH Secretary General.

[12]United Nations (1991). *Declaration of Principles and Guarantees for the Protection of Mentally Ill Persons and for the Improvement of Mental Health Care.*

Part III:
Human Rights for Elders

Julia Tavares de Alvarez

If we are to truly have an "Age of Rights," it must be one in which the rights of the aged are recognized. Older persons continue to face discrimination in employment and in access to credit. Elder abuse in the home and violence against older persons in the public sphere causes tremendous human suffering on a daily basis, even if it goes unreported.

There are two preconditions for an "Age of Rights" that will include aging. We must deal with the lack of sufficient resources in many areas, especially in our Third World, to provide other people with the basics of living, such as food. And at the same time, we must create a culture of human rights for older people that provides the social and political context for political and economic action. This is the heart of the matter.

The programmatic part of the human rights equation is fairly straightforward. In the industrial nations, the pressure of demographics will require adjustments in social security programs. This is beginning to happen, and while we can expect that the process of modifying these programs will be contentious, the task can be accomplished. Even in our Third World, where the demographic "Age Quake" will hit hardest, where vast numbers of elders, especially those over eighty-five, will strain scarce resources, a start can be made to deal with this issue. One approach that is gaining support is the development of age-appropriate economic opportunities, with easy credit for people in their sixties and seventies that allows them to set up small-scale enterprises.

But the key to securing and protecting the rights of older people is to create a culture of human rights that would motivate and sustain such measures. The sticking point is not demographics, but definitions; our main problem lies not in counting, but in consciousness.

What we see when we confront this problem depends on how we are looking at it. It may make sense to approach the securing of human rights for other groups in the context of their "victimization," but in the case of older people, the category is part of the problem. Looking at older people as "victims" victimizes them; it is more than a label, it is a libel and a self-fulfilling prophecy. The rights of older people cannot be grounded in such a fundamentally wrong concept of who they are and where they function in the social spectrum.

For too long older people have been portrayed as helpless, passive, and pitiful, little more than victims of the passage of time. They have been viewed as dependent, non-contributory wards of society, external to the main business of the world—people with needs who are no longer capable of deeds. Politically, the consequences of victimology, of this diminishing of the humanity of older people has been that they are less than full citizens. Part and parcel of this diminution has been an inattentiveness to their rights.

Human rights, of course, has been an issue at the United Nations from its beginning. The Organization's Charter, written in 1945, calls for all people "to practice tolerance and live together in peace with one another as good neighbors and to unite our strength to maintain international peace and security." Toward this end, the Charter sets as one of the aims of the United Nations the promotion of "respect for human rights and for fundamental freedoms for all without distinctions as to race, sex, language, or religion." The Charter, however, makes no mention of age. Three years later, the Universal Declaration of Human Rights enumerated similar distinctions. Article 25 did spell out the basic right to an adequate standard of living "in the event of unemployment, sickness, disability, widowhood, old age, or other lack of livelihood in circumstances beyond . . . control." But this passive presence is the only appearance older people make at the United Nations for several decades. In 1948, Argentina placed the status of older people on the agenda for discussion, but nothing was discussed. In 1969, Malta's similar restoration in the General Assembly met with a similar fate.

Finally, in 1978, the United Nations, forced by demographics to recognize the issue, funded the World Assembly on Aging, which was held in Vienna in 1982. The Assembly adopted an International Plan of Action on Aging[13] and called upon countries to review their laws with respect to protecting the rights of elders. Little came of this.

A decade and a half later the issue of elder rights was once again placed on the table, this time with greater urgency, propelled by the increasing pressure of demographics. In 1991, the United Nations adopted its Principles for Older Persons.[14] This document declared that older persons should have access to adequate food, clothing, shelter, and health care. It called for the establishment of physical and social environments for older people that would provide appropriate support services when needed. The Principles also advocated elder participation in the formation and implementation of policies that affect them. Finally, it asserted the right of older persons to live in dignity, with full participation in society.

The following year, an international conference, occasioned by the tenth anniversary of the adoption of the International Plan of Action on Aging, proclaimed 1999 the International Year of Older Persons.

Older people are finally gaining a measure of recognition. But this is no more than a start—mostly a cosmetic one. The demographic imperative will

---

[13]General Assembly resolution 37/51 of 6 August 1982, also published in UN Sales No. E.82.I.16.

[14]General Assembly resolution 46/91 of 16 December 1991.

accelerate in the next ten years. If we are to create the political and economic measures that will help us cope with worldwide population aging, we will first have to imbed respect for older people in all of our cultures.

Older people must rejoin the social matrix. We must stop fantasizing them as outsiders who need to be acted upon for their own good by a benevolent society that deigns to help them. Access to this important social interaction would carry with it political empowerment. Rights are, first of all, an attribute of citizenship. Citizens are members of the state, active inhabitants of the social realm. An associate membership will not do.

What should we do to return older people to civil society? Awareness of older people as socially important should be cultivated at an early age. The young cannot imagine that they too will age. Empathy for their elders is therefore often in short supply. Indeed, given today's attitudes about the value of youth, age is something to be feared. What are the prospects for securing the human rights of older people under these circumstances?

Younger people must see the world as a whole and recognize the interdependence of all people in a society of all ages. If they don't, it is wholly possible to foresee an "age war" over scarce resources, splitting the social ties that bind us together as our generation split the atom.

On a larger scale, we need to reconceptualize elder's rights and, indeed, the idea of human rights as a whole. We do not need another plea for special consideration for the human rights of yet another group.

The Universal Declaration of Human Rights proclaimed human rights as inherent to the human person and its scope extended to each and every human being. Yet, after the adoption of the Declaration in 1948, governments or specific groups felt that separate attention had to be paid to such groups and, therefore, advocated the adoption of separate declarations or treaties covering their human rights. This was the case, for example, with the rights of children, the rights of women, the rights of refugees, and the rights of indigenous peoples. As a result the UN codified, or is still in the process of codifying, the human rights of specific groups. It is doubtful, however, whether this trend has always been beneficial because one of the side effects of proclaiming rights of specific groups has been the occasional marginalization of such groups in the policy debates. Many lessons can be learned in this respect from the women's movement which is now advocating the mainstreaming of gender in all UN and other policy actions.

Aging, perhaps more than any other social-biological process, embodies the transforming social phenomenon of interdependence. Aging is related to dependence, but not just in the way we often hear about this connection. It is not a one-way street. We need older people just as much as they need us, and we ought to be able to depend upon them more than we do. The dependence, of course, is mutual: it is interdependent.

The struggle of older people for the recognition of their rights provides a unique perspective on how we might look at the fight for all human rights. Older people have not only lived through all of life's stages, they also encompass within their ranks many of the other categories under which we consider rights violations: women, people of color, various ethnic groups, people with disabilities, etc. In many ways, human rights for elders is a touchstone issue when considering human rights in general. The perspective of older people begins to show us that we must ultimately see the fight for human rights less through the paradigm of atomistic isolation of all "victimized" groups and more within a model of interdependent interaction that recognizes the irreducible mutuality of all people.

One could not better sum up this new conceptualization of human rights than did the President of the United States, Bill Clinton, in his 1998 visit to Africa. He said: "Democracy requires human rights for everyone, everywhere. For men and women, for children and the elderly, for people of different cultures and tribes and backgrounds. A good society honors its entire family."

Part IV:
Sexual Orientation and Human Rights in the United Nations

Julie Dorf

Over the past fifty years, sexual orientation issues have gone from being a topic discussed in embarrassed whispers in the halls of the United Nations to being recognized as a legitimate agenda item for its human rights mechanisms. Currently, the protections enshrined in the Universal Declaration of Human Rights (UDHR) and other international treaties are violated every day through murders, incarcerations, and infringements of fundamental liberties of expression and association directed at individuals and communities of sexual minorities. The attention given to these issues by the mechanisms in existence within the United Nations has been limited. Nonetheless, there has been significant progress, mostly within the last decade. This has been due to increased mobilization on the part of the NGO community and in some cases by certain governments, as well as a change in many societies' attitudes toward homosexuality.

BACKGROUND

While evidence of homoerotic and homosexual relations exist in most cultures and in various periods of history, actual social movements designed to advance the rights of sexual minorities and to fight human rights abuses aimed at these groups are a fairly recent phenomenon, most closely associated with public organizing in Western Europe, the United States, and Canada. But in truth, there are and have been movements in all inhabited regions of the world. Today, in hundreds of countries, thousands of grassroots groups are organizing around sexual rights and sexual identity. These NGOs range from large well-financed, officially registered groups in both the North and the South, to completely underground, illegal organizations without bank accounts or governmental or societal approval.

HISTORY WITHIN THE UNITED NATIONS

The first documented intervention in the United Nations in regard to sexual orientation took place in 1987, when The Economic and Social Council (ECOSOC) asked the UN Sub-Commission on the Prevention of Discrimination of Minorities to produce a report on the legal and social problems of sexual minorities.[15] The report was a dismal and insensitive failure, marked by ignorance about the individuals and communities which were its focus [1]. Fortunately, the report drew little attention inside or outside of the United Nations. The report claimed, for example, that "there would be fewer lesbians if men were able to be more affectionate, attentive and tactful." It displayed further fixation on theories of how to reduce homosexuality, rather than how to protect gays and lesbians from discrimination, by claiming that there would be fewer homosexual men "if men did not feel called on by the social model to achieve an exceptionally high level of sexual performance with their female partners."[16]

The subject of homosexuality did not arise again formally within the United Nations until the 1990s, when a number of different agencies, treaty bodies, and conferences began, randomly, to refer to or decide on sexual orientation issues in a much more informed fashion, probably due to increased NGO involvement as well as to sympathetic employees inside various UN bodies.

In 1991, the World Health Organization voted to delete homosexuality from its International Classification of Diseases, a decision that went into effect in 1993.[17] This decision, while it occurred after numerous countries' medical

[15]UN Document E/CN.4/Sub.2/1988/31 (1988). Jean Fernand-Laurent; Study on the Legal and Social Problems of Sexual Minorities.

[16]UN Document E/CN.4/Sub.2/1988/31 (1988), at 27-28.

[17]International Classification of Diseases, Chapter V, code 302.

professions had already declassified homosexuality in their equivalent national instruments, has had significant impact internationally.

Also in 1991, the United Nations Development Programme (UNDP) created its short-lived Human Freedom Index[18] which ranked countries by various indicators of democracy, including the right to have homosexual relations. There was much controversy about the Human Freedom Index: UNDP eventually ceased compiling the Index, while continuing to publish the annual Human Development Report, of which the index had been a part.

In 1993, the United Nations High Commissioner for Refugees (UNHCR) began issuing advisory opinions on political asylum cases dealing with individuals who were fleeing persecution due to their sexual orientation. A few countries had already begun interpreting the category of "membership in a particular social group" to include lesbians, gay men, bisexuals, and transgendered people, yet the UNHCR opinion and policy have been extremely influential in inducing a number of other countries, including the United States, to begin recognizing such cases. The policy of the UNHCR clearly states that "persons facing attack, inhuman treatment, or serious discrimination because of their homosexuality, and whose governments are unable or unwilling to protect them, should be recognized as refugees."[19]

Also in 1993, The International Lesbian and Gay Association (ILGA) applied for and, after much lobbying and a very close vote, received roster NGO status with the ECOSOC. During that first year, however, in what is still an unresolved scandal, their status was suspended after the United States, at the instigation of the conservative Republican Senator, Jesse Helms—claimed that ILGA had ties to pedophiles.[20] Even after ILGA expelled a few of its member organizations with ties to pedophiles, an unconvinced United States persisted in blocking its reinstatement to ECOSOC. Furthermore, the United States worked to ensure that any group with connection to ILGA is ineligible for NGO status in the ECOSOC, which has effectively meant that no organization representing sexual minorities has formal representation with one of the UN's most important bodies.

Despite this setback, however, in 1994 sexual minorities enjoyed what was probably the most important victory in the brief history of work on these issues within the United Nations. The Human Rights Committee (HRC) adopted a decision on the case of *Nicholas Toonen v. Australia,* a case of a man convicted under a sodomy law in Tasmania, Australia.[21] The decision clearly interprets the International Covenant on Civil and Political Rights (ICCPR) to protect the right to engage in adult same-sex sexual activities under both the privacy and

---

[18]Human Development Report, 1991, Oxford University Press, New York.

[19]UNHCR/PI/Q&A-UK1.PM5/Feb. 1996.

[20]Resolution of the ECOSOC, September 16, 1994. Also see US Congressional Record of the Senate, January 25, 1994, S 26-27.

[21]UN Document CCPR/c/50/D/488/1992 [1994].

the non-discrimination provisions of the Covenant. The Australian national government cooperated fully and enacted legislation banning such laws in the country, though the state of Tasmania took three more years before it finally repealed the law in 1997.

In 1995, the World Conference on Women in Beijing was the first occasion in the history of the United Nations when representatives of all the present member states debated inclusion of the term "sexual orientation" in one of the non-discrimination paragraphs of the conference's official final document, the "Platform for Action." While ultimately there was not enough global consensus for the words to remain in the document, this unprecedented debate raised awareness among all present. Numerous countries made formal statements acknowledging that they would interpret the document to include lesbian women.[22] Moreover, at this conference, concrete progress was made on sexual rights issues in general, including a passage that stated, "the human rights of women include their right to have control over and decide freely and responsibly on matters related to their sexuality."[23]

The Human Rights Committee has also issued criticisms of other governments for maintaining discriminatory laws, including sodomy laws. For example, in 1995 the HRC cited sodomy laws in the United States as needing to be repealed in response to the compliance report of the United States under the ICCPR.[24] Unfortunately, there are still twenty states in the United States with such laws on the books and the United States has given short shrift to the HRC's recommendations. Also cited were Romania and Hong Kong.[25]

UN GLOBE is a worldwide advocacy group of gay, lesbian, or bisexual employees of the United Nations. It was formed in 1996 by a group of employees from UNDP, UNICEF, UNFPA, and the UN Secretariat. UN GLOBE was granted official recognition by the Office of Human Resources Management. The group's main objectives are to attain equal rights and eliminate discrimination on the basis of sexual orientation, and to promote and support the United Nations in its global efforts to fulfill its principles of equal rights for all, including that of sexual orientation.

Also in 1996, the International Labor Organization (ILO), conducted a special survey on employment-based discrimination. In its conclusions and recommendations, the ILO specifically suggests that sexual orientation be

---

[22]Over twenty-five countries made public statements acknowledging that they would interpret either "other status" to include sexual orientation within the non-discrimination paragraph of the Platform (Paragraph 46) or the section acknowledging a woman's right to control her sexuality to include sexual orientation issues. These countries included Australia, Belize, Canada, Chile, the Cook Islands, Jamaica, Latvia, Israel, New Zealand, Norway, Slovenia, South Africa, and the United States.

[23]Report of the Fourth World Conference on Women: Beijing 5-15 September, 1995, UN Document A/Conf.177/20 (1995).

[24]UN Document GAOR, CCPR/C/79/Add 50, 6 April, 1995.

[25]UN Documents CCPR/C/79/Add.30 and CCPR/C/79/Add.57.

included in a new protocol that would extend the application of the ILO's 1958 Discrimination Convention. In 1996 and in 1997, UNAIDS formally recommended to the Commission on Human Rights and the Sub-Commission that countries consider the decriminalization of consensual same-sex sex acts as integral to their national efforts to prevent the spread of HIV. According to the International Gay & Lesbian Human Rights Commission, there are at least eighty countries in the world that still have anti-gay laws on their books today.[26]

This survey of events within the United Nations system is just one indicator of the increasing relevance of the UDHR in the protection of the human rights of sexual minorities. There are many other areas of international law, particularly other regional human rights bodies, where there have been other significant steps forward on cases involving sexual orientation issues not mentioned in this chapter. Additionally, there has been a clear and growing global consensus within NGO communities that these issues are important and require more attention in all regions of the world. International human rights NGOs (Amnesty International, Human Rights Watch, International Planned Parenthood Federation, and many others), are increasingly paying particular attention to sexual orientation issues in their mandates and in their work in general. The NGOs that represent individuals and communities of sexual minorities are increasing in number and scope, and are increasingly utilizing the human rights framework as a mechanism for ensuring their safety.

THE RELEVANCE OF THE UDHR

Although there is an interesting and valid debate about the universality of rights and about individual vs. collective rights, the UDHR as it stands is complete enough. Every article contained in the UDHR clearly applies to all individuals in society—this would obviously include lesbians, gay men, bisexuals, transgendered individuals, and anyone else who engages in private, consensual, adult sexual activities. The UDHR has one statement of limitation on the enjoyment of such rights: "In the exercise of his rights and freedoms, everyone shall be subject only to such limitations as are determined by law solely for the purpose of securing due recognition and respect the just requirements of morality, public order and the general welfare in a democratic society."[27] This limitation is used frequently by governments as rationale for discriminatory and oppressive legal and societal measures against those who are sexually different. This area must be scrutinized carefully and perhaps further defined for the UDHR to become a protective tool for sexual minorities.

---

[26]The International Gay & Lesbian Human Rights Commission, "A Global Overview: Criminalization and Decriminalization of Homosexual Acts," April 1997.

[27]Universal Declaration of Human Rights, Article 29, part 2.

Additionally, formally interpreting "other status" to include sexual orientation would be a useful next step in the utilization of the UDHR. Similarly, a broad interpretation of the family provisions, as was accomplished at the UN International Conference on Population and Development in Cairo in 1994, would be helpful in acknowledging the diversity of family structures that exist in the world today.

The next fifty years do not need to see the re-writing of every covenant and treaty that make up international human rights law. Rather, we must continue to update our interpretations—as has happened in the last decade—and realize that human rights are a living, breathing concept that apply to every individual and every community regardless of sexual orientation.

REFERENCE

1. L. R. Helfer and A. M. Miller, Sexual Orientation and Human Rights: Toward a United States and Transnational Jurisprudence, *Harvard Human Rights Journal, 9,* Spring 1996, at 97-98.

Part IV

Creating a Culture
of Human Rights

Chapter 18

Technical Cooperation in the Field of Human Rights, Past and Present, Reflections for Further Development

Jamal Benomar

INTRODUCTION

On the night of January 9, 1976 I was kidnapped from my home by the Moroccan secret police. This was the beginning of a long nightmare. I was severely tortured, held in a secret detention center for almost a year, handcuffed and blindfolded all the time, subjected to a summary unfair trial and sentenced to a twelve-year prison term. I was released after eight years, thanks to the tireless effort of Amnesty International and other human rights NGOs who adopted me as a prisoner of conscience, and I have been in exile ever since. Would this situation have been avoided if the United Nations had provided technical assistance to Morocco in human rights at the time? My answer is obviously no. UN work in this area can only be effective in countries where there is a strong political will to protect human rights, not in countries where violations are condoned and orchestrated at the highest level. Victims of human rights violations and NGO activities have long believed that the UN's advisory services and technical assistance program was a smoke screen for letting governments off the hook or an indecent way of helping repressive governments to graduate from the scrutiny of the public procedures of the UN Commission on Human Rights so that their appalling record would go unnoticed under a different item on the Commission's agenda. The truth of the matter is that up to the early 1990s this was very much the case. However, this program evolved since then from being the most marginal program to the most promising one only to be retrogressing under the new reorganization of the Office of the High Commissioner for Human Rights (OHCHR).

THE MANDATE

The Technical Co-operation Programme has been the most recent and fastest growing component of the UN Center for Human Rights, now the Office of the High Commissioner for Human Rights (OHCHR). This growth and new emphasis on technical cooperation represents a historic phase in the work of the United Nations in the field of human rights. The organization had already achieved tremendous success in the area of standard-setting and has begun to place more emphasis on implementation and compliance with international human rights standards.

The program was created as a result of a General Assembly resolution dated December 14, 1955 (926(x)) which authorized the Secretary-General to provide advisory services of experts, fellowships and scholarships, and seminars to member States upon their request. Provisions for regional and national training seminars were added, respectively, in 1967 and 1986.

The program was further enhanced by the following developments.

1. The creation of the Voluntary Fund for Technical Co-operation (VFTC) in 1987 by the Secretary-General to provide additional financial support for technical assistance projects aimed at implementing UN human rights standards.

2. The entry into force of key international human rights instruments and the development of Special Procedures and the treaty bodies, which has resulted in systematic recommendations for technical co-operation activities. Hence, there is a need to develop further the capacity within OHCHR and other parts of the United Nations to follow up on these recommendations and to implement them.

3. The Vienna Declaration and Programme of Action adopted by the World Conference on Human Rights in June 1993 placed a particular emphasis on technical co-operation. This emphasis reflected a new direction in the work which had already begun to give particular attention to preventive action and to the implementation of the existing, large and sophisticated body of international human rights instruments.

4. The Decade for Human Rights Education was launched in 1995 pursuant to General Assembly resolution 19/181 to contribute further to the promotion of a universal culture of human rights.

5. At its forty-eighth session, the General Assembly established the post of UN High Commissioner for Human Rights (resolution 48/141 of 20 December 1993). The mandate included the provision of technical co-operation programs in the field of human rights through the Centre for Human Rights and other appropriate institutions, and the coordination of relevant education and public information programs.

All of these developments dramatically increased the visibility of the program within the UN system as a key component of the UN human rights effort. This evolution has led to new and increasing demands, and hence to the need to develop new strategies for strengthening and refocusing the work program in the field of technical co-operation.

PROGRAM OVERVIEW

The strong legislative mandate of the program, the emphasis that has been placed on its importance, the increase in the resources currently available and its practical experience in the provision of technical assistance are essential elements which should precipitate a review of its strengths and weaknesses, an evaluation of its past performance, and the generation of new ideas for a new phase of development of the program.

Strengths

1. The program has widespread and unanimous support from Member States. The Vienna Declaration and Programme of Action (VDPA), and all recent resolutions of legislative organs of the United Nations, have stressed that priority should be given to its further strengthening and development. No other component of the UN human rights program has enjoyed this unprecedented unanimous and strong support from all stakeholders.

2. The program has developed during 1994-1997 new expertise and unique services. A serious effort has resulted in the development of new substantive material to support technical co-operation activities in the areas of law enforcement, national institutions, training material for judges and lawyers, prison officials, human rights education, and human rights and conflict resolution. The program's material in the area of administration of justice and human rights training for law enforcement officials is widely regarded as the best that is currently available. The current capability for strengthening national human rights institutions is also unique. The pedagogical material for the training of government officials on the technical preparation of reports to treaty bodies is also acknowledged to be the best material available.

3. The program has another comparative advantage which makes it unique: in addition to the work of its core staff, it benefits from the specialized expertise in human rights that exists throughout in the UN system. Experts from the various international treaty bodies, who themselves contributed to the recent development of international human rights jurisprudence, often work in the program by participating in needs assessment and advisory services missions and training activities. In addition, the program's strong interaction with Special Procedures and other expert bodies of the UN human rights system aids in the development of

substantive expertise and contributes to the development of high quality products and services.

4. Although the Technical Co-operation Programme has limited experience in methodologies and procedures of technical co-operation in general, the growth of the program in the last three years, has led to the development of new thinking on overcoming the many shortcomings that resulted during recent years. Internal and external audits undertaken in 1992, 1993, and 1994 have revealed a consistent pattern of mismanagement of the program. Efforts undertaken in 1995-1997 were in response to these audit recommendations. These efforts included the establishment and strict application of new methodologies and procedures for project development and management, full and extensive training of staff on project design, management, monitoring and evaluation as well as through concerted substantive program development activities (elaboration of training materials, model legislation, etc.). Consequently, the management of projects became significantly more efficient and systematic. Projects became regularly monitored and independently evaluated as a normal part of the project cycle. Periodic status reports on project activities and on the financial situation of the Voluntary Fund for Technical Co-operation have been prepared regularly as of 1995 and sent to all Member States, donors, and other partners in the UN system. In addition, regular and direct exchange of views and information with all Member States has enhanced the transparency of the program and led to contributions from many developing countries such as India, South Africa, and Mexico. As a result, annual voluntary contributions increased by nearly 50 percent during 1996-1997. Program activities have also increased by 209 percent while the number of technical co-operation staff was reduced by more than 50 percent.

5. Recognizing those positive developments, the Commission on Human Rights in its resolutions in 1997 welcomed progress made in the management of the program of advisory services and technical co-operation, notably the efforts made to apply more efficient procedures and training of staff in the area of proper identification, management, and evaluation, as well as the progressive development of clear objectives, strategies, and priorities for the effective management of the technical co-operation program.[1]

6. One other important strength of the program is the quality and dedication of a core expert staff who have accumulated in recent years considerable experience in this field, without whom the positive developments would not have occurred. It is therefore regrettable that this excellent team has now been disbanded as a result of the restructuring of the human rights secretariat.

---

[1] Commission on Human Rights resolution 1997/46: Advisory services, technical cooperation, and the Voluntary Fund for Technical Cooperation in the Field of Human Rights.

Weaknesses

The program has major weaknesses that hamper its development, some of which have already been identified in various audits:

1. Although considerable knowledge and expertise existed in the Centre for Human Rights (now OHCHR), the program has been unable for many years to apply appropriate methodologies for an effective transfer of expertise and know-how to Member States who aspire to acquire this knowledge. The development of an effective technical co-operation program was long inhibited by the lack of basic knowledge within the Centre on technical co-operation matters in general. Technical co-operation is a new priority area for the human rights program and its experience in this field until recently was very limited.

2. Before 1995, the program had no strategic management which requires the development of a collective vision or mission for the program, an assessment of the long-term opportunities and threats that could affect the vision, a mobilization of assets to address these opportunities and threats and an implementation strategy. No strategic planning was undertaken. To remedy this situation a strategic plan was developed in 1996, but it was never formally approved by top management.

3. The program lacked project management skills. Although the work of the program is project oriented, until 1995 projects were not formulated or designed on the basis of the framework and methodologies that currently exist in the area of project design, management, monitoring, and evaluation. Efforts to train project officers in this area have already started in 1995. New guidelines for project formulation have been drafted and applied, and by the end of 1997 a full manual outlining technical co-operation procedures, guidelines, formats, and methodologies was finalized.

4. The program does not have the necessary financial and administrative autonomy from the UN Secretariat to be able to deliver services to Member States efficiently. It has no self-financing strategy and is completely dependent on its modest allocation from the regular budget for technical co-operation of the UN system, and voluntary contributions from a limited number of donors.

5. The program is now overcommitted in terms of promises made to governments to develop technical co-operation programs and projects. Since up to 1995 no clear objectives were set and no priorities defined, all requests were accepted automatically although this was not advisable in some circumstances. The demand for technical assistance increased dramatically in the last two years. This "always yes" approach by top management continues (against the advice of program staff). The program in the new structure, under new management with no background in technical cooperation, with its current level of human resources, limited financial base and current UN secretariat procedures cannot implement all the projects for which there is already a commitment. In this context, the implementation rate remains low with the continuing lack of a

functioning Administration Unit. However, this was even worse prior to 1995. During 1994, only US $1,850,000 was disbursed although US $5 million was available in the Voluntary Fund for Technical Co-operation. Regular budget resources were not managed and planned properly either. By the end of June 1995, only half of the budget was obligated out of a total budget of US $4,129,000 US for the biennium. This meant that half the budget was returned and, since the financial authorities noticed this low level of expenditure, only half of this budget was authorized for the following biennium, further crippling the capacity of the program.

6. The program still has a long way to go to develop a number of substantive quality products and services that are in demand by Member States. Up to 1995, program development had consistently taken a back seat to project formulation and implementation. Obviously, the program cannot transfer knowledge and know how, which are the core concepts of technical co-operation, unless it has the tools and the reference and pedagogical materials to facilitate the transfer.

7. By 1995, as mentioned earlier, several excellent quality substantive services and products were already well developed, in the fields of police training, human rights and elections, and national institutions. However, other areas received only marginal and ad hoc attention. One example is the area of human rights training for judges and lawyers. Although several activities had been carried out in this field in the past, no systematic assessment had been done of what other institutions have produced. By 1995, few course materials had been developed and there were no pedagogical and resource materials, although most projects included a training component for the legal profession. Similar situations existed with respect to human rights and the media, human rights and prison personnel, curriculum development and teacher training on human rights, human rights and conflict resolution, and human rights and peace-keeping. A major achievement of the program is the serious work accomplished during 1995-1997 to develop substantive materials in all these areas in addition to a full manual on human rights monitoring for UN field operations, which was finalized at the end of 1997.[2]

8. The program is now facing another challenge in the area of quality control. Project personnel employed in the context of large technical assistance projects and in the context of "Field Operations" often do not apply the professional standards that the program developed in its approach to training and also in the areas of product design, management, monitoring, and evaluations, mainly because the core trained program staff has now been disbanded and the new program management has itself no training and experience in these areas.

[2] The result of this work has either been already published in the Professional Training Series of the OHCHR or in the pipeline for publication.

9. The program has long reflected the traditional bias of the UN human rights secretariat toward civil and political rights. The technical co-operation program attempted to break with this legacy. Two projects designed in 1996 which began implementation concurrently in 1997 were aimed at developing guidelines to integrate fully economic, social, and cultural rights, and to instill a gender perspective in all technical co-operation activities. Another project was also designed in late 1997 to develop substantive material and training of staff on economic, social, and cultural rights.

Opportunities

1. Member States are now unanimous about the need to develop an effective program of technical assistance in the field of human rights. This has been reflected in VDPA and subsequent resolutions of legislative bodies of the United Nations.

2. The establishment of the post of High Commissioner for Human Rights placed particular emphasis on the role of the High Commissioner in developing such a program. This presents a new opportunity for strengthening the program and increasing its visibility.

3. The VDPA has emphasized and strongly recommended that a comprehensive program be established within the United Nations in order to help states in the task of building and strengthening national capacities and adequate national structures, which has a direct impact on the overall observance of human rights and the maintenance of the rule of law.[3]

4. All stakeholders of the program have demonstrated their moral and financial support. Voluntary contributions are on the increase after several years of stagnation, rising from US $799,204 in 1987-1988, when the Fund was created, to more than US $25 million in 1997.

5. There is now a great potential for developing serious co-operation with other UN programs and agencies involved in technical co-operation in the field of human rights, such as UNDP and UNICEF. These programs and agencies desire more than ever to integrate human rights into all development efforts. Most projects developed by the program in 1996-1997 were the result of truly joint initiatives with UNDP field offices.

6. The global demand for technical assistance in the field of human rights has grown dramatically. Numerous countries around the world are now in transition to democracy, and therefore are in need of assistance to introduce constitutional human rights safeguards, legislative reforms, build new human rights and democratic institutions, and develop a culture of rights. Many countries have already ratified key international human rights instruments and subsequently

---

[3] See the Vienna Declaration and Programme of Action (A/CONF.157/23).

need assistance in bringing national legislation, policies, and practices into line with these international instruments. Nearly half the member states have requested assistance in this field in the last six years.

7. The United Nations now has a clear new objective: the promotion of democracy. This new objective is reflected in a number of recent resolutions of the UN legislative bodies and in numerous important UN initiatives such as the setting up of an Electoral Assistance Division in the Department of Political Affairs and the provision of assistance programs to strengthen the democratization process in post-conflict situations such as in El Salvador and Mozambique.

Threats

1. Although the VDPA has emphasized the need to develop technical assistance in the field of human rights, a survey of the distribution of current human and financial resources within the Office of the High Commissioner for Human Rights reveals that this may not be possible. Human resources allocated to technical co-operation were reduced by about 50 percent in late 1996. These resources have now been further reduced with the entry into force of the new structure of the Office in early 1998. The new structure integrates technical co-operation with investigatory and monitoring activities. The disadvantages and consequences of such a merger are significant. First, the purposes, methodologies, and procedures of these two sets of activities are completely different. Investigatory and monitoring activities and procedures are implemented in a highly charged political atmosphere. Their objective is to ascertain and expose to the world wrongdoing on the part of governments. By contrast, technical co-operation is almost totally de-politicized. Governments feel free to request such assistance in the knowledge that this request or anything that should result from it will not be used against them. This perception is particularly useful for governments who have shown themselves to be especially sensitive to external criticism but nevertheless recognize the need for outside help in developing national capacities, institutions, and structures which are the necessary preconditions for the exercise of rights and freedoms. Most Member States have voiced their opposition to this "merger" on numerous occasions. Commission on Human Rights resolution 1997/45 stressed "that the Centre's technical co-operation programme and the UN human rights monitoring will remain separate activities" (para 20). It should be noted also that all special rapporteurs, independent experts, and special representatives of the Secretary-General have also expressed, at their annual meeting in 1997, their disagreement with merging technical co-operation with monitoring activities. The Board of Trustees of the Voluntary Fund for Technical Co-operation, which is appointed by the Secretary-General, has repeatedly and strongly voiced its opposition to this "merger." There is only one explanation for the decision to ignore this advice. The restructuring of the human rights secretariat was carried in the context of the well known conflict which hampered its work during

1994-1997. The result of this restructuring largely reflects the individual interests of those who won the conflict than the interests, objectives, and priorities of the organization.

2. Technical cooperation has taken a back seat since field operations have become effectively, since 1994, the priority of the UN human rights program despite the lack of clear mandate in this area from UN legislative organs. These operations (the Rwanda style) are very costly, focus on monitoring civil and political rights only and producing catalogues of daily violations, and lead to no national capacity building. Most are donor driven initiatives and can only be initiated in countries where there is no strong government or no government at all. This strengthens the perception that the United Nations continues to use a double standard approach when dealing with violations worldwide by imposing its human rights field operations on the weakest member states only. It is significant to note that during 1994-1997 more than twenty-five million USD were spent on monitoring activities in Rwanda alone while in contrast only eleven million USD were spent for all technical cooperation activities worldwide. In late 1997, 10.2 percent of the total staff of the OHCHR in Geneva were assigned to technical cooperation in comparison to 59.4 percent assigned to the various monitoring activities (field operations, treaty monitoring, and special procedures). These figures do not include more than 200 monitors deployed in the field. The current over enthusiasm for field operations in the human rights community in the North is similar to the euphoria of the early 1990s concerning peace keeping operations. Although the United Nations has drawn valuable lessons in this area which have now been strictly applied (clear mandates, objectives, and exit strategies), when it comes to human rights field operations no lessons seem to have been learned yet. The largest human rights field operations, such as in Rwanda, continue to function with no agreed plan with the host country on what will be done, what will be produced, when and by whom, and what situation should exist when the operation ends. There is therefore no basis for planning and implementation and no framework which could provide the basis for an independent evaluation and the criteria by which the success or lack of success of the operation could be assessed.

3. The program remains marginal within the UN system. A survey of technical assistance activities revealed that most of the work being done in this area has been generated from within the UNDP in the context of the new emphasis on promoting good governance. UNDP's expenditure in this area is at least five times higher than that of OHCHR. Many UNDP country programs include components focusing on the strengthening of the administration of justice, judicial reforms, and the promotion of civil society. In most cases, these projects developed with no input from the OHCHR. In contrast to UNICEF, international human rights standards are often not reflected and promoted in the context of these UNDP activities. For the last two years substantive support from UNDP headquarters is being provided by a lay volunteer! However the personal

commitment of the UNDP Administrator to expand and improve this organization's work in human rights is already producing positive results. The UNDP is very likely to develop more as the premier agency in the provision of technical cooperation in this field.

4. Although the UNDP and other development agencies still do not have substantive technical capabilities in the area of human rights, it is possible for them to develop this capability in the medium term. This development will have tremendous implications for the program. Donors may feel more inclined to support efforts of UNDP, which has demonstrated over the years its capabilities to manage effectively technical co-operation, rather than the OHCHR, which has yet to prove its technical and management abilities.

5. The Department of Political Affairs and Peacekeeping Operations has and continues to provide technical assistance in the field of human rights and democracy in the context of conflict resolution and peace-keeping and post-conflict peace-building operations. The largest technical assistance programs in the field of human rights ever undertaken by the United Nations have, in fact, emanated and continue to emanate from these two departments within the UN Secretariat in countries including Cambodia, El Salvador, Mozambique, Haiti, and Guatemala.

6. The program has until now been absent from the process of formulation of UN country development programs. The program is not given the opportunity to provide input in the development of Country Strategic Notes and has not participated until now in the new UN Development Assistance Framework exercises at the county level despite all the official talks about the need to integrate human rights in all UN activities. Experience has shown that this integration will not happen by just focusing on servicing the new committees and task forces at headquarters in New York which seems to take a great deal of staff time in Geneva. Integration will only progressively develop in the context on a new emphasis on coordination at the country level, in the field, in the context of UN coordinated assistance in support of the countries national development objectives. Subsequently, technical assistance currently provided by the OHCHR does not fit in any UN institutional development framework and therefore remain at the margin of the UN coordinated action at the country level.

7. The trend in the UN system (outside the OHCHR) to develop technical capabilities and to carry out technical co-operation in the field of human rights is also coupled with another trend among bilateral donors to develop and strengthen their own national capabilities in this field.[4] For example, in the United States, several NGOs and university centers are the major contractors of USAID in this field with single contracts exceeding the total yearly expenditures of the VFTC.

---

[4] The current estimates for annual bilateral budgets that exist for assistance in the field of human rights/democracy/governance may exceed USD 500 million. SIDA (Sweden) alone has an estimated budget of USD 100 million in this field.

Furthermore, private firms in Washington have sprung up competing for lucrative USAID contracts. In the United States, at least $100 million is allocated yearly for technical assistance in this field. Most of this assistance is channeled through U.S. private companies. No international human rights standards are promoted in this context, but rather the promotion of the United States as a model for democracy and human rights.

8. The major UN agencies and programs which could benefit from the development of the program in the formulation and the implementation of technical co-operation in the field of human rights, democracy, and the rule of law have no practical working and institutional co-operative arrangements with the OHCHR. Memoranda of understanding have been signed with several agencies after several years of delay but these are general frameworks that lack practical arrangements. There is also no institutional structure for the program to permit their active participation and input in the development of the program activities.

9. A viable option to reverse this trend would be to establish a new structure that enables the High Commissioner to create an advisory board for the program under her leadership. The advisory board should include representatives of all major UN entities that have an interest in participating, supporting, and investing in a United Nations technical co-operation program in the field of human rights, democracy, and rule of law. The advisory board would therefore include high-level representatives from UNDP, UNICEF, ILO, UNESCO, DPA, DPKO, and representatives of recipient countries, major donors, and bilateral development agencies in addition to NGOs. Participation in the advisory board should be on the basis of an agreement to set up a single program for the United Nations that would create a concerted effort to help the international community develop a global, forward-looking, and proactive technical co-operation program to promote national capacity building in human rights, democracy, and the rule of law. The new program will then become the UN system's main body that will seek to achieve this aim. The new program should build on the strength and comparative advantages of its co-sponsors, the technical expertise of the OHCHR, and should have a mandate to facilitate coordination among its co-sponsors at national, regional, and international level.

10. It is against this background that the objectives and priorities of the program should be revisited. Under the new circumstances described above, the program should play more of a catalytic role within the UN system rather than an operational one. The program can be more successful in terms of reach and impact if it focused on the following:

- Build on the recent successful efforts in the area of program development to develop further more *substantive expertise*, training material, reference documentation, model legislation,etc.
- Research, documentation and wide dissemination of *best practices* in the area of national capacity building.

- Undertake *needs assessments and situation analyses* for selected interested countries in partnership with other UN actors at the country level.
- Offer expertise and resources for the development of *national plans of action (NPA)* by all the country's stakeholders including NGOs. The NPA should be based on the national development plan and cover all human rights, including economic, social and cultural rights, and rights of women. The NPA should analyze where the country is in terms of national capacity, where it wants to be, and how it can get there.
- Provide expertise for the formulation of a co-ordinated and joint UN system technical co-operation intervention using the *program approach,* rather than a project approach.
- Facilitate the development, at the country level, of *joint UN system work plans* centered on specified priority areas in support of the NPA, and taking into account the comparative advantage and specific mandate of the different UN agencies. Emphasis should be made on complementarity of action within the UN family, pooling of resources, and cost sharing.
- Facilitate the setting up of a *thematic and co-ordinating mechanism* at the country level under the leadership of the UN Resident Co-ordinator (human rights task force/theme group) to facilitate the development and implementation of the tasks described above.
- Undertake resource mobilization efforts to support the implementation of the NPA.
- Deploy *country advisors,* with a background in development co-operation, to assist the task force/theme group in the development of the needs assessment, NPA, joint UN technical cooperation interventions in support of the NPA. The Country Advisor should be a resource available in the UN system at the country level providing support for the design and implementation of all agencies projects and activities in the field of human rights. The country advisor should also support resource mobilization efforts on behalf of the national partners and the human rights task force/theme group.

Just 50 percent of the resources currently being spent on the human rights field operation in Rwanda could cover the cost of deploying forty country advisors in forty different countries. Resources of the VFTC would be better spent as seed money for the implementation of the activities described above rather than continuing to fund entire costly multi-year projects.

It is against this background that the following mission statement for the program could be useful. This statement is also followed by a set of guiding principles to support the mission statement and guide the program in its operations.

THE PROGRAM MISSION AND GUIDING PRINCIPALS

The Technical Co-operation Programme in the Field of Human Rights, Democracy and the Rule of Law should be a United Nations global program co-ordinated by the High Commissioner for Human Rights, which aims at promoting the incorporation of international human rights standards into national laws, policies and practices, building national and regional capacities and infrastructures for the promotion and protection of all human rights, democracy under the rule of law in the context of pursuit of national development objectives, and national programs and UN system co-ordinated interventions in support of these objectives.[5]

Guiding Principles

The past experience of the program has shown the need to develop principles in the form of a set of values and beliefs that aim at developing and defining guidelines for the program's activities. These principles would further clarify the direction, approach, and philosophy of the program, both inside and outside the UN system.

Principle 1 — Capacity Building

The program in developing technical co-operation activities should give particular emphasis to national capacity building strengthening, to enable governments to attain self-reliance. Program activities should be formulated and carried out in support of national development objectives through cohesive national programs. Program activities should be part of UN interventions and inputs to be merged with national and other external inputs in support of programs conceived by recipient countries.

Principle 2 — Partnership to Support Positive Change

The program's approach to technical co-operation should be based on respect for the countries' choices, national program, and strategies, and should avoid donor-driven development programs. It should only offer its outside perspectives on governmental objectives and programs in the context of dialogue. It is for the government concerned to define what it needs in terms of assistance

---

[5] This succinct statement sets forth the programme's purpose and philosophy, its fundamental reason for existence, its scope, and its unique characteristics as outlined in the various resolutions of the UN legislative authorities FTN (Economic and Social Council resolutions 277 (x) and 474 A (XV), 728 (XXIII), 1235 (XLII), 1503 (XI, VIII), and 1990/41, Commission on Human Rights resolution 8 (XXIII), General Assembly resolutions 7106 A (XX), 2200 A (XXI), 39/46, 45/158, 48/121, and 48/141, as well as the Vienna Declaration and program of Action.

and how to obtain this assistance. The program should neither impose its views on the type of assistance needed nor simply provide what is requested by government when its best technical assessment and professional judgment leads to the conclusion that what is requested is not feasible, does not conform with international human rights standards, and/or is not likely to be the most effective way of delivering technical assistance and meeting governmental objectives in this field.

Principle 3 — Participation

Capacity building for human rights will require active partnership among governments, civil society, and human rights organizations in particular, in formulating national plans of action in the field of human rights, in defining goals for the promotion and protection of human rights, and in the formulation and implementation of technical co-operation projects to promote the worldwide and national application of international human rights standards. The program should aim at enhancing participation by building broad constituencies and partnerships in the development and delivery of technical co-operation at the national level. It should seek actively the participation of local human rights NGOs in policy dialogue with government throughout all stages of the project cycle whenever appropriate.

Principle 4 — Women's Rights

A gender perspective should be integrated into all aspects of the program. In this regard, particular attention should be paid to strengthening national institutions and infrastructures better to protect and promote the human rights of women. The integration of a gender perspective should extend beyond the formal components of the program to include working methods and procedures as well as staff training. This integration should be achieved by taking into consideration the needs of women throughout the programming cycle, project design; the analysis of projects' impact on women and follow-up action at the monitoring and evaluation phases; and active participation of women and women's organizations in the formulation and implementation of technical cooperation activities.

Principle 5 — Vulnerable Groups

The program should assist member States to implementing international human rights standards relating to vulnerable groups such as children, persons belonging to minorities, indigenous people, and refugees, and should seek their active participation and partnership in the formulation and implementation of technical assistance projects.

Principle 6 — Human Rights in Sustainable Human Development

The program's mission should be part of the United Nations efforts to promote sustainable human development. Technical co-operation in the field of human rights, democracy, and the rule of law is one important dimension of sustainable human development and its central role in the promotion of peace and global human security.

Principle 7 — Technical Co-Operation is Not a Substitute for Scrutiny by UN Bodies

The provision of advisory services and technical assistance does not in any way reduce a government's accountability and responsibility for the promotion and protection of human rights. The development of technical assistance projects with governments should not exempt them from scrutiny by the various monitoring procedures established by the UN.

Principle 8 — Technical Co-Operation on the Basis of International Human Rights Standards

In developing technical co-operation with Member States, the program should apply international human rights norms and standards in all areas of assistance. In addition, the program should promote the realization of economic, social, and cultural rights since all human rights are universal, indivisible, interdependent, and inter-related and as such must be treated with no functional distinction or hierarchy vis-à-vis the various sets of rights.

Principle 9 — Assistance Within the Framework of the Program's Priorities and Procedures

Proposals for technical co-operation projects, whether originated as a result of actions of treaty bodies, Special Procedures mechanisms or other UN bodies, or as a result of direct requests from governments should be assessed on the basis of their compatibility with the mission of the program, its principles, goals and objectives, priorities, and availability of resources. All projects should be developed according to the program's guidelines for project formulation management, monitoring, and evaluation.

CONCLUSION

Technical co-operation in the field of human rights will very likely remain as an important component of the UN human rights program despite its current setback. The experience already accumulated is full of lessons learned. The current high profile given to human rights by the new Secretary-General and the High Commissioner, the unanimous consensus among Member States about the need to strengthen this area, and the strong legislative mandate of the program can only support its further development as an integral part of the new efforts of the Secretary-General and the High Commissioner to integrate human rights in all UN activities. For the first time, the program has an opportunity to truly play a catalytic role in the UN system which could have a wide impact. This requires moving from the usual "turf building" approach to developing a coordinating, substantive quality control function and mobilizing the technical and financial resources of the entire UN system. This does not mean that the program should have no operational activities at all. On the contrary, in addition to developing substantive products and services, the program should develop catalytic projects and programs from which lessons can be learned in order to disseminate best practices resulting from new approaches and innovative initiatives.

Chapter 19

Human Rights Education: The Humanizing of a Global Society

Peter Thuynsma and Heather Thuynsma

For the past fifty years the Universal Declaration of Human Rights (UDHR) has provided the legal principles which are fundamental to humankind. Its thirty Articles couch the very essence of humanist aspirations but it is the legal precepts that have drawn attention. Perhaps not enough attention went into helping general populations, societies, communities, and individuals to apply those tenets. Perhaps too little energy has been channeled into **helping** people to live as equals—in dignity, and with responsibility to each other.

There is often something narrow and restrictive about the way we think of "human rights education" (HRE). All too often it is classroom centered, and Western in concept. Training materials and manuals, portable as most are, are tailored to or seek to simulate classroom situations—as if HRE can only be learned in formalized teaching environments. Learning is a preconceived outcome that is often too constrictive, unvaried, and undynamic. Yet, HRE must be cognizant of current political and social developments. Citizenship education, democracy education, peace education are all vital aspects of HRE that need to draw more readily on the vibrant life experiences around us. HRE is, after all, humanitarian education that, in turn, forms the very foundation of lifelong learning and living. HRE is a state of mind—a state of mind that must be learned by everyone, for its success depends on everyone.

This chapter explores several textures of HRE, and provides a critique for not being aggressive enough in promoting a full understanding of human rights in nascent democracies. It is only since the launch of the *Decade for Human Rights Education* that the UN has advanced the fabric of rights knowledge. We probe the

253

export of a human rights' ethos through unique circumstances that encourage the practice of HRE, and our perspective is motivated by the African cultural maxim that: **I** am because **you** are, and **you** are because **we** are.

Several years after Angola's Independence from colonial rule, and deep into its civil war, a village elder asked a researching field worker: "When is this independence thing going to end?" More recently, a seventy-six-year-old South African who had voted for the first time in her life only four years previously commented on her country's rampant corruption by saying "I can't wait for this to end next year" (referring to the next scheduled elections).

Both statements reflect very interesting perspectives: the first by an illiterate person, the second by someone well-educated and informed. The first elder saw *Independence* as yet another social phase in her lifetime. The latter had an instinct that whatever was amiss now, could be changed at the next democratic election. In a recent assessment of the needs for South Africa's second democratic general election, an even more startling fact leaped out: most people felt that voting four years ago was enough. We've voted our leaders into office, now they have their jobs and must do it! seems to be the attitude.

Such are the hopes of those who know the democratic process, and the attitudes of those who do not. But however educated, the woman whose hopes are pinned to the forthcoming election may herself not fully understand the complexity of a democracy. Her dilemma was palpable when confronted with the following scenario:

> Democracy is inextricable from human rights. In its most elemental sense, democracy means *freedom*. The Human Rights concept, in its most fundamental sense, means *equality*. But, can we easily equate *freedom* and *equality*? Are they totally compatible?

Texturizing the scenario would be: a ten-year-old bouncing into a room. S/he spears a question at the nearest adult: "Are all people equal"? "Yes, is the likely reply. "Then can I have a driver's license and a credit card, please?" The adults are likely to break out in a stiff chuckle or burst into raucous laughter—followed by an answer that the child won't fully understand. Even seasoned human rights advocates will be hard pressed to discuss such dichotomous concepts. Then there are those little enigmas where tradition and religion fly in the face of basic democracy by admitting limited human rights. How feasible, alas, how logical, is it to allow some human rights and not others? We will revisit this dilemma in our remarks on cultural relativism further into this discussion.

In a similar vein, a legislated human rights ethos will empower a government while the inherent checks and balances will undoubtedly limit its authority— effectively empowering and disempowering it.

Such conundrums are amplified because democracy is a process, not a product. It braves debate and is often invigorated by amendment or review. In its guidelines and constitutional principles, it makes and influences policy and yet remains as amorphous as a people can allow. As easily as it can flow from an individual or a government's tongue, so too can it frustrate. How often has one not heard people whisper, only half humorously: democracy . . . so noble, but, oh so slow!

Nevertheless, a fully functioning democracy is vital if we are to guarantee our human-ness: our dignity, our freedoms, our rights to health care, and a healthy environment. Knowledge of the democratic system is imperative to forge a culture of accountability, responsibility, and mutual respect. Peace education is vital if we are to live in harmony yet retain our ability to assert and protest. These are lofty ideals for sure, but they are also imperatives if we are to acknowledge our full humanity.

Regrettably, we cannot quite rely on a mythical honor system to guarantee that our neighbors or our communities have the will or the stamina to subscribe to such a simple yet endearing morality. Angola and Mozambique are today recovering from their civil wars; South Africa is rebuilding after apartheid's savagery. Cracks are beginning to show in Zimbabwe's high road. Swaziland clings adamantly to its inflexible youthful monarchy. Zambia treads a fragile ledge between democratic interests and economic promise. Zaire was swiped away in favor of the *Democratic People's Republic of Congo*—whose political morality becomes more and more suspect each day. Slightly further afield, the help that Rwanda and Burundi are receiving after the mass genocide of two years ago, consists not only of development aid, but also of shipments of arms from South Africa—ostensibly to help stabilize the Great Lakes region!

This, believe it or not, geographically amounts to less than 5 percent of the globe. Yet it is at once a veritable microcosm of so many nations around the world who are fretting a democratic identity. Rwanda, most unfortunately, is not an African exception. We need only remember the "ethnic cleansing" of the former Yugoslavia. Ireland, Bosnia, Albania, Kosavo, the Mexican Chiapas, Cambodia, Tibet, Burma, and Timorean theaters are experiencing no less traumatic stresses—almost as if threats to humanist values are as prevalent as proselytizing them!

If it is indeed a dilemma of national character, then we can assume that questions like the following are sometimes (or oftentimes) played out behind the scenes: Shall we call ourselves a democracy? Or, shall we see electoral gestures as the limits of our democracy? Or, how shall we appease the IMF or World Bank? The only victims in such game-playing is everyone! And the victims in the African context have invariably grown out of Disraeli's caveat, so many years ago that:

A nation of sheep will breed a leadership of wolves.

SAMPLING THE SCOPE
OF HUMAN RIGHTS EDUCATION

HRE is a young academic venture with little published theory or criticism. For many of its advocates it is a tool with which to effect behavioral change— be it political or social. Many HRE workers are practitioners who concentrate their energies on classroom methodologies brimming with goals and activities. In stark contrast, there exists also a minority trapped in esoteric wrestlings and intellectual reification for its own sake. It is not, as it may appear, to be a lack of synthesis, but the diversity seems to call out for wider coordinated association of interests and talents.

In her succinct delineation of human rights education and human rights educators, Shulamith Koenig provides a list of why and how human rights should be promoted [1]. She advocates a holistic approach that engages the essential educational principles and sharpened gender sensitivities. She then calls for *expanding opportunities, encouraging effective educational projects, materials, a review of current and previous methods, mobilizing governments to engage in human rights education, endorsing and supporting new groups working in HRE, assessing the needs for a major,* and a *global strategy to strengthen all such efforts.* Although something of a rhetorical catalogue, Ms. Koenig's purpose is to help people learn that their human rights are universal and apply to everyone. She insists that governments are accountable to their national populations and to the world community, and that rights bestowed by governments are only as strong as the will of such governments. Finally, Koenig says,

> . . . social justice and human freedom can best be achieved through the realisation of human rights. . . . People need to know that the Universal Declaration of Human Rights contains the values that protect the spirit that promotes human dignity [1, p. 47].

The catalogue serves as a fine guideline, but implementation needs to be innovative, creative, and carry a lasting and measurable impact. There is no real mention of HRE as being culturally sensitive, as development, as promoting conflict resolution, reconciliation, or that it be rooted in the realities of the lives of people.[1] Ms. Koenig is among those who lobbied for the adoption of a Decade of Human Rights Education which, as is customary at the UN, carries with it a *Plan of Action.*

Within the *Plan of Action* there is a section that distills the meaning of human rights education into five overlapping areas:

---

[1] Taken, loosely, from the text of the *Final Document of the Conference-Workshop on Asia Pacific Human Rights Education for Development,* Manilla, Philippines, December 15, 1995.

   (i)   strengthening of respect for human rights and fundamental freedoms;

  (ii) developing the human personality and the sense of its dignity;

 (iii) promoting understanding, tolerance, gender equality, and friendship among nations, indigenous peoples, racial, ethnic, religious, and linguistic groups;

 (iv) enabling all peoples to operate effectively in a free society; and

  (v) furthering the activities of the UN in peace maintenance.[2]

For the hands-on HRE worker it is curious that it took the UN nearly forty-five years to proclaim this *Decade*. That this is standard UN practice is but cold comfort. Will it have an impact in promoting the dignity of humanity? Given the international support system, failure would seem impossible. However, it would be highly advisable that the following principles be included as the mainstay of all human rights work: participate, be impartial, non-defensive, tenacious, and cooperative/collaborative.[3] Above all, and as far as possible, human rights education must be proactive—HRE must work to instill an affirmative and an assertive sense of communal spirit which champions individual freedom in relation to, and with the consent of, community and society.

Implementing the *Plan of Action* is up to each member state and its civil society. Monitoring and global coordination is the responsibility of the UN High Commissioner for Human Rights in Geneva. The fact that the *Plan of Action* means to develop an international initiative that will drive momentum into national initiatives is utterly commendable. Implementation is crucial, yet the *Plan* spends almost no effort in outlining the theoretical imperative or the motivation for the national plans it hopes to spawn. It is not enough to point to the various international instruments as a theoretical justification. HRE is an educational exercise, a pedagogical program that by its very nature, means to subvert mindsets, modify behavior, and enrich intellects. As a consequence, we are attempting to transform large portions of global society and in many instances, battle ignorance and institutional adversities.

Human rights education, despite its innocuous ring, must be presented as:

- a standard to which everyone is entitled, and
- a tool with which to fight human rights violations.

---

[2] Report on the UN Decade for Human Rights Education (1994-2005) and public information activities in the field of human rights at the Fifty Second Session of the UN General Assembly, by the High Commissioner for Human Rights, Agenda Item 112(b) 1997.

[3] For a detailed discussion on implementing these principles, see [2]. This publication also contains an excellent discussion on core content, minimum core content, state obligation, and human rights indicators. This is a discussion that could clarify the concept of "limited rights" referred to earlier, far better than we have time or space to do.

Roland Hammer, the International Red Cross' director of international programs, asserts that HRE demands not just a legal approach, but a political one.[4] In perfect consonance is Clarence Dias' suggestion that we not concern ourselves with global implementation, but concentrate our synergies on local circumstances.[5] Both these suggestions bear heavily on our planning of human rights education over the next fifty years. Learning in the new millennium should mean applying education's four pillars: learning to be, learning to know, learning to do, and learning to live together. HRE shapes a person's, and therefore a society's, new identity and integrity. This, in turn, promotes dignity, equality, and freedom—we are therefore concerned with moral reasoning and social development [3].

It is primarily the cultural relativists that hold human rights and human rights education to be political. They argue that the local/regional cultural traditions (religion, politics, economics, and law) determine the existence and scope of civil and political rights enjoyed by individuals in a given stance—a stance with which even non-cultural relativists can find consonance. If this is so, then human rights and the UDHR cannot be seen as universal, say the relativists. They would argue further that human rights, in its Western sense, and as they appear in the UDHR, are incompatible with cultures whose values have been shaped by years of imposed colonial rule [4]. Nonetheless, relativists do admit that certain core rights should be respected universally. Among those rights are: the rights to life, the right not to be tortured or undergo cruel, inhuman, or degrading treatment or punishment, and the right to freedom of opinion [5].

More importantly, cultural relativists tend to diminish the government's role or responsibility to their constituents. Human rights educationists, of course, would disagree feverishly. To us, the role of the government is pivotal in promoting both human rights and democratic practices. Several new democracies have perished because governments have abdicated or neglected their responsibilities. A prime contemporary example is the Nigerian government which panders to the greed of a minority. In its high oil-price economy, Venezuela extended significant social programs to its people. When oil prices declined, it simply discontinued many of these programs. Official public relations had it that the government extended the social development and relief as gifts consequent to the healthy economy. When they were discontinued, the people who had come to see them as gifts, simply accepted that the gifts were now unaffordable. Activists, however, saw the programs for what they were—rights and entitlements, not gifts, and campaigned splenetically to have them reinstated [2].

---

[4] Roland Hammer, International Red Cross Mission Report on *International Consultation on the Pedagogical Foundations of Human Rights Education,* San Jose, Costa Rica, p. 4, July 1996.

[5] Clarence Dias, *Critique of the UN Decade of Human Rights Education's Plan of Action.* An address to *International Consultation on the Pedagogical Foundations of Human Rights Education,* San Jose, Costa Rica, July 1996.

Learners are palpable, thinking human beings, and HRE is a medium through which to address larger issues and one that can accommodate head-on engagement. Among the most vital of areas that demand engagement are the many facets of *Economic and Social Rights*. The entry point used by many HRE practitioners are the Articles of the UDHR that charge us to promote:

- the right to work (article 23);
- the right to an adequate standard of living, including food, clothing, housing, and medical care (article 25);
- the right to education (article 26).

These concepts are only apparently simple. The average citizen must not take the right to work to mean the right to a job. And, by whose definition do we assess an *adequate standard of living. . .* ? How, then, should we define and educate society about the responsibilities which human rights necessarily entail? The South African experience provides a useful explanation.

Not only has its democracy come about through a grueling bush war, world economic sanctions, and a negotiated revolution, but South Africa leaped idealistically into crafting the most harmonious, respectful, and best educated national society. As the economic powerhouse of southern Africa it hopes to cascade its successes throughout the southern African region, and perhaps even throughout the continent.

Most momentous of the transformational changes desired by the new SA government was a complete overhaul of the educational curriculum. It meant a radical move away from a separatist and highly discriminatory education that seemed hell bent on producing an inferior black workforce of *hewers of wood and drawers of water.* The target was largely to make the superior white educating process more universal. A whole new interdisciplinary curriculum has been drafted through vigorous consultation and which will meaningfully consolidate thirteen education departments into one national structure. The curriculum is based on specific outcomes and traditional subjects such as history, geography, literature, etc., have been replaced by eight distinct yet interrelated learning areas. Among the core learning areas are *Life Skills* and *Human and Social Sciences.* The *Life Skills* learning program, in particular, includes values-based education grounded on human rights principles.

Like veins coursing throughout the system, other human rights educational sub-curricula intersect with the major learning areas. A prominent example is environmental education. One practical application occurred when a primary school class was taken on a whale watch. Over the subsequent weeks, nearly every discipline drew on the experience: mathematics wrapped its work around size, volume, and displacement. Geography involved whale migrations and throughout the whole process learners were unobtrusively made aware of their responsibilities to wildlife and the environment. They learned about other cultures who depend on and respect sea life. More significantly, responsible trade, conservation, and economics become quietly infused as were values of respect and responsibility—the very basis of HRE.

Perhaps the lesson best learned from this fledgling but daring curriculum, is that human rights education is infused, entertainingly, subtly, and systemically. The learning begins almost informally with a live, interesting, even entertaining, contemporary activity. The focus is on holistic learning, drawing away from the dour formality of "teaching." Humanitarian responsibilities are interfaced with a practical context without preaching. "Learning," not "teaching," has become the hallmark of this new eclectic system drawn from numerous world models. But does that mean that HRE is so amorphous, so flexible as to be accommodated into any learning situation?

HUMAN RIGHTS, GLOBALIZATION, AND HUMAN RIGHTS EDUCATION: AN EXAMPLE

Business and human rights have traditionally been unlikely bedfellows. The corporate need to exploit cheap labor to maximize production has always been in conflict with human rights principles. In recent years, rights activism has seized the technological age with a vengeance and used the Internet, among other tools, as an inexpensive means to mobilize widespread awareness campaigns—thus intensifying the already hostile relationship.[6] Such campaigns have led to Levi-Straus' exit from Burma flicking in motion a domino trend that made it easier for Macy's, Liz Claiborne, and Eddie Bauer to leave the severely repressive Burmese politics behind. Similarly, Addidas, Nike, and Reebok were targeted for using child labor in the manufacture of some of their products. Unfortunately such punitive action is not the complete story, for as corporations withdraw they leave unemployment and misery in their wake.

Debra L. Spa's brisk-paced article in *Foreign Affairs,* narrates an encouraging scenario of corporate partnering to adopt codes of conduct [6].[7] In the past, multinational companies have always defended their use of unprincipled labor practices by citing "if we don't do it, our competitors will." Global competition only heightened the urgency of their defense. Lately they have come to realize that pressure against them is unlikely to abate. In actual fact, activist pressure is guaranteed to intensify and a larger clientele is likely to be made aware of inhumane underwritings. Anticipating a consumer backlash, many of the larger corporations have opted for collective action: if all firms adhere to the same

---

[6] Casa Alianza is one of many e-mail based campaigns enveloping the globe. Readers respond by e-mail to incidents involving human injustice. They write directly to the media and government officials. In most cases, these officials are inundated with mail and are obliged to take positive action.

[7] The preceding information on Levi-Straus et al. is also from Ms. Spa's insightful article.

standard, none is individually penalized. Firms adhere to the higher standards because public attention forces them to, and the more companies that comply, the easier it is for the less prominent ones to join. As this movement gains ground (along with the model factories initiatives), so too are human rights likely to improve. This is one of the rare encouragements in the debates around globalization.

But globalization has obviously gained a momentum too difficult to stop. For all its promise of prosperity, its concomitant effects remain disturbing. In many instances it threatens indigenous cultural values and, of course, harkens devastating consumerism. In plainer language, globalization is no more than neo-colonialism where the major trader or benefactor calls the shots. This has been met with relatively feeble resistance in the many developing countries who depend so heavily on foreign economies. One must assume that policy toward attracting such foreign investment will be deliberate and cautious. It should be a policy fully mindful of the perverse effects of building toward a global economy and a policy that vigilantly sees that:

- the opportunities that globalization presents are exploited in the interest of the common good, rather than to the exclusive advantage of a few;
- the growing and destabilizing gap between the haves and the have-nots presents a challenge to the entire international community;
- lowered trade barriers, lowered costs of transportation and communication, and mobility of capital are moving from traditional national markets to an integrated world market—which, if left unchecked, is often at the expense of national development;
- it promotes a sustainable human development in those nations with which it trades [7].

In reality, these strategies are underpinned by commercial overtones that are superficially political, and utterly cosmetic. In most instances, sponsoring high-profile development programs do little to effect a change in human values, i.e., legally, they comply with human labor laws; politically, they may appeal to acceptable social standards; and their commercial worth is tangible. Job creation and developing a sustainable market are vital, but social investment and development programs need to run much deeper. Human rights law may well be transmitted via the foreign work ethic, but this efficiency ethos begins and ends in the workplace. Little is transmutable and the experience remains a commodity applicable only to earning a wage. What else must be done?

The community must be taught about what it means to be human. All too often companies concentrate on economic upliftment but forget the role they can play in furthering the social human rights dimension. In their development programs they teach what it means *to be, to know,* and *to do* but not *how to live together in the new consumerist society.* Such programs need to help communities develop a sense of responsibility which, in turn, must be exercised with respect and dignity.

Human rights education, therefore, needs to piggy-back on this development thrust and infuse itself through traditional as well as *avant garde* educational principles. Should the very moral obligation drawn from international and local human rights instruments be used as either an overt or an unobtrusive ethos in all educative exercises, we may find a way to divert the globalization juggernaught in favor of the less privileged and more vulnerable.

A corporate partner needs to be proactive and assist its employees in fostering strong, lasting relationships between themselves and within their communities. Employees need to be taught moral competence, not merely moral values. By using innovative problem-based education, the firm can inculcate a comparable set of values and life skills as part of its training program. What is needed is not merely an awareness of the global work ethic, but also a practical sense of reciprocal responsibilities that can be applied to real everyday situations. This is the very stuff of human rights education. Without it, globalization is simply another form of exploitation; but add to it a tangible system of moral skills and respect, and prosperity becomes a goal everyone can aspire to and achieve.

CONCLUSION

In our opinion, HRE emerges as one of the most potent vehicles for conveying—not only a new set of values—but creating an awareness of the worth with which we are all born. HRE is (not simply conveys) the very substance and essence of being human while, at the same time, it emphasizes the responsibilities we have to one another. Should HRE scholars be able to galvanize their ideals, their educational principles, and their philosophies, we could produce a value system to safeguard us all.

REFERENCES

1. S. Koenig, Defending the Future, in *Human Rights: The New Consensus,* Regency Press (Humanity), London, pp. 43-47, 1994.
2. D. Buhl, *Ripple in Still Water,* International Human Rights Internship Program, Washington, D.C., pp. 14-17, 1997.
3. H. Starkey, Introduction, in *The Challenges of Human Rights Education,* Council of Europe/Cassel, London, p. 4, 1991.
4. I. G. Shivji, *The Concept of Human Rights in Africa,* Codesria Book Series, London, pp. 3-4, 1989.
5. D. Hill, Human Rights and Foreign Policy: Theoretical Foundations, in *Human Rights and Foreign Policy,* D. Hill (ed.), Macmillan, London, pp. 4-5, 1989.

6. D. L. Spa, The Spotlight and the Bottom Line, *Foreign Affairs,* pp. 7-12, March/April 1998.

7. J. Pooley, The Globalization of Oppression: Multinational Corporations and the Failure of Democracy, in *Perspective: Harvard-Radcliffe Liberal Monthly,* November 1995. http://hcs.harvard.edu/~perspey/nov95/democ.html. See also J. Brecher and T. Costello, *Global Village or Global Pillage.*

Voices

A Legacy for Everyone

Tracy Roosevelt

My father, who is a grandson of President Franklin Delano Roosevelt and Eleanor Roosevelt, likes to ask questions around the dinner table about what controversies and conflicts there are in our school and how we deal with them. Sometimes he draws parallels to events in Eleanor Roosevelt's life. In my mind, since I never knew my great grandmother, she seems to be a heroine—someone who always did everything right. When I say that, I am likely to get a description from my father about how Eleanor Roosevelt was considered ugly as a child, how her parents both died when she was very young, and how she overcame great obstacles to be lovingly called the "First Lady of the World."

All my life I have heard about how important it is to support issues such as human rights and equality. Eleanor Roosevelt has always been an example of one person who made a difference in the lives of so many people by standing up for human rights and the dignity of everyone. Because she was the First Lady, she had a unique opportunity to affect the lives of all Americans, but helping children was one of her major priorities. Her concern for the well-being of children may have grown from her work among the settlement house children on the lower East Side of New York City when she was in her late teens. She carried her concern for children throughout her life, and she worked hard as First Lady to include the rights of children in President Roosevelt's domestic programs. Later, when she was a Delegate to the United Nations, she drafted, among others, a section on children's rights in the Universal Declaration of Human Rights. Because of her public positions, she was able to accomplish so much to make children's lives better.

My favorite stories of Eleanor Roosevelt, however, are the ones in which she made a point or tried to influence equality in ways that anyone could do. During

World War II, she worked with a friend of hers who was the head of a company to get day care for children at his factory. The program became a model for others in the United States, and many children, who would have been left home alone while their mothers worked, were cared for. At a time in which there was wide-spread prejudice, she invited both black children and white children to play together at a White House party. Later, she invited children from a reform school to a garden party at the White House, shocking people who believed that these children were inferior.

Children and teenagers are often thought to be powerless in today's society, but I believe that everyone can take little actions like Eleanor Roosevelt's private efforts to further human rights, equality, and dignity. I believe there are "small" violations of human rights every day, and if we ignore them, they can become bigger and become accepted. Children and teenagers can fight the loss of human rights and dignity by standing up for what they believe even if the violation seems small at the time. For instance, I once went shopping with a black friend of mine and observed discrimination firsthand. While I was allowed to go in and out of the dressing rooms without being checked, my friend was followed and all her packages were checked every time she went into and out of the dressing rooms. She was even watched as she looked at clothes on the floor. Such behavior was outrageous, and we protested it, but it shows that black teenagers are often subjected to prejudice and a loss of dignity. There is no excuse for such behavior by a department store. Yet, I think many people tolerate it without expressing disapproval. It left me wondering what I would have done if my friend had been too poor to even consider going into the store to shop.

A school near mine which prides itself on being liberal and inclusive was also the site of an incident involving a human rights violation. While the class was studying "Facing History and Ourselves" which is an excellent curriculum that I have also taken, designed to teach teenagers about hate and human rights violations, an anonymous student put a swastika in the locker of one of the few black teens in the class. Instead of the school ignoring this terrible act or saying that it must have been an accident, the teachers took the opportunity to discuss what a hate crime is and how this action resulted in a loss of dignity for everyone. There were many meetings about it and many discussions about how such behavior diminishes everyone. While the school couldn't completely erase the hurt engendered by the act of putting a swastika in the black teen's locker, it used the hurtful act to expose hatred to the rest of the student body and to draw a valuable lesson.

I think there are many occasions like these when teenagers can stand up against hatred and human rights violations in their everyday life. When we hear someone saying something prejudiced or hateful or belittling to someone because of their race, we should have the courage to express our disapproval of such behavior. When we see an injustice, we should try to change it.

Perhaps some of us will be able to follow in the footsteps of Eleanor Roosevelt's public leadership for human rights. All of us, however, should be able to take actions to support human rights in our private lives, if we clearly and decisively protest when we see even a "small" example of a human rights violation. After all, teenagers today are the future. We will create the world of the twenty-first century. We must create a world without human rights violations.

Part V

Interface Between Global and Regional Protection and Promotion of Human Rights

Chapter 20

Interface Between Global and Regional Protection and Promotion of Human Rights: An African Perspective

M. Adama Dieng

At the time of the adoption of the Universal Declaration of Human Rights (UDHR), the majority of the African populations was subjected to colonial rule. Very few independent states from the Continent participated in the elaboration of the Declaration. With the exception of South Africa that abstained, all the other countries voted in favor of its adoption. The UDHR became the reference document for the then African leaders who were clamoring for independence, despite the fact that the Declaration did not recognize the right to self-determination. In 1957, Ghana became independent. The end of the 1950s and the early 1960s marked the realization for most African countries of independence. It is not surprising, therefore, that this right was affirmed in the two human rights Covenants adopted in 1966: the International Covenant on Civil and Political Rights (ICCPR) and the International Covenant on Economic, Social and Cultural Rights (ICESCR).

The Organization for African Unity (OAU) was founded on May 25, 1963. The main objectives of the organization were to liberate the Continent from colonialism and apartheid and "to promote international co-operation with due regard to the Charter of the United Nations and the Universal Declaration of Human Rights."

The aims of the Organization are set out in the Preamble of the Addis Ababa Charter and in its second Article.

Paragraph 8 of the Preamble reads as follows:

Persuaded that the Charter of the United Nations and the Universal Declaration of Human Rights, to the principles of which we reaffirm our adherence, provide a solid foundation for peaceful and positive cooperation among States.

This reference to the Universal Declaration is repeated in Article 2, clause 5:

The Organization shall have the following purposes . . . (e) promote international cooperation, having due regard to the Charter of the United Nations and the Universal Declaration of Human Rights.

Since the post-1960 independence movement and the decolonization process were inspired by the content of the Universal Declaration of Human Rights (1948) and other UN initiatives, it was not surprising that notions of human rights, constitutionalism, and democracy featured very prominently in the independence constitutions of several African states. The inclusion of elaborate Bill of Rights provisions in national constitutions was regarded as the best guarantee for democracy. A typical example was the constitution of the Federal Republic of Nigeria (1960) which was based on the European Convention of Human Rights and Fundamental Freedoms (1950). In Nigeria, the Report of the Minorities Commission, established to advise on constitutional safeguards to allay the fears of minorities, saw a Bill of Rights as an important tool for the advancement of democracy in emergent states. It stated:

Provisions of this kind in the constitution are difficult to enforce and sometimes difficult to interpret. Nevertheless, we think that they should be inserted. Their presence defines beliefs widespread among democratic countries and provides a standard to which appeal may be made by those whose rights are infringed. A government determined to abandon democratic courses will find ways of violating them, but they are of great value in preventing a steady deterioration in standards of freedom and the unobtrusive encroachment of a government on individual rights.

An analysis of the ongoing events in Nigeria and other states that adopted the Nigerian model shows clearly that the minimum conditions for democracy are non-existent. Issues of widespread illiteracy, lack of political will, and the absence of human rights education, account for part of the problem. A host of other factors as well led to the gradual erosion of democracy and respect of human rights in favor of repression.

Africa's quest for democracy and human rights in the immediate post-independence period was derailed by at least two countervailing forces: the preference for a single-party system of government and widespread military coups. Very few African states escaped these scourges. These are to be considered together because the justification for military intervention was often expressed as "liberation," "redemption," "salvation" from corruption, tyranny, and the dictatorship of the single-party system.

Following the adoption of the Universal Declaration of Human Rights in 1948, it was generally accepted that the implementation of the ideals it proclaimed would have to be pursued at three different levels: the national, regional, and universal.

As mentioned earlier, at the national level fairly successful efforts were made to secure at least a theoretical acceptance of the provisions of the Universal Declaration by means of constitutional provisions and national Bills of Rights. It has been long recognized, however, that the effective protection of human rights at the national level in many areas of the world is difficult to achieve, particularly in times of internal or external tensions. Executive action or subservient judiciaries tend to render ineffective the human rights guarantees in national laws. For these reasons, it has been accepted that international judicial supervision is essential. Due to both the difficulties of securing agreement at the universal level and the diversities in legal systems, efforts have been concentrated on securing the establishment of regional machinery for the protection of human rights.

The Council of Europe was the first to set up an international judicial machinery at the regional level to protect human rights by adopting the European Convention for the Protection of Human Rights and Fundamental Freedoms in 1950; originally consisting of the European Commission and Court of Human Rights. A recent initiative aimed at enhancing the efficiency of the system has led to a merger of the two organs into a single one.

Similar initiative to secure the establishment of analogous regional machinery for the protection of human rights were undertaken in Central America, Latin America, and on the South American continent as a whole. These efforts resulted in the adoption of the Inter-American Convention of Human Rights at a conference convened by the Organization of American States in Costa Rica in November 1969. The implementing mechanism under this system also consists of a Commission and Court.

The idea of developing an African mechanism for the protection of human rights was generated in January 1961 at the African Conference on the Rule of Law held in Lagos, Nigeria, under the aegis of the International Commission of Jurists (ICJ). The main conclusion that emerged from the Lagos Conference was that the dignity of the human person is universal, regardless of the different forms it may assume in one or another cultural environment. After twenty years of negotiations, which were dominated by purely political considerations, an African Charter on Human and Peoples' Rights was adopted. A Commission was put in place to implement the provisions of the Charter. A critical analysis of the mandate, capacity, and effectiveness of this machinery in the face of African realities, led to a call for the establishment of a Court which is expected to complement and reinforce the Commission's actions.

It is important to draw attention to Paragraph 4 of the resolution of the Lagos Conference (known in the history of human rights as the "Law of Lagos"). This Paragraph acknowledged the need for an interface between global and regional efforts aimed at protecting human rights by stipulating that:

> In order to give full effect to the Universal Declaration of Human Rights of 1948, the possibility of adopting an African Convention on Human Rights providing for the establishment of an appropriate tribunal and appeal procedures open to all individuals under the jurisdiction of the signatory States . . . be pursued.

Nevertheless, a little more than two years later, the 1963 OAU Charter did not provide for any system of promotion and protection of human rights.

The OAU's practical achievements in the field have been, by nearly unanimous judgment, somewhat limited. This is hardly surprising in view of the degree to which human rights are held to be within the internal jurisdiction of states, except for the right of peoples to self-determination, as indicated above.

BACKGROUND TO THE AFRICAN CHARTER

In June 1981, the 18th Assembly of the Heads of State and Government of the Organization of African Unity (OAU), meeting in Nairobi, Kenya, adopted the African Charter on Human and Peoples' Rights. The decision to adopt the African regional instrument for the promotion and protection of human and peoples' rights was the result of several years of deliberations, campaigns, and intensive diplomatic efforts.

A major breakthrough occurred in the 1970s during the regimes of Idi Amin (Uganda), "Emperor" Bokassa (Central African Republic), Macias Nguema (Equatorial Guinea), and other African dictators of that period. The unprecedented and massive violations of human rights at the time, prompted some criticisms within OAU circles, despite Idi Amin's chairmanship of the OAU in 1975. The refuge of "non-interference" which had hitherto characterized African politics and hindered any attempt to promote human rights ideals was being gradually defeated, thereby setting the stage for possible action in this area.

Resolution 115 (XVI), adopted by the Assembly of Heads of State and Government of the OAU at its 16th Ordinary Session held in Monrovia, Liberia from July 17-20, 1979, requested the OAU Secretary General to bring together a committee of high level African experts who were to be responsible for the preparation of "a preliminary draft of an African Charter on Human and Peoples' Rights, providing *inter alia* for the establishment of organs for the promotion and protection of human and peoples' rights."

A Preliminary Draft text was prepared by a group of African jurists who organized a meeting in Dakar in 1979. The meeting, attended by some twenty professors of law, judges, and advocates, endorsed the draft for presentation to a conference of plenipotentiaries.

Three important conclusions may be drawn from the drafting process: first, a sense of urgency prevailed in the late 1970s and early 1980s for the adoption of a human rights charter as a means of dealing with the grave violations occurring at that time. Second, the speed with which the draft was debated resulted in a number of compromises that weakened the instrument. Finally, the apparent lack of commitment and political will on the part of some states parties to implement the Charter may be explained in terms of these historical antecedents.

NORMATIVE CONTENT OF THE AFRICAN CHARTER ON HUMAN AND PEOPLES' RIGHTS

If it is agreed that all conventions reflect the cultural values of the regions where they have been adopted, the African Charter is no exception. Paragraph 5 of the Preamble clearly states that the Charter was drafted "Taking into consideration the virtues of their historical tradition and the values of African civilization which should inspire and characterize their reflection on the concept of human and peoples' rights. . . ."

This idea of the values of African civilization is embedded in the Charter under various aspects: morals, family, and positive African tradition as accepted by society. An analysis of its impact is worth undertaking ten years after the entry into force of the treaty.

As stated above, the drafters of the African Charter seemed to have perceived the treaty as a practical response to the human rights violations of the time. In the late 1970s, a number of important United Nations and regional human rights instruments, particularly those of the OAU, which had already entered into force, provided valuable reference for the drafting of the African Charter.

In its coverage of rights and duties, the African Charter is arguably the most comprehensive and innovative of all the existing original human rights instruments. In a single document, it covers civil and political rights on the one hand, and economic, social, and cultural rights on the other. It also incorporates the so-called third generation rights: the rights to peace, solidarity, a healthy environment, and development—matters that are of special relevance to the conflict-ridden and poverty-stricken African states. Furthermore, the inclusion of the concept of "duties" owed by individuals to the family, society, the nation, and the state, which has been rationalized as a peculiarly African conception of enjoyment of rights, raises interesting problems of enforcement.

Despite the peculiarities and innovative features of the African Charter, its drafters refer to existing human rights instruments to show their relevance and impact on the drafting process. Article 60 provides, in part:

> The Commission should draw inspiration from international law on human and peoples' rights, particularly from the provisions of various African instruments on human and peoples rights, the Charter of the United Nations, the Charter of the Organization of African Unity, the Universal Declaration of Human Rights, other instruments adopted by the United Nations and by African countries in the field of human and peoples rights as well as from the provisions of various instruments adopted within the Specialized Agencies of the United Nations of which the parties to the present Charter are members.

Apart from the UDHR and the International Bill of Rights, there are currently over seventy regional and global human rights conventions and declarations that could serve as useful reference points for drawing comparisons between their substantive provisions and those of the African Charter.

Individual Rights

A combination of civil and political rights, as well as economic, social, and cultural rights falls into this category under Articles 3 to 17. Specific rights covered are similar in wording to those reflected in the two UN Covenants, save that the latter go into greater detail and do not have the African Charter's "clawback clauses" (see below). The guarantees of the African Charter under this heading include: equality before the law and equal protection of the law (Art. 3); inviolability of human beings (Art. 4); respect for human dignity, status, and prohibition against slavery, the slave trade, torture, cruel, inhuman, or degrading punishment and treatment (Art. 5); the prohibition against being "subjected without free consent to medical or scientific experimentation" provided for under Article 7 of the Civil and Political Covenant is not reflected in the African Charter.

Similarly, the elaborate guarantees of Articles 9 and 10 of the Covenant regarding the right to liberty and prohibition against arbitrary detention are not found in the African Charter. Article 6 simply states:

> Every individual shall have the right to liberty and to the security of his person. No one may be deprived of his freedom except for reasons and conditions previously laid down by law. In particular, no one may be arbitrarily arrested or detained.

In view of the frequent use of arbitrary detention as a weapon against political opponents, stronger language and more elaborate guarantees would have provided better security. As a minimum, one would have expected such guarantees as being promptly informed of the reasons for the arrest, charges preferred, appearance before a judicial officer, and an enforceable right to compensation for unlawful arrest or detention, to have been included.

The right to a fair trial (Art. 7) embodies the presumption of innocence and the right to a defense and to trial within a reasonable time by an impartial court or tribunal. It also includes prohibition against *ex post facto* application of criminal laws. However, unlike Article 14 of the Covenant on Civil and Political Rights, there is no protection against trial *in absentia,* no provision for legal aid or assistance of an interpreter, no compensation for miscarriage of justice, and no protection against double jeopardy.

Clawback Clauses

One of the major weaknesses of the African Charter is the use of the so-called clawback clauses that impose severe limitations on the enjoyment of civil and political rights. Examples include the following:

Article 6 (Right to Liberty)

Every individual shall have the right to liberty and to security of his person. No one may be deprived of his freedom except for reasons and *conditions previously laid down by law.* (emphasis added)

Article 8 (Freedom of Conscience)

Freedom of conscience, the profession and free practice of religion shall be guaranteed. No one may, *subject to law and order,* (emphasis added) be submitted to measures restricting the exercise of these freedoms.

The problem with these clawback clauses is that they permit the imposition of restrictions by any law of the state, however arbitrary it might be. Perhaps guidance could be sought from the wording of the Universal Declaration and the Covenant on Civil and Political Rights on this issue. Although these two instruments recognize the logic and the need for limitations upon the enjoyment of these rights, they subject such laws to certain requirements essential for democracy. Under Article 21 of the Covenant, for example:

(2) No restrictions may be placed on the exercise of this right other than those imposed in conformity with the law and which *are necessary in a democratic society in the interests of national security or public safety, public order (ordre public), the protection of public health or morals or the protection of the rights and freedoms of others.*

Other Individual Rights

These include the right to participate freely in government (Art. 13), a crucial right in these days of the multi-party democracy; right to property (Art. 14), right to work under equitable and satisfactory conditions, and equal pay for equal work (Art. 15); right to enjoy the best attainable state of physical and mental health (Art. 16); right to education and freedom to take part in the cultural life of one's community (Art. 17).

Rights of the Family (Art. 18)

These include the rights of the aged and the disabled. The State is also obliged to "ensure the elimination of every discrimination against women and also ensure the protection of the rights of the woman and the child as stipulated in international declarations and conventions."

African women's groups are dissatisfied with this provision which simply incorporates women's rights by reference. They have called for an additional Protocol dealing with women's rights.

Peoples' Rights

These cover equality of all peoples (Art. 19); peoples' rights to existence and state assistance in liberation, struggle against foreign domination, be it political, economic, or cultural (Art. 20); free disposal of wealth and natural resources (Art. 21); the right to development (Art. 22); the right to national and international peace and security (Art. 23); and the right to a general, satisfactory environment favorable to development (Art. 24).

Individual Duties

The inclusion of "Duties of Individuals" spelled out under Articles 27 through 29 is another unique characteristic of the African Charter. These obligations include duties towards the family, society, the state, other legally recognized communities and the international community (Art. 27); the duty to respect and consider fellow beings without discrimination and to maintain relations aimed at promoting, safeguarding, and reinforcing mutual respect and tolerance (Art. 28).

Many have argued that these provisions reflect the African conception of rights, wherein the enjoyment of rights carries corresponding obligations. However, questions have been raised regarding the enforceability of these duties. Aside from tax evasion, which is a crime in most jurisdictions, can an individual be prosecuted, because he/she has not placed his/her physical and intellectual abilities at the service of his/her national community [Art. 29 (2)]? If such an individual were prosecuted by a state party, would such state action be compatible with the variety of individual rights guaranteed under the first chapter of the Charter? Put another way, could a state party validly stipulate the rendering of "individual duties" as a condition precedent to the enjoyment of the guaranteed rights?

In this year of the 50th Anniversary of the UDHR perhaps the time is probably right for a closer look at the inclusion of such provisions in a human rights treaty. The ongoing debate on whether the emerging concepts of responsibility are a threat to universality may benefit from some practical implementation of some of these articles.

In spite of the innovations already mentioned, legal protection of human rights remains inadequate in Africa, as exemplified by the continuing human rights violations in many states.

THE AFRICAN COMMISSION ON HUMAN AND PEOPLES' RIGHTS

Although the idea of an African human rights court was touted at the time of the actual drafting of the Charter, no consensus could be reached and the idea was dropped. It was felt at the time that a court of human rights was too controversial to gain endorsement by OAU member states.

Two organs were made responsible for the implementation of the Charter: first, an eleven-member African Commission on Human and Peoples Rights, and second, the Assembly of Heads of State and Government of the OAU, the latter being the final authority to act on recommendations made by the Commission. The wisdom of designating the OAU Assembly, a political body, as the final arbiter in human rights matters has often been questioned.

It is possible to argue that matters of human rights have far-reaching political implications for which ultimately a political solution taken by a political body is preferable to a purely legal one. Decisions of the Assembly carry enormous prestige. Offending states are more likely to be influenced to improve their human rights record by expressions of disapproval by fellow heads of State. The influence of former Presidents Julius Nyerere and Leopold Senghor on the OAU in the late 1970s regarding the adoption of the African Charter could be cited in supported of this argument.

On the other hand, the argument against leaving such a crucial responsibility to the Assembly is equally compelling. The Assembly meets only once a year. Its agenda is so full that it leaves little time to go into the merits of allegations against states. Furthermore, with the exception of very few known examples, African states are not known for their condemnation of fellow states. Indeed, despite the massive violations of human rights in Africa after the African Charter entered into force, no state has ever utilized the procedure of inter-state complaints provided for under the Charter (Art. 47).

Article 45 of the Charter, which gives the Commission an overly broad mandate covering a wide variety of academic, investigative, advisory, quasi-judicial, and judicial functions, raises the fundamental question of whether eleven legal experts. who are employed elsewhere and are thus working as part-time Commissioners only, are capable of discharging of such a mandate effectively? Perhaps more importantly from the standpoint of the public, it raises excessive expectations and hopes regarding the role of this implementing organ. It also imposes tremendous responsibility on the Commission itself.

A careful overview of the Commission's activities in the last ten years of its existence shows that an effective discharge of its mandate is largely dependent upon certain conditions that do not now exist. These include a fully functional and effective Secretariat; cooperation from States parties; support of Non Governmental Organizations (NGOs); and independence of action by the Commission.

From a victim's perspective, the most important of the requirements listed above would be the cooperation the Commission receives from states parties. Only a few states have formally complied with their obligations such as submitting periodic state reports, responding to the Commissioners' questions on their reports and facilitating the visits of Commissioners to their countries as part of the promotion campaign for the Charter. On the contrary, the majority of states parties who have not discharged their treaty obligations have yet to show signs of interest in doing so.

In the past few years, the Commission has cooperated with NGOs in workshops on NGO participation in the African Commission. Some progress has been made. However, many more high profile activities need to be undertaken by the Commission in order to maximize its effectiveness. And more resources must be provided to the Commission. A minimum pre-condition for effectiveness is that the Commission should have the necessary freedom of action and independence to carry out its mandate. However, provisions of Articles 58 and 59 of the Charter explicitly cast doubt on this matter and reveal a number of disturbing conclusions such as: the Commission's freedom of action is limited by the requirement in Article 58 (1); Article 58 (2) limits the independence of the Commission by subjecting the discharge of its mandate to the discretion of the Assembly, composed of political leaders of states against whom allegations of human rights abuses may have been made; the Principle of Confidentiality expressed under Article 59 (1) is a further limitation on the freedom of action of the Commission. This runs counter to the need for publicity.

In order to enhance the Commission's freedom of action and independence, there is a clear need for the amendment of Articles 58 and 59 of the African Charter. Furthermore, there is a need for willingness on the part of the members of the Commission to be reform-minded in their actions. It is sad to note that the will to be pro-active has been non-evident.

An evaluation of the Charter's "effectiveness" should attempt to determine the extent to which the basic goals of the Charter, as set forth in the Preamble, the promotion, and protection of human and peoples' rights, have been reasonably attained. One of the practical ways of judging whether these ideals have been or are capable of being translated into concrete action is through developing a set of criteria to measure them against, such as: adequacy of the Charter's provisions from the victims' point of view; public awareness of the guarantees and a willingness to utilize the complaints procedures; impact of the Charter on national institutions; the role of the Charter's implementation machinery—the effectiveness, viewed from the perspective of State's obligations: reporting, education, and guaranteeing the independence of the courts.

Any human rights instrument has little value unless the people whose rights are enshrined in it are aware of the guarantees and able to utilize it for their protection. To the credit of the African Charter, Articles 55 and 56 provide for a complaint procedure, entitled "Other Communications," as distinct from inter-state communications (Art. 47). Under the relevant provisions, complaints, and communications alleging violations of the rights guaranteed by the Charter may be sent to the African Commission by individuals and NGOs. Those filing the communications need not be the actual victims of the alleged violations. Since its establishment in 1987, the African Commission has held twenty-three ordinary sessions and one extraordinary session to review the human rights situation in Nigeria. More than 218 Communications have been received alleging violations of human and peoples' rights in Africa out of which more than half have been treated on the merits. There has been no inter-state communication filed with the African Commission. In light of the grave human rights situation on the continent, the only reasonable explanation for this inaction is lack of public awareness of the Charter and its complaints procedures. It is, thus, difficult to see the African Charter as a fully effective weapon for the promotion and protection of human and peoples' rights. And yet did the African States not undertake to respect these rights when they signed the United Nations Charter?

THE AFRICAN COURT ON HUMAN AND PEOPLES' RIGHTS

The idea of an African human rights court was elaborated in the "Law of Lagos" referred to earlier that called for the creation of such a judicial institution. The changing circumstances and political climate of Africa in the early nineties, characterized by increasing attempts toward democratization, presented a timely occasion and provided unique opportunities not only to take a fresh and critical look at the African Charter, the Commission and the latter's relations with the OAU Secretariat and Assembly, but also to seek ways of maximizing the role of the Commission.

In 1993, the ICJ, under the auspices of President Abdou Diouf of Senegal and then chairman of the OAU Assembly, convened a small group of African jurists and other human rights experts for a brain-storming session in Dakar. It was followed by several other meetings of experts to prepare a draft Protocol for the establishment of an African Court. This was reinforced by a strategic lobbying to get African leaders to subscribe fully to this idea and take concrete steps toward attaining the goal.

The Thirtieth Ordinary Session of the Assembly of Heads of States and Governments of the OAU, held in Tunis in June 1994, adopted a Resolution [AHG/Res. 230 (XXX)], requesting the OAU Secretary-General to convene a meeting of government experts to consider the question of the establishment of an African Court on Human and Peoples' Rights.

Subsequently, three meetings of OAU governmental experts to consider the ensuing draft protocol were organized. The meetings took place in Cape Town, South Africa, in September 1995 and in Nouakchott, Mauritania, in April 1997. The latter meeting was expected to be the final one, however, the Summit in Harare (1997) decided that another meeting should be organized, with an appeal for larger participation by Governments to seek to finalize the draft. The third and final meeting of experts which was followed by a crucial and successful meeting of Ministers of Justice and/or Attorneys General in December 1997 in Addis Ababa which finalized and adopted the draft protocol. The Assembly of Heads of State and Government of the OAU, meeting in Ouagadougou, Burkina Faso in June 1998, formally adopted the protocol. It is particularly encouraging that thirty Member States of the OAU have at the outset signed the protocol to the African Charter on Human and Peoples' Rights which establishes the new Court. The protocol requires fifteen ratifications to enter into force and its Article 5 allows the Court to receive cases directly from NGOs and individuals as well as States parties and African inter-governmental organizations.

CONCLUSION

In view of the efforts being deployed in various circles to ensure the enhancement of State Responsibility and to bring human rights permanently unto the Agenda of Africa's policy makers, one can safely say that the movement in favor of human rights is making headway. The struggle against violations of human rights in Africa will be long and tedious. It is not going to be an easy task—it must not be forgotten that the enthusiastic welcome accorded to the legal instruments carries no real weight in the field of human rights if their objectives are not explained to and understood by the people to whom they are to apply; hence the importance of the NGOs' role in teaching and propagating human rights.

Chapter 21

The Rebellion of the Vulnerable: Perspectives from the Americas

Susana Chiarotti Boero

A REGIONAL CONTEXTUALIZATION OF HUMAN RIGHTS IN THE AMERICAS

The geographical, ethnic, racial, and linguistic diversity makes of the Americas a rich mosaic with very complex realities in the economic, political, and cultural fields. In spite of this diversity there are some regional constants. In the political arena, for example, most of the Latin American countries are living through a process of formal democratization. The time of cruel dictatorships seems to be far away. There are no longer armed conflicts on a great scale, although in some countries the eradication of violence is not a concluded process.[1]

The building of democracy in the region is a slow and painful process with advances and setbacks. Passing from formal to real democracy is a complex task that requires the participation of multiple actors. Truth Commissions, as in El Salvador, and tribunals, such as the National Commission for the Disappeared (CONADEP) in Argentina, played an important role in limiting the impunity of those who violated human rights. At the same time, reactions of those involved in the dictatorships hindered investigations or, in some cases, closed them forever.[2]

---

[1] Colombia, Mexico, and Haiti are three countries where political violence is prevalent. Repression of the indigenous population is permanent in Chiapas, Mexico.

[2] Examples of these are the laws of true obedience and final point in Argentina. These laws were finally revoked on March 24, 1998. Another example is Peruvian law # 26 479 that granted general amnesty to military, police, or civil personnel, investigated or condemned in the struggle against terrorism.

Another constant in the Americas is that despite the prevailing racial diversity, political and economic power is exercised predominantly by white people. The presence of indigenous or black groups is scarce or non-existent in parliaments, the judiciary, or the executive.

In the juridical sphere, American countries follow one of two Western systems. The Roman system is followed by countries colonized by Spain (all Latin American countries, and some Caribbean countries) as well as Brazil, and these countries have codes inspired by the European ones. The Anglo-Saxon system is followed by countries colonized by England, such as the United States and Canada. This distinction is relevant in the area of human rights because the prevalence in some countries of codes inspired by European ones of the last century hinders the implementation of international norms that prohibit discriminatory practices. The persistence in countries that follow the Roman Law system of written procedures which are long and complicated, hinders and delays the resolution of cases. Such delays not only constitute denial of justice and a violation of human rights per se, but also block easy access to international human rights procedures.

THE REGIONAL SYSTEM OF PROTECTION AND PROMOTION OF HUMAN RIGHTS

The American Declaration of 1948 is generally considered as the starting point of the Inter-American system of protection of human rights, although in fact this Declaration was preceded by the Resolution of Lima in 1938 which first discussed human rights and possible mechanisms for their protection. The Inter-American human rights system is based on a series of legal instruments on a variety of subjects, some instruments being of a mandatory nature, i.e., treaties, others being declarations or resolutions that constitute general commitments or recommendations.

The Inter-American Commission on Human Rights, headquartered in Washington, D.C., had a limited mandate at its inception, yet gradually it expanded its scope.[3] In 1978, the Inter-American Convention on Human Rights entered into force. The states that ratified the Convention are subject to the broadened jurisdiction of the Commission. To date, the Commission has examined more than 15,000 communications about human rights violations, and has carried out investigations and on-site visits in several countries with positive results. It has also carried out a preventive function through recommendations

---

[3] At the Conference of Rio de Janeiro (1965), Resolution XXII established that the Commission could also receive petitions or communications about violations of human rights; it also incorporated the System of Reports, on site visits, etc. In 1969, after the First Protocol was signed in Buenos Aires, the Commission strengthened its juridical status.

addressed to certain governments. Following such recommendations, states have reformed laws that infringed upon human rights and improved internal procedures on human rights. The Inter-American Convention places emphasis on civil and political rights and stipulates that economic, social, and cultural rights will be subject to progressive development. This gap between categories of rights was bridged in 1988 through the adoption of an Additional Protocol on Economic, Social and Cultural Rights, called the Protocol of San Salvador. The Inter-American Convention, in article 2, establishes that states have the obligation to incorporate the provisions of the Convention in their national legislation and this has positive results in national systems.

The other body which is competent in the area of human rights in the Inter-American system is the Inter-American Court of Human Rights headquartered in Costa Rica. It is composed of seven judges elected by the General Assembly of the OAS in their personal capacity from among jurists of high caliber with knowledge in human rights. Their mandate is defined by the American Convention on Human Rights.[4] The Court may render decisions or advisory opinions. The Court's decisions are binding only for the countries which have accepted the jurisdiction of the Court.

Other human rights instruments of the Inter-American system include the Inter-American Convention for the Prevention and Punishment of Torture (1985), the Additional Protocol on the Abolition of the Death Penalty (1990), and the Inter-American Convention on the Prevention, Punishment and Eradication of Violence against Women (1994). The Inter-American system is complemented by the global one. Procedures to avoid duplication of efforts and to achieve the consistent interpretation of international instruments have been elaborated.

CONCEPTUAL ADVANCES AND OBSTACLES

In the last few years important conceptual advances took place, mainly in the field of women's rights. The Inter-American Convention on the Prevention, Punishment and Eradication of Violence against Women is unique in the sense that it allows individuals and institutions to petition the Inter-American Commission of Human Rights and the Inter-American Court of Human Rights for actions or omissions of the state regarding this issue.

This Convention not only reinforces the Convention on the Elimination of All Forms of Discrimination against Women (CEDAW), but also establishes mechanisms for enforcing its implementation in a regional context. Another significant achievement in the women's rights area was the creation of a post of Gender Rapporteur mandated to study the issue of discrimination against women.

---

[4] American Convention on Human Rights, articles 52 to 73.

In order to become more effective, the work of the Rapporteur should incorporate that of NGOs already engaged in monitoring activities.

At the national level some important achievements were registered in a few countries. Argentina, for example, twenty-two years after the military coup, repealed laws that guaranteed impunity for the military personnel that violated human rights. The Supreme Court of Paraguay recently declared crimes that violate human rights as imprescriptible, thus opening the way for the trial of three main torturers of the dictatorial regime (1954-1989).[5]

One of the biggest problems in the region is the disparity between the advances in the international arena and the realities at the national and local level. Two main tendencies are observed in the Americas. On the one hand, the governments of Latin America and the Caribbean generally ratify international treaties, but there is a great gap between the legal texts and the reality that their citizens experience. On the other hand, there is the position of the United States which is extremely reticent to ratify human rights treaties, although it participated actively in their elaboration. Thus, strategies for human rights advocates differ as well. While, in the United States, efforts focus on achieving ratification of human rights treaties, in Central and South America the emphasis is on implementing the legal obligations of governments.

Another important obstacle to the realization of human rights is the hierarchization of civil and political rights over economic, social, and cultural rights. This dichotomy is observed not only among governments but also in civil society, mainly non-governmental organizations. One explanation for placing more emphasis on civil and political rights for about three decades is the struggle in the 1970s and 1980s against the dictatorships and the brutal repression that accompanied them. The process of promoting and defending economic, social, and cultural rights is much slower. At this point it has slightly accelerated, mainly on the part of NGOs, after the Social Summit in Copenhagen in 1995.[6] However, these rights are granted much lower protection than that given to civil and political rights. A similar difficulty is observed in terms of incorporating new thematic human rights issues in national agendas, such as reproductive and sexual rights, and new beneficiaries, such as people with disabilities or homosexuals. The expansion of the agenda, whenever this has been achieved, is the result of the efforts of those affected by exclusion and marginalization. This has been the case, for example, with indigenous peoples whose presence has been very prominent at fora such as the World Conference on Human Rights.

---

[5] Report of CLADEM Paraguay, March 31, 1998.

[6] In different countries, human rights NGOs joined the Social Watch initiative, headquartered in Montevideo, Uruguay, that follows up the Copenhagen commitments.

THE INSTITUTIONAL ARENA:
CLAIMING JUSTICE, VICTIMS NEEDS, AND THE
INSTITUTIONAL RESPONSE

Major difficulties exist in obtaining sanctions for violations of human rights and reparations for victims. According to the American Convention of Human Rights, complaints may be submitted by individuals or organizations representing them to the Inter-American Commission of Human Rights after the victims have exhausted local remedies. The requirement of exhaustion of local remedies, although a common trait in international human rights treaties, is used as an excuse by many states to evade their international responsibilities. After examining the validity of such complaints, in a slow process, the Commission decides on the next steps to follow. Only states and the Commission itself are entitled to submit complaints to the Inter-American Court. As a consequence of such slow processes, only a very small number of cases reach the Court, the proportion being one case for every 1,500 communications. This gives victims the impression that the Commission acts as too tight a filter and that the Court is merely cosmetic.

Reservations to human rights treaties constitute another obstacle to the efficient functioning of the human rights system in the Americas. A case in point is the United States with the numerous reservations that it entered when ratifying the International Covenant on Civil and Political Rights.[7]

There are also logistical difficulties faced by people who want to use the Inter-American system of human rights since the location of the Commission is in Washington, D.C., USA, and the Court is in San Jose, Costa Rica. This places an enormous burden on the resources of human rights organizations from Latin America that want to make presentations to the Commission.

THE WORLD CONFERENCE ON HUMAN RIGHTS
AND ITS IMPACT IN THE REGION

The 1993 World Conference on Human Rights in Vienna, as well as its preparatory process, had an enormous impact in the continent. Organizations dealing with human rights, with indigenous people and women's rights, empowered themselves and linked up to the international human right's movement. Women's organizations from the whole continent participated actively and had their claims inserted within the human rights framework. Their capacity to

---

[7] The reservations include the interpretation of terms like "cruel, inhuman and degrading treatment," according to the 5th, 8th, and 14th Amendments to the Constitution.

use the human rights mechanisms for the defense of their rights increased in the years after the Conference through training.[8]

The statement in the final document of the Conference, the Vienna Declaration and Programme of Action, that human rights are interrelated, interdependent, and indivisible, gave strength to claims for the enjoyment of economic, social, and cultural rights which until then had been sidetracked. This also allowed the recognition, in subsequent years, of sexual and reproductive rights as human rights.

PRESSING HUMAN RIGHTS VIOLATIONS

The most pressing human rights problems of the past decade in the region can be grouped as follows: 1) problems connected with the increase of poverty, 2) problems connected with the activities of security forces, 3) ethnic-racial discrimination, 4) gender discrimination, 5) discrimination based on sexual orientation, and 6) the crisis of the prison system.

POVERTY

On February 13, 1998, human rights organizations met in the city of Cuernavaca in Mexico and agreed that the neoliberal economic model intrinsically generates a systematic violation of economic, social, and cultural rights, and that it increases social exclusion, poverty, and inequality in the enjoyment and exercise of rights.[9] Even in countries where this model shows a satisfactory growth index, it is accompanied by statistics of very high social cost. In Chile, for example, the distribution of resources has worsened, 10 percent of the richest controlling 45.8 percent of all wealth, as compared to 34.8 percent of all wealth before.[10] In the United States, more than 25 percent of the children are raised by mothers living in poverty.[11]

One of the most pressing issues in this panorama is child labor. Some experts call child labor a "strategy for survival," but this expression gives a misguided impression and diverts attention from the tragedy of child exploitation. In Sao

---

[8] CLADEM (Latin American and Caribbean Committee for the Defense of Women's Rights), for example, organized a Seminar in San Jose, Costa Rica, along with the IIDH, to train thirty women lawyers from twenty countries in the use of human rights mechanisms for the defense of women's rights.

[9] Commitments of Cuernavaca, Mexico, February 13, 1998.

[10] Commission on Human Rights, Report to the Sub-Commission on Prevention of Discrimination and Protection of Minorities, UN Doc. E/CN.4/Sub.2/1996/14.

[11] Koenig Shulamith, "A short analysis of Social and Economic Justice and Human Rights of Women in USA," presented at the Dialogue organized by DAW-CLADEM, at UN Headquarters, March 2, 1998.

Paolo, Brazil, alone, 500,000 children live and work in the streets. Child prostitution is soaring. One study found that in Bogota, Colombia, there is a 60 percent increase in the prostitution of girls by comparison to figures in 1990.[12]

Loss of social rights of workers is another characteristic of this era. Labor achievements of the last fifty years are being diminished or have been lost entirely. In many countries, governments have opened their doors to foreign capital looking for the highest possible profits and taking advantage of low labor cost. Such foreign companies do not respect the international labor standards of the International Labour Organisation. This process has been facilitated by the North American Free Trade Agreement.

Another example of violation of labor rights is the resurgence of "sweatshops" in the United States. According to the US General Accounting Office (GAO), business norms in such businesses are violated in terms of wages, child labor, health, and security in the workplace. Most "sweatshops" manufacture clothes for famous manufacturers, such as Esprit, The Gap, J.C. Penny, The Limited, Liz Claiborne, Patagonia, Ralph Lauren. It is estimated that there are 22,000 businesses of this type in the United States, working for some 1000 companies, and employing 80 percent Latin American and Asian women migrants.[13]

The vulnerability of migrant workers, especially those who are undocumented, is notorious with tragic human consequences. They are objects of abuse by employers, discrimination, and inhuman treatment.[14]

ACTIVITIES OF THE SECURITY FORCES

The repressive practices of security forces in countries of the region are of concern to the population. Violence by police and other security forces, including torture, summary executions, arbitrary detention, and other such violations, are common in the continent and with similar methodologies. Torture in places of detention is a constant and if the detainee is a woman, she is subject to sexual violation as well.[15] Some countries, although having ratified the Convention against Torture, do not recognize torture as a crime in their national penal codes.[16]

---

[12]Caja de Herramiontas, Bogota, Colombia, #23, November 1994

[13]Isis International, Women in Action # 2, "Made in the U.S.," Manila, 1996.

[14]CELS, Annual Report on the situation of human rights in Argentina, Buenos Aires, 1996.

[15]Thousands of testimonies in Latin America prove this point, such as National Human Rights annual reports, the CONADEP investigation in Argentina ("Nunca Más"). CLADEM Brazil sent the testimony of Maria Almeida Teles, from Sao Paulo, February 27, 1998.

[16]This is the case in Peru, where on July 7, 1988, the Congress of the Republic ratified the Convention against Torture, while the national penal code did not recognize torture as a crime. APRODEH "So near death." Report on violation of Human Rights in Peru, Lima, 1997.

Impunity often accompanies such human rights violations. Factors that contribute to impunity include complicity nets inside police institutions, operation in a strongly militarized framework, and lack of democratic control within the security forces. Impunity is compounded by police corruption, and abuse of authority, influence, and power.

ETHNIC-RACIAL DISCRIMINATION

In some areas racial discrimination reaches painful levels. In most, it has economic, social, and cultural characteristics. This type of discrimination affects both the North and the South of the continent. In the United States, for example, 15 percent of the whites are poor, as compared to 49 percent of the blacks (see note 11).

In Canada, aboriginal peoples have often been deprived of their land, and their standard of living is significantly lower than that of the rest of the population.[17] In Guatemala, the indigenous population lives in extreme poverty (73.8% are extremely poor in the Department of Solola where 95% of the population is Mayan).[18] In Peru, sterilizations of black and indigenous women have been carried out, without most of them being aware of permanent effects of such sterilization. In Chile, the Mega-I deforestation project Ralco will threatens to flood around fourteen Mapuche cemeteries and seventy archaeological sites.[19]

GENDER DISCRIMINATION

Gender discrimination is prevalent throughout the Americas. Very serious difficulties exist in terms of accepting the participation of women in political and social life. Women's participation in Parliaments is 12.9 percent in Lower Houses and 11.5 percent in Upper Houses.[20] In all countries, in both urban and rural areas, illiteracy is higher among women than among men. Formal legal barriers exist hindering the advance of women toward equality.

[17]Royal Commission on Aboriginal People: People to People, Nation to Nation: Highlights from the 1996 Report, Canada, 1996.

[18]FUNCEDE, Municipal Diagnosis, Central America Serviprensa, Guatemala, 1995.

[19]Popular and Indigenous Chilean Network, Report of March 20, 1998.

[20]Inter-Parliamentary Union, Annual Report, January 1, 1998.

DISCRIMINATION ON THE BASIS OF SEXUAL ORIENTATION

Despite advances achieved in the area of gay and lesbian rights, thanks largely to the advocacy of their groups, severe setbacks have been experienced in recent years. Discrimination and persecution persist. The situation is different among the countries of the North, whose philosophies have another approach to privacy and where the organization of groups and networks is more advanced. In southern countries, society in general prefers to maintain silence on the subject of homosexuality, and homosexuals must keep their sexual orientation secret in order to maintain their employment or their social or political position.

THE CRISIS OF THE PRISON SYSTEM

In all countries of the region, the prison system is in crisis. Overpopulation and the resulting negative conditions for the health of prisoners are oftentimes disastrous. Many prisoners are detained for years without a trial and juvenile offenders have to share facilities with adults. Others suffer torture and ill treatment.

NGO MOBILIZATION

Civil society makes a major effort to guarantee the exercise and enjoyment of human rights. Thousands of organizations on the whole continent work tirelessly to monitor the implementation on the part of governments of international treaties. In the last few years, electronic advances have helped these organizations to connect at local, national, and international levels. Through these networks, they denounce violations of human rights, circulate petitions and are able to work in solidarity with each other. The participation of NGOs from the Americas in a series of global conferences organized by the United Nations in the 1990s strengthened these organizations and their links.

Some of these organizations have initiated pioneering projects that demonstrate their creativity in human rights issues. The Institute of Gender, Law and Development, an NGO under CLADEM, has taken the initiative of creating a "community of human rights." In July 1997, the city of Rosario in Argentina was declared a "Community of Human Rights." A variety of public authorities, organizations, and educational institutions participated in this effort and committed themselves to transform Rosario into a community where all people could enjoy their human rights. The Universal Declaration of Human Rights was widely disseminated and training courses were conducted for teachers and the police as part of these efforts.

FUTURE DIRECTIONS

The building of real democracy and of full respect for human rights in the continent is a task that involves all—governments, civil society, and the international community. Governments must enhance their human rights policies and close the gap between the international treaties they have accepted and the reality experienced by their citizens.

At the same time, the international regional mechanisms should be improved to offer more expeditious and effective justice. There is no reason why, in this era of electronic progress, the justice system cannot be reformed to serve the cause of human rights. Moreover, the extensive centralization of the Inter-American human rights machinery should be corrected by creating sub-regional offices that would allow citizens quicker access to international justice.

Finally, people belonging to disadvantaged groups should make use of the mechanisms for the protection of human rights and demand, from governments and NGOs alike, to incorporate human rights into their agendas.

ASSESSMENT AND CHALLENGES

Although some Truth Commissions proved countless cases of human rights violations and identified perpetrators, the Inter-American system has not taken effective measures to sanction them or to provide reparations to the victims.

Inhuman jail conditions, the systematic practice of torture, illegal executions, and forced disappearances in some countries have been properly documented. The answer to these serious violations is slow, bureaucratic, and demonstrates an attitude of indifference to human rights on the part of governments.

Human rights defenders are frequently threatened and do not enjoy enough protection. Many pay with their life for promoting human rights and denouncing their violations.

The death penalty was reintroduced in some countries of the region, undermining the abolitionist orientation of the Organization of American States (OAS).

In the face of the multiplicity of problems, the answer of the Inter-American system is very weak and the system does not respond to the serious needs of the region. The following points require urgent attention:

- The human rights bodies of the OAS must have more autonomy.
- Civil society must increase its participation in the monitoring process and evaluation of the implementation of human rights treaties.
- More human rights NGOs of the region must be given consultative status with the Economic and Social Council of the UN.

- Commitments to address gender discrimination are still very weak. The post of Gender Rapporteur must have an appropriate budget, commensurate with the challenge of the task, i.e., the elimination of discrimination against women. The Rapporteur should give more emphasis to women's life conditions rather than to formal equality. Funds must be granted to women's organizations to assist in the monitoring process.

The Inter-American system must prove that it has more than a token commitment to human rights.

Chapter 22

Protection of Human Rights in Asia and the Pacific: Think Universal, Act Regional?

Vitit Muntarbhorn

In the decade preceding 1997, the Asia-Pacific region was admired extensively for its record economic growth and growing confidence as a leader in the economic field, out-performing other regions. However, the 1997-98 period has witnessed a radical reversal of trends in a number of key countries in this region. There has been an economic crash of gargantuan proportions with rapid depreciation of national currencies and extensive bankruptcies, caused by profligate expenditure, over-borrowing, excessive investment in the real estate sector, inadequate regulation, and an admixture of vested interests and cronyism. This has resulted in a decidedly less confident region which now has to borrow extensively from abroad to replenish its coffers and whose future performance depends upon a process of restructuring the national economy on terms dictated from outside. The economic growl of the so-called Tigers has become the anemic meow of the Siamese cat.

There are dire repercussions. Millions are now out of work. Social expenditure on sectors interlinked with marginalized communities is declining markedly, and it is feared that more people will be pushed into situations of exploitation and neglect. Political strife is rife in some corners of the region. Yet, the economic debacle is also a blessing in disguise. It has enabled the region to question its economic and political bases, as well as their legitimacy. Was the crash due to economic malaise, political problems, or both? Can there really be a cure for economic ills unless there are also political pills? As it is increasingly recognized that the economic mess was greatly due to political discrepancies heightened by the complicity between some governments, politicians, and vested interests and by top-heavy administrations that tended to be elitist rather than pluralistic, there is thus an opportunity for key changes with a more popular appeal.

All these issues are linked, to a greater or lesser extent, with human rights. The glow of economic success in the pre-1997 phase was always illusory, in the sense that it was never complemented by adequate distribution of income or resources. Growth was never sufficiently complemented by equity. Economic, social, and cultural rights were never adequately implemented to spread wealth and resources to the populace. While some groups were reaping huge profits during that phase, there was always a hollow ring behind the deceptive economic aura: poorer groups were becoming poorer and richer groups were becoming richer. Side by side with this phenomenon, in several countries there was, and still is, an opaque political system based upon authoritarian streaks which repress democratic aspirations. Civil and political rights, such as self-determination, freedom of expression, and freedom of association, linked with the demands of good governance, transparency, and accountability, were and still are denied in parts of the Asia-Pacific region by undemocratic regimes.

One of the basic truths emerging from the above situation is that economic problems cannot be solved by economic solutions alone. These problems are inherently rooted in political conditions, and they need political as well as economic solutions. In 1998, at the time of the preparation of this study, it is intriguing to observe that those countries with the more liberal and democratic governments are recovering from the crash more easily and evidently than illiberal regimes burdened with the economic mess. Transparency and popular participation through the democratic process enable the remedies to be adopted and applied more effectively than the converse case of opacity and authoritarianism. Concomitantly, it is only through a democratically elected government, and respect for freedom of expression and assembly, that the abuse of power leading to the economic miasma can be prevented or attenuated.

The Asia-Pacific lesson for the new millennium is that economic and political considerations are ultimately interrelated. Growth needs to go hand-in-hand with equity and democracy. Economic, social, and cultural rights are indivisible from civil and political rights. Human rights, development, and democracy are inextricably intertwined. If these are almost self-evident platitudes, are they readily accepted by the countries of the region?

THINK UNIVERSAL?

The question to what extent do Asia-Pacific countries think universally and accept international human rights standards is an enigma which has plagued the region for many years. While Asia-Pacific countries voted for the 1948 Universal Declaration of Human Rights, one Prime Minister of the region recently called for its review, thereby raising a question whether that Declaration is universal or sufficiently universal. This ambivalence is further highlighted by a number of developments in the region.

First, many countries of the region have not yet become parties to several key international human rights treaties. This is particularly the case with regard to the 1966 International Covenant on Civil and Political Rights, the International Covenant on Economic, Social and Cultural Rights and the two Protocols affiliated with the former. At a recent seminar organized by the United Nations in Teheran involving Asia-Pacific countries, it was found that just over half of the forty-four countries represented were parties to the two Covenants, with only between two and six countries being parties to the two Protocols. However, in fairness, it should be noted that all countries of the region are parties to the Convention on the Rights of the Child.

Second, several Asian countries have been vocal exponents of the Asian values' argument, namely, that there are Asian values, such as respect for authority and the primacy of the community over the individual, different from Western values that are inherently individualistic rather than communitarian. On analysis, this type of reasoning may simply be a tool of some authoritarian regimes to suppress individual rights, especially freedom of expression and association which are at the heart of democratic aspirations. This undercurrent is related to the next observation.

Third, although Asia-Pacific governments adopted, with the rest of the world community, the 1993 Vienna Declaration and Programme of Action of the World Conference on Human Rights, they did so reluctantly. In the process leading to the World Conference, many of these governments were reticent to recognize and guarantee the universality of human rights, especially the primacy of international standards over national laws and practices. In the lead-up to the World Conference, Asia-Pacific Governments met in Bangkok in 1993 to assert that universality must go hand-in-hand with (and may have to be subjected to) regional and national particularities. By implication, international human rights standards are not necessarily primordial and may have to bend to national and regional contexts. This was highlighted further by their advocacy of state sovereignty and non-interference in the internal affairs of a state. By contrast with such a position, the international standpoint is that state sovereignty is not absolute, and that the protection of human rights cannot be considered to be interference in the internal affairs of a state.

By contrast, in 1993 over 100 Asia-Pacific non-governmental organizations (NGOs) adopted the Asia-Pacific (Non-Governmental) Declaration of Human Rights[1] which favored the universality of human rights as follows:

---

[1] *Our Voice: Bangkok NGO Declaration on Human Rights,* Asian Cultural Forum on Development, Bangkok, pp. 242, 244-245, 1993.

We can learn from different cultures in a pluralistic perspective and draw lessons from the humanity of these cultures to deepen respect for human rights. There is emerging a new understanding of universalism encompassing the richness and wisdom of Asia-Pacific cultures.

Universal human rights are rooted in many cultures. We affirm the basis of universality of human rights which afford protection to all of humanity, including special groups such as women, children, minorities and indigenous peoples, workers, refugees and displaced persons, the disabled, and the elderly. While advocating cultural pluralism, those cultural practices which derogate from universally accepted human rights, including women's rights, must not be tolerated.

As human rights are of universal concern and universal in value, the advocacy of human rights cannot be considered to be an encroachment upon national sovereignty.[2]

The formula adopted at the World Conference in Vienna was to reaffirm the universality principle as follows:

5. All human rights are universal, indivisible, and interdependent and interrelated. The international community must treat human rights globally in a fair and equal manner, on the same footing, and with the same emphasis. While the significance of national and regional particularities and various historical, cultural and religious backgrounds must be borne in mind, it is the duty of States, regardless of their political, economic and cultural systems, to promote and protect all human rights and fundamental freedoms.[3]

Fourth, where Asia-Pacific governments are ready to advocate human rights, there is a tendency to prefer the economic, social, and cultural rather than civil and political aspects. In concrete terms, there is a preference for "bread/rice" over "ballots," or economic development over democracy. This orientation has been advanced by these governments in the discourse over the right to development. While the UN resolution on this right in the mid-1980s clearly spelled out the interdisciplinary nature of such a right as comprising civil, political, economic, social, and cultural components, the push from Asia-Pacific governments has veered toward the economic and social components rather than the holistic approach. This orientation suggests that in the practice of these governments, in concrete terms, they prefer the divisibility rather than the indivisibility of human rights.

Fifth, it was the Asia-Pacific governments that influenced the drafting of the 1993 Vienna Declaration and Programme of Action of the World Conference on

[2] Note 1, pp. 198-199.

[3] United Nations, *World Conference on Human Rights: The Vienna Declaration and Programme of Action June 1993*, United Nations, New York, p. 30, 1993.

Human Rights to underline not only issues of universality and indivisibility, but also objectivity and non-selectivity. In other words, they were and are against double standards (thus against "selectivity") on the one hand, and against unilateral action taken against a state considered to have violated human rights (thus against "subjectivity") on the other hand.[4] In regard to the latter, the preferred forum for action would be the UN, and even in such setting, Asia-Pacific countries would prefer a non-confrontational approach.

Sixth, in conceptual terms, many Asia-Pacific governments prefer to highlight responsibilities or rights with responsibilities rather than human rights alone. At best, this could lead to a balance between the rights and obligations of all persons and communities. At worst, it could be distorted by illiberal governments to constrain the exercise of human rights in that the responsibilities argument would enable the interests of the state and the community to prevail over the individual on the one hand, and the national security and stability arguments to prevail over social movements seeking change and the quest for democratization on the other hand. This debate is currently heating up due to a proposal from the Interaction Council to the UN to adopt a universal declaration of human responsibilities.[5] Intriguingly, the declaration fails to address the issue of the duties or responsibilities of governments, while advocating a panoply of responsibilities for everyone else. Asia-Pacific countries are likely to be proponents of this Declaration. However, as a counterbalance to this, in 1998 the non-governmental sector spearheaded by FORUM-ASIA is advocating a Universal Declaration on the Duties of Governments and Other Power Groups.

There thus remain conceptual problems concerning how governments view human rights in the region and a divergence between the universal outlook and the parochial standpoint. Despite such a chasm, is some action possible to promote and protect human rights in the region?

ACT REGIONAL?

In this context, there is the well-known fact that unlike in Europe, Africa, and the Americas, there is no regional inter-governmental human rights treaty, mechanism or system for the promotion and protection of human rights in the Asia and Pacific region. The lacuna is partly due to the lack of political will and partly due to the lack of homogeneity in the region; it is perhaps too vast and eclectic for a comprehensive regional system.

Yet, some identifiable action is already taking place at the regional level, although at a modest pace. For the past few years, with the support of the United Nations, Asia-Pacific countries have met annually to discuss the issue of regional

---

[4] Paragraph 32 of the Vienna Declaration and Programme of Action, note 3, p. 41.

[5] Interaction Council, *A Universal Declaration of Human Responsibilities*, 1997.

arrangements for the promotion and protection of human rights. A range of regional workshops have been held in the following venues: Manila 1990, Jakarta 1993, Seoul 1995, Kathmandu 1996, Amman 1997, and Teheran 1998.

In Amman, a range of measures was underlined by the workshop, including a step-by-step and building blocks approach based upon the needs in the region; ratification of international human rights instruments; promotion of national institutions and national plans of action; recognition of the work of NGOs and the role of civil society; promotion of the right to development; advocacy against human rights conditionality; attention for vulnerable groups; support for not only universality but also objectivity and non-selectivity of human rights; more technical cooperation; more information sharing; more national capacity building; more confidence building measures; more programs for regional cooperation, e.g., strengthening institutions, the right to development, human rights education, and national plans of action.[6]

A formal regional system for the protection of human rights was not yet feasible. However, various activities could be undertaken to improve understanding, education, networking, and capacity-building. These would be step-by-step measures, building blocks of confidence, rather than a comprehensive system which would be too ambitious.

That approach was continued in 1998 at the Teheran Workshop, with more concrete developments highlighted by the Workshop Conclusions as follows:[7]

- reaffirmation of the universality, indivisibility, and interdependence of human rights "in a region proud of its rich cultures, religions and diversities";
- reaffirmation of the commitment to the Vienna Declaration and Programme of Action;
- emphasis on a step-by-step and building blocks approach;
- commitment to developing and strengthening national capacities, in accordance with national conditions, as the strongest foundation for regional cooperation;
- adoption of a Framework for Regional Technical Cooperation for the promotion and protection of human rights.

The concrete outcome from Teheran was the consensus for a regional technical cooperation program, with financial back-up and other support from the United Nations, in the following areas:

- national plans of action for the promotion and protection of human rights and the strengthening of national capacities;

---

[6] C. Dias, *From Building Blocks to Next Steps: The Task Ahead at Teheran,* background paper for the Sixth Workshop on Regional Arrangements for the Promotion and Protection of Human Rights in the Asian and Pacific Region, Teheran, p. 15, 1998.

[7] UN Doc. E/CN/1998/50 (March 1998), p. 11.

- human rights education;
- national institutes for the promotion and protection of human rights;
- strategies for the realization of the right to development and economic, social, and cultural rights.

Clearly, human rights activities are possible despite the lack of a regional human rights system. They are particularly pertinent in four areas.

1. National Plans of Action on Human Rights

This is new to most countries, although some countries such as Nepal and the Philippines are now experimenting with them. Thailand recently set up a committee to draft such a plan in view of the 50th anniversary of the Universal Declaration of Human Rights. Such plans usually involve training, dissemination and education, capacity building, law and policy reform, networking, and help for marginalized groups. In practice, the plans should have specific time frames so as to propel operationalization and monitoring of implementation.

2. Human Rights Education

The impetus for this is provided in part by the fact that the international community is currently in the midst of the United Nations Decade for Human Rights Education. Some countries such as Japan have already adopted such a national plan. In 1997, the United Nations developed a series of Guidelines for National Plans of Action for Human Rights Education comprising these steps: establishing a national committee for human rights education; conducting a baseline study; setting priorities and identifying groups in need; developing the national plan; implementing the national plan; reviewing and revising the national plan.[8]

These are coupled with various underlying educational activities such as non-discrimination and participatory learning.

3. National Human Rights Institutions

The United Nations has been promoting these institutions in the 1990s and it has adopted various principles concerning the functions and role of such institutions ("The Paris Principles").[9] Two principles are particularly pertinent:

---

[8] UN Doc. A/52/469 and Add. 1 (October 1997).

[9] United Nations, *National Institutions for the Promotion and Protection of Human Rights. Fact Sheet No. 19,* United Nations, New York/Geneva, p. 12, 1993.

independence of these institutions and pluralism of composition, implying broad popular participation.

A number of human rights institutions, especially national human rights commissions, have emerged with government blessing in the region. They exist in Australia, New Zealand, India, Indonesia, the Philippines, and Sri Lanka. Although Iran has such a mechanism, there is a question concerning its independence. Thailand and Cambodia have mechanisms under Parliament, while under Thailand's 1997 Constitution, an independent National Human Rights Commission is due to be established. A network of these institutions has been formed with the help of Australia. The network met in Australia in 1996 and in India in 1997 and adopted a declaration to promote greater capacity-building of these institutions for more education, training and information collection and dissemination.

Despite initial scepticism toward some of these institutions when they were first established, they have proved themselves to be effective on many fronts. The Indian Commission, for instance, has tackled the issue of preventive detention and abuse by law enforcers, as well as child trafficking and prostitution.[10] The Indonesian Commission has not shied away from the issue of investigating human rights violations in East Timor, even though this was a very slippery political slope.[11]

Evidently, this is a growth industry which should be fostered. However, it is important that these institutions not merely pay lip service to human rights or act as a facade for government transgressions.

4. Realization of the Right to Development

As noted earlier, the issue is not new and there was a UN resolution on the subject in the mid 1980s. One danger is that some government quarters may wish to limit themselves to the economic components while failing to address the political components of this right. At the heart of the resolution mentioned was the issue of equity, in particular, how to distribute income and other resources to marginalized groups. There is an international perspective linked with the unbalanced international framework of trade, development, and aid on the one hand, and the national framework which is unbalanced in its economic, social, and political policies on the other hand. A key concern will be to foster best practices of equity policies, such as more social safety nets for the needy, more access to education, more empowerment of women and marginalized groups, more access to micro-credit, more access to slums and rural areas, and more distribution of land, income, and other resources coupled with popular participation.

[10]See, for example, *National Human Rights Commission Annual Report 1995-96,* National Human Rights Commission, Delhi, 1996.

[11]See, for example, *The National Commission on Human Rights Indonesia Annual Report 1994,* National Commission on Human Rights, Jakarta, 1995.

While the above considerations indicate that an entry point has been iden-tified at the regional level between governments and the United Nations in terms of a program to promote and protect human rights, one should not forget that irrespective of inter-governmental initiatives, there is already a host of non-governmental activities in the region for the promotion and protection of human rights. In 1997, for instance, NGOs, under the leadership of the Asian Human Rights Commission, adopted the Asian Human Rights Charter based upon this premise:

> We must move from abstract formulations of rights to their concretisa-tion in the Asian context by examining the circumstances of specific groups whose situation is defined by massive violations of their rights. It is only by relating rights and their implementation to the specificity of the Asian situa-tion that the enjoyment of rights will be facilitated.[12]

That Charter targeted for action the rights of vulnerable groups such as women, children, the disabled, those with AIDS, workers, students, prisoners, and detainees. Various concrete measures were advocated as follows: strengthen the guarantees of human rights in national constitutions; ratify international human rights instruments; review domestic legislation and administrative practices for consistency with international standards; maximize the role of the judiciary in enforcing human rights; enable social organizations to litigate on behalf of the victims; establish National Human Rights Commission(s) and other specialized institutions for human rights protection; recognize Peoples' Tribunals which are not based on adjudication but which help to raise consciousness of problems based upon moral and spiritual foundations.

As to the sub-regional level, the Asia-Pacific region is home to a number of inter-governmental, sub-regional organizations such as the South Pacific Forum, the Gulf Cooperation Council, The South Asian Association for Regional Cooperation (SAARC) and the Association of South-East Asian Nations (ASEAN). Bridging Asia, the Middle East, and Africa are the Arab League and the Organisation of the Islamic Conference (OIC). However, they are organiza-tions with the aim of economic/political, and to a lesser extent social, cooperation rather than human rights. Could they be encouraged to adopt a sub-regional human rights system?

In 1990, the OIC adopted the Cairo Declaration on Human Rights in Islam. In 1994, the Arab League came closest to a sub-regional human rights system by adopting the Arab Charter on Human Rights which establishes a mechanism to monitor state compliance by means of periodic reports.[13] However, the Charter is not yet in force and it is too early to appraise its work, although one should be

---

[12]*Human Rights Solidarity,* Volume 13 (February 1997), pp. 39; 40 (Article 23).

[13]See note 6.

vigilant against lowering international standards to respond to national and regional particularities.

In 1993, the ASEAN Inter-Parliamentary Organisation (AIPO) adopted the Human Rights Declaration of AIPO but it did not provide for a sub-regional human rights system. That Declaration is also unbalanced since it provides room for subjecting human rights to human responsibilities on the one hand, and for constraining human rights by means of national and regional particularities on the other hand.[14]

Despite the above, ASEAN could be heading toward some human rights-related programs, even though these would not be advocating a sub-regional human rights system immediately. Working Groups for a human rights mechanism in ASEAN have been formed. In 1997, members met in Kuala Lumpur and agreed on the following:

- develop the process of establishing a regional human rights mechanism in an orderly and systematic manner;
- establish links between the civil society and ASEAN governments to build confidence and consensus concerning the contents of such mechanism;
- establish national working groups in the pursuit of such process;
- promote research on pressing issues such as the rights of children and women;
- organize regional conferences on common issues, such as the status of women and children, and promote dialogue between ASEAN and non-governmental organizations on these issues;
- advocate the establishment of a national human rights mechanism in every country of ASEAN, while noting that the existence of national commissions in every member State is not a necessary prerequisite to the establishment of a regional human rights mechanism;
- regularize contact between the steering committee of the Kuala Lumpur Workshop and ASEAN officials;
- explore the possibility of drafting an ASEAN Convention on Human Rights.

Other organizations have attempted to deal with some specific human rights issues, although not explicitly under the rubric of human rights. For instance, SAARC has adopted a Decade for the Girl Child to help end gender discrimination and promote access to education by girls. It is now drafting a convention against human trafficking to counter the phenomenon whereby many victims are traded between countries for the sex trade and other contemporary forms of slavery.

---

[14]V. Muntarbhorn, Regional Protection of Human Rights in Asia: Projects, in *Collection of Lectures*, International Institute of Human Rights, Strasbourg, pp. 515-533, 1997.

From these examples, one can see that at the sub-regional level inter-governmental activities for the promotion and protection of human rights are possible, even though not necessarily leading to a human rights system and even though not called human rights. To these should be added the fact that there is a wealth of non-governmental activities in the various sub-regions. For instance, in 1996, NGOs adopted the Alternative ASEAN Declaration on Burma calling for respect for human rights and reversion to human rights in that country.

At the national and local levels, the spread of national human rights commissions, national human rights plans, and human rights education has already been noted. A number of state mechanisms also exist which can be used to promote and protect human rights, even though not called human rights institution(s) or mechanism(s). These include the system of courts and other state organs which interrelate with the lives of people. There are also non-formal protectors of human rights, such as the mass media and NGOs. In supporting the plurality of promoters and protectors of human rights, one should not be naïve about the role of governments in less-than-democratic societies. They are likely to constrain the work of such actors if the latter are seen to be questioning the status quo. This is why international solidarity and support are crucial to back up those working in the field. Even in democratic societies, there is a need for vigilance against state intrusion and manipulation.

DIRECTIONS

Particularly at the inter-governmental level, the directions that are emerging are becoming clearer on several fronts. At the regional level, despite the absence of a human rights system, a variety of activities is possible, linked with the impetus from the United Nations under the rubric of technical cooperation programs that entail national action plans, education, institution building, and concretization of the right to development.

In this setting, there is a key linkage between the global/universal and the regional/sub-regional/national/local levels. Ultimately, the crux of the interaction will have to be at the national/local level, since it is the area where the most needed changes are identifiable and where people's lives and livelihood are at stake. This is qualified by the fact that in an increasingly globalized setting, there are many cross-border issues which may lead to human rights violations of a borderless kind.

Apart from concretizing the directions identified above, the Asia-Pacific region should set a Human Rights Agenda for the New Millennium to address those areas where national performance is still deficient or ambivalent, as follows:

• accession to international human rights instruments and effective implementation;

- withdrawal of reservations to international human rights instruments;
- democratization and multi-party system;
- people-based constitution and constitutional process;
- reform of national security laws to reflect human security;
- elimination of preventive detention and promotion of due process of law;
- promotion of freedom of expression, assembly, religion, and thought;
- accountability of public officials and an end to impunity;
- promotion of an independent and transparent judiciary and other modes of dispute settlement accessible and affordable to the people;
- eradication of poverty and concretization of equitable policies to distribute land and other resources;
- development of safety nets, such as social security, for those in need;
- respect for the rights of vulnerable groups including women, children, the disabled, migrant workers, displaced persons, refugees, minorities, indigenous communities, victims of environmental degradation, the elderly, and those with HIV/AIDS;
- improvement of the criminal justice system and humane treatment of suspects, prisoners, and detainees;
- capacity-building of law enforcers to promote integrity and counter corruption;
- promotion of community participation and civil societies, including NGOs and the mass media;
- elimination of corporal punishment and capital punishment;
- eradication of negative traditional practices;
- protection of the environment;
- sustainable development activities;
- conflict prevention, resolution, and cross-cultural understanding between different ethnic groups;
- dissemination of human rights to a broad public, including power groups such as government officials, politicians, religious leaders, and the business sector;
- enhancement of local, national, sub-regional, and regional capacities, programs and interchanges for the promotion and protection of human rights.

To achieve such perspective, the catalysts must have a much broader composition than the traditional government agencies or personnel. As one marches toward the new millennium, civil society, NGOs, the mass media, the business sector and other non-state actors, including non-government armed groups, must be mobilized to respect human rights.

The interface between universal standards and regional responses will have to be monitored and measured by how, and how much, it can help to nurture the knowledge, attitudes, and behavior of all such catalysts, to personify a humane society.

ACKNOWLEDGMENTS

The author wishes to thank warmly the following for providing some of the information for this study: J. Pace, B. Burdekin, I. Hamilton, G. Onojima, and the Office of the UN High Commissioner for Human Rights. All views expressed are personal.

Chapter 23

Human Rights and Victims' Rights in Europe

Gudmundur Alfredsson

Europeans tend to be quite proud of their regional organizations and the human rights standards and procedures adopted under their auspices. This is true, in particular, of the requirements for democracy and freedom associated with membership in the Council of Europe. The 1950 European Convention on Human Rights and Fundamental Freedoms (European Convention) is a deserving flagship, with the European Court of Human Rights (the Strasbourg Court) in the captain's seat.

To a lesser degree, the pride extends to other instruments adopted and monitoring procedures set up by the Council of Europe and the Organization for Security and Cooperation in Europe (OSCE). Other regional and sub-regional organizations enter this picture, but the human rights input, albeit growing, is so far either marginal or minimal when compared with the Council of Europe and the OSCE.

This chapter has a twofold focus in line with the overall themes of the book: on the interface between international and European human rights efforts and on victims in a variety of contexts. It addresses minority rights, inasmuch as they continue to be violated with relative impunity in Europe, and concludes with some overall impressions and a list of issues not dealt with for reasons of space.

INFLUENCE OF THE UNIVERSAL DECLARATION OF HUMAN RIGHTS

The Universal Declaration of Human Rights served as an inspiration for the drafters of the European Convention. Its fifth preambular paragraph states that

European Governments which share political traditions, freedoms, and the rule of law are taking "the first steps for the collective enforcement of certain of the rights stated in the Universal Declaration." The influence is also shown by the choice of topics and wording of many articles in the Convention, and it is reinforced by the case law of the Strasbourg Court [1].

The Universal Declaration was adopted by General Assembly resolution 217 (III), with the text of the Declaration contained in Part A of the resolution. In Part B, the right of petition was acknowledged as an essential human right in line with constitutional approaches common to many countries [2]. The Council of Europe moved faster than the United Nations with the European Convention and its authorization of petitions.

The European Convention has been a successful tool of collective enforcement. States Parties by and large comply with decisions handed down by the Strasbourg Court. A few States have incorporated the Convention into national legislation [for a sub-regional survey, see 3], and both national courts and the European Court of Justice in Luxembourg apply it. In Central and Eastern Europe, newly democratic States have sought membership in the Council of Europe as a regional stamp of approval for their improved human rights and rule of law records.

A more recent example of the interface between international and regional developments is the adoption, in 1983, by the Council of Europe of the European Convention on the Compensation of Victims of Violent Crimes. The preparatory process leading to this Convention coincided with the drafting and adoption in 1985 of the UN Declaration of Basic Principles of Justice for Victims of Crime and Abuse of Power.[1]

VICTIMS

As to the protection of victims in human rights instruments, the main categories addressed are victims of human rights violations, of national and international crimes, and of official abuse, but the standards and responses vary in scope and strength.

A quick electronic search of human rights texts reveals that the term "victim" appears pervasively in contexts relevant to Europe. Such references come up with regard to the overall categories of human rights violations and crimes, as well as specifically in connection with genocide, ethnic cleansing, racism, hate speech, media violence, land possession, wars and international conflicts, land mines, murder, rape, torture and inhuman treatment, disappearances, slavery, sexual

---

[1] Adopted by General Assembly resolution 40/34 of 29 November 1985, upon recommendation from the Seventh UN Congress on the Prevention of Crime and Treatment of Offenders held in Milan in 1985. The Sixth Congress in Caracas in 1980 had also dealt with the issue.

exploitation, forced evictions, terrorism, and corruption. The persons and groups affected include women, children, minorities, and not least the Roma, indigenous peoples, migrant workers, displaced persons, and refugees. All of these references have justice and the well-being of people in common, but they also demonstrate potential overlaps and/or possible conflicts between human rights and victims' rights. In particular, it is important that the emphasis on victims does not counteract the rights of the accused in the administration of justice. The rights of victims will not be fully realized until this conflict has been resolved.

VICTIMS OF HUMAN RIGHTS VIOLATIONS

Traditionally, the term "victim" has meant victims of human rights violations, as evidenced by international and regional instruments. A good example is article 25,1 of the European Convention, stipulating that individuals submitting petitions to Strasbourg must claim "to be the victim of a violation" by States Parties of rights set forth in the Convention. The person concerned must be directly and personally affected or injured by the act or omission at issue; in this way, class actions and submissions on behalf of unrelated individuals are generally ruled out [1, pp. 39-40; for case-law summary see 1, pp. 39-52].

As to remedies, instruments provide for access to justice, restitution, compensation, rehabilitation, and/or assistance. The European Convention foresees compensation to victims of certain violations. Article 3 of Protocol VII, in case of a miscarriage of justice, provides that a person punished as a result of wrong conviction shall be compensated according to the law or practice of the State concerned. Another relevant clause, prescribing an enforceable right to compensation for victims of unlawful arrest or detention, is article 5,5 of the European Convention. International instruments contain parallel standards, and international petition and other monitoring procedures elicit similar responses.[2]

It is interesting to note that several instruments address acts occurring in private life, requiring States to regulate and even criminalize certain private behavior. One example is the 1965 International Convention on the Elimination of All Forms of Racial Discrimination which prescribes effective protection and remedies, including the right to seek just and adequate reparation or satisfaction for damage suffered (article 6). Another example is the UN Declaration on the

---

[2] *The Study on the Right to Restitution, Compensation and Rehabilitation for Victims of Gross Violations of Human Rights,* by Special Rapporteur Theo van Boven, submitted to the UN Sub-Commission on Prevention of Discrimination and Protection of Minorities in document E/CN.4/Sub.2/1993/8. His revised basic principles and guidelines, now also referring to violations of humanitarian law, are currently under UN consideration, see document E/CN.4/1997/104. A recent example of a monitoring response is the report by Special Rapporteur Bacre Waly Ndiaye on extrajudicial, summary or arbitrary executions, in UN document E/CN.4/1998/68; in a chapter devoted to the rights of victims, he points out that compensation is rarely paid for violations of the right to life.

Elimination of Violence against Women[3] which calls for victim access to mechanisms of justice, effective remedies, rehabilitation, specialized assistance, and other support services (article 4, paragraphs d and g).

Active protection for victims, and other witnesses, against retaliation and reprisals because of evidence and testimony they may provide in the course of establishing that a human rights violation or crime has taken place[4] needs a more prominent place in international and regional monitoring bodies. Such protection can take the form of confidentiality for authors of complaints[5] or other effective security measures.[6] The right to privacy also plays a role in these considerations.

VICTIMS OF NATIONAL AND INTERNATIONAL CRIMES

A different aspect of the term "victim" appears in the 1985 UN Declaration of Basic Principles of Justice for Victims of Crime and Abuse of Power. "Victim" is defined as a person who suffers harm, including physical or mental injury, emotional suffering, economic loss, or substantial impairment of fundamental rights, through acts or omissions that are in violation of criminal laws operative within Member States. The term may extend to family members, dependents, and persons who have suffered harm in assisting victims or in preventing victimization (paragraphs 1 and 2).

The 1983 European Convention on the Compensation of Victims of Violent Crimes generally follows this definition. The UN Declaration on Victims and the 1983 Convention point to a number of suggested remedies, such as access to justice, fair treatment, restitution, compensation, assistance, and prevention of victimization. The 1983 Convention goes further inasmuch as the States Parties agree, when compensation for a victim is not fully available from other sources, to contribute to the compensation for the loss of earnings, medical and eventual funeral expenses, and/or loss of maintenance (article 4) in the case of certain grave crimes (article 2). A vague monitoring mandate is given to the Council of Europe's Committee on Crime Problems (article 13).

A number of European States have taken steps to meet these requirements, but it may be argued that their approach is necessarily tied to countries of affluence as compared to States facing more serious human rights problems, such as the realization of the rights to food, health, and education. Compensation under

---

[3] Adopted by General Assembly resolution 48/104 of 20 December 1993.

[4] For a practical example, see the latest report to the UN Commission on Human Rights on the human rights situation in the Sudan by Special Rapporteur Gaspar Bíró who, in document E/CN.4/1998/66, part IX: "Reprisals," condemns specific incidents of this kind.

[5] Like for the 1503 complaints procedure, see paragraphs 4b and 7c of UN Economic and Social Council resolution 1503 (XLVIII) of 27 May 1970.

[6] As in those foreseen in the draft declaration on human rights defenders, see article 12,2 in UN document E/CN.4/1998/98.

the 1983 Convention is to be paid by the State on whose territory the crime was committed and basically only to European nationals (article 3); the latter has an unfortunate discriminatory element as it seems to be more concerned with costs than justice.[7]

A non-governmental organization, the European Forum for Victim Services, has set forth principles and demands for strengthening the rights of victims of crime. Because of the long-term and detrimental consequences of crime for victims, their families and society as a whole, the rights of the victim should be accorded the same priority as those of the accused. The criminal justice system should acknowledge the legitimate interests of victims, treat them with respect and dignity, and ensure that the process of dealing with the offender will not increase the distress or add to the victims' problems. Other victims' rights should cover privacy, receiving and providing information, legal advice, protection against further violence or harassment, and the obligation of democratic societies to alleviate adverse consequences that crime imposes on victims and their families.[8]

There is merit to the assertion of victims' rights in the criminal justice process. A victim should not have to feel as if he or she is on trial, with the consequent denial of dignity and invasion of privacy. At the same time, it is important to ensure that the focus on the rights of victims of crime will not deny the accused his or her rights. A balance must be maintained. International and regional standards about fair trial have been adopted for a reason, and a far-reaching victim-oriented shift in the balance could result in conviction of the innocent or excessive and cruel punishment.

Victims of international crimes are not specifically mentioned in the UN Declaration and the 1983 Convention, if only because national laws are expected to follow suit when the international community has criminalized certain behavior. When the national response to such crimes has been totally inadequate, as in the former Yugoslavia, the international community has established its own criminal tribunals, but the little that has been done for the victims has mostly been by way of humanitarian assistance and not through the criminal justice process.[9]

---

[7] Compare with paragraph 3 of the UN Declaration of Basic Principles of Justice for Victims of Crime and Abuse of Power which bars discrimination based on, inter alia, nationality.

[8] These comments draw on two pamphlets produced by the European Forum for Victim Services: *Statement of Victims' Rights in the Process of Criminal Justice,* 1996, and *The Social Rights of Victims of Crime,* 1998. The address of the European Forum is Cranmer House, 39 Brixton Road, London SW9 6DZ, United Kingdom; fax 44-171-5825712.

[9] In report E/CN.4/1998/68, Bacre Waly Ndiaye regrets that the tribunals are not accompanied by compensation schemes for victims or their families. Less known than the UN criminal tribunals in the Hague is the Human Rights Chamber for Bosnia & Hercegovina, an international court set up under the Dayton Agreement and based in Sarajevo, which is more geared toward victims; its first volume of *Decisions on Admissibility and Merits 1996-1997* was published in Sarajevo in May 1998.

Already in 1948, the Convention on the Prevention and Punishment of the Crime of Genocide[10] foresaw the existence of an international penal tribunal (article VI) as well as jurisdiction for the International Court of Justice in disputes between States Parties (article IX). Now, the expected adoption[11] of an international criminal code and of a statute for an international criminal court may further enhance the international role, as described in detail in Chapter 9 of this volume. The draft statute addresses several aspects of victims' rights; in addition to deterring future crimes, reparations to victims would be considered, identities of testifying victims would not be disclosed, and victims could participate in the proceedings as part of a healing process.[12]

VICTIMS OF ABUSE OF POWER

In addition to the above-quoted reference to criminal abuse of power in the UN Declaration of Basic Principles of Justice for Victims of Crime and Abuse of Power (paragraph 1), the Declaration extends the term's coverage to persons who suffer under "acts or omissions that do not yet constitute violations of criminal laws but of intentionally recognized norms relating to human rights" (paragraph 18); reference is also made to serious abuses of political or economic power (paragraph 21). Remedies to victims should include restitution, compensation and the necessary material, medical, psychological, and social assistance (paragraph 19).

This type of abuse could encompass corruption by public officials. In this connection, reference can be made to the UN Code of Conduct for Law Enforcement Officials[13] and UN Guidelines on the Role of Prosecutors[14] More significantly, the Council of Europe is currently preparing a framework convention against the corruption of public officials and elected representatives which is intended to tackle the phenomenon not only as a trade or competition problem, but also as a threat to democracy, the rule of law, equality, and human rights.[15]

---

[10]This Convention was adopted by General Assembly resolution 260 A (III), on 9 December 1948, the day before the adoption of the Universal Declaration. Thus, 1998 will see two fifty year anniversaries as far as major international human rights instruments are concerned.

[11]At the UN Diplomatic Conference of Plenipotentiaries on the Establishment of an International Criminal Court, which was held in Rome from 15 June to 17 July 1998.

[12]As highlighted in the UN publication *Bringing Justice to the Victims,* DPI/1960/C of May 1998.

[13]Adopted by General Assembly resolution 34/169 of 17 December 1979. It says that law enforcement officials shall not commit acts of corruption and that they shall oppose and combat all such acts (article 7).

[14]Adopted by General Assembly resolution 45/166 of 18 December 1990. It says that prosecutors shall give due attention to crimes of public officials, including corruption and abuse of power (paragraph 15). It also says that prosecutors shall consider victims' views and concerns and ensure that they are informed about their rights under the 1985 Declaration.

[15]The Council of Europe homepage at <http://www.coe.fr> leads the user to a number of working group reports and studies on corruption.

The weakness is in the form; a framework convention is supposed to allow flexibility to ratifying States for the eventual incorporation of common principles rather than firm rules with a biting monitoring mechanism.

MINORITIES AND INDIGENOUS PEOPLES

Violations of the rights of minorities and of persons belonging to minorities remain perhaps the main human rights problem in Europe. Discriminatory patterns in the economic and political fields persist, combined with indignities and threats to identities and cultures. Crime is also present; even genocide is taking place in Europe in this modern day and age. A number of violent internal conflicts have obvious potential for international spillovers. Many other minority situations are unresolved. Political solutions to minority situations on an uneven, case-by-case basis result in continuing discrimination, and groups should not have to resort to violence as a tool for solving their problems.

Equal enjoyment of all human rights and non-discrimination must be extended to minorities. The rights must be applied on an objective and non-selective basis, by judicial or quasi-judicial organs relying on the rule of law. Democracy is good for human rights, but minority rights must be enshrined in constitutional and legislative guarantees with available and accessible remedies, in line with international standards, because majority rule is not necessarily friendly to or understanding of group concerns.

Minority-specific measures, as set forth in many international instruments, are intended to make sure that persons belonging to minorities enjoy the same rights as everyone else. In fact, this must be achieved by way of special and concrete measures so that groups and their members enjoy a position comparable with the majority. Special measures do not constitute privileges; they are rooted in the rule of equal enjoyment, just as is non-discrimination.

European instruments are soft on special measures. The 1992 Charter on Regional or Minority Languages and the 1994 Framework (that word again) Convention for the Protection of National Minorities are somewhat disappointing, as they originate with the Council of Europe which has a good record and a strong emphasis on the rule of law and an advanced system of monitoring institutions with impressive and respected case law. Instead, in these two treaties, State actions constitute the point of departure[16] rather than the rights of minority members, let alone the rights of groups. Even the selection by a State of some rights and areas of protection and not others is tolerated. The monitoring is left to weak institutions reviewing State reports rather than the Strasbourg Court.

---

[16]Repeated formulations refer to States recognizing and promoting rights and creating favorable conditions rather than saying outright that minorities or persons belonging to them shall have certain rights and that States must introduce special and concrete measures for their realization.

Political instruments of the OSCE contain special measures for minorities; these texts also reflect a new thinking about dialogue and confidence-building for security reasons. Respect for human rights is seen as a method of prevention which is a lot less costly than conflict control or restoration of peace. Much of the OSCE success rests with the High Commissioner on National Minorities who facilitates dialogue between the parties for prevention purposes; Max van der Stoel of the Netherlands, the first High Commissioner, has made very good use of a limited mandate.

With reference to treaty rights, complaints avenues, other monitoring instances and minority access and participation established in a series of texts under UN,[17] ILO,[18] and UNESCO auspices, it would seem clear that international instruments and procedures offer more effective protection of minority rights than those of the Council of Europe and the OSCE.

A FEW CONCLUDING OBSERVATIONS

It is interesting to note that international organizations have moved first or are ahead of the European institutions with regard to some of the standards and procedures referenced above. The issue may be academic, since most European States have accepted the international avenues, but the results of the comparison are nevertheless somewhat surprising.

Many other issues could be brought up as regards the human rights performance of European States. These would include the privilege of affluence when it comes to national implementation, reservations to treaties, margins of appreciation and other sovereign ways of safeguarding regional or national particularities, reluctant cooperation with international monitors, a relative lack of attention to economic, social, and cultural rights, and technical assistance in the field of human rights. Selective criticism of the human rights record of non-European countries based on self-interests relating to trade, security, colonial relations, or other foreign policy considerations should also be noted.

The European Convention and the Strasbourg Court lend credibility to efforts of European States to export their human rights positions, since they have subjected themselves to serious standards and monitoring mechanisms. There are, however, notable shortcomings in the European performance; thus, the time is not ripe for anniversary celebrations.

---

[17]For a collection of relevant texts, see G. Alfredsson and G. Melander, *A Compilation of Minority Rights Standards. A Selection of Texts from International and Regional Human Rights Instruments and Other Documents,* Lund: the Raoul Wallenberg Institute, Report No. 24, 1997.

[18]There is no regional counterpart to ILO Convention No. 169 on Indigenous and Tribal Peoples in Independent Countries, but there are indigenous groups on Europe's northern rim and the Roma may qualify as a tribal people under the ILO text.

REFERENCES

1. P. van Dijk and G. J. H. van Hoof, *Theory and Practice of the European Convention on Human Rights and Fundamental Freedoms* (2nd Edition), Kluwer Law and Taxation Publishers, Boston, pp. 435, 437, 1990.
2. A. Eide and G. Alfredsson, Introduction, in *The Universal Declaration of Human Rights. A Commentary*, A. Eide et al. (eds.), Scandinavian University Press, Oslo, pp. 5-16, at p. 13, 1992.
3. M. Scheinin (ed.), *International Human Rights Norms in the Nordic and Baltic Countries,* Nordic Human Rights Publications and Martinus Nijhoff Publishers, The Hague, 1996.

Chapter 24

Human Rights in East and Central Europe

Malgorzata Fuszara

The task of evaluating the state of implementation of human rights in East and Central Europe for the last fifty years, i.e., since the adoption of the Universal Declaration of Human Rights, is very difficult. There are several reasons for this.

The first is a result of the many changes in the region during those years. The fifty years should thus be divided into several periods. In some of them human rights violations prevailed; therefore, we will mainly speak about the most common forms of those violations. Characteristic of other periods in East and Central Europe were citizens' demands or even struggles for human rights against totalitarian regimes, followed by repression and more violations of human rights. Finally, we will consider the period that started around 1989, when the state and society's transition to democracy called for a system allowing genuine protection of human rights. It is obvious that the past fifty years cannot be presented as a homogenous picture.

The second difficulty results from important differences among the countries of East and Central Europe, including those from the viewpoint of protection as well as violation of human rights. The differences among the countries stem from, among other factors, their history, their status before the 1990s, and especially from different events that preceded or accompanied the transition period. The region that now bears the name of "East and Central Europe" consists of countries that regained independence or became independent states as a result of the fall of the USSR, including Lithuania, Latvia, Belarus, and Ukraine. It also consists of countries belonging to the Soviet Bloc as a result of the Yalta Treaty (often against the will of their citizens) but which were independent states for the past fifty years, such as Poland, Hungary, Romania, and Bulgaria. Finally, there are countries in which transition meant profound changes: the fall of old structures and creation of new states in a peaceful way (Czechoslovakia) or through armed conflict (former Yugoslavia, where fundamental human rights have been severely violated). Countries like the latter deserve a separate analysis; however, since a full discussion of them is beyond the purview of this chapter, we will treat them as examples to illustrate general questions regarding the protection of human rights in the region.

The third difficulty stems from the fact that before 1989 many human rights violations remained unknown to the public. Sometimes this was done deliberately by governments to keep international public opinion disinformed; sometimes it resulted from the desire to avoid certain problems and to keep up a myth of equality, lack of discrimination, and protection of rights. Some of these problems have been disclosed and discussed only recently, leading to a false impression that they are a result of the transformation. The general improvement in the field of human rights protection in East and Central Europe comes together with a debate on social groups whose rights are endangered as well as violations of individual rights. Whether individual or group rights are now more endangered than before or whether—which seems more probable—the dangers existed before but had never been disclosed, is not an easy question to answer. The absence of a free press and access to information and the imposition of censorship resulted in a situation where the knowledge of human rights violations of many social groups was scarce, especially with regard to women and ethnic minorities, whose rights will be discussed separately below.

IMPLEMENTATION OF HUMAN RIGHTS IN EAST AND CENTRAL EUROPE UNDER THE COMMUNIST REGIMES

The shortest description of the status of human rights under the communist regimes is that there is no right included in the Universal Declaration of Human Rights that was not violated during that period. Private correspondence was checked, phones were "bugged"—the right to privacy was violated. Well-known opposition leaders were banished from their countries, various people were forced to emigrate—the right to stay in one's own country was violated. Refusal to issue passports or systematic difficulties in obtaining passports were violations of the right to free movement. Examples abound. It is even hard to say that the communist authorities have ever, if only in theory, treated implementation of human rights seriously. It is noteworthy that of eight countries who abstained during voting on the Declaration in 1948, the majority (6) were East and Central European countries. And although their official explanation was different, it is clear that communist representatives were reluctant to support the Declaration from the very start [1]. In their view, international protection of human rights was an instrument of international policy and not a tool to be used by citizens or independent organizations [2].

There were both legal and practical obstacles to the implementation of human rights under communist regimes.

The communist legislatures created a series of obstacles to the implementation of human rights in East and Central European countries. Despite their ratification of basic international human rights conventions, these countries' authorities stressed that the fact of ratification was not enough for the law to be binding within a given country. Specific legislation was necessary for that.

Thus, the courts did not refer to international conventions and the citizens could not treat them as instruments for demanding their rights. However, the question of whether it was necessary to transform international law into national law or whether it was binding directly had always remained controversial. The former view prevailed in most cases. In 1987, the Polish Constitutional Tribunal declared that international conventions ratified by Poland that had not been transformed into law were binding only as regards international relations and were not relevant to judgments by Polish courts.[1]

Another obstacle to the implementation of human rights was a method of transforming fundamental human rights into internal law which, under communist regime, often resulted in the total denial of certain rights. The Declaration's rights were frequently included in the country's constitution, but their practical implementation was subject to laws that, in practice, effectively denied them. For instance, the right to work and choose a job freely (Art. 23 of the Declaration), which was included in a majority of the constitutions of communist states, co-existed with bills directed against the so-called "social parasites," i.e., persons who did not work. The laws concerning such fundamental rights as freedom of speech and freedom of association are another example. The Polish Constitution of 1952 included a declaration on the freedom of assembly (Art. 71); however, legislation in 1962 introduced the total denial of this law in practice. Organizers of meetings—"meetings" meant also gatherings of several persons— had to apply for permission to hold them. Reasons for refusal could be based upon such unclear criteria as "being in opposition to social interest." No independent control of the implementation of the law existed. The situation changed in 1990 with the introduction of a new law based on the principle of freedom of assembly.

---

[1] Judgment of August 25, 1987, published in: Supreme Court Judgements. December 1987, No. 12, item 199. See also: Jewgenij Usienko: Prawo miedzynarodowe a prawo wewnetrzne w ZSRR (International law and national law in USSR) in: Prawo miedzynarodowe a prawo wewnetrzne w swietle doswiadczen panstw socjalistycznych, (International law and national law in socialist countries) Ossolineum, Wroclaw 1980 pp. 53-68; Petko Radionow: Prawo miedzynarodowe a prawo wewnetrzne w Ludowej Republice Bulgarii, (International law and national law in Bulgaria) ibidem pp. 69-84; Nae Androne: Prawo miedzynarodowe a prawo wewnetrzne w Socjalistycznej Republice Rumunii (International law and national law in Romania), ibidem pp. 105-112; Antonin Kanda: Prawo miedzynarodowe a prawo wewnetrzne w Czechoslowackiej Republice Socjalistycznej (International law and national law in Czechoslovakia) ibid. pp. 113-116.

Under the communist regime, the East and Central European countries introduced many laws that were in direct opposition to basic concepts of human rights. For example, in 1967 Albania declared itself the "first atheist country in the world" and introduced a law forbidding religious practices. Consequently, many people were arrested and sentenced to prison, even persons who participated in a holy mass celebrated at a private home.[2] In Bulgaria, ethnic Turks were arrested and imprisoned for following the Islamic custom of having their sons circumcised.[3] In many countries, including Czechoslovakia, people were imprisoned for distributing illegal publications,[4] and in Poland and Hungary, as elsewhere in the region, men were imprisoned for refusing military service.[5] In the majority of cases, verdicts were based upon laws that stood in contradiction to internationally recognized human rights.

However, if the law itself was not contradictory to human rights, the rights were still not realized, due to various practical obstacles erected by the totalitarian regimes to make protection of human rights even more difficult. Laws were thus used or interpreted in such a way that fundamental human rights were often violated. Sometimes the very construction of the laws made it easy in practice to violate human rights. In Bulgaria in the 1980s, the Turkish people were forced to change their names to "Slavic" ones. The procedure was presented as voluntary.[6] People were forced to stop wearing their traditional clothes, using their language in public, and celebrating their traditional holidays [3]. In the German Democratic Republic people were arrested not only for attempting to cross the border illegally, but also for applying repeatedly but without success for permission to emigrate.[7] The law itself permitted them to do so; nevertheless another regulation on "impeding the activity of public bodies" (Art. 214 of the Penal Code) was used to persecute them. In many countries, in spite of the legal right to an independent court trial, this right and many others were often violated, especially as concerns political prisoners. Summary justice procedures were applied and the rights of the accused were often ignored. Some political cases were even submitted for trial to institutions outside the judiciary system. Yearly reports of Amnesty International cite cases of violence, inhuman treatment of prisoners, and risks to life and health resulting from treatment in prisons in all East and Central European countries.

---

[2] Amnesty International Report 1987, p. 280.
[3] Amnesty International Report 1987, p. 283.
[4] Amnesty International Report 1987, p. 285.
[5] Amnesty International Report 1987, pp. 205, 305-306.
[6] Amnesty International Report 1988, p. 195.
[7] Amnesty International Report 1987, p. 292.

PERIOD OF THE
STRUGGLE FOR HUMAN RIGHTS

These difficulties in realizing basic human rights did not mean, however, that they had no influence upon the situation in East and Central European countries under the communist regime. Such influence was mainly in the citizens' thoughts of a wider system of norms that included their rights and the possibility of fighting for these rights even within the communist system.

Violations of human rights by these countries' legal systems had never been accepted by the majority of their citizens. Sociological research on law in countries where such research could be carried out showed that many citizens demanded respect for human rights and rejected their violation by the legal system. This research revealed their deep belief in natural law and that no state-approved law could change their understanding of this law as imperative and existing independently from national law, and their deep conviction that human rights were for everyone no matter what the actual law was [4]. This concept of law was especially vivid during periods of struggle against these totalitarian regimes. Let us recall the events in Hungary in 1956, in Czechoslovakia in 1968, and in Poland in 1956, 1970, and 1980. The most explicit example was in Poland in 1980 when, among twenty-one demands of the Gdansk workers, the right to establish free and independent trade unions, which is one of the rights included in the Universal Declaration of Human Rights, was at the top of the list. The workers referred to ILO Convention No. 87 that had been ratified by Poland. Other top priorities were a free press and the release of political prisoners, which proved that human rights were internalized deeply, despite many years of communist brainwashing and violations of these rights.

The Polish people did not regain their rights in 1980. Repressions followed. Martial law, which was introduced in December 1981, violated human rights and introduced severe penalties for any attempt to demand them. Political activists were imprisoned, correspondence was monitored and phones were bugged, associations were suspended, and activists were punished if they continued their work. The right to move freely throughout the country was limited, many publications were banned, gatherings were forbidden, and forced labor was introduced. Penalties for violation of these regulations included the death penalty and summary justice procedures were introduced [5]. Nevertheless, both the opinion polls and the events in the following years proved that a deeply internalized concept of human rights as everyone's rights, no matter whether justified or not by existing law, survived the period of communist regimes. The changes that began after 1989 created the possibility of fully executing these rights. Unfortunately, this has not happened in all of these countries. It is necessary to comment on the positive as well as the negative aspects of the transition period.

HUMAN RIGHTS IN EAST AND CENTRAL
EUROPE AFTER 1989

After 1989, many countries of East and Central Europe began revising their human rights systems, and began a process of adjustment of the existing national law and practice to the international human rights norms. Prior to 1990, Eastern and Central European countries did not belong to a regional system for protection of human rights. Following the dissolution of the Soviet Union, many of these countries joined the council of Europe and signed and ratified the European Convention on the Protection of Human Rights and Fundamental Liberties. Among them, by 1997, Albania, Bulgaria, Czech Republic, Estonia, Hungary, Lithuania, Poland, Romania, Slovakia, and Slovenia had ratified this convention, and even more countries (Croatia, Latvia, Moldova, Russia, Ukraine, and the former Yugoslav Republic of Macedonia) had signed it. The convention permits individuals to submit complaints against their country alleging violations of rights protected by it. This provision has been used extensively. In 1996, Polish citizens submitted 1127 complaints; only French, Italian, and British nationals sent more complaints to Strasbourg, the seat of the Council of Europe, in that year. Also in 1996, there were 415 complaints from Romania, 177 from Hungary, 169 from the Czech Republic, 165 from Slovakia, 90 from Bulgaria, 41 from Lithuania, and 34 from Slovenia.[8]

In another turning point concerning the applicability of international law, many East and Central European constitutions now state that international law is binding directly in their countries. For instance, the Polish Constitution of 1997 declares that international conventions ratified by Poland become part of the internal legal system and are applied directly (Art. 91). A similar declaration is included in the Bulgarian Constitution [Art. 5 (4)], the Russian Constitution [Art. 15 (4)], and the Estonian Constitution (Art. 123). In these countries, there are now no legal obstacles to treating international conventions as a legislative source. However, problems still arise due to the lack of tradition in the courts of referring to international law, or even to the constitution itself [6].

Fundamental changes in constitutions, or even the preparation of new constitutions, presented a natural occasion for discussion of human rights, their legal implications, and enforcement [7, 8]. In many countries, institutions monitoring the implementation of human rights, such as ombudspersons, constitutional

[8] See: M. A. Nowicki: Europejski system ochrony praw czlowieka ("European System of Protection of Human Rights"), M. Krzyzanowska-Mierzewska, M. A. Nowicki: Sprawy polskie przes Europejski Komisja Praw Czlowieka (Polish cases in European Commission of Human Rights) in: Polak w Radzie Europy (Poland in Council of Europe). Warsaw 1997, pp. 77-96. On ratification see: Chart of Signatures and Ratifications: Convention for the Protection of Human Rights and Fundamental Freedoms, Council of Europe, Update 05/05/1998.

courts or constitutional tribunals were established. The majority of East and Central European countries introduced the "Swedish" type of Ombudsperson who controls not only public administration, but the justice system as well. It differs from the "Danish" type, more popular in West Europe, who controls only public administration. Despite the introduction into the constitution of the institution of Ombudsperson by many East and Central European Countries (e.g., Bulgaria, Estonia, Hungary, Lithuania, Poland, and Russia), no one was appointed for some time (e.g., Bulgaria), and in others (e.g., Sergie Kovalov in Russia) the Ombudsperson's important work led to dismissal. But in most of these countries the Ombudsperson has become a very important part of the national "machinery" for monitoring the implementation of human rights [9-12].[9] They created a basis for citizens to defend their rights as well as to monitor possible violations. The literature demonstrates that the Universal Declaration of Human Rights, international conventions and declarations were used as examples while working on constitutional revisions in these countries [13].

The change after 1989 is so great that it is difficult to compare the situation before and after that year. Freedom of association, the right to hold meetings, freedom of speech, the right to choose freely where to settle and to travel are now widely exercised by the citizens of these countries. Obviously, this does not mean that violations of human rights do not take place. There are spheres where such violations are abundant. Especially numerous are complaints concerning the police force,[10] judiciary,[11] bad conditions in prisons,[12] and discrimination in obtaining citizenship in newly-created states.[13] The most common violations of these rights concern primarily two groups: ethnic minorities and women. These will be addressed later in this chapter.

In several countries of East and Central Europe, human rights continue to be grossly and systematically violated. For example, in Belarus, journalists are arrested and other measures undertaken against the independence of the press. Control over the media results in censorship of the opposition and in the denial of the citizens' right to choose freely their vote. Brutality by the police forces is a violation of the right to freedom of assembly. Arbitrary arrests, including arrests

---

[9] On Ombudspersons see also: art. 55 of the Constitution of Romania, art. 32 B of the Constitution of Hungary, art. 93 of the Constitution of Croatia, art. 159 of the Constitution of Slovenia, art. 103 of the Constitution of Russia, art. 55 of the Constitution of Ukraine, art. 208-211 of the Constitution of Poland.

[10] For instance, in Hungary, Amnesty International Report 1997, p. 176; in Bulgaria, p. 100.

[11] For instance in Poland International Helsinki Federation for Human Rights 1997, p. 200; Lithuania, p. 169.

[12] For instance in Romania International Helsinki Federation for Human Rights, Annual Report 1997, p. 211; in Russia, pp. 222-223.

[13] For instance in Czech Republic, Human Rights Watch World Report 1998, pp. 252-253; in Latvia International Helsinki Federation for Human Rights, Annual Report 1997, pp. 164-165; in Slovenia, pp. 235-236.

of members of Parliament, the lack of an independent judiciary, and deplorable prison conditions[14] are the most often quoted examples of human rights violations. There are also forced movements of populations,[15] and suppression of religious freedom.

All forms of violations—massive ethnic extermination, rape, murder, torture, deportation, demolition of religious sites, violation of freedom of speech, religion, association, and assembly—can be found in the former Yugoslavia [14-16]. The UN Special Rapporteur on Human Rights there, Tadeusz Mazowiecki, resigned from his post in 1995 when he concluded that his documentation on crimes evoked no reaction within the international community and no help for the victims of these terrible crimes. The weakness of his mandate, he said, was dramatized by the fact that only once during those three years was he invited to speak to a Security Council meeting, and his presentation had to be very brief. The Commission on Human Rights, by which he was appointed, could not launch any concrete action aiming at ending the tragic events in that country [17, 18].

ETHNIC MINORITIES—THE ROMA EXAMPLE

Even in countries with a high awareness of human rights, violations of ethnic rights are common [19-20], especially as regards the Roma people living in this region. It is estimated that approximately five million Roma live in East and Central Europe, most of them in the suburbs of larger cities [21]. The Roma were openly discriminated against under the communist regime, mainly through forced settlement. Those who did not comply were persecuted on the pretext of violating other regulations, such as laws on assembly, traffic laws, and obligatory registration while visiting a place [22]. Since 1989 the Roma in most countries of the region have not been persecuted; however, there are countries where legal discrimination of ethnic minorities is permitted, including of the Roma. For instance, the Bulgarian Constitution bans formation of political organizations based on ethnic grounds [Art. 11 (4)].[16] On the other hand, in some countries with no discriminatory regulations of this kind, the Roma are often subject to aggression and many of them complain about the weakness of legal protection against such acts. For instance, in Romania, as many as thirty acts of aggression against the Roma were submitted to courts in 1990-1995 that either never came to trial or ended in suspended sentences and minor penalties.[17] The Roma also faced

---

[14]Country Reports on Human Rights Practices for 1996, 105th Congress 1st Session, February 1997, str 847-859, International Helsinki Federation for Human Rights, Annual Report 1997, str 31-43, Amnesty International Report 1997, str 88.

[15]Country report by Committee on Human Rights "Viasna-96" Belarus, unpublished report. Property of the author.

[16]International Helsinki Federation for Human Rights, Annual Report 1997, str 60.

[17]International Helsinki Federation for Human Rights, Annual Report 1997, p. 212.

aggression in Slovakia,[18] and the Czech Republic, where many of them could not obtain citizenship after the division of the former state,[19] and in Hungary,[20] Bulgaria,[21] and numerous other countries. Such acts are usually based on prejudice, and the fact that the authorities are usually reluctant to take a firm stand against it only adds to the conflict.

WOMEN'S RIGHTS

Sociological research, legal analysis, statistical data, and local as well as the reports of international organizations show inequality of opportunity between women and men in all countries of the region [23-28]. Everywhere women's representation in parliaments has dropped drastically and women's representation in other decision-making bodies remains very low. East and Central European women have difficulties in obtaining jobs; in spite of their high level of education, women are over-represented among the unemployed and discriminated against in the process of getting a job, including by gender-defined job offers. Sexual harassment in some countries is of epidemic proportions. The laws of the previous period included some "privileges" for women such as maternity leave, child care leave, and leave from work in case of illness of a child or family member. Such regulations, while contributing positively to women's performance of their traditional tasks, in fact locked into place the woman's duty to take care of other members of the family, especially children, and maintained the traditional division of roles in the family. These regulations endanger women's status, especially in the labor market, by creating an impression of women being less effective workers. In many countries, this is accompanied by ideologies promoting women's unique role as mothers and caretakers. Stereotypes of women and men are reproduced in school manuals and in the media, especially in advertisements. At the same time, the situation of women is often associated with many problems that have so far been treated as taboo, making it even more difficult to start a genuine public debate on women's issues. Unknown in scope, but probably very wide, are the phenomena of violence against women, rape, traffic in women, sexual harassment at work, and wage gaps. Virtually nothing is being done by the authorities to analyze these questions and even less to solve them. Many elements point to the conclusion that the governments of East and Central European countries neglect gender discrimination and even the international conventions that they willingly ratified. Hope lies primarily in the activities of the non-governmental sector. It is worthwhile to emphasize that, although under the

---

[18]International Helsinki Federation for Human Rights, Annual Report 1997, p. 23.

[19]Human Rights Watch, World Report 1998, p. 252.

[20]Human Rights Watch, World Report 1998, p. 261.

[21]International Helsinki Federation for Human Rights, Annual Report 1997, pp. 60-61.

communist regimes equality of men and women was a myth, many women worked and many had access to education. Thus, it is very unlikely that women will accept traditional roles and traditional infringements upon their rights. However, inequality of opportunity and lack of protection of rights is common to all countries of the region.

INSTEAD OF AN EPILOGUE

It is difficult to write about human rights protection in a region as new as "Eastern and Central Europe." It is even more complicated if we consider not only political, but also economic, social, and cultural rights. During the communist regime, many problems were hidden. For instance, in principle there was no unemployment; in reality, this meant a high level of "hidden unemployment" and, as a result, a relatively low level of income for almost everyone. Many social services, such as kindergartens, were subsidized and thus more broadly available than now. On the other hand, censorship and other restrictions made access to many goods like books or a free press much more difficult than now, even if they were less expensive. Also, the economic costs of the transition to a market economy was harder on some groups (e.g., the less educated and those in rural areas) than others. We also must bear in mind that implementation of human rights is not equal among these countries. A group of states in this region has achieved great progress in this respect. They are now democracies, where human rights protection is quite advanced. This does not mean, however, that violations of human rights do not occur. No country in the world is free of them. Yet, these countries have created procedures for human rights monitoring, as well as mechanisms for complaint, including complaints to international tribunals. What makes us anxious is that infringement of the rights of groups, such as women, does not evoke serious reactions on the part of authorities and political elites.

There are also countries where human rights are constantly violated, and war crimes are still committed. The process of creating human rights protection in the region has thus not come to fruition. There are two possible outcomes: the democratic part will grow slowly but steadily until it includes the entire region, or the region will split into two parts: a democratic one and a totalitarian one. We must continue to hope that, at least in a more distant future, the optimistic ending will be achieved and the rights included in the Universal Declaration will be protected throughout the whole region.

REFERENCES

1. J. Michalski, Z. historii Powszechnej Deklaracji Praw Czlowieka (From the History of Universal Human Rights Declaration), in *Chrzescijanin w swiecic (Christians in the World), 123,* pp. 81-91, 1983.

2. M. A. Nowicki, Kilka uwag o ochronie praw czlowieka (Some Remarks on Protection of Human Rights) Prawa czlowieka. in *Komitet Helsinski w Polsce (Bulletin of the Helsinki Committee in Poland)*, 5, pp. 15-18, 1989.

3. M. Fiucher, *Minorities in Central and Eastern Europe*, Council of Europe Press, Strasbourg, 1994.

4. J. Kurczewski, *The Resurrection of Rights in Poland*, Clarendon Press, Oxford, 1993.

5. M. Fuszara, Prawo- stan szczegolny czy normalny? (Law: A Special or Normal State), Res Publica 1987 No. 2 str 21-31; M. Fuszara, The Law—A Special or Normal State? in *Tidskrift for Rattssociologi*, 5, pp. 133-148, 1988.

6. E. Letowska, Promocja praw czlowieka w dzialalnosci polskiego ombudsmana (Human Rights Promotion in the Activity of the Polish Ombudsman), *Biuletyn Rzecznika Praw Obywatelskich (The Ombudsman Office Bulletin)*, 13, Warszawa, pp. 5-46, 1992.

7. G. Halmai, The Protection of Human Rights in Poland and Hungary, in *Human Rights in Eastern Europe*, I. Pogany (ed.), Edward Elgar Publishing Press, pp. 149-167, 1995.

8. B. Bowring, Human Rights in Russia: Discourse of Emancipation or Only a Mirage? in *Human Rights in Eastern Europe*, I. Pogany (ed.), Edward Elgar Publishing Press, pp. 87-109, 1995.

9. J. Kurczewski, The Politics of Human Rights in Post-Communist Poland, in *Human Rights in Eastern Europe*, I. Pogany (ed.), Edward Elgar Publishing Press, pp. 111-134, 1995.

10. J. Priban, The Constitutional Court of the Czech Republic and a Legal-Philosophical Perspective on the Sovereignty of the Law, in *Human Rights in Eastern Europe*, I. Pogany (ed.), Edward Elgar Publishing Press, pp. 135-148, 1995.

11. R. Mullerson, Perspectives on Human Rights and Democracy in the Former Soviet Republics, in *Human Rights in Eastern Europe*, I. Pogany (ed.), Edward Elgar Publishing Press, pp. 47-85, 1995.

12. G. Fetkova, *Fundamental Rights and Freedoms in Constitutional Case-Law in Slovac Republic*, unpublished paper, in type form, property of the author; Marten Oosting: Contributions on Ombudsmanship, National Ombudsman of the Netherlands, Hague.

13. W. Osiatynski, Rights in New Constitutions of East Central Europe, *Columbia Human Rights Review*, 26:1, 1994.

14. N. Howen, Significance of a War Crimes Tribunal for the Balkans, in *Monitoring Human Rights in Europe*, A. Bloed (ed.), Kluwer Academic Publishers, pp. 261-283, 1993.

15. R. Wieruszewski, Case Study on the Former Yugoslavia: The International Mechanisms, Their Efficiency and Failures, in *Monitoring Human Rights in Europe*, A. Bloed (ed.), Kluwer Academic Publishers, pp. 285-303, 1993.

16. A. Uzelac, Pacyfikacja (Pacification), *Gazeta Wyborcza*, 52:3 III, p. 1, 1998; A. Uzelac, Dwie Prisztiny (Two Prisztinas), ibid. p. 8.

17. T. Surdel and J. Kalabinski, Mazowiecki rezygnuje (Mazowiecki Resigns), *Gazeta Wyborcza*, 28, VII, p. 1, 1995.

18. D. Warszawski, W. Bartoszewski, S. Ogata, H. Koschnik, and M. Abrams, Miedzy glupota a nienawiscia, *Gazeta Wyborcza*, 204:2/3 IX, pp. 6-8, 1995.

19. V. Bogdanor, Overcoming the Twentieth Century: Democracy and Nationalism in Central and Eastern Europe, in *Human Rights in Eastern Europe*, I. Pogany (ed.), Edward Elgar Publishing Press, pp. 1-15, 1995.

20. P. Dunay, Nationalism and Ethnic Conflicts in Eastern Europe: Imposed, Induced or (Simply) Reemerged, in *Human Rights in Eastern Europe*, I. Pogany (ed.), Edward Elgar Publishing Press, pp. 17-45, 1995.

21. M. Foucher, *Minorities in Central and Eastern Europe*, Council of Europe Press, Strasbourg, 1994.

22. A. Bartosz, *Nie bój sie Cygana. Fundacja Pogranicze*, Sejny, 1994.

23. E. Baalsrud (ed.), *Free and Equal? Female Voices from Central and Eastern Europe*, Norwegian Equal Status Council, No. 2, September 1992.

24. N. Funk and M. Mueller (eds.), *Gender Politics and Post-Communism*, Routledge, 1993.

25. B. Einhorn, *Cinderella Goes to the Market*, Verso, London, 1993.

26. M. Fuszara, Market Economy and Consumer Rights: The Impact on Women's Everyday Lives and Employment, in *Economic and Industrial Democracy, 15*:1, February 1994.

27. A. Posadskaya (ed.), *Women in Russia: A New Era in Russia's Feminism*, Verso, London, 1994.

28. J. W. Scott, C. Kaplan, and D. Keates (eds.), *Transitions, Environments, Translations. Feminists in International Politics*, Routledge, New York and London, 1997.

Voices

Vaclav Havel
President, Czech Republic

A number of diverse texts have played fundamental roles in human history. The Universal Declaration of Human Rights differs from all the others primarily in one respect: its impact has not been meant to remain confined within one culture or one civilization. From the very outset, it has been envisaged as a universal, so to speak planetary, set of principles to govern human coexistence, and it has gradually become the point of departure for countless successive guidelines defining the rules of a worthy life together for the people and nations on this Earth. Texts of such fundamental nature are not easily born. The Declaration was obviously the fruit of a very special climate right after World War II, when all humanity realized that if the world wanted to prevent repetitions of such apocalyptic horrors, it had to rise above the various particular interests or concerns of prestige, and to agree on a certain fundamental code.

The life of the Universal Declaration of Human Rights has been marked by contradictions.

On the one hand, the Declaration has notably predetermined the direction of the United Nations in the fifty years that have followed. Its imprint is borne by many ensuing UN documents, as well as by hundreds of international treaties and constitutional instruments of individual nations. It was also present in the background of the well-known Final Act of the 1975 Helsinki conference. The emphasis placed in that document on human rights helped to put an end to the bipolar division of the world. It added momentum to the opposition movements in the communist countries who took the accords signed by their governments seriously, and intensified their struggle for the observance of human rights, thus challenging the very essence of totalitarian systems.

On the other hand, it is also true that human rights have been violated, ignored, or suppressed in many countries of the world—in some of them in milder forms, in others very brutally—throughout the fifty years since the Declaration was adopted. This is not surprising: the immensely complex world that we live in can hardly be changed overnight simply by passing a declaration.

Nevertheless, I believe that the frequent breaches of its principles have been by far outweighed by the historic importance of this global commitment. For the first time in history, there has been a valid, and globally respected, instrument holding up a mirror to the misery of this world: a universal standard with which we can constantly compare the actual state of affairs, to which we can point, and in whose name we can act, to combat injustices if need be. Since everyone has subscribed to this standard, few would venture to criticize it as such. This means that all those who commit substantial violations of its principles must face this historical reality.

To put it simply: the life of all those who scorn human rights is much more difficult with the Declaration in place, than it was before. For this reason we must not allow the subject of human rights and their consistent enforcement to be quietly relegated to a second- or third-class status as an inconvenient and politically inexpedient issue. Massive violations of fundamental human rights, which clearly include the right to life, are, in fact, often invoked to explain or defend national or state interests, and are, unfortunately, becoming an everyday reality which, in the past decade, we could watch in almost a live transmission. The genocide in Rwanda, the killing in Chechnya, Bosnia and Herzogovina, the situation in Tibet, North Korea, Burma, Cuba, and Kosovo—this is but a part of the list of events we have to bear in mind. Backed by the provisions of the Universal Declaration of Human Rights, we should be able to confront these threats to human life, freedom, and dignity, or at least to always clearly identify them.

Why have human beings the prerogative to enjoy any human rights? I often ask myself this question and, time and again, I come to the conclusion that this is something essentially different, and much more profound, than a mere contract among people who have found it practical to have their rights articulated and guaranteed in some way or other, and to have an instrument restricting, automatically, the rights of those who could, or would wish to, deny them their rights or jeopardize their exercise. In formal terms, the Declaration, indeed, takes the form of a contract or covenant, like the hundreds of thousands of laws or regulations governing human coexistence. This covenant, however, derives from certain paradigms, established notions or preconditions that need no further explanation. For example, in one way or another, the concept of human dignity permeates all the fundamental human rights and human rights documents. We find this so natural that we see no point in asking what human dignity actually means, or why should humanity possess it; nor do we inquire why it is practical for us all to recognize it for one another.

I am convinced that the deepest roots of what we now call human rights lie somewhere beyond us, and above us; somewhere deeper than the world of human covenants—in a realm that I would, for simplicity's sake, describe as metaphysical. Although they may fail to realize this, human beings derive their dignity, as well as their responsibility, from the world as a whole; that is, from that in which they see the world's central theme, its backbone, its order, its direction, its essence, its soul—name it as you will.

The world has markedly changed in the past fifty years. There are many more of us on this planet now; the colonial system has fallen apart; the bipolar division is gone; globalization is advancing at a dizzying pace. The Euro-American culture that largely moulded the character of our present civilization is no longer predominant. We are entering an era of multiculturalism. While the world is now enveloped by one single global civilization, this civilization is based on coexistence of many cultures, religions, or spheres of civilization that are equal, and equally powerful.

These different worlds naturally have their different historical, spiritual, political, and moral traditions. More and more often, we witness clashes between these traditions and the human rights notion embodied in the Universal Declaration of Human Rights. Many times, an alleged contradiction has simply served as an ignoble pretext for various autocrats who have sought to legitimate their evil actions by pointing out the "otherness" of their cultures. On other occasions, however, the incongruity is real, and the various standards developed by the Euro-American world are truly perceived in all sincerity as an alien creation that can perhaps be respected, but not inwardly embraced. Moreover, some find this creation much too secular, much too mundane, much too material, claiming that it fails to pay regard to the higher authority that is the only source of all moral imperatives and all the rights that are derived from these imperatives, or safeguarded by them.

What can be done in this situation?

I see one viable course in placing emphasis on the spiritual source of human rights. This is something that will not make these rights an alien phenomenon for the non-European or non-American worlds; on the contrary, it may bring them closer to these realms. First and foremost, however, it may bring them closer to us who come from the Euro-American environment, for we seem to be the ones who are most inclined to lose sight of the spiritual dimension of the values we believe in, and of the metaphysical origin of the rights we claim; and to regard producing documents like the Universal Declaration of Human Rights simply as a kind of good business.

Most importantly, the primeval foundations of all the main religious systems of the world contain, in different forms, the same basic principles, and the same moral imperatives. The various religions differ tremendously in accentuation, in spirit, in character, and in liturgy, but somewhere deep down we always find the same fundamentals—the same call for humility before that which is around us and above us, for decency and for solidarity; the same reference to the memory of the universe where all our nations are proven for their true worth; the same emphasis on our responsibility for the whole world.

I do not think that the United Nations, today, could adopt a document whose significance would match that of the Universal Declaration of Human Rights. I believe that we should make an effort to highlight the spiritual dimension and spiritual origin of the values guarded by the United Nations, and to translate this also into the Organization's practical activities. If a better future for this world lies in the realm of spirit, of moral order, and of a renewed sense of responsibility for this world, who but the United Nations should be the one to restate this again and again?

The UN should look for ways in which the entire system that is aimed to foster human rights, and all the other rights and responsibilities shared by humanity today, could be more deeply implanted in this spiritual foundation.

In addition, I think that the United Nations and the various UN agencies, committees, and commissions should, in an increasing measure, instil their efforts with a systematic concern for human rights. All their actions should be rooted in, related to, or derived from, the concept of human rights. This might, perhaps, create a climate in which there would not be so much particularism, so much indifference, so much tolerance for obvious evil, motivated by egoism or by economic or geopolitical interests. To my mind, the biggest problem of today's multipolar world—a world which has witnessed a reawakening of hundreds of atavistic national interests—does not lie in evil as such, but in tolerance for evil.

It would be marvelous if every man and woman knew that the United Nations is their organization. It is my wish for us all, that the post-war attempt, called the United Nations, succeeds and thrives. It is my hope that the Universal Declaration of Human Rights, whose birth we are commemorating this year, will not be just a dream about what humanity's position should be like in this world. May it gradually turn, in all countries, into a living reality.

Part VI

The Trauma of Human Rights Denial and Violation

Chapter 25

The Impact of Traumatic Human Rights Violations on Victims and the Mental Health Profession's Response

Brian Engdahl, Marianne Kastrup,
James Jaranson, and Yael Danieli

This chapter surveys the growing understanding of the traumatic impact of human rights violations. This understanding has developed over time through work by the mental health and other professions with victims of such violations. This work has had a profound effect on the mental health professions, creating a wellspring of concern that challenges them to be creative and humane in their responses. The chapter is a contribution to the ongoing efforts of those working toward the healing of the victims and ensuring against future victimization.

TRAUMATIC HUMAN RIGHTS VIOLATIONS: DELINEATION OF THE PROBLEM

The label "human rights violations" exposes the inadequacy of (particularly) legalistic language that connotes the legal provisions violated rather than the enormous gravity and intolerable impact on individuals, families, communities, and even entire societies and nations. The term is a euphemism, an evasion, and a denial of the awfulness of the experiences and the ways in which they may "sear the souls of the survivors" [1]. Further complicating our task is the difficulty in distinguishing human rights violations that occur within the devastation of war from those that occur in other circumstances (i.e., the arrest, torture, and "disappearance" of thousands in Argentina and Chile and other instances of abuse of power, such as violence against women and rape, and child abuse). According to a survivor, the abuses are suffered in a "common pool [of] political crimes . . . Thus, the seeds of fear and mistrust are planted and germinate, resulting in silence on the part of the people and yielding the torturers a harvest of total domination" [2]. Therefore, we use a definition of traumatic human rights violations which encompasses damage done by "plans to persecute and destroy individuals, classes, ethnic groups or religious sects, regardless of absolute numbers involved" [1].

These experiences often cannot be put into words, although there have been numerous eloquent attempts by Holocaust survivors, among others, to describe them. They may only be encoded as powerful negative feelings, painful physical sensations, or horrific imagery of the events. The psychobiological trauma of starvation, untreated disease, experiences of persecution, psychological shock (or numbing), and head injury may further interfere with recall and verbal description of the traumatic experiences. While ordinary stressful life events seem to release a strong need for sharing in victims, extreme traumatic events may result in the conspiracy of silence [3], with victims sharing neither their experiences nor the aftermath [4, 5]. A study of torture victims found that fewer than one out of ten victims disclosed details of their experiences to their close relatives after their release [6]. Certain experiences are seldom revealed unless specifically asked about by another who is perceived as trustworthy and, therefore, as a potential source of support.

Of the population with traumatic violations of human rights, those most often treated by health professionals may be divided into the following overlapping groups.

Refugees

In 1995, the estimated number of refugees forced into migration was twenty-three million people [7]. Because they did not cross political borders, an additional twenty-six million internally displaced persons are not classified as "refugees." When they are included, it can be estimated that the world situation includes approximately forty-nine million forced migrants. Refugees and asylum seekers face psychological challenges including demands of adjustment to a new country, often with racial or religious discrimination, and the losses of their homeland, culture, social ties, and former economic status [8]. Most of these individuals migrated due to the forces of war and ethnic strife. Many had refugee camp and/or concentration camp experience, and a significant proportion were exposed to systematic torture and related trauma; the additional traumata of the exile may worsen the consequences of torture.

Torture Survivors

There are no reliable estimates of the prevalence of torture in the world. Because of the politically sensitive nature of the issue, epidemiologic studies are difficult, if not impossible, to conduct. The only data available are those published by human rights organizations such as Amnesty International (AI), although they probably represent only a fraction of all human rights abuses in the world; the 1997 Report of AI listed over 150 countries known for some form of human rights violation in the previous year [9].

An analysis of the 1992 AI report demonstrated the nature and global distribution of human rights violations [10]. In 1991, systematic torture was reported in ninety-three of the 204 countries. Reports of torture were more common from regions affected by political unrest, including mass demonstrations, outbreaks of violence, killings, coup attempts, civil war, separatist or guerilla groups, and armed tribal conflict. Systematic torture and/or ill treatment were also reported in 25 percent of the western European and North American countries. Little is known about the prevalence of torture among various at-risk populations. Five percent to 35 percent of the world's refugees may have had at least one experience of torture [11]. In some refugee groups living in Western countries the prevalence of a history of torture may be as high as 70 percent [12]. Similarly, some studies of non-political prisoners suggest that the prevalence of torture in some prison populations may be as high as 85 percent [13].

Prisoners of War

Wars, political unrest, and civil upheavals in the last fifty years led hundreds of thousands of individuals to experience forced captivity and attendant maltreatment. In 1998, 56,700 American POWs are estimated to be alive [14]. Surviving civilian prisoners taken in the context of international conflicts include an estimated 75,000 European Jewish Nazi concentration camp inmates [15] and about one million non-Jews [16]. Many POWs as well as civilian prisoners were intentionally subjected to beatings and torture at the hands of their captors; still others suffered untreated medical conditions, food and shelter deprivation, armed attack, and forced relocations.

Other Victim/Survivor Groups

Although reliable estimates are not available, soldiers not captured during combat and civilians (including children) exposed to armed conflict [17, 18] likely constitute even larger groups than those detailed above. More recently, the stress of UN peace-keeping has been recognized to have adverse effects on thousands of participants [19]. There are an estimated twenty-six million internally displaced persons [7]. Their displacement is forced and invariably associated with violence [20], carrying with it the potential burden of negative psychological and social consequences. Enormous numbers of people have not been traumatized collectively, but perhaps less dramatically and alone, such as victims of crime [21, 22], survivors of abuse and violence against women [23, 24], and victims of other human rights violations [25], such as contemporary forms of slavery [26] and maltreated non-political prisoners [27].

TRAUMATIC HUMAN RIGHTS VIOLATIONS:
SHORT- AND LONG-TERM CONSEQUENCES

Systematic attention was first paid to victims/survivors of human rights violations in the aftermath of World War II. This attention was drawn by the extremely gruesome and heinous maltreatment that prisoners were subjected to in Nazi Germany [28] and Japanese prison camps [29]. Many studies documented the serious and chronic effects of massive trauma, including fear, paranoia, depression, anxiety, and personality change [e.g., 30]. A "concentration camp syndrome," characterized by fatigue, irritability, restlessness, anxiety, and depression was characteristic. Furthermore, the post-World War II rate of schizophrenia among refugees in Norway was found to be five times higher than the rate among the non-refugee Norwegian population [31]. A high rate of schizophrenia was also found among European refugees in Australia, but not among Jewish refugees, who instead had a high rate of the concentration camp syndrome [32].

Across most groups studied, trauma exposure most frequently precipitates a *core group* of symptoms that are currently best represented by the diagnostic category of posttraumatic stress disorder (PTSD) in the DSM-IV [33] and the ICD-10 [34]. Even though the full syndrome as defined by Western diagnostic systems may not apply to all survivors [35], posttraumatic stress symptoms appear in non-Western survivors and are therefore not ethnocentric [36]. PTSD symptoms include re-experiencing of the traumatic events through intrusive memories, avoidance of trauma reminders, withdrawing behavior, and chronically elevated arousal, as illustrated in the words of a refugee who had recently escaped from a war situation when interviewed about PTSD symptoms: "All the villagers have nightmares and trouble sleeping. Everyone is fearful of wandering too far from the village and no one talks about the bad things that have happened. It is better not to think about the past . . . there is too much trouble right now. We are always nervous, on guard and suspicious. We have to be . . . the military attack any time, and usually at night. The things you ask about are natural in all of us" [37].

Difficulties in concentration and memory are common, subjectively very distressing, and, in certain cases, related to illness and head injury [38]. Irritability and emotional numbing may lead to serious social, occupational, and family problems, including unemployment, criminal behavior, domestic violence, and divorce [39]. The psychological and physical problems of torture survivors may further contribute to their social and economic disability in the host country, apart from the familial difficulties. Estimates of the enormous economic costs of exposure to trauma are being developed [40], along with calculations of the costs and benefits of treating the consequences.

Studies conducted across many cultures further suggest that exposure to severe trauma can provoke other mental health symptoms among survivors, some of which are influenced by culture [35]. Among refugees, the primary symptom difference apparently linked to cultural differences occurs with reported rates of substance abuse. For example, unlike the higher rates seen with American combat veterans, trauma-exposed Asians tend to have lower rates of alcoholism. But among Central American refugee males, substance abuse is fairly common [41]. A second cultural difference seems to be the need for detailed recall and recollection of the traumatic experience(s), and the willingness to retrieve such information. In some reports, Indochinese tend to minimize their problems and are reluctant to talk about the event(s). When compelled to tell their stories, they tend to have marked exacerbation of symptoms, especially re-experiencing, nightmares, and intrusive thoughts. This may relate to their Buddhist culture, with its sense of fate and personal shame about terrible deeds done by their countrymen. Alternatively, South American refugees seem to be more willing and perhaps even helped by the experience of recalling and describing the trauma in detail [42, 43].

Refugees

A differential effect was found among clients at a Southeast Asian clinic: the PTSD rate was 92 percent among Cambodians, 93 percent among the Mien, and 54 percent among the Vietnamese [44]. Of thirty children exposed to Central America warfare, ten had PTSD [45]. In a study of Chilean and Salvadorian migrants, those with torture experiences had higher rates of PTSD than those who had neither torture nor trauma [46]. Among Ethiopians, 27 percent of eighty-seven of the Jews moving to Israel had moderate to severe psychological symptoms [47]. Among thirty-eight young Afghan refugees, thirteen had PTSD, depression, or both [48].

Under threat of forced repatriation, asylum seekers must endure a prolonged waiting period during which basic services are often inadequate. In a study of Tamil migrants in Australia, it was found that asylum seekers had trauma and psychiatric symptoms similar to other refugees, but they also had increased post-migration stress related to their insecure residency status [49]. Among Cambodian adolescents, war trauma was found to relate to PTSD symptoms while post-migration stress related to depression [50]. Bosnian survivors of "ethnic cleansing" were found to have current PTSD rates of 65 percent and 35 percent for depression [51]. The effects of massive trauma on Bosnian families and individuals were severe and well-described [52].

Survivors of Torture

Most of the refugees who have also experienced torture are in a particularly vulnerable position. Reports of Afghan refugees in Pakistan indicate a high prevalence of severe trauma and torture. The most common psychological symptoms among those exposed to torture were anxiety and depression. Substance abuse had also increased in this group [53]. In a recent controlled study [54], when Tibetan refugee torture survivors were compared to non-tortured refugees, they were found to have more PTSD symptoms, higher anxiety and depression scores, and more physical complaints.

Prisoners of War (POWs)

Uniformly, studies from the United States demonstrate that former POWs manifest high rates of persistent and debilitating psychiatric disorder. A four- to five-fold excess of hospitalizations for psychoneurosis was found among World War II POWs of Japan and POWs of Germany compared with their controls, and excess mortality was found among POWs of Japan, primarily due to accidents and tuberculosis [55]. In a later study that included POWs of North Korea, there were significantly more hospitalizations for anxiety reactions, alcoholism, "nervousness and debility," other psychoneurotic reactions, and schizophrenic disorders [56]. POWs held by Japan were more physically and psychiatrically disabled than those held by Germany or North Korea due to the harsher treatment suffered at the hands of the Japanese.

In a community sample of POWs ($N = 262$), over half met lifetime criteria for PTSD and 30 percent met criteria for current PTSD, even forty to fifty years after the traumatic events [57]. The most severely traumatized group (POWs held by Japan) had lifetime rates of 84 percent and current rates of 58 percent for PTSD. Those who were tortured or who witnessed the torture of others were at particular risk for PTSD, even forty to fifty years later. Nearly two-thirds of lifetime PTSD cases were complicated by another psychiatric disorder; nearly half of current PTSD cases also met criteria for another psychiatric disorder [58]. PTSD almost always emerged soon after trauma exposure and alcohol abuse at the same time as PTSD; panic disorder arose equally often at the time of PTSD onset and after PTSD onset; and depression most often followed PTSD. Lifetime PTSD increased the risk for lifetime panic disorder, major depression, alcohol abuse/dependence, and social phobia. Current PTSD increased the risk for current panic disorder, dysthymia, social phobia, major depression, and generalized anxiety disorder. Interestingly, few of these survivors had ever sought mental health treatment.

A recent survey of U.S. civilians held as POWs by the Japanese ($N = 129$) included the largest number of female POWs yet reported ($N = 58$) [59]. They reported symptoms indicating a lifetime PTSD rate of 37 percent and a 15 percent current rate. Consistent with the findings of a recent survey of the U.S. population [60], when exposed to comparable levels of trauma, females were at significantly greater risk of developing lifetime PTSD than were men. From these studies we conclude that the majority of POWs experience significant problems with anxiety upon release from captivity. For some, these symptoms tend to decrease over time. For others—especially those with PTSD—there is a stable and persisting course for decades, and for still other individuals the occurrence of subsequent stressful life events often leads to a secondary depression or to the worsening of an existing depression.

TRAUMATIC HUMAN RIGHTS VIOLATIONS: REHABILITATIVE ASPECTS

The Tasks of Caregiving

Caregivers for survivors come from a myriad of backgrounds. These include health, in particular mental health, and social services professionals; religious leaders, lawyers, politicians, human rights activists, but also concerned persons and volunteers, with or without formal training, and survivors themselves who advocate for survivors and attempt to meet their needs. The agendas and conceptual models of these groups often conflict; nor is there unanimity as to rehabilitative models within a given group. The roles of training and education, treatment of victims, research, preventive efforts, expert testimony as well as public education and advocacy are not easily blended. As a result, the tasks may appear overwhelming and the focus of the field diffuse [61].

Rehabilitative Methods

The complexity of the aftermath of gross violations of human rights calls for a multiplicity of therapeutic methods and modalities.

General Medical Approach

Allodi highlights the complexities confronting physicians who care for survivors of traumatic human rights abuse [62]. While strongly supporting psychiatric diagnostic specificity, he goes beyond the prevailing disease classifications and identifies the needed sensitivity to interpersonal issues. Many experts have emphasized a holistic approach in which trust and the doctor/patient relationship are critical. In a complementary manner, other medical specialists should provide their assessments to objectify physical consequences of abuse, identify organic factors presenting as psychiatric disorder, reassure the survivor, and set the stage for ensuing psychotherapeutic treatment [63].

Psychotherapy

Many therapists have emphasized psychodynamic insight, understanding, and reintegration of the trauma as major treatment components for survivors. They describe trauma's propensity for "splitting off" parts of the personality and impairing the individual's ability to connect with earlier "good objects and self-representations." They emphasize in-depth exploration of the traumatic experiences to allow processing and integration of the traumatic memories. Other therapists, in describing their "relational psychotherapy," look to psychotherapy to "get things started again" and to put trauma in the past [64]. The differential effects of psychotherapy should be studied with particular emphasis on long-term follow-up studies, the value of group therapy, and the value of indigenous treatment approaches [65], many of which have never been systematically evaluated.

Insight therapy is used by the Rehabilitation and Research Centre for Torture Victims (RCT) in Copenhagen [66]. Cognitive-behavioral [67] and psychodynamic approaches [68] have been central to treatment. Other therapies include supportive, desensitization, family, group [69], play, psychosocial, and testimony [66] or working with the families of the disappeared [70].

Pharmacological Treatment

PTSD has known biological correlates [71] such as disruptions in various physiological and neuropsychological systems that may be ameliorated through the use of medications. With the high incidence of head injuries, malnutrition, and inadequately treated disease among survivors of traumatic human rights violation, it is crucial to address the effects of each in treatment efforts. In the treatment of severely traumatized patients, it is often advisable to aggressively treat pharmacologically the intrusive symptoms of impaired sleep, nightmares, hyperarousal, startle reaction, and irritability. Drug treatment [72] should be used to: 1) decrease overwhelming symptoms which require rapid reduction for the patient to function and/or to have less pain; 2) provide help if no psychotherapy is available or if psychotherapy is proceeding but ineffectively; 3) facilitate psychotherapy by reducing hyperarousal, intrusions, numbing, and avoidance so that a more optimum mix of mental functioning is available for psychotherapy; 4) reduce co-morbid symptoms, particularly panic and depression; 5) improve impulse control in the presence of rage and violence; and 6) control episodic rage or violence, where an anti-kindling agent may be especially helpful.

Psychotropic agents from virtually all of the major categories have been used to treat survivors of extreme trauma. The findings, both from research and from clinical experience, indicate that prescribing smaller doses of psychotropic medications than recommended for Caucasians can effectively treat survivors who belong to non-Caucasian groups [73]. Both pharmacokinetic (metabolic) and pharmacodynamic (brain receptor) influences have been demonstrated [74]. Alternatives [75] or supplements to medication, such as acupuncture, hypnosis, relaxation, massage, or medicinal teas have also been used, but scientific support for the efficacy of these treatments is minimal.

Treatment On Site/In the Field

Continued strife within a nation often remains the major cause of human rights violations and at the same time constitutes the single biggest obstacle to the rehabilitation of survivors where threats to life and security confront the survivors and the health care professionals who serve them. Even when freed from detention, political prisoners continue to suffer the stress caused by possible recapture or reprisals from the agents of the state who violated their human rights in the first place. If the society in which the survivors live continues to tolerate human rights violations, rehabilitation can never be fully achieved.

Many effective activities are action-oriented and short-term. Experience has proven that providing direct material and economic aid to survivors and their families contributes immensely to over-all adjustment [76]. Treatment strategies are most effective when they can utilize local sources of social, cultural, and organizational support. Health professionals may conduct training for human rights organization service workers who often are among the first to see survivors of human rights violations. Materials for training and family/public education in such situations have been developed [76].

For survivors with psychological problems, individual counseling and psychotherapy, family and group therapy can be helpful. Treating the survivor's medical problems invariably improved his or her psychological condition. Physical therapy, medications, or surgical procedures help the survivor regain trust that may have been lost in other people because of the traumata experienced.

Treatment is rarely initiated until months and often years after the human rights violations. The treatment often occurs, if at all, in a country of asylum far from the survivor's native land. International agencies and the world community respond to crises, such as violence in the former Yugoslavia, with as much physical support as they can muster. Many health care workers from a wide range of specialties have significant roles to play in such crises. However, attention to the psychological consequences continues to be delayed until some later date when the confusion and chaos have subsided. Unfortunately, as we know from the treatment of soldiers during wartime, neglecting these consequences early on may make the recovery process more difficult and prolonged [77].

Acute stress disorder symptoms may be best treated "on site." The U.S. military regularly employs psychiatrists and other mental health professionals in war zones, drawing on principles developed in Israel, as represented in the "P.I.E." model of stress disorder treatment [78], where treatment is provided in Proximity to the area of battle, Immediately, and with the Expectation that symptoms will subside and that the individual will return to a normal functional level. Although such treatment for combatants involves ethical issues regarding the "good of the patient" versus the "good of the military," many of the techniques used for timely intervention to mitigate traumatic reactions could certainly be, and sometimes are, employed in refugee camps [79]. Similarly, in disaster areas, mental health workers not only triage and treat acute reactions, but educate and give support to the survivors regarding the nature of posttraumatic reactions, often by defining them as "normal reactions to abnormal experiences."

Interventions also take place in transit camps outside the survivors' home country, and in the countries of final resettlement [80]. To reach a large number of survivors, agencies must coordinate their service delivery and devote effort to training and supervising paraprofessionals in the affected countries. A successful application of these principles in the former Yugoslavia has been described [81]. Further principles for treatment and service development are provided by Cunningham and Silove [82].

Treatment Research

Reviewing the definitive evidence about the relative efficacy of various psychological treatment methods, Gerrity and Solomon conclude that definite evidence is lacking due to methodological limits of the studies [83]. The biological and pharmacological aspects of PTSD treatment are often crucial to patient improvement [84].

In a unique treatment outcome study of concentration camp survivors, Drozdek assigned 120 refugees from Bosnia and Herzegovina (now living in the Netherlands) either to six months of group psychotherapy, pharmacological therapy, or its combination in the treatment of PTSD [80]. The treatment was initiated within three months of release from the prison camps. All treatments yielded positive short-term effects, with some positive effects observable three years later. The elderly benefited less from intervention than did younger participants. More treatment research is needed to identify those interventions that are most effective for survivors.

Rehabilitation following particularly gross violations of human rights should address not only the traumatized individual, but also the family, community, society, and even the nation. In addition, continuing elements need to follow in time the initial treatment and are essential to a comprehensive rehabilitation program. The individual needs to know that society as a whole knows and understands what has happened. A true healing process includes apology, reparations, education, commemorations, and other events acknowledging what has happened. Genuine rehabilitation must work for redress and justice as well as for the restoration of dignity to the victim/survivor, and be set in a sociopolitical context in which the experience and the pain are shared by the society (and nation). To break the intergenerational chain of transmission [5], the story must be told accurately and the public records secured, and mechanisms for monitoring and preventive intervention established to ensure against repetition.

It is increasingly recognized that impunity for the perpetrators contributes to social and psychological problems and impedes healing in the survivors [67] by adversely affecting bereavement, inducing self-blame, and eroding moral codes. Justice denied is a persistent irritant to the victim/survivor's psychic wounds. Impunity becomes a new traumatic factor that renders justice as well as closure impossible, leads to a loss of respect for law and government as well as a subsequent increase in crime [85]. We lack systematic data as to how survivors appraise the sociopolitical process for perpetrators and how efforts to bring perpetrators to justice and provide compensation may affect the healing process.

ETHICAL IMPLICATIONS
IN THE REHABILITATIVE WORK

More attention is being given to the reactions and well-being of those who care for trauma survivors [86, 87]. A critical element for therapeutic recovery of traumatic reactions is a "safe" environment, one that includes, even requires, substantial empathy. The intensity of the therapeutic process and the arousal in both the patient and the therapist in response to the traumatic reports can produce unique countertransference (or empathetic strain) reactions. "Countertransference" in this context is used broadly to encompass all emotional reactions a therapist has toward a patient. Empathetic strain may be divided into two categories: 1) over-identification (enmeshment, over-involvement, and the loss of boundaries); or disequilibrium (uncertainty and unmodulated affect); and 2) avoidance (withdrawal or blank screen facade and intellectualization); or repression (including denial and distancing) [88]. The effects of countertransference reactions can be severe within trauma treatment centers in which caregivers can regularly experience disruptive and painful psychological effects, including suffering some of the symptoms of the patients or responding with disbelief and cynicism [89]. These reactions may explain some of the strife that often troubles and challenges trauma rehabilitation programs [90]. The principles that should govern ethical practice in order to avoid therapeutic pitfalls and countertransference reactions are derived from biomedical ethics and reflect a "deontological" position, i.e., that there are features of human acts other than their consequences that make them right or wrong. Several useful principles have been articulated [91]. These principles applied to PTSD are hierarchical, as follows:

1. Fidelity. The most important ethical principle is the establishment of a doctor-patient relationship based on trust, honesty, confidentiality, predictability, and consistency.

2. Non-maleficence. The second principle is to do no harm. Traumatized patients have already been harmed, deceived, and brutalized often in unpredictable and arbitrary ways. Insensitivity, minimizing patients' problems, pushing patients into therapy and in life to do more than they can, and over-identifying all can have harmful effects.

3. Beneficence. This is an obligation to provide competent treatment, reduce suffering, and promote health based on a sound scientific foundation.

4. Autonomy. This is the respect of and encouragement for the survivor's independence; the survivor is an active partner in the treatment program.

5. Self-Interest. During the intense treatment of the traumatized patient, the therapist must be able to meet his or her own needs in a healthy manner. Therapists may need to limit the number of patients and/or limit their involvement in other stressful professional or community activities. Some, however, may choose to become involved with various advocacy groups to protest unjust acts. Developing a supportive network of colleagues and friends is probably a necessity for this kind of work.

6. Justice. Justified indignation against wrongs and survivor endured may be encouraged. The therapist should support the survivor to protest injustice in whatever manner he or she feels comfortable. In the absence of supportive treatment, individuals called to make public statements about atrocities inflicted on them must abandon their avoidance and may experience increased PTSD symptoms. In other cases, legal and social needs may be at variance with the personal needs of the survivor, who may be fearful or made vulnerable by such demands for expression. For example, in post-apartheid South Africa, the lengthy hearings conducted by the Committee for Truth and Reconciliation have provided a forum for many survivors of traumatic human rights violations to describe their experiences and the impact such experiences have had upon their lives. The benefits and costs to victims giving testimony have yet to be determined, in the absence of assurances of justice, adequate treatment, or compensation. The United Nations Commission on Human Rights (UNCHR) recently considered reviewing a consolidated claim against the government of Japan representing over 200,000 former POWs of Japan and their surviving spouses in Canada, Great Britain, the United States, the Netherlands, New Zealand, and Australia. It is widely recognized that the Imperial Japanese Army perpetrated gross violations of human rights against POWs during World War II. The UNCHR was asked to consider the issue of Japan's guilt in this matter, as it had agreed to do in the case of the Asian "comfort women." After seven years of effort by the War Amps/Hong Kong Vets of Canada (the UNCHR-recognized NGO presenting the claim), the UNCHR declined to consider the claim, dashing the hopes of the survivors who had been waiting over fifty years for some official review and action on their claim.

CONCLUSION

The provision of sound psychological interventions employed as quickly as possible for the survivors of traumatic human rights violations is vital, promoting recovery and the building of new lives. There is an understandable tendency for relief efforts—governmental as well as non-governmental—to emphasize basic survival, e.g., safe water, food, and shelter. But "rushing to the scene" with only the tools to treat bodily injuries, however commendable, is not enough. Later, when their bodies have healed, it is the nightmares and the emotional turmoil that haunt victim/survivors. This chapter presents background and themes essential to a dialogue between the human rights community and the mental health community, hopefully pointing the way ahead to a collaborative, mutually supportive and reinforcing human rights agenda. Ultimately, stopping traumatic human rights violations would help prevent the epidemic of posttraumatic stress disorder that plagues untold millions worldwide.

REFERENCES

1. B. Simon, Obstacles in the Path of Those Who Care for Survivors of Human Rights Violations, *International Journal of Law and Psychiatry, 16,* pp. 427-440, 1993.
2. D. Ortiz, The Survivor's Perspective: Voices from the Center, in *Mental Health Consequences of Torture and Related Trauma: Preliminary NIMH Report to the South African Truth and Reconciliation Commission,* T. Keane and E. T. Gerrity (eds.), NIMH, Bethesda, Maryland, 1998.
3. Y. Danieli, On Not Confronting the Holocaust: Psychological Reaction to Victim/Survivors and Their Children, in *Remembering for the Future, Theme II: The Impact of the Holocaust on the Contemporary World,* Pergamon Press, Oxford, pp. 1257-1271, 1988.
4. Y. Danieli, The Treatment and Prevention of Long-Term Effects and Intergenerational Transmission of Victimization: A Lesson from Holocaust Survivors and Their Children, in *Trauma and its Wake: Vol. I,* C. R. Figley (ed.), Brunner/Mazel, New York, pp. 295-313, 1985.
5. Y. Danieli (ed.), *International Handbook of Multigenerational Legacies of Trauma,* Plenum Press, New York, 1998.
6. L. Weisaeth and I. Lind, A Follow-Up Study of a Tortured Norwegian Ship's Crew, in *Wartime Medical Services,* J. E. Lundeberg, U. Otto, and B. Rybeck (eds.), proceedings of the 2nd International Conference, Swedish Defense Research Institute (FOA), Stockholm, pp. 397-412, 1990.
7. R. DeMartino and U. von Buchwald, Non-Governmental Efforts in the Psychosocial Care of Traumatized Peoples: The Contribution of Non-Governmental Organizations, in *International Responses to Traumatic Stress,* Y. Danieli, N. S. Rodley, and L. Weisaeth (eds.), Baywood Publishing, Amityville, New York, pp. 193-217, 1996.

8. S. Ekblad, B. Ginsburg, B. Jansson, and L. Levi, Psychosocial and Psychiatric Aspects of Refugee Adaptation and Care in Sweden, in *Amidst Peril and Pain: The Mental Health and Wellbeing of the World's Refugees,* A. Marsella, T. Bornemann, S. Ekblad, and S. Orley (eds.), American Psychological Association, Washington, D.C., 1994.

9. Amnesty International, *Amnesty International Report,* Amnesty International Publications, London, 1997.

10. M. Basoglu, unpublished data.

11. R. Baker, Psychosocial Consequences for Tortured Refugees Seeking Asylum and Refugee Status in Europe, in *Torture and Its Consequences: Current Treatment Approaches,* M. Basoglu (ed.), Cambridge University Press, New York, pp. 83-106, 1992.

12. M. Basoglu, Prevention of Torture and Care of Survivors: An Integrated Approach, *Journal of the American Medical Association, 270*:5, pp. 606-611, 1993.

13. M. Parker, O. Paker, and S. Yuksel, Psychological Effects of Torture: An Empirical Study of Tortured and Non-Tortured Non-Political Prisoners, in *Torture and Its Consequences: Current Treatment Approaches,* M. Basoglu (ed.), Cambridge University Press, New York, pp. 72-82, 1992.

14. C. Stenger, *American Prisoners of War in WWI, WWII, Korea and Viet Nam, Desert Storm, and Somalia,* VA Advisory Committee on Former Prisoners of War, U.S. Dept. of Veterans Affairs, Washington, D.C., 1998.

15. H. Epstein, *Children of the Holocaust,* Putnam, New York, 1979.

16. P. Thygesen, K. Hermann, and R. Willanger, Concentration Camp Survivors in Denmark: Persecution, Disease, Disability, Compensation, *Danish Medical Bulletin, 17,* pp. 65-108, 1970.

17. D. Reichenberg and S. Friedman, Healing the Invisible Wounds of Children in War: A Rights Approach; The Contribution of the United Nations Children's Fund (UNICEF), in *International Responses to Traumatic Stress,* Y. Danieli, N. S. Rodley, and L. Weisaeth (eds.), Baywood Publishing, Amityville, New York, pp. 307-326, 1996.

18. N. Dubrow, N. I. Liwski, C. Palacios, and M. Gardinier, Helping Child Victims of Violence: The Contribution of Non-Governmental Organizations, in *International Responses to Traumatic Stress,* Y. Danieli, N. S. Rodley, and L. Weisaeth (eds.), Baywood Publishing, Amityville, New York, pp. 327-346, 1996.

19. B. Egge, M. Mortensen, and L. Weisaeth, Soldiers for Peace: Ordeals and Stress; The Contribution of the United Nations Peace-Keeping Forces, in *International Responses to Traumatic Stress,* Y. Danieli, N. S. Rodley, and L. Weisaeth (eds.), Baywood Publishing, Amityville, New York, pp. 257-282, 1996.

20. M. Petevi, Refugee Trauma, Protection and Assistance: The Contribution of the United Nations High Commissioner for Refugees, in *International Responses to Traumatic Stress,* Y. Danieli, N. S. Rodley, and L. Weisaeth (eds.), Baywood Publishing, Amityville, New York, pp. 161-192, 1996.

21. E. Vetere and I. Melup, Victims of Crime: The Contributions of the United Nations Crime Prevention and Criminal Justice Program, in *International Responses to Traumatic Stress,* Y. Danieli, N. S. Rodley, and L. Weisaeth (eds.), Baywood Publishing, Amityville, New York, pp. 15-80, 1996.

22. I. Waller, Victims of Crime: Justice, Support and Public Safety—The Contribution of Non-Governmental Organizations, in *International Responses to Traumatic Stress,*

Y. Danieli, N. S. Rodley, and L. Weisaeth (eds.), Baywood Publishing, Amityville, New York, pp. 81-99, 1996.

23. C. A. Brautigan, Overcoming Victimization through Equality and Non-Discrimination: The Contribution of the United Nations Commission on the Status of Women, in *International Responses to Traumatic Stress,* Y. Danieli, N. S. Rodley, and L. Weisaeth (eds.), Baywood Publishing, Amityville, New York, pp. 347-365, 1996.

24. R. Harris, Dealing with Violence Against Women: The Contribution of Non-Governmental Organizations, in *International Responses to Traumatic Stress,* Y. Danieli, N. S. Rodley, and L. Weisaeth (eds.), Baywood Publishing, Amityville, New York, pp. 367-382, 1996.

25. J. Welsh, Traumatic Stress and the Role of NGOs: The Contribution of Non-Governmental Organizations, in *International Responses to Traumatic Stress,* Y. Danieli, N. S. Rodley, and L. Weisaeth (eds.), Baywood Publishing, Amityville, New York, pp. 131-159, 1996.

26. E. Stamatapoulou, United Nations Action from the Victims' Perspective: The Contribution of the United Nations Centre for Human Rights and the High Commissioner for Human Rights, in *International Responses to Traumatic Stress,* Y. Danieli, N. S. Rodley, and L. Weisaeth (eds.), Baywood Publishing, Amityville, New York, pp. 101-129, 1996.

27. P. Daudin and H. Reyes, How Visits by the ICRC Help Prisoners Cope with the Effects of Traumatic Stress: The Contribution of the International Committee of the Red Cross, in *International Responses to Traumatic Stress,* Y. Danieli, N. S. Rodley, and L. Weisaeth (eds.), Baywood Publishing, Amityville, New York, pp. 219-255, 1996.

28. R. Hilberg, *The Destruction of the European Jews,* New Viewpoints, New York, 1973.

29. G. Dawes, *Prisoners of the Japanese,* Morrow, New York, 1993.

30. L. Eitinger, The Symptomatology of Mental Disease among Refugees in Norway, *Journal of Mental Science, 106,* pp. 947-966, 1960.

31. L. Eitinger, The Incidence of Mental Disorders among Refugees in Norway, *Journal of Mental Science, 105,* pp. 326-338, 1959.

32. J. Krupinski, A. Stoller, and L. Wallace, Psychiatric Disorders in East European Refugees Now in Australia, *Social Science and Medicine, 7,* pp. 331-349, 1973.

33. American Psychiatric Association, *Diagnostic and Statistical Manual of Mental Disorders (4th ed.),* Washington, D.C., 1994.

34. World Health Organization, *International Statistical Classification of Diseases and Related Health Problems, Tenth Revision (ICD-10),* WHO, Geneva, 1992.

35. A. J. Marsella, M. J. Friedman, and E. H. Spain, Ethnocultural Aspects of PTSD: An Overview of Issues and Research Directions, in *Ethnocultural Aspects of Post-traumatic Stress Disorder: Issues, Research, and Clinical Applications,* A. J. Marsella, M. J. Friedman, E. T. Gerrity, and R. M. Scurfield (eds.), American Psychological Association, Washington, D.C., pp. 105-130, 1996.

36. M. J. Friedman and J. M. Jaranson, The Applicability of the Posttraumatic Concept to Refugees, in *Amidst Peril and Pain: The Mental Health and Wellbeing of the World's Refugees,* T. Marsella, T. Bornemann, S. Ekblad, and J. Orley (eds.), American Psychological Association, Washington, D.C., pp. 207-227, 1994.

37. D. Silove and J. D. Kinzie, *Survivors of War Trauma, Mass Violence, and Civilian Terror: An Overview, Mental Health Consequences of Torture and Related Trauma:*

Preliminary NIMH Report to the South African Truth and Reconciliation Commission, T. Keane and E. T. Gerrity (eds.), NIMH, Bethesda, Maryland, 1998.

38. A. E. Goldfeld, R. F. Mollica, B. H. Pesavento, and S. V. Farone, The Physical and Psychological Sequelae of Torture, *Journal of the American Medical Association, 259,* pp. 2725-2729, 1988.

39. B. Masaki and L. Wong, Domestic Violence in an Asian Community, in *Working with Asian Americans: A Guide for Clinicians,* E. Lee (ed.), The Guilford Press, New York, 1997.

40. A. Rupp and E. Sorel, Conceptual Models: Economic Consequences, in *Mental Health Consequences of Torture and Related Trauma: Preliminary NIMH Report to the South African Truth and Reconciliation Commission,* T. Keane and E. T. Gerrity (eds.), NIMH, Bethesda, Maryland, 1998.

41. P. J. Farias, Emotional Distress and its Socio-Political Correlates in Salvadoran Refugees: Analysis of a Clinical Sample, *Culture, Medicine and Psychiatry, 15,* pp. 167-192, 1991.

42. P. Morris and D. Silove, Cultural Influences in Psychotherapy with Refugee Survivors of Torture and Trauma, *Hospital and Community Psychiatry, 43,* pp. 820-824, 1992.

43. C. Rouseau and A. Drapeau, The Impact of Culture on the Transmission of Trauma: Refugees' Stories and Silence Embodied in Their Children's Lives, in *International Handbook of Multigenerational Legacies of Trauma,* Y. Danieli (ed.), Plenum Press, New York, 1998.

44. J. D. Kinzie, J. K. Boehnlein, P. Leung, L. Moore, C. Riley, and D. Smith, The High Prevalence Rate of PTSD and its Clinical Significance among Southeast Asian Refugees, *American Journal of Psychiatry, 147,* pp. 913-917, 1990.

45. W. Arroyo and S. Eth, Children Traumatized by Central American Warfare, in *Post-Traumatic Stress Disorders in Children,* S. Eth and R. S. Pynoos (eds.), American Psychiatric Association Press, Washington, D.C., pp. 101-120, 1985.

46. M. Thompson and P. McGarry, Psychological Sequelae of Torture and Trauma in Chilean and Salvadoran Migrants: A Pilot Study, *Australia and New Zealand Journal of Psychiatry, 29,* pp. 84-95, 1995.

47. A. Arieli and S. Aycheh, Psychopathology among Jewish Ethiopian Immigrants to Israel, *Journal of Nervous and Mental Disease, 180,* pp. 465-466, 1992.

48. R. Mghir, W. Freed, L. Raskin, and W. Katon, Depression and Post-Traumatic Stress Disorder Among a Community Sample of Adolescent and Young Afghan Refugees, *Journal of Nervous and Mental Disease, 183,* pp. 24-30, 1995.

49. D. Silove, I. Sinnesbrink, A. Field, V. Manicavasagan, and Z. Steel, Anxiety, Depression and PTSD in Asylum-seekers: Associations with Pre-Migration Trauma and Post Migration Stressors, *British Journal of Psychiatry, 170,* pp. 351-357, 1997.

50. W. H. Sack, S. McSharry, G. N. Clarke, R. Kinney, J. Seeley, and P. Lewinsohn, The Khmer Adolescent Project: 1. Epidemiologic Findings in Two Generations of Cambodian Refugees, *Journal of Nervous and Mental Disease, 182,* pp. 387-395, 1994.

51. S. M. Weine, D. F. Becker, T. H. McGlahan, P. Lamb, S. Lazrove, D. Vojuoda, and L. Hyman, Psychiatric Consequences of "Ethnic Cleansing": Clinical Assessments and Trauma Testimonies of Newly Resettled Bosnian Refugees, *American Journal of Psychiatry, 152,* pp. 536-542, 1995.

52. S. M. Weine, D. Vojuoda, S. Hartman, and L. Hyman, A Family Survives Genocide, *Psychiatry, 60,* pp. 14-39, 1997.

53. A. Dadfar, The Afghans: Bearing the Scars of a Forgotten War, in *Amidst Peril and Pain: The Mental Health and Wellbeing of the World's Refugees,* A. Marsella, T. Bornemann, S. Ekblad, and J. Orley (eds.), American Psychological Association, Washington, D.C., 1994.

54. T. H. Holtz, Refugee Trauma vs. Torture Trauma: A Retrospective Controlled Study of Tibetan Refugees, *Journal of Nervous and Mental Disease, 186,* pp. 24-34, 1998.

55. B. M. Cohen and M. Z. Cooper, *A Follow-Up Study of World War II Prisoners of War,* (Veterans Affairs Medical Monograph), U.S. Dept. of Veterans Affairs, Washington, D.C., 1954.

56. G. W. Beebe, Follow-Up Studies of World War II and Korean War Prisoners, II: Morbidity, Disability, and Maladjustments, *American Journal of Epidemiology, 101,* pp. 400-422, 1975.

57. B. E. Engdahl, T. Dikel, R. E. Eberly, and A. S. Blank, Jr., Posttraumatic Stress Disorder in a Community Sample of Former Prisoners of War: A Normative Response to Severe Trauma, *American Journal of Psychiatry, 154,* pp. 1576-1581, 1997.

58. B. E. Engdahl, T. Dikel, R. E. Eberly, and A. S. Blank, Jr., The Comorbidity and Course of Psychiatric Disorders in a Community Sample of Former Prisoners of War, *American Journal of Psychiatry,* in press.

59. M. K. Potts, Long-Term Effects of Trauma: Post-Traumatic Stress Among Civilian Internees of the Japanese During World War II, *Journal of Clinical Psychology, 50,* pp. 681-698, 1994.

60. R. C. Kessler, A. Sonnega, E. Bromet, M. Hughes, and C. B. Nelson, Posttraumatic Stress Disorder in the National Comorbidity Survey, *Archives of General Psychiatry, 52,* pp. 1048-1060, 1995.

61. J. M. Jaranson and M. K. Popkin (eds.), *Caring for Victims of Torture,* American Psychiatric Press, Washington, D.C., 1998.

62. F. Allodi, The Physician's Role in Assessing and Treating Torture Survivors, in *Caring for Victims of Torture,* J. M. Jaranson and M. K. Popkin (eds.), American Psychiatric Press, Washington, D.C., pp. 89-106, 1998.

63. N. R. Holtan, How Medical Assessment of Victims of Torture Relates to Psychiatric Care, in *Caring for Victims of Torture,* J. M. Jaranson and M. K. Popkin (eds.), American Psychiatric Press, Washington, D.C., pp. 107-113, 1998.

64. S. Varvin and E. Hauff, Psychotherapy with Patients Who Have Been Tortured, in *Caring for Victims of Torture,* J. M. Jaranson and M. K. Popkin (eds.), American Psychiatric Press, Washington, D.C., pp. 117-129, 1998.

65. E. Duran, B. Duran, M. BraveHeart-Jordan, and S. YellowHorse-Davis, Healing the American Indian Soul Wound, in *International Handbook of Multigenerational Legacies of Trauma,* Y. Danieli (ed.), Plenum Press, New York, 1998.

66. P. Vesti, K. Helwig-Larsen, and M. Kastrup, Prophylactic Measures Concerning Doctor Involvement in Torture, in *Caring for Victims of Torture,* J. M. Jaranson and M. K. Popkin (eds.), American Psychiatric Press, Washington, D.C., pp. 185-199, 1998.

67. M. Basoglu, Behavioral and Cognitive Treatment of Survivors of Torture, in *Caring for Victims of Torture,* J. M. Jaranson and M. K. Popkin (eds.), American Psychiatric Press, Washington, D.C., pp. 131-148, 1998.

68. E. Bustos, Psychodynamic Approaches in the Treatment of Torture Survivors, in *Torture and Its Consequences: Current Treatment Approaches*, M. Basoglu (ed.), Cambridge University Press, New York, pp. 333-347, 1992.

69. Y. Fischman and J. Ross, Group Treatment of Exiled Survivors of Torture, *American Journal of Orthopsychiatry, 60*:1, pp. 135-142, 1990.

70. D. Kordon, L. Edelman, D. Lagos, and D. Kersner, Forced Disappearance: A Particular Form of Torture, in *Caring for Victims of Torture*, J. M. Jaranson and M. K. Popkin (eds.), American Psychiatric Press, Washington, D.C., pp. 203-227, 1998.

71. C. Grillon, S. M. Southwick, and D. S. Charney, The Psychobiological Basis of Posttraumatic Stress Disorder, *Molecular Psychiatry, 1*, pp. 278-297, 1996.

72. A. S. Blank, Jr., *A Biopsychosocial Review of the Pharmacotherapy of PTSD*, presented at the Fourth European Conference on Traumatic Stress, Paris, 1995.

73. J. M. Jaranson, Psychotherapeutic Medication, in *Mental Health Services for Refugees*, J. Westermeyer, C. L. Williams, and A. N. Nguyen (eds.), U.S. Government Printing Office, No. [ADM] 91-1824, Washington, D.C., pp. 132-145, 1991.

74. K. Lin, R. Poland, and D. Anderson, Psychopharmacology, Ethnicity and Culture, *Transcultural Psychiatric Research Review, 32*, pp. 3-40, 1995.

75. J. P. Hiegel, Use of Indigenous Concepts and Healers in the Care of Refugees: Some Experiences from the Thai Border Camps, in *Amidst Peril and Pain: The Mental Health and Wellbeing of the World's Refugees*, T. Marsella, T. Bornemann, S. Ekblad, and J. Orley (eds.), American Psychological Association, Washington, D.C., pp. 293-309, 1994.

76. A. A. Parong, Caring for Survivors of Torture: Beyond the Clinic, in *Caring for Victims of Torture*, J. M. Jaranson and M. K. Popkin (eds.), American Psychiatric Press, Washington, D.C., pp. 229-242, 1998.

77. N. M. Camp, The Vietnam War and the Ethics of Combat Psychiatry, *American Journal of Psychiatry, 150*, pp. 1000-1010, 1993.

78. I. Manor, R. Shklar, Z. Solomon, Diagnosis and Treatment of Combat Stress Reaction, *Journal of Traumatic Stress, 8*, pp. 247-258, 1995.

79. L. Fletcher, K. Musalo, D. Urentlicher, and K. Pratt, *No Justice, No Peace: Accountability for Rape and Gender-Based Violence in the Former Yugoslavia*, International Human Rights Group, Washington, D.C., 1993.

80. B. Drozdek, Follow-Up Study of Concentration Camp Survivors from Bosnia-Herzegovina: Three Years Later, *Journal of Nervous and Mental Disease, 185*, pp. 690-694, 1997.

81. S. Witterholt and J. M. Jaranson, Caring for Victims on Site: Bosnian Refugees in Croatia, in *Caring for Victims of Torture*, J. M. Jaranson and M. K. Popkin (eds.), American Psychiatric Press, Washington, D.C., pp. 243-252, 1998.

82. M. Cunningham and D. Silove, Principles of Treatment and Service Development for Torture and Trauma Survivors, in *International Handbook of Traumatic Stress Syndromes*, J. P. Wilson and B. Raphael (eds.), Plenum Press, New York, pp. 751-763, 1993.

83. E. T. Gerrity and S. D. Solomon, The Treatment of PTSD and Related Disorders: Current Research and Clinical Knowledge, in *Ethnocultural Aspects of Posttraumatic Stress Disorder: Issues, Research, and Clinical Applications*, A. J. Marsella, M. J. Friedman, E. T. Gerrity, and R. M. Scurfield (eds.), American Psychological Association, Washington, D.C., pp. 87-102, 1996.

84. J. R. T. Davidson and B. A. van der Kolk, The Psychopharmacological Treatment of PTSD, in *Traumatic Stress: The Effects of Overwhelming Experience on Mind, Body, and Society,* B. A. van der Kolk, A. C. McFarlane, and L. Weisaeth (eds.), The Guilford Press, New York, pp. 510-524, 1996.

85. Y. Danieli, Justice and Reparation: Steps in the Process of Healing, in *Reining in Impunity for International Crimes and Serious Violations of Fundamental Human Rights,* proceedings of the Siracusa Conference 17-21 September 1998: Vol. 14, Christopher C. Joyner (ed.), International Review of Penal Law, pp. 303-312, 1998.

86. Y. Danieli, Confronting the Unimaginable: Psychotherapists' Reactions to Victims of the Nazi Holocaust, in *Human Adaptation to Extreme Stress: From the Holocaust to Vietnam,* J. P. Wilson, Z. Harel, B. Kahana (eds.), Plenum Press, New York, pp. 219-238, 1988.

87. B. Smith, I. Agger, Y. Danieli, and L. Weisaeth, Emotional Responses of International Humanitarian Aid Workers: The Contribution of Non-Governmental Organizations, in *International Responses to Traumatic Stress,* Y. Danieli, N. S. Rodley, and L. Weisaeth (eds.), Baywood Publishing, Amityville, New York, pp. 397-423, 1996.

88. J. P. Wilson and J. D. Lindy (eds.), *Countertransference in the Treatment of PTSD,* The Guilford Press, New York, 1994.

89. J. D. Kinzie and J. K. Boehlein, Psychotherapy of the Victims of Massive Violence: Countertransference and Ethical Issues, *American Journal of Psychotherapy, 47,* pp. 90-102, 1993.

90. J. M. Jaranson, The Science and Politics of Rehabilitating Torture Victims: An Overview, in *Caring for Victims of Torture,* J. M. Jaranson and M. K. Popkin (eds.), American Psychiatric Press, Washington, D.C., pp. 15-40, 1998.

91. J. K. Boehlein, J. D. Kinzie, and P. K. Leung, Countertransference and Ethical Principles for Treatment of Torture Survivors, in *Caring for Victims of Torture,* J. M. Jaranson and M. K. Popkin (eds.), American Psychiatric Press, Washington, D.C., pp. 173-183, 1998.

Chapter 26

The Role of Health Professionals in Protecting and Promoting Human Rights: A Paradigm for Professional Responsibility

Susannah Sirkin, Vincent Iacopino,
Michael Grodin, and Yael Danieli

In every sector of society, professionals have begun to play critical roles in promoting and protecting human rights: journalists have convened to discuss their responsibilities when they are the first international witnesses of massacres, war crimes, and genocide;[1] business executives have met to develop corporate codes of conduct in relation to labor conditions in general and child and prison labor in particular, as well as trade and aid in countries where gross human rights violations are the norm;[2] international humanitarian workers, agonized over the manipulation by warlords and genocidal killers of their presence and provision of aid, have begun to discuss their responsibilities to develop human rights protocols;[3] clergy of many faiths have used their pulpits, sometimes at great personal risk, to call for an end to injustices and human rights violations; artists, writers, and musicians have organized human rights actions and events for years, and have stood in solidarity with embattled colleagues.

---

[1] Reporting from the Killing Fields: A Conference on Genocide, Crimes Against Humanity, and War, Berkeley, California, April 5-7, 1997.

[2] See Businesses for Social Responsibility website <www.bsr.org>.

[3] J. de Milliano, *The MSF Perspective on the Need for Cooperation between Humanitarian Organisations and Human Rights Organisations,* from Conference on the Cooperation between Humanitarian Organisations and Human Rights Organisations, Final Report of the Conference held in Amsterdam, the Netherlands, pp. 12-16, 1996.

357

Lawyers have numerous and obvious, specific roles in the struggle for human rights: developing and advocating for international human rights law, trying human rights cases in domestic, regional, and international courts, training human rights lawyers, and supporting the development of judicial systems that protect human rights.

Of all professionals, however, those who take on the ethical oath to protect and promote human life and health, have a unique obligation and contribution to make to human rights. It is a responsibility that has yet to be fully realized. In this chapter, we seek to elaborate on the special connection between health and human rights, the record of health professionals in human rights advocacy, and the betrayal that occurs when members of the health professions engage in or support violations of human rights. We also address the critical role that health professionals must play in attending to and advocating for the healing of the individual, and his or her family, community, society, and nation in the aftermath of traumatic human rights violations.

THE RELATIONSHIP BETWEEN HEALTH AND HUMAN RIGHTS

Health professionals have a responsibility to protect and promote human rights.[4] This is both because human rights violations have devastating health consequences and because protecting and promoting human rights (civil, political, economic, social, and cultural) can be the most effective means of ensuring the positive conditions for health.[5] A global society must recognize the inherent dignity and equality of all members of the human family.

Throughout history, society has charged healers with the duty of understanding and alleviating causes of suffering. As we enter the twenty-first century, the nature and extent of human suffering have compelled health providers to redefine their understandings of health and the scope of their professional interests and responsibilities. Despite a century of technological progress, poverty, hunger, illiteracy, and disease continue to plague the world community. Today, 1.3 billion people live in deep poverty, and over 85 percent of the world's income is concentrated in the richest 20 percent of the world's people. Seven hundred fifty million people go hungry every day. Nine hundred million adults are illiterate, two-thirds of whom are women. More than one billion people have no access to health care or safe drinking water [1, pp. 30-38]. Each day 40,000 children die from malnutrition and disease, lack of clean water, and inadequate sanitation.[6]

---

[4] See Health and Human Rights Consortium Web Site <www.healthandhumanrights.org>

[5] Health is defined as a "state of complete physical, mental and social well-being, and not merely the absence of disease or infirmity." Declaration of Alma Ata. World Health Organization, Primary Health Care. Geneva: World Health Organization, 1978.

[6] World Summit on Children, 1990.

In the past century, the world has witnessed ongoing epidemics of armed conflicts and violations of international human rights, epidemics that have devastated and continue to devastate the health and well-being of people around the world. Armed conflicts have claimed the lives of more than one hundred million people in the twentieth century, and increasingly, civilians have become the victims of war and internal conflicts. Today, 90 percent of war-related deaths are civilians. Twenty-six major civil conflicts raged in 1995. Torture, disappearance, and political killings are systematically practiced in dozens of countries, and tens of millions of landmines threaten the lives and limbs of civilians. In 1995, one in every 200 persons in the world was displaced as a result of war or political repression [1, pp. 5-9].

Health professionals have a great stake in the Universal Declaration of Human Rights, because the document provides the underpinning for the professions' goals of alleviating suffering and promoting the conditions for health and well-being of all people. These goals represent an ideal that cannot be achieved unless the fundamental rights set forth in the UDHR are recognized, respected, protected, and fulfilled. The observance of the 50th Anniversary of the UDHR is an occasion for institutions within the health sector to explore and embrace the critical link between human rights and health.

Historically, human rights have not been among the expressed concerns of health practitioners. Medical training has not yet incorporated human rights into the standard curriculum, and traditional concepts of medical ethics relate primarily to the doctor-patient relationship and the treatment of disease devoid of analysis of societal issues surrounding the patient, his or her community or political, cultural, or economic environment. When conceptualizations of health and human suffering are devoid of human rights concerns, health practitioners can become both willing and unwilling participants in human rights violations. Sometimes, such violations even serve the interests of individual practitioners and may sustain the interests of the state and other actors.

Before reviewing the myriad ways in which health professionals can promote and protect human rights, it is essential to confront the potential within the professions to collaborate in abuses. Health professionals must face the history of a sordid collusion in human rights violations throughout the twentieth century—and sound an alarm at the continued betrayal of their professions on virtually all continents.

THE INVOLVEMENT OF HEALTH PROFESSIONALS IN HUMAN RIGHTS ABUSES

After World War II, the Allies prosecuted the major surviving Nazi war criminals in an international military tribunal. That trial created new international law and can be properly seen, together with the adoption of the 1948 Universal

Declaration of Human Rights, as the birth of the international human rights movement. The trial produced the Nuremberg Principles that recognize that there are crimes against peace, war crimes, and crimes against humanity, and that individuals can be punished for committing these crimes even if such violation is consistent with the laws of their own country, and even if they were "obeying orders" [2].

The 1946-47 trial of Nazi doctors (the Doctors' Trial) documented the most notorious example of physician participation in war crimes and crimes against humanity, specifically murder and torture in the guise of human experimentation [3]. Hitler called upon physicians not only to help justify his racial hatred policies with a "scientific" rationale (racial hygiene), but also to direct his euthanasia programs and ultimately the Nazi death camps. Almost half of all German physicians joined the Nazi Party [4].

Nazi medicine was formed and nurtured by a symbiosis of National Socialist ideology and social Darwinism, mixed with the theory of racial hygiene that viewed some racial and ethnic groups as subhuman and gave physicians an ideological excuse to use their skill to harm people in the name of the state. There is a series of recurrent themes in Nazi medicine: The devaluation and dehumanization of defined segments of the community, the medicalization of social and political problems, the training of physicians to identify with the political goals of the government, fear of the consequences of refusing to cooperate with civil authority, the bureaucratization of the medical role, and the lack of concern for medical ethics and human rights [4]. Nazi physicians failed to see themselves as physicians first, with a calling and an ethic dedicated to healing and caring for the welfare of human beings. Instead, they were seduced by power and ideology to view the state as their "patient" and to see the extermination of an entire people as "treatment" for the state's health.

How could physicians serve as agents of state repression? How could physicians use their skills to torture and murder, rather than to heal and help? Sadly, there is incontrovertible evidence of the continuing involvement of physicians in crimes against humanity [5]. The extent of the involvement of physicians in contemporary human rights violations is horrifyingly broad: the examination of prisoners prior to torture, the monitoring of torture victims, the resuscitation and medical treatment of prisoners after torture, as well as the falsification of medical records, death certificates, and certifications after torture. Physicians also carry out and supervise capital and corporal punishments to which prisoners are sentenced after judicial hearings. Physicians continue to be involved in unethical human experimentation.[7] Physicians and psychologists have also collaborated with brutal regimes to develop and advise on interrogation techniques including

---

[7] Final Report of the Advisory Committee on Human Radiation Experiments, U.S. Government Printing Office, October 1995. See also [6].

sensory deprivation and brainwashing [7]. Physicians have violated medical neutrality during periods of peace and conflict [8]. Finally, they have been silent witnesses to intentional harm and social injustice as well as the neglect of human medical and social needs. For example, in South Africa, government policies under Apartheid were based on indignity and dehumanization. In the past, health professionals, through acts of commission and omission, facilitated and systematically legitimized the debasement of humanity. Under Apartheid, health personnel failed to document forensic evidence of torture and ill-treatment, breached principles of confidentiality, delivered health services on a highly discriminatory basis, and neglected the health consequences of extreme racial disparities in poverty, illiteracy, unemployment, and other social determinates of health. As of this writing, professional organizations, scholars, NGOs, and others within the health sector are examining the role of the health professions under Apartheid, developing recommendations for reform and promoting measures to prevent such abuses in the future.[8]

What circumstances and preconditions facilitated these human rights abuses? What were the personal, professional, and political contexts that not only permitted but encouraged these human rights abuses? Why and how did doctors become involved? In examining these profoundly important questions, several recurrent themes have emerged: the devaluation of certain members of society, persistent blaming of the victims of abuse, training physicians to identify with a political cause, fear of refusing to cooperate, bureaucratization of the medical role, and lack of concern for medical ethics [5]. Physicians who resist may be marginalized from their own professional groups. Also, they may themselves be jailed, tortured, and murdered. In recent years, health professionals in Turkey have been prosecuted for treating victims of human rights violations, and health professionals in several countries have disappeared, been arrested, or threatened for treating the sick and wounded in internal armed conflicts or in the course of the violent suppression of public demonstrations.[9]

Additional factors that may facilitate human rights violations within the health sector include: limited conceptualizations of health and human suffering, ineffective leadership of health sector organizations, inadequate accountability among health personnel, lack of independence in the health sector, and lack of human rights and bioethics education. Of course, one cannot exclude the sad fact that some health professionals are witting and willing participants in human rights violations through some major flaw in character and moral standing.

---

[8] The American Association for the Advancement of Science and Physicians for Human Rights, *Human Rights and Health: The Legacy of Apartheid,* submission at the request of the Truth and Reconciliation Commission, Boston, 1998.

[9] Amnesty International, *Prescriptions for Change: Health Professionals and the Exposure of Human Rights Violations,* AI Index: ACT 75/01/96, London, 1996; Physicians for Human Rights, *Torture in Turkey & Its Unwilling Accomplices,* Boston, 1996.

Physicians who use their special skills and knowledge to violate human rights not only violate the rights of their victims, but betray their obligation to their profession. The standing of the entire profession suffers when physicians act as agents of the state to destroy life and health. Physicians themselves should benefit from the articulation of clear international standards that prohibit the use of physicians by the state to violate human rights [9].

Just as it took the world's lawyers and physicians working together to bring the Nazi Physicians to justice at Nuremberg, it will take the worlds lawyers and physicians working together to prevent wholesale violations of human rights and to support proactively the growth of human rights worldwide. In 1996, Global Lawyers and Physicians (GLP) was established to help accomplish this goal. The world's physicians and lawyers, because of both their moral authority in defending life and justice and their privileged positions in society, have special obligations to humanity and must work together transnationally to identify and publicize physicians, lawyers, and judges involved in human rights abuses. It is our obligation to understand how and why physicians dedicated to health and healing can turn to torture and murder in the service of their country so that repetition of this betrayal of humanity can be avoided. Whenever politics or ideology treat people as objects, we all lose our humanity. Medical ethics devoid of human rights become no more than hollow symbols [9].[10]

THE ROLE OF HEALTH PROFESSIONALS IN PROTECTING AND PROMOTING HUMAN RIGHTS

Although individuals within the health professions have violated their professional oaths, participated in abuses, or acquiesced to human suffering by remaining silent, for the past two decades physicians and other health professionals have also contributed their specialized skills and experience to exposing human rights violations, documenting their serious health consequences, and addressing the needs of victims. Thousands of individual physicians and other health professionals and dozens of national, regional, and international medical and health organizations have adopted human rights principles into their understanding of their professional obligations and incorporated them into codes of ethics.

In Chile, Turkey, and Uruguay for instance, where torture was or has been widespread, medical leaders organized to oppose the practice, condemn medical participation, hold participants in abuses to account, and treat thousands of victims. In the USSR in the late 1970s and early 1980s, courageous Soviet

[10]See Global Lawyers and Physicians (GLP) Web Site <www.bumc.bu.edu/www/sph/lw/GLPHR.htm>

psychiatrists risked long prison sentences to speak out in opposition to the wrongful confinement of dissidents in psychiatric hospitals.

In the 1980s, the anti-apartheid National Medical and Dental Association of South Africa and others documented torture, denial of health care, and other abuses of political detainees. They, too, set up clinics to provide rehabilitative services to survivors of police brutality and prison camps. Amnesty International launched medical groups in many countries to mobilize the profession in its campaigns against torture, the death penalty, and the abysmal health conditions of individual prisoners of conscience. In 1977, the American Association for the Advancement of Science organized a Clearinghouse on Science and Human Rights, initiating medical and scientific delegations to study specific human rights problems and explore the unique contribution of science to the protection of human rights. Together with Argentine doctors, scientists, and students, for instance, they pioneered the use of DNA in the identification of the bodies of the "disappeared" from Argentina's "dirty war" of the 1970s.

In 1986, Physicians for Human Rights (PHR) was established, constituting the first formally-organized group of medical scientists working in the United States to promote human rights worldwide.[11] Since then, similar groups have emerged in Denmark, India, Israel, the Palestinian Authority, South Africa, the United Kingdom, and elsewhere. In the Netherlands, the Johannes Wier Institute has also organized physicians to promote human rights since the mid-1980s.

Physicians, scientists, and other health professionals such as nurses, psychologists, and public health workers fulfill an important need in the worldwide struggle for human rights. Because of their training, they are uniquely qualified to play an important role in human rights investigation, fact-finding, documentation, advocacy, and treatment. Scientists can conduct autopsies, uncover graves, identify remains, and determine cause of death. The evidence doctors and scientists uncover is now routinely used in courts and tribunals to bring perpetrators to justice and hold governments accountable for violations. Health professionals can conduct surveys to quantify in stark figures the morbidity and mortality that result from such violations of human rights as torture, excessive use of force by police and military, and use of chemical weapons and landmines. Medical and psychological examinations and collection of victim histories can provide objective and forceful evidence of abuse by governments and can alert the international community to refugee crises and populations at risk due to hunger, disease, abuse, or neglect [10-12]. Medical and psychological documentation of human rights abuses is more difficult to refute than oral or written testimonies, and is often retrievable even after the witnesses' voices have been silenced.

In addition, when they are well organized, health professionals can put pressure on governments that violate human rights. The grounding of their

---

[11]See PHR Web Site <www.phrusa.org>

concerns in professional ethics and their recognized commitment to health render their voices particularly powerful. During the past decades, numerous specialists have made contributions to documentation and advocacy for human rights: internists, pathologists, pediatricians, psychiatrists, psychologists, epidemiologists, gynecologists, nurses, midwives, toxicologists, burn specialists, prison health workers, orthopedic surgeons, social workers, and medical ethicists have conducted investigations, published articles in medical journals, spoken at hearings, presented evidence in national trials, regional courts and the ad-hoc international criminal tribunals for the former Yugoslavia and Rwanda, conducted training sessions, and mobilized their colleagues to promote human rights. Health professionals have also played a central role in documenting the occurrence of rape and child abuse, estimating their incidence, assessing physical and psychological consequences, and helping to develop community-based strategies for helping victim/survivors.

Physicians and their professional associations have mobilized in defense of colleagues who have been imprisoned, tortured, or otherwise abused for performing their duties and adhering to the ethical standards mandating appropriate treatment of the sick and wounded regardless of political affiliation. Major professional societies, such as the British Medical Association, as well as prestigious institutions such as the Institute of Medicine in the United States, have established human rights committees.

Increasingly, health professionals are also engaging in prevention strategies. It is not enough for those whose work is to protect and promote health, to regard their human rights obligations as limited to treating and alleviating the consequences of abuses, reporting on violations, and conducting campaigns after abuses have occurred. The effort to prevent human rights violations extends to monitoring the early signs of outbreaks and to inoculating society against epidemics of abuse through education in tolerance, non-violence, conflict resolution, and basic human standards. Most importantly, health professionals must view addressing the need for truth, justice, and commemoration for victims of human rights abuse as essential to prevention. Failure to meet these needs will open the door to repetition of cycles of violence and revenge, as well as leave a debilitating legacy of trauma for the next generation [13].

THE ROLE OF HEALTH PROFESSIONALS IN ADDRESSING GLOBALLY THE NEEDS OF VICTIMS OF HUMAN RIGHTS ABUSES

In addressing the needs of victim/survivors, health professionals must see their role in a comprehensive, integrated manner, from the perspective of the totality of the individual's life, as a member of a family, community, society, nation, and the world. To respond effectively to victim/survivor needs, health professionals should be cognizant of their complexity so that they can make informed choices about how to meet them. This will usually be done in collaboration with other relevant professionals such as lawyers, journalists, human rights organizations, community activists and leaders, in addition to cooperative governments and United Nations bodies. In addition to obvious medical treatment, among the important survivor needs and recommended health professional responses are the following.

Acknowledgment by the Caregiver

For decades, survivors of human rights violations have been doubly victimized: first by the abuse itself, and subsequently by a conspiracy of silence that frequently surrounds the victims. Most victims need to tell their story. And they need others to listen to them. Among the first and foremost listeners should be caregivers. In order to listen to and subsequently acknowledge the trauma story, the caregiver must overcome the numbing, denial, avoidance, distancing, and bystander's guilt that frequently accompany the hearing [14]. Whereas society has a moral obligation to share its members' pain, psychotherapists and other health professionals have, in addition, a professional, contractual obligation. When they fail to listen, explore, understand, and help, they participate in the conspiracy of silence and may inflict further trauma on the survivor [14].

Acknowledgment by Society

Recovery from trauma, at least at the cognitive level, involves the ability to develop a realistic perspective of what happened, by whom, to whom, and accepting the reality that it had happened the way it did. Formal and public establishment of the historical record, compilation of eyewitness and survivor accounts, investigation into the roles, motives, and strategies of perpetrators, can validate this perspective for the survivor and the larger society. In the experience of South American psychologists who have worked for years with victims of repression "the victims know that individual therapeutic intervention is not enough. They need to know that their society as a whole acknowledges what has happened to them. . . . Truth means the end of denial and silence. . . . Truth will be achieved only when literally everyone knows and acknowledges what happened during the military regime . . ." [15]. Health professionals have a role to play in supporting and participating in the revelation of these truths, whether through truth commissions, national or international courts and tribunals, or articles, books, archives, and films.

Justice

For victims of serious human rights violations, truth without justice is, in most cases, empty. Impunity for criminals who rape, torture, and kill is an insult to the dead and to survivors and their loved ones. Failure to bring individual perpetrators to justice risks the collectivization of guilt, and can encourage renewed cycles of violence and revenge. Fifty years after Nuremberg, the functioning of two international criminal tribunals to prosecute war crimes, crimes against humanity and genocide in former Yugoslavia and Rwanda, as well as serious prospects of the establishment of an International Criminal Court are cause for hope [16]. Forensic pathologists, archaeologists, anthropologists, radiologists, odontologists, and geneticists, have been and must continue to be central players in the efforts to collect evidence, and promote criminal prosecution of perpetrators of human rights violations. Psychologists and social workers must work with and provide support for witnesses. All health professionals need to view the establishment of justice as a critical part of the healing of individual victims and societies.

Measures of Individual Redress Such as Reparation, Restitution, Compensation

Establishing guilt and enforcing punishment for abusers is a real and important form of redress for victims. But victims still need a tangible or symbolic statement from society that they have been grossly wronged. And they should have a right to monetary or other recompense. Reparations for damages, such as restitution of property and possessions or lost income, both real and symbolic compensation for the harm done, and rehabilitation can accomplish the reestablishment of victims' equality of value, power, and self-esteem [17].

Commemoration and Education

There is a deep human need for rituals of mourning and commemoration that transcends all cultures, religions, and society. In the aftermath of gross human rights violations and the devastation caused by war, starvation, and epidemic disease, there is a need for shared context, shared mourning, and shared memory. From the hills of Guatemala, to the villages of Kurdistan; from the parishes of Rwanda to the fields of Srebrenica in Bosnia, forensic scientists who have exhumed graves with Physicians for Human Rights have felt the intense need of the victims for ceremonial reburial, for mourning rituals, and for monuments and memorials. And when all of the bodies cannot be found, recovered, or identified, the anguish of survivors who still wait for the truth and cannot yet grieve fully is incalculable. Recording death and ensuring burial with dignity are essential to demonstrate the value of human life. Mental health professionals in particular, have much to offer in working with individual victims, clergy, and communities to develop and ensure appropriate rituals for reburial, mourning, and commemoration. They can also be instrumental in advocating for special resources to be devoted to memorial and commemoration.

REGARDING HUMAN RIGHTS EDUCATION

The millions of trained health professionals around the world have yet to embrace fully the notion that human rights are essential for human health. Health professionals should understand that human rights are interdependent and indivisible; that the realization of any one right depends on the realization of other rights. The spectrum of human rights that may affect health includes a broad range of possibilities: civil, political, economic, social, cultural, and others. This understanding will only emerge through human rights education for health professionals.

For health practitioners to promote health and well being, human rights concerns need to be integrated into health education. Throughout the world they have been ill-equipped to address human rights abuses because medicine in the twentieth century has focused almost exclusively on the treatment of disease. But a disease focus marginalizes their roles in society and consequently neglects social conditions that affect health and well being. A prevention orientation offers a more comprehensive perspective that can remove some of these limitations.

Over the past five years, curricular studies in health and human rights have begun to develop in the health sector [18]. Such studies provide students with a basic understanding of human rights issues that are relevant to health professionals and enable students to acquire the knowledge and skills necessary for preventing and alleviating the human suffering caused by human rights abuses. Also, continuing education courses have taught practitioners to document human rights violations and to provide care for survivors of human rights abuses. Hopefully, these pioneering efforts represent the beginning of a global movement for human rights education that will transform effectively the aspirations of the Universal Declaration into action.

The inclusion of human rights in the curriculum of health professionals carries significant implications: it challenges them to redefine health and well-being and focus on causes of human suffering that have been neglected in the past. It requires health professionals to move beyond the traditional physician-patient relationship, and is likely to interfere with the traditional self-protection of the profession and the financial self-interest which is at the core of many health care systems. Furthermore, efforts to integrate human rights into health education are limited by leadership, organization, funding, and policy within the health sector. While no human rights culture can be legislated, many professions have instituted ethical and human rights standards for themselves. The health profession in every country must discipline its own members who violate these standards. But traditional codes of ethics must also extend beyond the doctor-patient relationship to address the relationship between the professional and the larger community. Public health proponents increasingly understand that they must address directly the underlying societal issues that determine, to a large extent, who lives and who dies, when and of what. And human rights activists are ever more aware that limitations to health care based on discrimination exacerbate myriad human rights violations [19].

Notwithstanding these challenges, health and all other professionals, cannot stand by as silent witnesses to the incalculable human suffering caused by human rights violations on a daily basis on a staggering scale worldwide. At stake is not only individual and community well-being and the credibility of all professionals, but the safeguarding of our humanity for centuries to come.

REFERENCES

1. R. L. Sivard, *World Military and Social Expenditures, 1987-1988,* WMSE Publications, Leesburg, Virginia, 1996.
2. M. Cherif Bassiouni, *Crimes Against Humanity in International Criminal Law,* Martinus Nijhoff Publishers, Dordrecht, The Netherlands, pp. 1-48, 1992.
3. G. Annas and M. Grodin (eds.), *The Nazi Doctors and the Nuremberg Code: Human Rights in Human Experimentation,* Oxford University Press, New York, 1992.
4. M. Grodin and G. Annas, Legacies of Nuremberg: Medical Ethics and Human Rights, *Journal of the American Medical Association, 276*:20, pp. 1682-1683, November 27, 1996.
5. *Medicine Betrayed: The Participation of Doctors in Human Rights Abuses,* Report of a Working Party, British Medical Association, Zed Books, London, United Kingdom and Atlantic Highlands, New Jersey, pp. 1-8, 1992.
6. D. J. Rothman, Ethics and Human Experimentation: Henry Beecher, Revisited, *New England Journal of Medicine, 317*:19, pp. 1195-1199, 1987.
7. R. J. Lifton, *The Nazi Doctors: Medical Killing and the Psychology of Genocide,* Basic Books, New York, pp. 1-18, 1986.
8. B. Levy and V. Sidel, *War and Public Health,* Oxford University Press, New York, 1997.
9. M. Grodin, G. Annas, and L. Glantz, Medicine and Human Rights: A Proposal for International Action, *Hastings Center Report, 23*:4, pp. 8-12, 1995.
10. M. J. Toole and R. J. Waldman, Refugees and Displaced Persons: War, Hunger and Public Health, *Journal of the American Medical Association, 270*:5, pp. 600-605, 1993.
11. H. J. Geiger and R. M. Cook-Deegan, The Role of Physicians in Conflicts and Humanitarian Crises: Case Studies from the Field Missions of Physicians for Human Rights, *Journal of the American Medical Association, 270,* pp. 616-620, 1993.
12. R. Desjarlais, L. Eisenberg, B. Good, and A. Kleinman (eds.), *World Mental Health: Problems and Priorities in Low Income Countries,* Oxford University Press, New York, 1995.
13. Y. Danieli (ed.), *International Handbook of Multigenerational Legacies of Trauma,* Plenum Press, New York, 1998.
14. Y. Danieli, Confronting the Unimaginable: Psychotherapists' Reactions to Victims of the Nazi Holocaust, in *Human Adaptation to Extreme Stress,* J. P. Wilson, Z. Harel, and B. Kahana (eds.), Plenum, New York, pp. 219-238, 1988.

15. D. Becker, E. Lira, M. Moses, I. Castillo, E. Gomez, and J. Kovalskys, Therapy with Victims of Political Repression in Chile: The Challenge of Social Reparation, *Journal of Social Issues, 40*:3, pp. 133-149, 1990.
16. E. Stover, In the Shadow of Nuremberg: Pursuing War Criminals in the Former Yugoslavia and Rwanda, *Medicine and Global Survival, 2*:3, pp. 140-147, 1995.
17. Y. Danieli, Preliminary Reflections from a Psychological Perspective, in *The Right to Restitution, Compensation and Rehabilitation for Victims of Gross Violations of Human Rights and Fundamental Freedoms,* T. C. van Boven, C. Flinterman, F. Grunfeld, and I. Westendorp (eds.), Netherlands Institute of Human Rights, Special Issue No. 12, pp. 196-213, 1992.
18. J. Brenner, Human Rights Education in Public Health Graduate Schools, *Health and Human Rights, 2*:1, pp. 129-139, 1996.
19. J. Mann, S. Gruskin, M. Grodin, and G. Annas, *Introduction to Health and Human Rights: A Reader,* Routledge, New York (1998 in press).

Voices

Freedom: Press, Speech, Expression

Terry Anderson

In nearly thirty years as a journalist, I have seen about every kind of human rights violation that can be perpetrated by man. I have observed and interviewed victims and their victimizers. I have counted bodies, listened to the groans of the wounded and dying, and heard their children cry.

For nearly seven years, I was a hostage, a prisoner without even the minimal rights that a convicted criminal would have in most countries.

What remains most prominently in my mind out of all those experiences is not the suffering, not the destruction, not the deaths, but the consistent dignity with which the victims faced their fate, the strength they found in the midst of disasters that make even hardened reporters shake their heads in wonder. For every evil oppressor, for every violent war-lover, for every power-hungry and greedy dictator, I have seen thousands of decent, brave people summon strength beyond belief, and compassion beyond understanding.

To believe that these ordinary people, without power or wealth, are not entitled to the basic rights put forth so eloquently in the Universal Declaration of Human Rights requires a moral blindness that, fortunately, is increasingly rare.

In the past decade or so, following the end of the Cold War, we have seen country after country move from totalitarian and tyrannical forms of government toward freedom, toward open societies, toward the acceptance and observance of individual rights. Millions of people are living today in a greater degree of freedom than they have ever had before. And that will continue because the Universal Declaration has become part of the world's culture. Fifty years ago, the declaration was considered by many to be simply an idealistic statement of goals, a dream that would never be achieved. Today, we can recognize it as a statement of truths, becoming more and more of a reality.

I am proud that my profession, journalism, has played a part in the increasing triumph of freedom. In my work with the Committee to Protect Journalists, which monitors attacks on the press around the world and works on behalf of jailed journalists, I am constantly inspired by the dedication and sacrifice of thousands of reporters around the world. These people go to work every day not knowing if it will be the day they go to jail, or are beaten or kidnapped or murdered. Twenty-six journalists were killed last year for reporting the truth. Another 129 were imprisoned by their own governments.

Just recently, I spoke with a young African reporter who was returning to his country in the face of a brutal dictatorship. Dozens of his colleagues are already in jail there. Others have simply disappeared after being picked up by security forces. This reporter knew his chances of remaining free, and maybe even alive, were slim. But he, like others before him, was going back.

Why do they do this? More importantly, why do their oppressors do this to them? Because they know how important a free and active press is. They know that they cannot oppress others, cannot deprive people of their basic rights, unless they first muzzle or frighten the press.

Freedom of the press, freedom of speech, freedom of expression are the most basic of rights, without which no other rights can be established, or long exist.

Part VII

Mainstreaming Human Rights

Chapter 27

Peace, the Security Council and Human Rights

Andrew Clapham

Since the end of the Cold War, there has been a growing recognition of the importance of human rights not only to development but to peace itself. We have learned in lesson after lesson that democracy enables development and sustains its success by empowering the individual and distributing its fruits equitably. We have learned that respect for human rights ensures peace between groups and peoples, both within and between states. We have learned, finally—from Latin America to South Africa—that telling the truth about human rights abuses is a precondition for national healing and reconciliation. What is needed now is for us to draw the right lessons for the future of human rights. As we embark on that journey, we need look no further than the past decade's conflicts and uncivil wars to know that the human right of groups and ethnicities to live with their identities is critical to peace itself.
Louise Frechette, Deputy Secretary-General of the UN, June 1998[1]

It is sadly ironic that, as we commemorate the founding of the United Nations and 50th anniversary of the Universal Declaration of Human Rights, the phrases "crimes against humanity" and "genocide" have returned to our everyday vocabulary. In such an age people throughout the world look to the Security Council, as the UN organ with primary responsibility for international peace and security, not to turn away, but rather to take decisive action to preserve the foundations of peace and security—in other words, to prevent and stop the very worst human rights violations in the world. We have been asked to take a victim's perspective as we look at the different roles played by the United Nations. We are

---

[1] DSG/98/08, 4 June 1998, handing over ceremony of Palais Wilson to the UN in Geneva.

forced to conclude that most victims looking toward the Security Council will be filled with feelings of despair and disappointment. In fact, talking about victims in this context may not be the most helpful approach. The victims of Security Council action or inaction may actually be dead. Perhaps a more constructive viewpoint would be to look at the issues through the eyes of the survivors and potential victims of massive human rights violations.

During the Cold War the blockage in the Security Council could be explained by the antagonism between the two blocs. Since the end of the Cold War, the failure to act is less comprehensible. The Security Council prevaricated over the war in the former Yugoslavia, the genocide in Rwanda, and the continuing massacres in Burundi. And where the Security Council has acted, victims may be just as confused as to why they are seemingly being punished by their supposed saviours.

I. THE ISSUE OF HUMAN RIGHTS AT THE INTER-STATE LEVEL

If we step out of the role of the victim for a moment and see the issue through the eyes of governments, we have to admit that government representatives have become comfortable with doctrinal debates about the superiority, priority, or interdependency of different sets of rights. This is a way of carrying on group politics at the United Nations by other means. It is also a way of avoiding discussion of the bigger human rights problems of our times. For example, why do states pretend they were powerless to intervene in cases of genocide in the 1990s?

If one studies what was said by the main players at the time of the Rwandan genocide, two main hesitations emerge, at least on the part of the United States, and in many ways it was the prevarication of the United States that prevented early action by the Security Council. First, the so-called "Somalia syndrome" meant that American politicians and diplomats were wary of having dead or wounded U.S. soldiers paraded on CNN for voters at home to see and feel humiliated. Second, suspicion of the United Nations and a sense of creeping supranationalism meant that the United States was not prepared to authorize the United Nations or be part of a UN-led operation.[2] The result: a stalemate and the

---

[2] For details of what was going through the minds of US officials at this time, see M. N. Barnett, "The Politics of Indifference at the United Nations: The Bureaucratization of Peace-keeping and the Toleration of Genocide," mimeograph on file with the author, publication forthcoming in *Cultural Anthropology*. I have discussed these events and some of the other themes touched on in the current chapter in more detail in "Human rights and the prevention of humanitarian emergencies" in *War and Destitution: The Prevention of Humanitarian Emergencies*, Volume III of the forthcoming three volume series *War, Hunger and Displacement: The Origins and Prevention of Humanitarian Emergencies*, E. Wayne Nafziger and Raimo Väyrynen (eds.), WIDER, United Nations University.

loss of hundreds of thousands of lives, and a sense that rhetoric about rights and promises of "never again" are not worth very little. Of course the Rwanda case is a hard case, and does not deny the human rights project, but it begs the question: what is being done by states to meet the challenge of being prepared to prevent massive violations of human rights amounting to genocide? The answer is—not a lot.

In his *Agenda for Peace,* Secretary-General Boutros Boutros-Ghali had proposed volunteer peace-enforcement units (in the nature of a provisional measure under Article 40 of the UN Charter).[3] He later outlined how he envisaged this working:

> An even more radical development can now be envisaged. It happens all too often that the parties to a conflict sign a cease-fire agreement but then fail to respect it. In such situations it is felt that the United Nations should "do something." This is a reasonable expectation if the United Nations is to be an effective system of collective security. The purpose of peace enforcement units (perhaps they should be called "cease-fire enforcement units") would be to enable the United Nations to deploy troops quickly to enforce a cease-fire by taking coercive action against either party, or both, if they violate it.

Having stressed that the operations would still have to be authorized by the Security Council, and would be under the command of the Secretary-General, he continued:

> But the concept goes beyond peacekeeping to the extent that the operation would be deployed without the express consent of the two parties (though its basis would be a cease-fire agreement previously reached between them). UN troops would be authorized to use force to ensure respect for the cease-fire. They would be trained, armed, and equipped accordingly; a very rapid response would be essential.[4]

Although the Security Council and the General Assembly have offered little encouragement to the Secretary-General in his appeal for such units, a public

---

[3] An Agenda for Peace: Preventive diplomacy, peacemaking and peacekeeping (Report of the Secretary-General pursuant to the Statement adopted by the Summit Meeting of the Security Council on 31 January 1992, UN Doc. A/47/277-S/24111, 17 June 1992 at para. 44. Article 40 (which is part of Chapter VII of the Charter) reads: "In order to prevent an aggravation of the situation, the Security Council may, before making the recommendations or deciding upon the measures provided for in Article 39, call upon the parties concerned to comply with the provisional measures as it deems necessary or desirable. Such provisional measures shall be without prejudice to the rights, claims or positions of the parties concerned. The Security Council shall duly take account of failure to comply with such provisional measures." The Secretary-General stressed that he was not referring to the agreements between the Security Council and member states which Article 43 of the Charter foresees. He saw this latter issue as a much longer-term project relating to the provision of troops to "deal with acts of aggression" (at para. 44).

[4] "Empowering the United Nations," *Foreign Affairs,* (1992/3) 89-102 at 93-4.

debate on this and similar options is underway and may eventually turn the tide of governmental skepticism.[5] When the survivors and potential victims speak up in this context, we may be able to move away from the State-centered debate about sovereignty toward a more meaningful discussion about effective protection. In the meantime, some steps have been taken to ensure stand-by arrangements. These units are supposed to be ready for departure within fifteen to thirty days from the time of the official request.[6] This is a softer option and avoids the impression of giving the Secretary-General a "UN army," something that had been troubling some member states. Whether the stand-by arrangements will prove satisfactory remains to be seen. The arrangement has been described by UN officials as only as good as a travellers' cheque that has not been countersigned. When it comes to the crunch the United Nations still has to get the second signature and it is, of course, at this crucial point that national governments prevaricate.

It is suggested that the real solution is a properly trained multinational rapid deployment force which can be sent following a Security Council decision and which is not dependent on the vagaries of national politics. Moreover, the mandate of such a rapid deployment force could go beyond the "cease-fire enforcement" envisaged by the Secretary-General and cover such human rights tasks as the protection of civilians, reporting serious violations of international humanitarian and human rights law, arresting and surrendering internationally indicted criminals (where an international tribunal exists to issue the indictment), laying the foundations for the establishment of a civilian police force which operates in conformity with international criminal justice standards, and helping to establish national procedures to ensure accountability and compensation for the victims of the crisis.[7] This may seem over-ambitious but such timely action probably could have prevented the further deterioration of the situation following the fragile

---

[5] Most recently, see the recommendation of the Independent Working Group on the Future of the United Nations that "a UN Rapid Reaction Force be established for urgent deployment on the decision of the Security Council," at page 22 of *The United Nations in its Second Half-Century* (copies available from the Ford Foundation). The issue was taken up by the Canadian Government at the 50th General Assembly with the launch of their report *Towards a Rapid Reaction Capability for the United Nations* (September 1995). The Canadian model foresees a 5,000 military and civilian multi-functional force to be rapidly deployed under the control of an operational-level headquarters upon authorization of the Security Council. See also the report commissioned by the Canadian Department of Foreign Affairs: "Human Rights Principles and Practice in United Nations Field Operations," by Paul LaRose-Edwards, Draft 2.1, January 1996.

[6] DPI Press Release SG/2010, 22 June 1994.

[7] Compare the Report of the Independent Working Group on the Future of the United Nations which looks at the question in the broader context and would accord rapid reaction forces the following tasks: "establish a UN presence; provide security for UN personnel or for evacuations; establish one or more safe areas for the civilian population; limit escalation and assist in ending the violence; provide limited humanitarian assistance in emergency circumstances; assess and report on the situation to the Secretary-General and the Security Council." At page 22 of *The United Nations in its Second Half-Century* (1995).

peace agreements in Rwanda, Angola, and Liberia.[8] Military, police, and civilian personnel would have to be UN servants and trained as members of the multinational rapid deployment team and not simply hired out as national contingents. It is this sort of preparedness and commitment that could prevent contemporary forms of violent conflict and massive human rights violations. To concentrate on the machinery for monitoring and enforcing cease-fires may be to miss the point. Contemporary conflict seems likely to continue to revolve around attempts to eliminate the "other" in our midst.[9] A lead from the Security Council could empower the United Nations to prevent future catastrophes.

II. A NEW ROLE FOR HUMAN RIGHTS IN THE WORK OF THE UN SECRETARIAT

The UN Secretary-General, Kofi Annan, as part of his reform program, made a series of internal changes that have reoriented the role of human rights within the Organization. In his July 1997 package, he stated that he had reorganized the Secretariat's work program around five core missions of the United Nations. Four of these core missions now have executive committees that involve the relevant UN departments, programs, and funds. These four committees are: peace and security, economic and social affairs, development cooperation, and humanitarian affairs. The fifth core mission is human rights. Human rights does not have an executive committee, but is "designated as cutting across and therefore participating in, each of the other four."[10] The strengthening of the New York Office of the High Commissioner for Human Rights and the participation of the High Commissioner, Mary Robinson, in these Committees represents a most important development in the way in which human rights issues are being dealt with within the parts of the secretariat that deal with peace and security issues.

However, we should point out that this new cross-cutting role gives rise to a number of dilemmas. The peace and security executive committee is chaired by the Under-Secretary-General for Political Affairs. The stated mission of the United Nations in this field revolves around two functions: preventive action and peace-making. The Secretary-General currently has preventive action

---

[8] A. Clapham and M. Henry, Peace-Keeping and Human Rights in Africa and Europe, in *Honoring Human Rights and Keeping the Peace*, A. Henkin (ed.), Aspen Institute, Washington, D.C., pp. 129-160, 1995.

[9] See Roberto Toscano "Guerre, violence civile et éthique: La diplomatie à la lumière de Levinas," *Esprit,* pp. 152-172, July 1997. "Le conflict contemporain entre groupes est un défi bien plus direct lancé à l'éthique que le conflit international classique ne l'a jamais été. La victime de la violence organisée, aujourd'hui, a souvent un visage réel et familier. La violence procède alors du désir de se débarrasser d'un visage intolérablement familier mais différent, d'un visage qui suscite une tension permanente à laquelle on est incapable de résister. C'est, en bref, le chemin vers un synthèse narcissique, pour ne pas dire autiste, où le Soi est seul et incontesté parce que l'Autre a été éliminé." At 163-4.

[10]"Renewing the United Nations: A Programme for Reform," Report of the Secretary-General. UN Doc. A/51/950, 14 July 1997 at para. 28.

mandates in Afghanistan, Bougainville, Burundi, Cambodia, Cyprus, East Timor, El Salvador, Georgia, Guatemala, Haiti, Liberia, Myanmar, Sierra Leone, Somalia, Tajikistan, and the former Yugoslav Republic of Macedonia. The new label of "preventive action" conceals the essentially diplomatic role which the United Nations has to play in these places. Demands to include human rights concerns in a cross-cutting way are going to sound a discordant note. Those engaged in preventive diplomacy are going to be concerned with keeping open channels of communication and getting their interlocutors to come closer together. Human rights accusations can seem divisive and confrontational. It may therefore be better to keep them separate and not to contaminate the diplomatic discourse. The dilemma for the secretariat and the leadership in the executive committee on peace and security is how to accommodate the human rights dimension without undermining their chances of peace-making.

This is how Margaret Anstee, Special Representative of the Secretary-General for Angola, saw the conundrum:

> [T]here is no doubt that monitoring of human rights must be given a prominent place in the mandate and staffing of UN peacekeeping missions. The accusation of not speaking out sufficiently has not been limited to matters of human rights but extends to all breaches of the Peace Accords. This raises a fundamental question of judgement, and of style. I am convinced that, while it is perfectly right and proper for NGOs, particularly those involved in human rights, to speak out plainly against abuses—indeed it is their duty and their *raison d'être* to do so—the position of the United Nations, when it is functioning as a mediator, is necessarily more nuanced. This by no means entails turning a blind eye to wrongdoing, but rather dealing with it in a less public manner that will not put negotiations at risk—that is, in direct talks, or by raising the matter through whatever monitoring mechanism may have been set up (in this case the CCPM [Joint Political Military Commission]). This does not mean that public disavowal or criticism will never be resorted to, but that they will be used sparingly, in carefully selected cases. A careful balance has to be maintained between avoiding ructions that could imperil the whole delicate negotiation and allowing offenders to go scotfree. It is almost invariably the case that both parties to a conflict transgress—there are no pure innocents in situations of this kind—even though one may be worse than the other, and it is therefore of the utmost importance to apportion blame scrupulously between them, according to their relative degrees of compliance.[11]

[11]M. Anstee, *Orphan of the Cold War: The Inside Story of the Collapse of the Angolan Peace Process, 1992-3*, pp. 529-530, 1996. See also pp. 88-89, "The President also expressed the hope that UNAVEM could investigate the human rights situation in UNITA-controlled areas. I was obliged to point out that human rights had not been included in our mandate, I had neither the resources nor qualified people to undertake such a task. I forbore to add that if I had they would have had to investigate both sides."

I would suggest that what is needed is a paradigmatic shift in thinking about human rights. Rather than perceiving human rights issues as inevitably controversial and counterproductive, the time may have come to see human rights norms as part of the framework for dialogue. The issue is more one of a *clash of cultures* than of inherent *antagonism*. The culture within the departments of the secretariat that deal with preventive action, peace-making, peace-keeping, and peace enforcement is determined by the overriding sense that things can only be accomplished by ensuring consent and cooperation from the relevant member states. On the other hand the human rights messenger often seeks to transmit a message that will inevitably upset the state of relations between the United Nations and the member state concerned. The ethics of the human rights movement suggest that one cannot selectively withhold complaints in order to retain cordial relations with governments. Both sides need to question their approach and see if they cannot combine to produce a creative tension, which would allow the United Nations to capitalize on its leverage, so as actually get improvements in the long-term human rights situation, and not just smooth relations with governments and factions in the short term. From the perspective of the survivor, the United Nations is only as credible and trustworthy as the energy and commitment they put into taking up the atrocities which have just taken place under their noses. There is a sense, which permeates all UN activity, that progress comes through smooth cooperation with governments. But now that the United Nations is increasingly operational, the time has come to realize that effective progress also depends on accommodating the needs and aspirations of survivors.

One can unearth similar tensions in the other core missions. In the case of humanitarian assistance the conflicts can be very concrete. Why should the United Nations take up human rights issues with a belligerent party when it will only result in lack of access to populations in need? But the ethical dilemmas are just as sharp. If the population in need is sheltering war criminals and future *genocidaires* what sort of humanitarian assistance is that—and is it ethical? When this choice presented itself in Zaire, the UN High Commissioner for Refugees appealed for a security force to separate the war criminals from the innocent civilian population. No such force was forthcoming. We are therefore forced to return to the responsibilities of governments at the interstate level (referred to in Part I previously).

III. THE IMPORTANCE OF RESPECT FOR HUMAN RIGHTS IN THE WORK OF THE SECURITY COUNCIL[12]

The Security Council has recognized the importance of human rights issues with regard to its work concerning the maintenance of international peace and security. Although in the past human rights were considered subjects for another place, to be dealt with by different diplomats, the Security Council more recently has in some cases requested human rights reports from the Secretary-General in the context of the Security Council's peace-keeping operations.[13] Moreover, the Council now often provides for a human rights component in some of its operations set up to address armed conflict. This has been the case with regard to El Salvador, Cambodia, Angola, Liberia, Bosnia and Herzegovina, and Georgia. In fact, the Council's recent Resolutions and Presidential Statements regularly reaffirm the Council's concern for human rights, and in 1997 dealt with related issues such as the importance of having appropriately trained UN civilian police,[14] the need to respect the rights of personnel endeavoring to carry out international humanitarian assistance, as well as the importance of recognizing that massive displacements of civilian populations can cause threats to international peace and security.[15]

But, despite these developments, it seems that there is still a tendency to see human rights work as somehow an *obstacle* to conducive political progress. What is really needed is a change so that human rights are seen as another instrument in the tool box we have on hand, to tackle emerging conflict, and help the Security Council know what action might be taken to avert conflict. If the Security Council wants to grasp the causes and solutions to armed conflict it has to pay greater attention to the human rights violations that *lead to* armed conflict, that *fuel* armed conflict, that are *weapons of war* within the armed conflict, and that, if not addressed, will lead to *further* conflict and *further* threats to international peace and security.

So, what is being proposed is nothing more than taking human rights issues into account when attempting to fulfill the Security Council's role under the UN Charter of maintaining and restoring international peace and security. Unfortunately, in much modern armed conflict the civilian population has become the target of attack by the belligerents. Knowledge about these human rights abuses can assist the Security Council in seeking to find

---

[12]This section is based on the presentation made by Pierre Sané, Secretary-General of Amnesty International, to the members of the Security Council, 15 September 1997. I have tried to keep some of the original tone so that this section represents victim-orientated advocacy rather than cool commentary.

[13]For example, Resolution 1020 (1995) on Liberia.

[14]Presidential Statement PRST 1997/38, 14 July 1997.

[15]Presidential Statement PRST 1997/34, 19 June 1997.

solutions to these situations. No one is suggesting that the Security Council should become a human rights debating chamber. Nor are we suggesting that the existing human rights mechanisms should be discarded. We are also not suggesting that human rights issues should be used as factors that automatically lead to sanctions or the use of military force. What follows is a review of some of the phases during which human rights discussion can prove useful in the Security Council's work.

Prevention

The new emphasis on preventive action and preventive diplomacy implies that the United Nations and the diplomatic community are receiving information about ongoing tension and potential conflict. Human rights reports can provide such information; yet the process for their examination takes place away from discussions on preventive action. Where there are attempts to raise human rights issues in the Security Council during this phase, such discussion is somehow seen as inappropriate at this time. But human rights reports can enable a clearer picture to emerge for early warning and early action purposes. In this phase one has the chance again to prevent, not only human rights violations, but also a potential armed conflict. It is well known that the UN Commission on Human Rights' own expert on extrajudicial executions warned in August 1993 that Burundi and Rwanda would be drenched in blood unless urgent preventive measures were taken.

Role of Reporting and Investigation During a Conflict

At all stages of armed conflict it seems that the political players involved in trying to resolve the crisis have considered human rights complaints or investigations troublesome, rather than central to any mediation or conflict resolution efforts. But ignoring or downplaying human rights issues during a conflict in fact leads to serious discontent and antagonism toward the United Nations and the "international community," among the factions and the local population. We might suggest that attention to human rights issues, as well as proper human rights reporting and investigations, in fact fulfill a number of functions.

First, when massacres of civilians and serious violations of international humanitarian law are discussed at the level of the Security Council, this is the first step in the parties realizing they will be held accountable for their actions. Second, accurate and timely human rights investigations can dispel propaganda and rumors which only fan the flames of conflict. In many of today's armed conflicts the perception that vicious atrocities have been committed against one's own people has been the fuel used by leaders to ignite feelings of injustice and demands for retribution against the "other." Soldiers then go on to commit further atrocities and the conflict spirals. This has been recognized by UN Special

Rapporteurs on Human Rights as they seek to sift the truth from the war propaganda. To ignore proper human rights reporting during armed conflict is to surrender to the best propaganda machine. The importance of on-site investigations by UN peace-keeping operations has also been recognized by the Secretary-General's Special Representatives heading operations such as those the Security Council established in Angola and Mozambique. Third, by investigating, reporting, and following up human rights violations in times of armed conflict, one can dispel the sense on all sides that it is futile to play by the rules, as no one cares, and this has no relationship with the political forces that will combine to end the war and assist the new government. Fourth, by studying human rights reports in armed conflict one can start to understand some of the causes of war and the underlying grievances, inequalities, demands, and aspirations that feed the conflict and instability. If the Security Council is to maintain and restore international peace and security it needs to address these issues in designing its responses. A human rights perspective suggests that ad hoc strategies, that rely solely on emergency assistance projects to solve deep-rooted conflicts, are destined to fall apart in a short time and require the renewed attention of the Security Council all over again. The Council has authorized expensive and comprehensive operations for Cambodia, Angola, and Bosnia and Herzegovina. Although the Council approved human rights work as part of the program for each of these countries, the failure to take human rights issues seriously in the long term bodes badly for each of these cases. Political will now could save billions of dollars and thousands of lives later on.

Post-Conflict Peace Building

The Charter mandates the Security Council to make recommendations on what measures need to be taken to maintain or restore international peace and security. Much of the Security Council's work focuses on conflicts which have recently ended. But these are actually "high maintenance" situations. It is suggested that maintaining peace in the post-conflict period means constant attention and work. These situations need considerable investment for the countries involved to be able to return to normalcy. This means institutions such as the police and the judiciary functioning effectively in a way that conforms to international human rights and criminal justice standards.

Unfortunately, the Security Council often seems prematurely relieved to be able to close the dossier on a situation before ensuring that the political will and economic resources have been mustered to solidify the gains which have been made through political mediation or peace-keeping. Although there are many UN agencies involved in reconstruction, this sort of reconstruction is likely to be more effective when it is approached in the context of the political work of the Security Council. The Security Council's work needs to continue to be informed by the human rights dimension of the problems it is dealing with. Human rights need not be seen as confrontational activity that ought to be confined to the conference rooms of Geneva. We hope that human rights work can be seen as the cement for *maintaining* lasting peace and preventing new cycles of violence.

There is another aspect of prevention that seems to get passed over, namely, that in the post-conflict phase there is often a chance for the United Nations and its programs and funds to help the authorities to put in place national institutions to promote and protect human rights. There is also an opportunity to train and restructure the police and military so to reduce the likelihood of a renewed cycle of human rights violations. In some cases such as Haiti, El Salvador, and Guatemala there has been interest in such programs; but in other cases there have been no significant Security Council-backed activities. Suggestions for national human rights commissions and retraining of the police, for countries such as Liberia and Angola, have not been taken up by the Security Council. In these war-ravaged societies the best form of prevention of further conflict may be initiatives to strengthen national human rights institutions and training. This is a low-cost endeavor considering the implications of renewed conflict.

International Criminal Justice and the Role of the Council

Experience shows that long-term reconciliation after an armed conflict is not possible unless justice is central to the search for peace. Sweeping aside the question of responsibility for atrocities during an armed conflict only leads to renewed cycles of violence and impunity. Sometimes reprisals are immediate; sometimes the wounds erupt many years later. It is clear that the Security Council action to establish individual accountability in the former Yugoslavia and Rwanda has in fact led to some changes in behavior and different orders being issued. Unfortunately, the lack of proposals from the Security Council to follow up its concern about crimes against humanity and serious violations of humanitarian law in Burundi and Cambodia only seems to embolden the parties in those countries, and sends a message to leaders elsewhere that the authority of the United Nations can be successfully challenged.

Many of the human rights violations committed during armed conflict will involve crimes over which the proposed new International Criminal Court will have jurisdiction. Clearly, there should be some role for the Security Council to ensure that the perpetrators are tried by this new Court so that the Council is not forced to establish additional *ad hoc* tribunals. On the other hand, the new Court must be truly *independent* and be perceived as such.

Arms Transfers and a Renewed Role for the Council

Similarly, the analysis of arms flows to areas of armed conflict can help to determine responsibility for human rights violations, and, if action is taken, atrocities and abuses can be prevented. Without taking a general position on sanctions or boycotts, human rights organizations, such as Amnesty International, oppose in specific instances the transfer of military and security equipment, as well as training and personnel, that can reasonably be assumed to contribute to human rights abuses. Human rights reports in such cases (for example with regard to Afghanistan and Rwanda) can support efforts of the United Nations, including those taken by the Security Council. The Secretary General's reform program proposes that a new Department of Disarmament and Arms Regulation will interact with the Security Council. That might facilitate the development of a more systematic approach to studying the transfers of arms where these lead to human rights abuses and provoke instability and threats to international peace and security.

Article 26 of the UN Charter gives the Security Council responsibility for formulating plans for the establishment of a system for the regulation of armaments, in order to promote the establishment and maintenance of international peace and security.[16] Yet, as the UN passes the fifty year mark, there is barely any international system applicable to the control of conventional arms transfers. Perhaps the time has come for the Council to start to fulfill this responsibility. The Security Council must recognize that it is not simply *illicit* traffic in arms that is leading to persistent human rights abuses, but also many cases of governments' irresponsible, albeit *authorized,* transfer of arms that contribute to such abuses. The International Code of Conduct on Arms Transfers launched by the Nobel Peace Laureates represents a useful starting point for the future regulation of arms flows to conflict zones where such arms are being used to commit human rights abuses.

Women's Rights in Armed Conflict

The importance of undertaking full investigations into all acts of violence against women during war was stressed by the international community in the Beijing Declaration and Platform for Action (paragraph 145e). The Security Council must pay specific attention to the fact that a huge percentage of victims of armed conflict are women and they face particular violations in armed conflict such as rape and sexual slavery. In this context it is important that where the

---

[16]Article 26 reads in full: "In order to promote the establishment and maintenance of international peace and security with the least diversion for armaments of the world's human and economic resources, the Security Council shall be responsible for formulating, with the assistance of the Military Staff Committee referred to in Article 47, plans to be submitted to the Members of the United Nations for the establishment of a system for the regulation of armaments."

Security Council decides to establish commissions of inquiry that all such UN investigations fully incorporate a gender perspective so that gender-based abuses are recognized and qualified women participate in such investigations. The Security Council also needs to ensure that the gender dimension is not overlooked in UN peace-keeping, including by ensuring that UN personnal respect the rights and dignity of women at all times. In the Beijing Declaration and Platform for Action, governments recognized the need to take into account gender-sensitive concerns in developing training programs for all relevant personnel involved in United Nations peace-keeping and humanitarian aid (paragraph 145(g)). The pocket size cards produced by the UN Department of Peacekeeping Operations Training Unit represent a start but the rules need to be spelled out in more detail. The relevant rules state:

> We will never:
> Commit any act that could result in physical, sexual or psychological harm or suffering to members of the local population, especially women and children; Become involved in sexual liaisons which could affect our impartiality, or the well-being of others.

Children as Victims in Armed Conflict

Millions of children are directly affected by armed conflict: killed, maimed, displaced, orphaned, and psychologically traumatized. Present estimates suggest that there are more than 250,000 child soldiers. The protection of children in war must be given high priority and should be considered as a matter of course by the Security Council every time it elaborates peacekeeping and demobilization mandates.[17] Unless programs for demobilizing child soldiers are built into Security Council mandates for UN operations, these child soldiers will be re-recruited into tomorrow's conflict. In this work the Security Council can be guided by the Convention on the Rights of the Child, ratified by all but two UN member states. States should be urged to support measures to increase the protection of children from abuses in armed conflict.

CONCLUDING REMARKS

As we commemorate the 50th anniversary of the Universal Declaration of Human Rights we should avoid the temptation to argue over the priorities that

---

[17]Following the publication of the Graça Machel report (UN Docs A/51/306 and A/51/306 Add. 1) in 1996, the General Assembly created the post of Special Representative for Children in Armed Conflict Res 51/77, 12 December 1996. Olara Otunu has been appointed to this post and will have a number of professional staff working with him. This new office should be in a position to influence the Security Council in this field. It is of particular interest that Otunu was himself once the Ugandan Representative on the Security Council.

should be given to abstract notions of responsibility and right in international relations. Governments should seize the universal commitment to the Declaration to use human rights texts as instruments for structural change in countries around the world. We need to emphasize the utility of a human rights approach for creating societies based on accountability, the rule of law, participation, and the provision of basic needs. Indeed, on July 28, 1997 Secretary-General Kofi Annan spoke enthusiastically about these aims:

> Our human rights field operations are helping build national as well as non-governmental institutions for the promotion and protection of human rights. I am pleased and proud to say that we now have more staff working on human rights issues in the field than at Headquarters. All these efforts yield another important dividend: they help to combat crime and corruption, which thrive where laws and civic institutions are weak.[18]

Taking human rights issues out of the realm of inter-governmental debate and into the field of UN programs to combat crime and corruption on the ground may leave some human rights thinkers feeling uncomfortable. But the human rights debate has run out of steam. The ethical conundrums now relate to concrete choices to be made by the United Nations and its member states in designing solutions on the ground. The time has come to find practical solutions for the victims of human rights around the world.

[18]Statement at the International Conference on Governance for Sustainable Growth and Equity, July 28, 1997, SG/SM/6291.

Voices

We Also Have the Right to Dream

Rosa Anaya Perla

When asked to write for this book I was excited, and all these ideas came to my mind, but when I sat down to write, nothing came out. Here I had the opportunity I was waiting for, to tell everybody my story. How much, as a child, I had experienced violations of my human rights. Then I realized that my story wasn't my story; it was the story of all the Salvadoran children who lived a war and had to fight to survive. I have been fighting for my people my whole life, and my family's story is only one piece of a big puzzle that has to be seen all together in order to understand.

So please don't read this if you are not going to see our face on the paper. Don't read this if you have never learned to read with your heart. Only then will you understand what I am trying to say.

What are human rights? I would like to know. Sometimes human rights are only a whole bunch of papers and numbers, and maybe the pictures of people crying for a lost brother, sister, mother, father, or just a good friend. Human rights workers often forget that each one of those numbers, each face in the pictures, has a name and feelings, that they all laugh and cry, get angry and walk on the same planet. Most important, many times we forget that they all have a story to tell. Those stories are the stories we are not allowed to forget, even if they are the most terrible ones, not in order to hate, but not to let those terrible things happen again. We have to learn to listen to others so that they can listen to us; then we will start looking at each other as human beings and understand what that really means. So now allow me to tell my people's story.

My parents were both born in a country where almost everybody was poor and wealth was owned by a few families who also had control over the land, the businesses, and the military. The rich used to say that if the problem in the country were the poor, well, kill them.

389

My father, Herberth Anaya Sanabria, had to struggle for food and to get an education since he was a little boy. He knew that it wasn't right that his mother had to work very hard for very little money and that her boss, who didn't do anything, had everything he wanted.

My mother, Mirna Perla Jimenez, was one of five children whose mother had to struggle alone to raise them. She had to go to school without shoes and had to sell the books from the previous year to get new ones. She was lucky since, while many children had to work for their families' food, her mother insisted that only education could help them in the future, and not the few cents that they could get at the moment, even though they needed the money.

They both began to fight against the injustice in my country, because they knew that being poor here was a sin to the ones in power. They also knew that speaking for human rights meant death for them. No one was allowed to speak out for themselves or others, but they didn't care. They didn't want to see more children working in the streets, and more people dying because they didn't have money for medicine or for food.

The things that were happening in my country were very horrible. The continuing war was taking too many lives. People were asking only for what they had the right to have: not a million dollar house, but only a place to live, food, a good job, and education for their children. I remember that during the war it was common to find ten bodies on the road with a sign saying: "killed for being Communists." Things like that happened daily. Everybody who lived in the countryside was accused of being a guerrilla. Every time that the soldiers went to a town and committed a massacre, nobody was left alive. The young ones were killed for being guerrillas, the old because they helped them, the children because they would be the future guerrillas.

These are the kind of things that caused my parents to start to fight for human rights. When my mother was two months pregnant with me, she was captured and tortured with electric shocks to her belly so that she would tell who was working with her. They wanted to rape her but she wouldn't let them. She thought she wasn't going to live. She knew that whoever was captured by the death squads was never seen again.

As a little girl one of the games I played was to count the crosses on the side of the roads, signifying that someone was assassinated there. I could never finish counting them.

People were being tortured, killed, disappeared, because they would tell the truth, or fight for better conditions in the schools and for jobs. My father and a group of people founded the non-governmental Human Rights Commission so the people had a place to go and tell what had happened to them and speak out for the ones that were afraid to speak.

One by one, the human rights workers were assassinated.

My father was always telling us about death, knowing that his work was dangerous. He was captured in May 1986 and tortured for fifteen days in the policia de hacienda. He had always been a strong man and no matter what happened, he took his people's suffering and transformed it into strength for himself. When my mother went to see him for the first time after the fifteen days of torture, she thought that he was going to be laughing at the soldiers and was going to be ready to keep working. But he looked at her and started crying. It had been too much. She says it was the first time she saw him cry with so much pain, so she told him what all the people he once helped were doing to find him and protest his capture. She said, "the people are standing up for you because they know you have been standing up for them." He looked up, dried his tears, and came out like a new man ready to keep up the fight and help as many as he could.

He was in jail for several months as a political prisoner. He kept working with the other human rights workers who were also in jail, interviewed the prisoners and prepared a book about the torture they were subjected to. Over forty torture methods are described there. This book was presented to Pastor Idruejo from the United Nations who visited them in the jail. When he was out, the government told him, even on national television, to leave the country or they would kill him, but he told us (me and my brothers and sisters) that he couldn't leave his people alone. He couldn't walk away knowing that story of the hunger and suffering wasn't going to be told by anybody else. He couldn't let his people down. He had decided that the only way he was going to be silent was if they killed him. When he came out of jail, he was working harder for the ones who were tortured and killed. Even though by this time there was a slight change in El Salvador, a President elected by the people, my father wanted to make them respect human rights, not only in speeches, but in real life.

On the morning of October 26, 1987, when I was ten years old, my father, who was going to take us to school, went to the parking lot first to start the car. When I got near the car I heard little whistles, saw my dad fall to the ground, and two men running away. I didn't realize what was happening. I couldn't move. I could see my father's face under the car. He seemed scared but at the same time a look of peace in his eyes made me think that he was OK. Suddenly, I returned to the house to tell my mother, who ran out to see my father. I told my brothers and sisters (Miguel, 9; Gloria, 8; Rafa, 6; Edith, 5) what had happened. We didn't know that he was dead. My grandmother, who was very Catholic, always said that the first ones God listens to are the children, so we all knelt down in front of the image of Jesus and prayed and cried so my father wouldn't die, but he was already dead. We couldn't understand. We thought that maybe we didn't pray hard enough. I have never seen a funeral so big. There were hundreds and hundreds of people. I felt happy to know that my father helped so many people and had sacrificed his life for others, for telling the truth. One of the things I remember every time I feel down and that keeps me going is that at the funeral an old lady in a very torn, dirty dress and without shoes, her face reflecting her sorrow for many deaths, came up to my mother and said: "He helped me find my son who was captured by the death squads. I love him like he were my son." My mother couldn't say anything. She knew that she was one of many mothers my father helped in the nation he had given his life for. She took my mother's hand and gave her five cents and said "it is all I have but take it for your children." Those five cents meant more than all the money in the world. It came from our people, the ones that had nothing and still gave my father the little they had. After the funeral, the ones who killed him came back, burned all the flowers that covered his grave, and left a sign saying "if we could kill him again, we would."

My father and many others were killed for the truth. Archbishop Oscar Arnulfo Romero, Marianela Garcia Villa, and there are those whose names we don't even know, who now are only numbers under the category of "Assassinated during the civil war in El Salvador," were killed fighting for a better country and human rights. But they are still alive and will be as long as the people remember what they gave their lives for: those living in poverty, for children dying of hunger and people working for very low wages, for a place where there would be no more orphans. Even if they wanted to kill them again, they couldn't because they are alive in our hearts, as long as we fight their fight.

Like me, many children in El Salvador have lost their parents. I still have my mother, and I was able to bury my father. Many other children did not even know who their father was, others don't have any relatives. They may still be looking for them, hoping to know if they are dead or just lost in the past. These children have survived on their own. Some had to fight in the war, for they knew that in a way they were going to change something in El Salvador.

The war in my country may be over, but the reasons it broke out to begin with are still here, and the children of the war are paying the price of violence in a different way. They kill each other for no more reason than for belonging to different gangs. They have the same problems and live in the same poverty, but kill each other for living one block away. We still see big malls being built for the rich, while children under five years of age have to work in the streets selling candy or anything they can carry. Even though less than 2 percent of our forests remain, the rich want to cut down the last trees to build expensive houses for themselves, while the rest of the people live in shacks built out of plastic and boxes.

There is still much to do in my country. I hope that for the next book I can write about how great life is here, and that young people and children are being heard by the adults when it comes to solving problems that affect us too, rather than just calling us the lost generation that solves violence with violence. We didn't start it. Now they blame us for their own creation, and say that the past was for us. They paid by their blood so that future generations could live peacefully. But until then must we still pay with blood for what should already belong to us: the basic human rights not just for me but for all the people of my country and the world?

What I have learned is that you cannot start saving the world if you have not first listened to your own child, and ask him or her what he or she feels. If you want to give your life for others, let your own family be the first to understand your fight. I learned this from the best teachers I have had, two of the most important persons in my life: my three-year-old daughter, Lindiwe and my one-year-old son, Herberth. They were able to teach me and the people around them that children come into the world with no hate or anger. They don't ask if you are a farmer or a president. They give their love to whoever asks for it, even to people they don't know. Children can see your heart and the feelings you have. We are the ones who teach them hate or love for others. This you don't learn in a book or from the best University or the most intelligent person. These things we learn from being humble and letting the children teach us what they do best, giving love to others no matter who they are. The children are the best human rights workers because they teach by their example.

Chapter 28

Human Rights, Development, and Environment

Clarence J. Dias

The Charter of the United Nations emphasizes three interdependent and inter-related goals: PEACE, DEVELOPMENT, AND HUMAN RIGHTS. There is no peace where human rights are systematically violated and where there is no development to bring about poverty elimination. The absence of peace creates conditions that make development difficult and that breeds massive and wide-spread violations of human rights. Respect and promotion of human rights, how-ever, creates an environment favorable to both peace and development.

In his Foreword to a Harvard Law School symposium commemorating the 50th Anniversary of the UN, then Secretary-General Boutros Boutros-Ghali emphasizes:

> In 1945, the founders of the United Nations identified peace, development, human rights and international law, as the four cornerstones of the Charter. Increasingly, we have come to understand that these elements of the UN Charter are linked and intertwined.[1]

It is indeed important to emphasize, as a matter of practical significance, these four "cornerstone" objectives:

- Lasting peace must be built upon respect for the human rights of all people.
- Development is the key to the progressive realization of human rights.
- Human Rights provide the value framework and the criteria for account-ability for *all* UN activities with respect to peace and development alike.
- International law is the vehicle to achieve these purposes.

[1] 36 *Harvard Journal of International Law*, pp. 267-272 at 267 (1995).

Clear though these interlinkages between human rights, development, and environment are, somewhere down the line during the past fifty years, the UN seems "to have lost the plot."[2] At grassroots level and among the NGO community, there is keen appreciation of a fourfold complementary relationship between human rights, environment, and development:

- Development projects which degrade the environment also produce violations of human rights.
- Development projects which condone the violation of human rights in the process of the implementation of such projects also tend to condone conduct which degrades environments.
- Development projects which consciously aim at protection of the environment also end up promoting the greater realization of human rights.
- Development projects which consciously seek to protect and promote the human rights of the poor also end up protecting the environment.

Despite the relationship between human rights and environment being so self-evident, reality provides innumerable examples of the sort typified by Pulicat Lake in Tamil Nadu, India. This inland lake has, for decades, provided sustenance and livelihood to communities of subsistence fisherfolk who live around the lake. However, the balance between nature and man has been disturbed in recent years. Large-scale infrastructure development in Tamil Nadu has resulted in the displacement of a large number of communities of other subsistence fisherfolk involved in fishing in the ocean. These communities have been resettled around Pulicat Lake. As a result, the resources of the lake are overburdened and both communities of fisherfolk find themselves unable to sustain their livelihoods. The resultant conflict over scarce resources has taken a violent turn and many human rights abuses have resulted. The government authorities were quick to blame this conflict on Hindu-Muslim differences, thereby evading their own accountability for a clearly man-made developmental disaster. Pulicat Lake has become a poignant reminder of the essential need to interlink human rights, development, and environment. Fortunately, recent developments with the UN system are helping it find once again the human rights "plot" that it had lost:

- Over the past decade, the UN has convened what it has come to refer to as the UN Global Conference Continuum on Development—to arrive at a new global consensus on development epitomized by the articulation of the human right to development.

[2] To use the trenchant words of the UN High Commissioner for Human Rights, Mary Robinson, in her first public lecture, after assuming office, delivered at Oxford University, 11 November 1997. See Mary Robinson, *Realizing Human Rights: "Take hold of it boldly and duly . . .",* Romanes Lecture 1997, UN Department of Public Information, DPI/1937/E-98-00426-February 1998.

- Over the past few decades, the UN has established a significant number of "special procedures and mechanisms" under its Commission on Human Rights through which the relationships between human rights and environment have been carefully elaborated.
- Following the recommendation of the UN World Conference on Human Rights (Vienna, 1993) the UN General Assembly has created the office of a UN High Commissioner for Human Rights with a mandate to coordinate and implement all aspects of human rights within the United Nations system-wide.
- In 1997, upon assuming office, the current UN Secretary-General, Kofi Anan, unveiled his plan for reorganization of the United Nations so as to "mainstream" human rights in *all* of the activities of the United Nations: peace-keeping, humanitarian assistance, economic and social affairs, and development. This holds out the promise of a UN system whose effectiveness is truly enhanced as a result of interlinking human rights, development, and environment.

THE HUMAN RIGHT TO DEVELOPMENT

Commencing with the World Summit on Children, the United Nations has organized a series of world conferences in Rio (on environment and development), Vienna (on human rights and development), Cairo (on population and development), Copenhagen (the World Summit on Social Development), Beijing (on women and development), Istanbul (on habitat and development), and Rome (the World Food Summit) which have helped redefine development and clarify the relationships between human rights and development. This endeavor was long overdue.

Development, as it has come to be practiced over the past fifty years, has itself become a cause rather than a cure of human rights violations. In the name of development, indigenous peoples have been forcibly evicted from their ancestral domains and their resources plundered. Green Revolution agriculture has left a legacy of exhausted soil, chemically poisoned water, an erosion of biodiversity, and monocrops which are vulnerable to megablights. Reckless and ultra-hazardous industrialization is destroying the global environment—creating global climate change and damage to the Earth's ozone layer. It has also produced tragedies like Bhopal and Chernobyl in which thousands of lives have been lost and horribly mutilated across generations. Moreover, for too long, development has been equated with economic aggrandizement alone. Development has come to be about *having more and more* rather than about also *being more*. In such a situation, all too often the paradox has been proven that more may well be less and that, indeed, less may well be more in terms of environmental sustainability. The linkage between human rights to development has helped bring about a normative redefinition of development as sustainable human development. The very *raison d'etre* of development is promoting the well-being of the people and progressively realizing *all* human rights of *all*. Moreover, the human right to development, as detailed in a 1986 Declaration by the General Assembly and as reaffirmed in the series of UN global conferences during the 1990s, clearly affirms the fundamental human right of participation. Linking human rights to development is essential to ensure that no more will development displace people, destroy their communities and devastate their environment.

The human right to development, set out in the General Assembly Declaration mentioned above, reaffirms that development is an inalienable human right of every person and all peoples to exercise full and complete sovereignty over all their natural wealth and resources in pursuit of their economic, social, and cultural development.[3]

Development is defined as "a comprehensive economic, social, cultural and political process, which aims at the constant improvement of the well-being of the entire population and of all individuals . . . in which all human rights and fundamental freedoms can be fully realized."[4]

The human right to development includes several component rights:

- *Rights of Participation.* Every *person* and all *peoples* are entitled to "active, free and meaningful participation in development" (Preamble, DHRD) and as an "active participant" (Article 2, DHRD) to "*contribute* to, and *enjoy* economic, social cultural and political development (Article 1(1), DHRD).
- *The Right to be "the central subject of development"* (Article 20, DHRD) which constitutes the right to people-centered, human development where people and their well-being come first, ahead of *all* other developmental objectives and priorities.
- *The Right to "fair distribution of the benefits from development"* (Preamble, DHRD).
- *The Right to nondiscrimination in development* "without distinction of any kind such as race, color, sex, language, religion, political or other opinion, national or social origin, property, birth or other status" (Preamble, DHRD).
- *The Right to Self-Determination.* "The human right to development also implies the full realization of the right of peoples to self-determination, which includes . . . their inalienable right to full sovereignty over all their natural wealth and resources" (Article 1(2), DHRD).

---

[3] Preamble and Article 1 of the UN Declaration on the Right to Development (DHRD).

[4] Preamble and Article 1(1) of the UN Declaration on the Right to Development.

- *The Right to "the free and complete fulfillment of the human being"* with "full respect" for "human rights and fundamental freedoms" (Article 1(2), DHRD).
- *The Right against trade-offs. Every human person* and *all peoples* have the right to "the implementation, promotion and protection" of "all human rights and fundamental freedoms . . . civil, political, economic, social and cultural." (Article 6(2) and Preamble, DHRD). "The promotion of, respect for and enjoyment of certain human rights and fundamental freedoms cannot justify the denial of other human rights and fundamental freedoms." "All human rights and fundamental freedoms are indivisible and inter-dependent." (Preamble, DHRD).

The Declaration on the Right to Development also imposes several duties upon States:

- *The Duty "to ensure full exercise and progressive enhancement of the right to Development"* (Article 10, DHRD) which includes:
  - (i) *"the right and duty to formulate appropriate national development policies"* (Article 2(3), DHRD);
  - (ii) *the duty to "undertake, at the national level, all necessary measures* for the realization of the right to development" (Article 8(1), DHRD);
  - (iii) *the duty "for the creation of national conditions* favourable to the realization of the right to development" (Article 3(1), DHRD).
- *The Duty to ensure "active, free and meaningful participation"* (Article 2(3), DHRD) and to "encourage popular participation in all spheres as an important factor in development" (Article 8(2), DHRD).
- *The Duty not to discriminate* in development on the basis of "race, sex, language or religion" (Article 8(1), DHRD).
- *The Duty "to eliminate obstacles in development* resulting from failure to observe civil and political rights as well as economic, social and cultural rights" (Article 6(3), DHRD).
- *The Duty "to eliminate the massive and flagrant violations of the human rights* of people and human beings" (Article 5, DHRD) and to eradicate "all *social injustices"* (Article 8(1), DHRD).
- *The Duty of "promoting,* encouraging and strengthening *universal respect"* for all human rights and fundamental freedoms (Article 6(1), DHRD).

The human right to development, as set out in the 1986 UN Declaration detailed above, has been reaffirmed by consensus at UN global conferences in Vienna, Cairo, Copenhagen, and Beijing, as a *"universal and inalienable right and an integral part of fundamental human rights."* It has been accorded priority by the UN High Commissioner on Human Rights, the UN General Assembly and, most recently, the UN Commission on Human Rights.[5] It represents a global consensus on the relationship between human rights and development. It promises to usher in a new era of development cooperation on human rights bridging the traditional North-South divide that has, for too long, impeded effective realization of all human rights for all.

THE HUMAN RIGHT TO ENVIRONMENT

Environmental degradation very often leads to human rights violations. Similarly, human rights violations often lead to environmental degradation. There already exists[6] thousands of international environmental law instruments and yet the results are disappointing in terms of enforcement. There also exists a large number of international human rights law instruments along with an elaborate UN system of procedures and mechanisms for monitoring implementation of such laws and for documenting violations thereof. It is, therefore, unnecessary to debate whether there exists, in international law, the right to environment. More importantly, where environmental degradation results in human rights violations (e.g., of the right to life, to health, to livelihood), it is imperative that human rights norms and procedures be applied.

In 1989, the UN Sub-Commission on Prevention of Discrimination and Protection of Minorities initiated a study on human rights and the environment. In 1991, the UN Commission on Human Rights endorsed the appointment by the Sub-Commission of a Special Rapporteur on Human Rights and the Environment. The Rapporteur, Ms. Fatma Zohra Ksentini, submitted a series of reports culminating in a final report in 1994 which detailed the many interlinkages between human rights and the environment. Drawing upon these reports, a group of international law experts on human rights and environment produced a *Draft Declaration of Principles on Human Rights and the Environment* which sets out the legal framework for a holistic human rights-based approach to environmental protection and which is annexed to the final report of Special Rapporteur Ksentini. Key aspects of the *Draft Declaration* bear highlighting:

- All persons have the right to a secure, healthy, and ecologically sound environment.
- All persons are entitled to be free from discrimination regarding actions and decisions that affect the environment.

---

[5] See, for example, the Oxford address of the High Commissioner supra note 2, UN General Assembly resolution 52/135 of 12 December 1997 and Commission on Human Rights Resolution 1998/72.

[6] For a review, see A. Kiss and D. Shelton, *International Environmental Law,* Transnational Publications Inc., Graham and Trotman Publishers, New York (1991) and B. Ruster and B. Simina, *International Protection of the Environment (2nd series, 1994).*

- All persons have the right to an environment adequate to meet equitably the needs of present generations without impairing the similar right of future generations.
- All persons have the right to freedom from pollution and environmental degradation that threaten life, health, livelihood, and well-being within, across, or outside national boundaries.
- All persons have the right to information concerning the environment.
- All persons have the right to active, free, and meaningful participation in planning and decision-making activities that impact on the environment including the right to a prior assessment of environmental impacts of proposed developmental actions.

The pioneering and timely work of the Special Rapporteur on Human Rights and the Environment has paved the way for the UN system, its member states, and for "we the peoples of the United Nations" to address, meaningfully, the inter-linkages between human rights, development, and the environment.

OUR COMMON FUTURE

Today we are witnessing a so-called paradigm shift from *development through aid* to *development through trade and investment.* Such a shift has serious environmental and human rights implications evident today, for example, in the newly and rapidly industrializing provinces of China. The New World Order panacea of globalization, trade, and economic liberalization, privatization, and deregulation is converting development into a process of social Darwinism: producing hordes of development victims and development displaced persons and growing numbers of marginalized peoples whose very rights of subsistence are being denied existence. Now, more than ever, there is an urgent need for advocacy efforts around human rights, development, and environment to break the vicious cycle of poverty and powerlessness, and replace it with a much-needed cycle of empowerment.

Moreover, Copenhagen (and the World Summit on Social Development) was just the first stop for the Global Express on its headlong rush toward privatization, free trade, and free markets: *free* for the licentiousness of multinational and national corporations. Corporations are to be the new vehicles of social development. Their expanded role will inevitably result in increased impacts, both on human rights and the environment. It is an urgent priority, therefore, that multi-national and national corporations be held strictly accountable to the standards of international human rights law. What is at stake, here, is that most precious of all human rights: the right to be human. What is at stake, here is, indeed, our common future.

Chapter 29

Changing Forces and Non-State Actors in the Struggle for Human Rights

Russel Lawrence Barsh

By making UN Member States accountable for their treatment of individuals, the post-1945 framework for achieving universal respect for human rights was a break with the past. International law had previously been concerned chiefly with the behavior of States toward other States. But in other ways, the UN approach to human rights remained enslaved to pre-war realities. Nowhere is this more evident than in the key assumption of human rights conventions and machinery that States are the principal violators and (paradoxically) chief defenders of human rights.

The old European club of strong imperial States had already begun to disintegrate by 1919, when the Versailles Peace Treaty created both the League of Nations and the International Labour Organisation (ILO). The ILO reflected new conditions associated with the globalization of capital and mass organization of labor. Its constitution refers to three "social partners"—labor, employers, and government—and accords official standing and voting power to each of them. This recognizes that the protection of workers' freedom, health, and safety could only be achieved fully by engaging the cooperation of non-governmental actors in legislation and implementation. The architects of the ILO constitution appreciated the fact that real power in the new, highly industrialized world would be accumulated in the hands of capital—and that governments would be powerless to protect their citizens without the support of capital, or labor, or (ideally) both.

Any remaining illusion of preeminent State power should have been dashed by the worldwide depression of the 1920s-1930s, that States proved powerless to manage. The subsequent establishment of the Bretton Woods system—the World Bank and the International Monetary Fund—reflected the conclusion of powerful European and North American States that they could not ensure the stability of their own societies without the support of global bankers capable of counter-balancing the movements of private capital. The recent catastrophic collapses of southeast Asian currencies, preceded by the collapse of the Mexican peso, provide evidence of growing power and instability of private financial markets. Devaluations can lead to the severe hardships, unrest, and political volatility that the founders of the Bretton Woods system blamed for the rise of Nazism in the 1920s.

Contemporary initiatives to promote global capital mobility and trade liberalization through the World Trade Organization and regional free-trade blocs have their origins in the GATT, another product of the strategic rethinking of global economic relations which began in the 1940s. Western political and busi-ness leaders had foreseen a post-war era dominated by the ideological struggle between capitalism and communism—and that the ultimate weapon of capitalism would be the accumulation of wealth and the visibility of public prosperity within the West. This could be accomplished through the promotion of trade, investment, and growth within the West, and between the West and the South. One significant result of the promotion of trade has naturally been growth in the power and mobility of corporations.

The United Nations Charter does not reflect these important changes in the structure of world power. It relies on States to make decisions and, on the whole, to implement them. The United Nations' economic role was restricted to mobiliz-ing economic aid through cooperation among States. Economic regulatory func-tions were left to the Bretton Woods system and GATT, neither of which was effectively bound to respect the decisions of the UN General Assembly. While NGOs were given an important foothold by the consultative provisions of the Charter, the Charter's drafters were thinking solely of humanitarian relief agencies such as the International Committee of the Red Cross, and scientific bodies. Members States were seeking technical advice and assistance with aid programs, not sharing power with what they perceived to be a new class of powerful actors on the world stage.

Were the original UN Member States so myopic? The UN system was designed by the same States that had built the Bretton Woods system and GATT as well as the ILO. They realized that the rise of Nazism has been facilitated by debt, severe inflation, labor unrest, unemployment, and depression in post-1918 Germany. They believed that international security in the future would depend as much on economic stability as upon the rule of law and social justice. Hence the separation of functions between the UN and international economic institutions was deliberate, and it had the effect of insulating the governance of world capitalism from the ideological struggles and social policy concerns that world leaders expected to preoccupy the UN. An unfortunate consequence of this separation of functions has been a gradual erosion of the ability of the UN to achieve its Charter aims in the field of human rights.

While UN Member States engaged in endless sterile debates about the inter-dependence of all human rights, and about whether economic well-being is a "right" or a social goal, there was a widening gap between the work of the UN and the activities of international economic institutions. The "Debt Crisis" of the 1970s, and subsequent controversy over the structural adjustment policies of the IMF, put the two complementary global governance systems into direct conflict. Human rights hung in the balance. Debt and structural adjustment were clearly causing hardship and suffering among the poorest sectors of society. It was debatable whether human rights would be fostered in the long term or merely sacrificed in the short term.

Industrialization in the South meanwhile led to increasingly disruptive externally-assisted development projects, resulting in new forms of poverty, disorder, and grassroots resistance, as well as a growing concentration of wealth in the hands of new national entrepreneurial elites. The accumulation of power in the private sector outstripped the institutional development of the State and civil society in many countries.

It must also be acknowledged that the Cold War itself led to the rapid build-up of military technology and power in the South, as the West and the East positioned themselves in strategic areas and promoted proxy wars. Militarization increased the potential for oppression by strong States. In weak States, militariza-tion simply created new centers of oppressive power outside the State, or loosely affiliated with some elements of State leadership.

Thus, the tools of international cooperation and ideological competition— macroeconomic policies, aid, trade, investment, and military assistance— combined to strengthen non-State actors such as transnational corporations, national entrepreneurs, and paramilitary groups. In weak States, the capacity of non-State actors to abuse human rights with relative impunity was enhanced considerably. The State itself nonetheless remained the main target of the UN human-rights machinery.

WORLD POWER IN THE NEW CENTURY

The unravelling of the Soviet Union in 1991 brought an end to East-West ideological rivalry. New political polarities have begun to emerge, however, creating a challenging environment for the implementation of human-rights instruments in the coming century.

In the UN context, two reorientations can be identified. In ideological terms, the East-West confrontation has been replaced by a North-South debate over global economic equity. In terms of global governance, the United Nations has moved from an East-West bipolarity, to a temporary American unipolarity.

Trade integration will eventually restore a kind of weak bipolarity to world politics, as two major trading blocs emerge: a European-Western Asian bloc centered in the European Community, and a Pacific Rim bloc dominated by the United States and Japan. The absorption of large industrializing countries such as China, Indonesia, Brazil, and Mexico into these two trade blocs foresees the lessening of North-South tensions. Thus, while there may be a new Europe-Pacific bipolarity, it will play itself out within the context of a shared free-market ideology. Russia and China will undoubtedly continue to undergo major economic and social upheavals, but each is already aligned aspirationally with either the European or Pacific trade blocs.

As the framework of the global balance of power shifts from ideological contests to trade competition, governments will shift their political loyalties from the United Nations system to trade fora such as the World Trade Organization and regional free-trade bodies. As European and American strategic priorities shift from avoiding global nuclear war and managing conventional proxy wars to creating a favorable climate for trade (including intervening in local conflicts wherever they threaten trade), support for the United Nations will weaken and the role of the United Nations will be seen increasingly as promoting political stability rather than investing in social and economic justice.

The rising influence of trade institutions is accompanied by a growing role of corporations in international negotiations—not only indirectly by advising and influencing governments, but also as official participants, for instance as members of the business advisory council of the Asia-Pacific Economic Co-operation (APEC) process. It is plausible that industry will enjoy a consultative and informal negotiating role in trade fora parallel to the role that NGOs have won in ECOSOC bodies and global UN conferences.

Assuming that the trend toward global trade liberalization persists, the role of corporations as actors on the national and international stages will continue to grow, and may eclipse the power of governments. In the proposed Multilateral Agreement on Investments (MAI), corporations are seeking standing to challenge national laws directly at international trade tribunals. In many countries, moreover, transnational corporations already enjoy, or will likely enjoy in the future, greater political influence than governments through the use of their job-creating and advertising capability.

Greater mobility and economic power for corporations creates greater potential for abuses, and greater likelihood of impunity. Corporations' activities can have sweeping ecological, social, and cultural impacts on host countries, leading to changes in health, redistributions of income and power, and even internal migration. At the same time, corporations can respond to government pressure by mobilizing their employees politically, shaping public opinion through the mass media, influencing government officials directly through financial contributions, rewarding governments indirectly through investment decisions—or punishing governments by means of disinvestment. Faced by a resolute government or intransigent adverse public opinion, corporations can exit and re-invest where the climate is more hospitable.

The illusion of strong governments nevertheless persists in UN debates on human rights. This may be partly due to the fact that a few of the old Great Powers have survived, and continue to project themselves economically and militarily into other regions of the world. It may also reflect an awareness that many of the evils in our world are being perpetrated by groups acting in the name (but not necessarily under the control) of States, such as national armies, security forces, and paramilitary groups.

NEW TOOLS FOR HUMAN RIGHTS

Industry will overtake the State as a focus of human-rights concerns, while gradually freeing itself from State control. UN machinery directed at States will become less effective, because the power of States to control the private sector will gradually erode. Human-rights advocates must seek alternative tools that are capable of applying direct, effective pressure directly on corporations, and they must recognize the possibility that the UN system may not be the most effective institution to wield those tools.

Conceptually, the simplest approach to the task of reaching new, non-State actors is somehow to include them within existing human-rights instruments and machinery. It could be argued, for example, that corporations are responsible for observing existing human-rights treaties where they are "citizens" of State Parties. This would be analogous to the practice of the ILO to regard trade unions and industry associations as "social partners" with the State. As such, trade unions and industry are both entitled to participate in drafting new standards, and bound to cooperate in implementing those standards after they have been ratified by States.

It could also be argued that every individual citizen of the State, including corporate owners and managers, is bound by the States' treaty obligations to respect human rights. Only one UN human-rights instrument, the 1948 UN Convention on the Prevention and Punishment of the Crime of Genocide, expressly imposes duties on individual citizens, however.

During the Cold War, UN Member States were polarized on the question of individual responsibility. Some governments tried to deflect criticism of their human-rights records by stressing the duty of citizens to respect State authority. The West responded by focussing UN attention on individual's right to dissent. With the end of the Cold War, it may now be possible to speak not only of the individual's right to dissent, but of individual liability for contributing to abuses of human rights, in the spirit of the Nuremburg Principles.

In the West, at least, there has been a renewed interest in the establishment of an international criminal court. Thus far, this revived mechanism has been used selectively, in the form of ad hoc tribunals for Rwanda and the former Yugoslavia limited to "crimes against humanity" as defined by the Genocide Convention and four Geneva Conventions. People in the South might look more favorably on the establishment of an international criminal court if the corporate executives responsible for disasters such as Bhopal could be prosecuted and punished for poisoning civilians in the same manner as soldiers who shot civilians. It might also be useful to give national courts transboundary jurisdiction over rights-abusers based on the precedent of the Genocide Convention. The United States has already adopted this principle to a limited extent in its municipal law.

Ultimately, we must all grasp the reality that violations of human rights are committed by individual people, whether they act behind the institutional mask of a State, a private corporation, or an ethnic or political movement. The most comprehensive means of reaching non-State actors is to reach individuals, regardless of their institutional disguises. This is especially true in the case of corporations, which can shield their decision makers from "pain" by shifting the costs of compliance and penalties to their employees and customers. Paying penalties for abusing individual human rights could simply become another "cost of doing business" unless managers face the risk of personal consequences. Indeed, national courts in the West have imposed penalties on individual corporate executives in a growing number of cases involving death or serious injuries.

There is one other potential lever of accountability against corporations: a direct attack, under international trade law, on the ability of corporations to profit from the violation of human rights. Under current conceptions of free and fair trade, States must accord equal treatment to all producers and their products, irrespective of nationality. States cannot discriminate against a foreign firm, nor subsidize a domestic firm such that it gains a competitive advantage at home or abroad. Subsidies may take a number of different forms, from cash grants and tax relief to the use of government facilities or prison labor. Any exporter that relies on such means to undersell its competitors is guilty of an unfair trade practice (dumping). Allegations of dumping can lead to a trade-dispute panel which, if satisfied of the truth of the complaint, can award compensation and authorize retaliatory trade actions such as punitive tariffs.

One drawback is *standing* to invoke trade-dispute mechanisms. The official participants in trade disputes are States, acting on behalf of industry groups or corporations. As indicated earlier, however, corporations are seeking standing to bring complaints against governments under the MAI, and this may open the door to the recognition of corporate liability as defendants. Motivated by narrow self-interest, moreover, corporations may be more aggressive than States in challenging unfair trade practices. States avoid pressing human rights issues with key military partners, for example, or with countries with which they enjoy a large favorable balance of trade. Corporations directly affected by dumping would be inclined to pursue their complaints without regard to governments' wider strategic aims.

Some human rights violations lend themselves readily to this approach, including any involuntary, inadequately compensated, or hazardous labor, or the exploitation of a minority or indigenous people, or other kinds of discrimination which have the effect of reducing the cost of export production. Inadequate protection of public health and safety in the design of products and production processes also lends itself to trade action. It is possible (but difficult) to make a case for dumping in the suppression of civil and political rights, such as freedom of speech and assembly, where there are effects on unionization, or on corporate accountability for the health and safety of workers and the public. The precise nature of the abuse is not as important as evidence that there is an effect on the pricing of exports.

The use of trade mechanisms to hold corporations accountable for violating human rights, or for profitable collaborations with repressive regimes, recalls international efforts in the 1970s to combat *apartheid* by boycotting corporations for doing business in South Africa. The most effective boycotts were highly selective, targeting firms that were demonstrably benefiting from *apartheid* by enjoying cheap, unorganized, intimidated labor. The approach suggested here would differ in two respects. Complaints would be directed at individual firms or specific industries, and would be based on evidence that they were reaping an unfair advantage from abuses of human rights—not merely doing business in a repressive country. Successful complaints would not necessarily result in a complete exclusion of target companies' exports, moreover, trade panels would be more likely to recommend a countervailing tariff as a remedy. Such a tariff, equal to the cost advantage enjoyed by the target companies, would be tantamount to a tax on abusers of human rights.

Recalling the history of the long struggle against *apartheid* reminds us that one of the most powerful weapons of human-rights defenders against corporations can be "consumer exit"—consumers' purchasing decisions. Consumers can be mobilized to boycott the products of rights-abusers, or—perhaps a more fruitful idea for the next century—selectively choosing the products of firms that can be certified as rights-respecters. The latter tool has been adopted by many international environmental NGOs, for instance, in the campaign to eliminate the use of extremely long drift nets on the high seas. Labeling brands of canned tuna as "dolphin safe" quickly disciplined non-conforming corporations economically, and facilitated the adoption of a moratorium on the use of drift nets by the UN General Assembly. We might envisage some future use of "human-safe" labels such as "not produced with child labor."

The main difficulty with certification schemes is agreeing on some credible, independent body to establish valid standards and do the certifying. Collaboration between NGOs and industry associations might prove the best solution, judging from recent experience with environmental certification.

If the next century is indeed an era of free trade, growing corporate power, and the primacy of trade law, then advocates for human rights must address the extent to which corporations can be made directly responsible for respecting the principles contained in the Universal Declaration of Human Rights. We must recognize that the same global changes which are augmenting corporate power are weakening States, and creating a new generation of relatively strong international trade and financial institutions. The best course of action is to abandon the illusion of strong States, and find ways of importing human-rights standards into the new arenas of world power: trade regulation and consumer choice.

Chapter 30

The Poorest Teach Us the Indivisibility of Human Rights

Alwine A. de Vos van Steenwijk

Mr. and Mrs. Simon are traditionally members of the nomadic population. However, as a result of their poverty, they no longer travel. Currently, they live with their children, ranging in age from five to twelve, and an elderly uncle, in two trailers set up at the end of a road, surrounded by woods and cultivated fields in the vicinity of several other families.

They have been camping there for three and a half years, after having lived for twenty-seven years in a trailer in a large urban center in the same department.[1] Five or six years ago, they were put under a great deal of pressure by local authorities who urged them to move into a trailer park. Mr. Simon refused because in the park he would have been prohibited from carrying on his activities as a scrap-metal dealer. Following this refusal, the family was chased out of its home by the police. Later, they were once again forced off another property they had managed to rent. They felt branded as outcasts everywhere. They made up their minds to seek a hiding place in the deserted area where they currently live, in the hope of not having to endure any more evictions.

So great is their fear of "being reported to the authorities" that they avoid, as much as possible, contacts with institutions and even with neighbors. This is why their children do not attend school, and their only address is a Post Office box.

Mr. Simon has managed to obtain the minimum social integration income.[2] This income comes with an obligation to accept all proposals for job training or placement that aim to promote the social integration of recipients. Mr. Simon

---

[1] Political and administrative units into which the French Republic is divided.

[2] In 1988, France included a *revenu minimum d'insertion* (RMI) to the country's social welfare programme. The RMI is an income that guarantees the poor a minimum standard of subsistence.

does not believe that he could feel comfortable in these training sessions. Now thirty-five years old, he feels that he can continue earning his living from salvaging scrap-metal. The vehicle he uses is no longer fit to transport water, let alone scrap metal. However, he has no choice.

The Simon family represents millions of households found in all industrialized countries and, in different proportions, in developing countries. They represent family groups and individuals who live in old flats, streets, and neighborhoods; in dilapidated housing projects and clusters of makeshift dwellings. In such places, insecurities are cumulative: lack of income, unemployment, substandard education and training, lack of professional qualification, and poor health due to the impossibility of hygiene and lack of medical care. It is within these human groups that the whole set of social, economic, and cultural rights are endangered.

The International Movement ATD Fourth World was founded in 1957 by Father Joseph Wresinski, who was himself born into an impoverished household in Angers, France, in 1917. In 1956, at his bishop's request, Father Joseph went to live in an emergency camp for the homeless on the outskirts of Paris. Observing what he called "collective extreme poverty," he concluded that "those people would never escape as long as they were not welcomed as a whole, as a people, in those places where other people held debates or led struggles. They had to be there, on equal terms, in all places where people discuss and make decisions, not only about the present, but also about people's destiny and the future of humanity" [1]. It was in this camp, with the families living there, that Father Joseph laid the foundations of an international movement committed over the long-term alongside the poorest families to asserting their dignity and their rights. The goal of this movement was, as the Heads of State and Government throughout the world were to promise in March 1995 at the World Summit for Social Development in Copenhagen, to "exercise the rights, utilise the resources and share the responsibilities that enable them to lead satisfying lives and to contribute to the well-being of their families, their communities and humankind."[3]

The International Movement ATD Fourth World has been at the forefront of NGO and governmental activity in support of the poor in developed countries. Very poor families in Europe insisted that ATD Fourth World permanent volunteers be present wherever extreme poverty exists in the world. Thanks to these families, ATD Fourth World began working alongside very poor families throughout the world.

In 1985, awareness was growing of the persistence of poverty and even of the emergence of what some called "new poverty" caused by the evolution of the

---

[3] United Nations. *World Summit for Social Development 6-12 March 1995*. Copenhagen Declaration on Social Development, paragraph 9. New York: United Nations Department of Public Information, 1995.

economic crisis. This led to Father Joseph Wresinski's appointment as Rapporteur of the French Economic and Social Council on chronic poverty and lack of basic security. Between 1985 and 1987, the Council embarked on an in-depth exploration of the flagrant violations of human rights endured by the poorest families. In its Policy Statement and Report in February 1987, the Council offered the following definition:

> A lack of basic security is the absence of one or more factors that enable individuals and families to assume basic responsibilities and to enjoy fundamental rights. Such a situation may become more extended and lead to more serious and permanent consequences. Chronic poverty results when the lack of basic security simultaneously affects several aspects of people's lives, when it is prolonged and when it severely compromises their chances of regaining their rights and of reassuming their responsibilities in the foreseeable future [2].

Speaking to the UN Commission on Human Rights later that same year, Father Wresinski stressed "the interdependence that exists between liberties, civil and political rights, and economic, social and cultural ones. Without basic security, liberty is jeopardised. At the same time, when liberties are not exercised, basic security is not guaranteed." On the basis of this observation, he asked that a study be undertaken "in the context of the interdependence and the indivisibility of civil, cultural, economic, political and social rights, examining the manner in which human groups living in a situation of extreme poverty in industrialized and in developing countries can indeed enjoy these rights and exercise the responsibilities that are granted them."[4]

After the death of Father Wresinski in February 1988, his cause was taken up by a number of governments, with Leandro Despouy, then the Ambassador of Argentina to the United Nations, circulating a draft resolution. However, due to pressure from Western countries and the reticence of some developing countries, the draft was withdrawn.

It is necessary to recall that in 1988 international policy was still characterized by East-West tension and political blocs. This appeared in the area of human rights through a confrontation over the pre-eminence of one category of rights over another. Eastern bloc countries deemed it essential to guarantee the enjoyment of economic, social, and cultural rights before civil and political rights could be implemented. Western bloc countries insisted that the establishment of representative governments, ensuring the full enjoyment of civil and political rights, was an indispensable prerequisite for the achievement of economic, social, and cultural rights. Therefore, the assertion that extreme poverty constitutes a

---

[4] Father Joseph Wresinski's speech on 20 February 1987 addressing the Commission on Human Rights in Geneva.

violation of all human rights jeopardized the Western theory that priority be accorded to civil and political rights.

At the same time, some developing countries—without denying that extreme poverty affects the enjoyment of human rights—feared that a resolution confirming this would turn against them, adding one more argument to the attacks of which they felt themselves victims in the area of civil and political rights. Alone and opposed in many respects, Argentina withdrew its project, but its contribution at least kept the issue in people's minds.

In 1989, France took up this theme. Joining forces with Argentina, it submitted a draft resolution. There were many reservations to overcome. First of all, it was necessary to reassure developing countries that under no circumstance would such a resolution aggravate the attacks of which they were already the targets in the area of human rights. As for Western countries, it was necessary to leave behind the ideological debate over the hierarchy of human rights. Eastern bloc countries, on account of the emphasis on economic, social, and cultural rights, agreed to back the resolution. The Soviet Union became its co-author, a fact that did not improve the mood of many Western countries.

The resolution was finally adopted by consensus, without being put to a vote. Several states, especially the United States and Japan, expressed their deep scepticism about this approach. During the debate, they indicated that, in their opinion, extreme poverty should not be treated within human rights bodies because it is purely an economic and social issue. Various Western countries held this critical attitude for several years. It frequently resurfaces, as it did recently in a debate over the European Parliament's 1996 annual report on respect of human rights in the European Union. This caused a split within the Parliament as to whether a chapter about poverty should be included in the report.

THE SPECIAL RAPPORTEUR'S MANDATE

Year after year, by overcoming various obstacles, by adopting resolutions, always by consensus, and by mobilizing more and more countries, the sponsors of this project, among whom France continues to play a central role, succeeded in defining a framework for the study. In resolution 1990/15, the Commission on Human Rights requested the Sub-Commission on Prevention of Discrimination and Protection of Minorities to examine extreme poverty and social exclusion. In resolution 1992/27, the Sub-Commission appointed Mr. Leandro Despouy as the Special Rapporteur for the study entitled, "Human rights and extreme poverty."[5]

---

[5] See also General Assembly resolutions 49/179 (1994); 51/97 (1996); ECOSOC resolutions 1993/13; 1993/44; Commission on Human Rights resolutions 1989/10; 1991/14; 1992/11; 1993/13; 1994/12; 1995/16; 1996/10; 1997/11, and Sub-Commission on Prevention of Discrimination and Protection of Minorities resolutions 1992/27; 1993/35; 1994/41; 1995/28; 1996/23.

His tasks were to:

> Take advantage of the experience and the thinking of the poorest and those
> committed to their defence in order to make extreme poverty a better-known
> phenomenon; bring to the public eye the efforts the very poor make in order
> to be able to exercise their rights and participate fully in the development of
> the society in which they live; and enhance the conditions enabling such
> persons to become partners in the realization of human rights.

Over the years, several events contributed to and served as guidelines
for the Special Rapporteur's work: the International Year of the Family in
1994; the World Summit for Social Development held in Copenhagen in March
1995; and the seminar *Extreme Poverty, Denial of Human Rights* that took
place in New York in October 1994 as a result of cooperation between the UN
Centre for Human Rights and the International Movement ATD Fourth World.
For the first time in the history of the United Nations, this seminar brought
together individuals living in extreme poverty and international human rights
experts.

The Special Rapporteur submitted to the Commission and the Sub-Commission a preliminary report and two interim reports, as well as a report on the
seminar, *Extreme Poverty, Denial of Human Rights,* before presenting his final
report to the Sub-Commission in August 1996 and to the Commission in March-
April 1997.[6]

The main feature of this report lies in the manner in which it was written: in
close partnership with the population under consideration, the victims of extreme
poverty and social exclusion. Relying on non-governmental organizations that
have long-term, grassroots commitments to these population groups, the Special
Rapporteur did his utmost to include in his report and draw recommendations
from their points of view, thinking, and analyses. A questionnaire was sent to
States, intergovernmental organizations, and non-governmental organizations. He
studied family monographs[7] outlining the history of very poor families, from
around the world, over several generations as well as testimonies published in the
Fourth World Human Rights Chronicles [3]. Direct consultations and dialogue
took place during both the seminar *Extreme Poverty, Denial of Human Rights* and
People's Universities.[8]

---

[6] See documents E/CN.4/sub 2/1993/16; 1994/19; 1995/15; 1995/101; and 1996/13.

[7] The Special Rapporteur referred to the monographs of families from four continents published in
This is How We Live—Listening to the Poorest Families (Fourth World Publications, Landover, MD,
U.S.A., 1995), translated from the original French *Est-ce ainsi que des familles vivent?* This study was
published on the occasion of the International Year of the Family.

[8] Fourth World People's Universities bring together adults living in extreme poverty with other
members of society in order to share experiences, learn more about extreme poverty, provoke a
dialogue, and create partnerships.

His report observed that when people living in extreme poverty are told about human rights, they say: "This is not for us." However, the very poor endowed with and entitled to human rights and, by virtue of their resistance to hardship, they are elevated de facto to the rank of defenders of human rights.

The report studies three fundamental principles of human rights and twelve specific rights. For each one, it refers to the international texts at the foundation of these rights. It analyzes them in the light of examples taken from the experience of the poorest, illustrating to what extent general principles and specific rights are constantly transgressed at the bottom of the social ladder.

The tree fundamental principles which frame the set of texts that are the foundation of human rights are:

— **The equal dignity of all human beings:** "It is not right that we are treated like this—we are human beings, after all," very poor people often say. "We feel as though we are dogs. But the dog kennels in the center of town have water and electricity, and we do not. This is really an injustice." These affronts to dignity follow people living in extreme poverty to the very end of their lives. A volunteer working closely with a family living in a shantytown in Latin America witnessed a woman who had illicitly taken in her sick brother who was discharged from the hospital. Upon finding out that the man was dying, the landlord threatened eviction unless he was taken out into the street at night so that he would not have to pay for moving the body. The "unknown person" found dead in the street was buried anonymously. Such situations are so revealing of extreme poverty that the United Nations Development Programme (UNDP) has included among its indicators the inability of poor people to provide their dead with a decent funeral.

— **The principle of equality and non-discrimination:** according to the report, the "principle of free movement of persons within the European Union expressly excludes those who cannot prove they have sufficient means not to require assistance by the host country." A poor couple, each born in a different country within the European Union, illustrates this. Following the couple's marriage, the woman changed her nationality to that of her husband. Twenty years later, they divorced and the woman decided to return to her native country with her seven children. Having few resources, they eventually found themselves living in the streets. In desperation, the mother applied for social assistance. Since she was no longer a citizen of her country of birth, she was not entitled to the social assistance income. In addition, they were threatened with deportation. She filed a petition with the European Parliament which decided that the right to free movement within the European Union did not apply to her because she was neither a salaried worker, nor a student, nor a retiree, nor financially independent. Ironically enough, due to changes in the national legislation, the mother was later entitled to social assistance even though she did not have the right to remain in the country.[9]

— A concatenation of misfortunes demonstrates **the indivisibility and interdependence of human rights:** one Latin American participant in the seminar *Extreme Poverty, Denial of Human Rights* testified: "Without shelter, drinking water, electricity, adequate food, work, a minimum income, or other resources, one simply cannot conceive of living a life in good health, having one's children go to school, participating in local activities, including annual festivities or even birthday parties, participating in any political process as citizens or even having one's family life respected."

Reviewing twelve specific rights, the Special Rapporteur compared extreme poverty to apartheid or slavery. In his opinion, each of these situations involves a denial of human rights: there are individuals who are no longer regarded as human beings. "Poverty is the new face of apartheid," President Nelson Mandela declared during the World Summit for Social Development at Copenhagen.

We must, therefore, reach a new awareness of extreme poverty by changing our outlook, understanding, rising above prejudice and accusation, and learning the right way to react. "The rich have drawn a curtain over the poor, and on it they have painted monsters," wrote English sociologist Charles Booth at the end of the nineteenth century. It is essential to support the daily efforts of the extremely poor. Their acts reveal a fighting spirit, albeit one that results in small achievements, occasional triumphs, and many defeats. We should foster trust and mutual understanding, and accept the poorest as partners. We should be determined to reach them and to constantly to take up the search for all who are absent, all who are left behind. Only in this way will we attain a development that excludes no one. "Only as they rediscover their full range of rights and responsibilities shall we see emerging in all their splendour the human beings behind the poverty-scarred faces," wrote Leandro Despouy, before presenting a series of recommendations to international agencies and Member States of the United Nations.

In this year, 1998, we commemorate the fiftieth anniversary of the Universal Declaration of Human Rights by rallying around the theme "All Human Rights for All," which recalls the theme of the gathering celebrating the 25th anniversary of ATD Fourth World: "Full Rights for All." The Commission on Human Rights has made new commitments as a consequence of the Despouy Report. By

---

[9] See petition 240/1991 submitted to the European Parliament by Mrs. C. Lepied.

requesting that the High Commissioner on Human Rights give priority to the issue of human rights and extreme poverty, it asked her to ensure that this issue be on the agenda: of the evaluation session of the World Conference on Human Rights ('Vienna + 5'), of the half-way point evaluation of commitments made during the World Summit for Social Development ('Copenhagen + 5'); and throughout the International Decade for the Eradication of Poverty. Furthermore, the Commission decided to appoint an independent expert who will make a substantial contribution to these evaluations and activities and prepare, if need be, a Declaration on Human Rights and Extreme Poverty.

In April 1996, the Council of Europe adopted a revised version of the European Social Charter providing in its new article 30 a right to protection against the threat of poverty, and in its article 31 a right to housing.[10] At the same time, it paved the way for an improved system for monitoring commitments made by States that have signed the Social Charter through a collective complaints procedure which is open to NGOs enjoying consultative status with the Council of Europe.

It is, after all, in the "International Day for the Eradication of Poverty" that the message of Father Wresinksi and the poorest around the world is completely fulfilled. This day was established on October 17, 1987, and was recognized officially by the General Assembly of the United Nations in December 1992. The Commemorative Stone in Honour of Victims of Extreme Poverty affirms the dignity of victims of human misery, hunger, violence, and ignorance. It was inaugurated in October 1987, on the Plaza of Human Rights and Liberties, the Trocadero Plaza, in Paris. Replicas have been laid throughout the world—among them in October 1996 at the United Nations' headquarters in New York. All those who come together around the Commemorative Stone or one of its replicas, on October 17th of each year and the 17th of each month, invite us to join them in proclaiming:

"Wherever men and women are condemned to live in extreme poverty,
human rights are violated.
To come together to ensure that these rights be respected
is our solemn duty.
Father Joseph Wresinski."

---

[10]Council of Europe. Directorate of Human Rights. European Treaties Series, n° 163 and 158.

REFERENCES

1. J. Wresinski, *Les Pauvres sont l'Eglise* [translation from the original French], Entretiens avec Gilles Anouil, Collection Les Interviews, Editions Le Centurion, Paris, 1983.
2. French Economic and Social Council, *Chronic Poverty and Lack of Basic Security (Grande pauvreté et précarité économique et sociale),* Rapporteur J. Wresinski (trans.), NEW/Fourth World Movement, Fourth World Publications, Landover, Maryland, 1994.
3. International Movement ATD Fourth World, *Fourth World Chronicle of Human Rights,* Editions Quart Monde, Paris, 1989, 1990-1991. (A 1993 edition exists in French, *Cahiers du Quart Monde-Oser la paix!*)

Voices

Is this America?
The New Freedom Bus Travels
the Country

Cheri Honkala

She laid the blanket down, folding and tucking the corners of the light blue comforter turned brown. Tonight her son will lie beneath the stars again, but she felt relief knowing that it would not rain tonight. Crouched on her milk crate she began her nightly lookout role, entertaining her mind with dreams of a better tomorrow in order to endure another cold, sleepless night being homeless in America.

Ms. Betty had worked hard all her life. Now in the late days of her life she was raising a child again. Each morning she would rise and feed her granddaughter a bowl of cereal, bathe her, and get her dressed. Yet even this joy would be taken from Ms. Betty. You see, there was a house fire and her granddaughter was taken by "child protection" because Betty and the child, unable to find affordable housing, were living in the half burned house.

She watches the snow as it covers the front sidewalk of her little row house on Mercer Street and then instructs her children to go get ready for baths; little Charlie drips with chocolate syrup covering him head to toe. She makes her way upstairs knowing what she must do. The children have gone too long without a bath and she must not put it off—not even for one day. As she grabs Billy, the youngest, and places him in the tub, they joke and giggle as she turns on the faucet and tilts him back to wash his hair, then within seconds, the cold pierces his entire body. The howl he lets out is so deep. Tears run like water off his little cheeks. Her entire body is now needed to restrain him as he kicks and cries. In the dead of winter with no gas to heat the house she must find the strength to bathe her four children with no hot water.

This is America. Where people suffer from unemployment, hunger, and homelessness in an affluent country. Where some people have the choice to lay their children down in any of several houses and other children are laid down to sleep beneath a bridge. These are the roads that lead to the New Freedom Bus traveling across America, documenting economic human rights violations caused by welfare reform. For over sixty years our country has had a safety net; today it is being totally eliminated. We filled this bus with poor and homeless people from across the United States who have become today's freedom fighters. We are bound and determined to speak and fight for ourselves. We are stopping in over thirty cities across the country this month. From the North to the South, East to West, urban to rural we are collecting the stories of how poor people like us are hurting in America, and we are committed to telling their stories to the world. On July first, we marched to the United Nations, demanding an end to the human rights violations in the United States.

We commemorate the 50th Anniversary of the Universal Declaration of Human Rights by committing ourselves to teaching everyone about their basic human rights and by making known the economic human rights violations occurring in this country. Through this activity we are building a movement for true freedom from unemployment, hunger, and homelessness.

Epilogue

Addressing the Gap Between Rhetoric and Reality

Mary Robinson
United Nations High Commissioner
for Human Rights

At this year's Commission on Human Rights there was a rare moment of hope, a moment of unity and common purpose as the fifty-three member governments agreed on the text of a declaration on human rights defenders and sent it for formal adoption on Human Rights Day 1998.

We were all very pleased: there was a feeling that we were making a difference, there in the vast meeting rooms of Geneva's *Palais des Nations,* that somehow the world would be a safer place for those who stand up for human dignity. The feeling didn't last for long. On 18 April, gunmen posing as a television crew murdered Eduardo Umaña Mendoza in his office in Colombia. Mr. Umaña was one of his tortured country's most prominent human rights defenders. The reasons for his death could be guessed from his list of clients: guerrilla leaders, indigenous people, trade unionists, and the families of the "disappeared."

Shortly after the Commission ended, Guatemala's Monsignor Juan Gerardi Conedera published a report detailing the military's involvement in human rights violations during his country's long and brutal civil war. Two days later, the elderly bishop was bashed to death.

I raise these two cases because they are reality checks. They remind us that human rights are not theoretical, they are life and death issues. There are women and men like Mr. Umaña and Msgr. Gerardi in every country: people, known and unknown, who have a sharp sense of right and wrong, who cannot be silent in the face of oppression and cannot live comfortably when others suffer. The

423

Declaration on Human Rights Defenders honors them and seeks to provide them a small measure of protection. However, I have no illusions: brave men and women will continue to pay a high price for their commitment to protect the vulnerable and oppose injustice.

My priority throughout this human rights year has been to rekindle some of the vision of 1948 in governments, in NGOs, in academic circles, and even in the jaded ranks of the media to develop the idea that this is a time for making some sober assessments and, on the basis of new understandings, to recommit ourselves to the principles of the Universal Declaration.

I find it strange that we use the language of "mechanisms and machinery" to describe the international community's efforts to improve respect for human rights. It is certainly not well-designed or well-oiled machinery. Unlike the Universal Declaration, which was adopted in one fluent and inspired effort, the human rights system since then has been built up through a series of slow, often painful, steps. The results are predictably uneven. Only one of the major human rights treaties has almost universal ratification—the Convention on the Rights of the Child; many governments which have ratified human rights treaties have failed or are late in reporting to the treaty bodies; Special Rapporteurs of the Commission on Human Rights are often ignored and excluded from countries they seek to visit, and the Commission itself is sometimes unable, for political or other reasons, to address urgent human rights issues.

Contributors to this book have rightly noted the shortcomings in the United Nation's human rights program. I share many of their concerns. Both the Commission on Human Rights and the Office of the High Commissioner have begun detailed reviews of the so-called "special procedures"—the system of working groups, special rapporteurs, and independent experts. The reviews are separate, but there will be close consultation and cooperation, ensuring that our efforts are consistent and complementary. The common aim is to develop a new consensus on how the Commission can effectively address both country specific situations and broader thematic concerns and to enhance the quality of our support for these measures.

At the same time, there will be a detailed review of the treaty body system with assistance from two universities—one from an industrialized country and one from a developing country. I have a particular concern to ensure not only the effectiveness of the mechanisms available to promote and protect human rights, but also that they complement and reinforce each other. These elements are essential objectives of the review process.

These initiatives acknowledge the need to revitalize our work in human rights both to discard what no longer works and take advantage of new possibilities. The agenda of the Commission itself is now in a process of change. Thankfully, the motivation isn't political but, in the words of Ambassador Jacob Selebi of South Africa who chaired the 54th session, "to have an agenda that reflects what is happening in the world today."

That is where we must focus rather than be caught up in the processes that take place in Geneva, New York, and diplomatic/academic gatherings around the world. One of the toughest challenges I set for myself when I arrived in Geneva as High Commissioner in September 1997 was to be a moral voice on behalf of victims. My motivation was the awareness of the gap between discussions in inter-governmental gatherings and the pain of people on the ground.

Ambassador Selebi's closing comments to the Commission on Human Rights eloquently highlighted this gap when he spoke of a young man, rendered stateless and with an uncertain future, who had visited Geneva and asked that the Commission do something about his own plight and that of more than one hundred thousand of his countrymen. Nothing was done and Ambassador Selebi reflected on his own sense of failure.

I carry many similar memories with me: of the sixteen-year-old girl rescued from forced prostitution in Cambodia and now wondering what her future might hold; in Rwanda, the women attempting to recover their lives shattered by the 1994 genocide and their continuing insecurity; and of my inability to provide for the starving children who reached out to me in Somalia.

My Office has just moved to the splendor of the Palais Wilson on the shores of Geneva's Lake Leman. While grateful to the Swiss authorities for their generosity, I want to be sure that we do not become comfortable, that we do not forget what our work is about. I am planning to install a flame at the entrance of the Palais Wilson—a flame that will be kept lit to remind all who visit and all who work there, that violations continue and that our work must be on behalf of the victims and aimed at preventing further violations.

Just two months after taking office last year, I spoke of a worry that many in the United Nations appeared to have "lost the plot" and allowed their work to answer to imperatives other than those set out in the UN Charter. I suggested that this distraction from the core principles of the Charter could be a root cause of much of the criticism that is leveled at the Organisation—couched in terms of complacency, of bureaucracy, of being out of touch, and, certainly, of being resistant to change.

Now there are changes which, as they are carried through, should set the United Nations system being driven by human rights principles—the principles of the Charter and of the Universal Declaration. I have termed this "regaining the lost purpose of the United Nations." Secretary-General Kofi Annan's leadership has been decisive in questioning the gap between the rhetoric and action on human rights; pointing out that, for the victims, most action comes too late; and stressing the role of human rights in preventing conflict, using reports to my Office, the Commissioner, and General Assembly as early warning and diagnostic tools.

There is a growing awareness of the human rights dimension of the United Nations' roles in economic development, in humanitarian assistance, in social and economic policy making, and in peace and security. The same message should be disseminated in Washington in the World Bank and International Monetary Fund—agencies which have tended to see their impacts solely in macroeconomic terms rather than in the realization of economic and social rights of people.

On another front, my Office receives requests virtually every week from countries looking for help in setting up national human rights institutions. When such institutions or commissions conform to the "Paris Principles" providing for their legislative or constitutional foundation, resourcing and independence, they can make a decisive contribution to promoting and protecting human rights where it matters most—at the country level. In Kampala, the members of the Ugandan Commission told me of their desire to open branch offices around the country so people could learn of their rights and know that there is a body empowered to ensure that those rights are respected. It takes courage and foresight for a government to set up such a body and, through its operation, take ownership of shortcomings across the full spectrum of human rights.

The great defenders of human rights have been the non-governmental organizations—some are famous while many others do valuable work with lower profiles. My Office is committed to building effective links with all of them. The United Nations human rights program is small and my plan is to keep it that way but to have an impact disproportionate to our size through effective partnerships with NGOs, with national institutions, with academic institutions, and others committed to the same principles.

The record of the past fifty years does not encourage any "business as usual" approach. Twice in this decade we have witnessed genocide. Rape has become a weapon of war. Torture, arbitrary detention, and disappearance remain commonplace. Hundreds of millions live in extreme poverty, suffering from malnutrition, disease, and a lack of hope. Many billions of dollars have been spent and much rhetoric expended for disturbingly little result. This massive failure of implementation shames us all.

What I am proposing, and working as High Commissioner to achieve, is a new partnership in which governments, the UN systems, NGOs, and broader civil society recognize their responsibilities in realizing human rights. Governments might talk about "internal affairs" but the reality is different: rights do not stop at borders. NGOs and civil society can raise their voices and do valuable grassroots work, but their work alone is insufficient.

I believe that such a partnership, globally and at national levels, is possible. It will come through a better understanding of what is meant by human rights. As High Commissioner I have a responsibility to bridge the gap in perceptions about human rights and foster a rights-based approach across the whole spectrum of civil, cultural, economic, political, and social rights, to enhance understanding of the right to development as the synthesis of other rights and to include women's rights as human rights.

The debate on human rights has not been helped by those who are partisans of one or more rights and who seek to deny the legitimacy of other rights, or by those who use human rights standards to judge and condemn others. When I said I would be the "voice of the victims" there was an expectation that the High Commissioner would become the "chief accuser" and I have been criticized for failing to take public positions on some cases. I will live with the criticism because my role needs to combine a judicious mix of public and private diplomacy. Its value, I hope, will be measured in enhanced protection for the victims and the vulnerable rather than in media coverage.

Finger pointing does not help build any new consensus on human rights. This can come only by genuine dialogue based on respect for the views of others and a willingness to listen and truly hear what is being said, across national boundaries and across differences in tradition and belief. There may not be universal models for implementing human rights standards, but there is recognition that the principles themselves are universal and the birthright of all people.

In the same spirit, my Office has begun public discussion of the use of benchmarks in economic, social, and cultural rights to explore various possibilities of measuring progress in the realization of rights that are too often regarded as ill-defined, fuzzy, and somehow not as legally "hard" as other human rights.

There is nothing ill-defined or fuzzy about being deprived of the basic human rights to food and clean water, clothing, housing, medical care, and some hope for security in old age. As for legal toughness, the simple fact is that the 138 governments which have ratified the International Covenant on Economic, Social and Cultural Rights have a legal obligation to ensure that their citizens enjoy these rights.

This raises some difficult policy decisions; difficult but not impossible. South Africa, for example, has now committed itself to providing clean drinking water within easy reach of all residences over the next five years. That is an important human rights policy objective and arguably a better use of scarce national resources than a new airport or new military aircraft.

The Universal Declaration might have been adopted in 1948 by only forty-eight states, but it was reaffirmed by 171 states in Vienna in 1993 who declared with admirable clarity that "all human rights are universal, indivisible and interdependent and inter-related. The international community must treat human rights globally in a fair and equal manner, on the same footing and with the same emphasis." There are countries with an exemplary record in civil and political rights who continue to neglect economic, social, or cultural rights of many of their people. And there are countries that have made great strides in economic and social rights, but have failed to make progress on civil and political rights. We do wrong to emphasize some rights and neglect others.

We should be on our guard against allowing the debate on human rights issues to be purely political and used as an arena to replace the East-West Cold War with an equally sterile North-South tension. This would be a betrayal of the hopes still alive for a better post-Cold War world and a betrayal of our responsibility to deliver on the promise of the Universal Declaration and the UN Charter for "social progress and better standards of life in larger freedom" for all.

There are practical challenges ahead and many have been suggested in this book. They deserve close consideration. When I spoke to the 54th Commission on Human Rights, I posed my own challenges, recognizing that some might be easier than others, but that all could be tackled, learning from successes and failures equally.

Challenges to Governments:

- to end violations against women, children, minorities, and migrants, and to end racial discrimination;
- to ratify international human rights treaties;
- to adopt national plans of human rights action and include human rights in national economic priority setting;
- to ensure human rights education for all;
- to establish national human rights institutions;
- to make progress toward eradicating poverty;
- to recognize and protect the cultural and other rights of indigenous and minority groups.

Challenges to NGOs and to individuals:

- to reinforce education and information on human rights;
- to develop wide partnerships and broader approaches for action on human rights;
- to alert governments and UN bodies to violations and dangers of violations;
- to make human rights and respect for human dignity a part of daily life.

I believe that most governments and certainly all sectors of civil society would agree that these points should be policy priorities for national and local administrations. In many ways the issues outlined above would, if implemented, serve to underpin any security policy and provide the basis for stable economic growth.

It has become fashionable to call such human rights policy imperatives "good governance." But we should not be shy about using the language of rights. It is the language of hope, of liberation, and of empowerment. It is language that emerged out of the horrors of the Holocaust, the atomic and fire bombings, starvation and sufferings of the two world wars, from a gathering in Paris fifty years ago of ordinary men and women prepared to offer humanity an extraordinary vision. They were people who believed that by working together, great change was possible. It is also, therefore, the emergence of responsibility to secure the rights of others.

This book, written and edited by individuals with their own strong commitment to human rights, is a welcome contribution to a new process of change and a valuable reminder of how much must be done if we are to bridge the gap between our rhetoric and the reality in the lives of many people on every continent. The diversity of the authors and their views is equally welcome—there is no one way to realize human rights. It is a field where every culture, every tradition, and every individual can make their own contribution.

Contributors

GUDMUNDUR ALFREDSSON, Candidatus juris (University of Iceland Law School, 1975), M.C.J. (New York University Law School, 1976) and S.J.D. (Harvard Law School, 1982). The author worked with the UN Secretariat 1983-95, most of that time at the Centre for Human Rights in Geneva. He is now Co-Director and Professor at the Raoul Wallenberg Institute for Human Rights and Humanitarian Law, University of Lund, Sweden.

S. JAMES ANAYA is Professor of Law at the University of Iowa. Since early 1997 he has been on leave from the University of Iowa to serve as Special Counsel to the Indian Law Resource Center, a U.S.-based non-governmental organization with consultative status at the United Nations. Professor Anaya received his B.A. from the University of New Mexico (1980) and his J.D. from Harvard (1983). He has been a consultant for numerous organizations and government agencies in several countries on matters of human rights and indigenous peoples, and he has represented indigenous groups from many parts of North and Central America before courts and international organizations. Professor Anaya has been a visiting professor at Harvard Law School, the University of Toronto, and the University of Tulsa. His teaching and research interests include international law and organizations, indigenous peoples, and human rights. Among his numerous publications is his book, *Indigenous Peoples in International Law* (Oxford University Press, 1996).

RUSSEL LAWRENCE BARSH was at the United Nations from 1981 to 1993 representing the Mikmaq Nation, coordinating Four Directions Council (an organization of North American indigenous peoples in consultative status with ECOSOC and the ILO) and writing technical studies for the UN Centre for Human Rights, UNDP, and the UN Centre on Transnational Corporations. He is currently Associate Professor of Native American Studies at the University of Lethbridge in Alberta, Canada, where he directs the Strategic Network for Indigenous Peoples, an information exchange project focusing on corporate investment and development practices. His book, *Effective Negotiation by Indigenous Peoples* (written with Krisma Bastien) is available in both English and Spanish editions from the ILO.

431

GRAZIANO BATTISTELLA holds a degree in political science, and director of the Scalabrini Migration Center in Quezon City, Philippines, and editor of the *Asian and Pacific Migration Journal* and *Asian Migrant*. Before working in the Philippines, he was in Italy and in the United States. While in New York, he participated in the working group of the United Nations that drafted the Migrant Workers Convention. He has organized the Philippine Migrants Rights Watch—a network of NGOs dedicated to the protection of migrants—and is a member of the International Migrants Rights Watch Committee.

JAMAL BENOMAR was a prisoner of conscience for eight years in Morocco and was held incommunicado, handcuffed, blindfolded, and tortured for nearly a year. He has an interdisciplinary background in development studies, economics, political science, and international human rights law. He holds degrees from the University of Rabat (Morocco), Sorbonne (Paris), and a doctorate from the University of London. He was an associate researcher and lecturer at the University of Paris, Africa specialist at the international headquarters of Amnesty International (London), Director of Human Rights Programs at The Carter Center of Emory University (Atlanta), and Head of technical cooperation at the OHCHR, (UN Geneva). He worked as senior consultant to UNDP, USAID, DANIDA, and other international agencies on issues concerning human rights, rule of law, governance, and development cooperation.

SUSANA CHIAROTTI BOERO, Argentinean, lawyer. Director of the Institute of Gender, Law and Development in Rosario, Argentina. Regional Coordinator of CLADEM (The Latin American and Caribbean Committee for the Defense of Women's Rights). Susana has worked in human rights and women's organizations in Bolivia and Argentina. She has participated in many international conferences, seminars and forums on human rights and women's rights. She is a visiting professor in the Master's Degree Program in Gender at the National University of Rosario, where she coordinated a seminar on gender and legislation. Susana integrates the team of Professors at the annual international seminar, "Human Rights of Women," held in Lima, Peru. She has several publications.

EUGENE B. BRODY, M.D., was President of WFMH, 1981-1983 and has been its Secretary General since then. He is also Professor and Chairman Emeritus of Psychiatry, University of Maryland, Visiting Professor of Psychiatry, Harvard, and Editor-in-Chief, *Journal of Nervous and Mental Disease*.

ANDREW CLAPHAM is Associate Professor of Public International law at the Graduate Institute of International Studies in Geneva. He teaches international human rights law and public international law. From 1991 to 1997 he was the Representative of Amnesty International at the United Nations in New York and he dealt in particular with issues relating to the Security Council, peace keeping, human rights field operations, and the new High Commissioner for Human Rights. His publications include *Human Rights and the European Community: A Critical Overview* (1991) and *Human Rights in the Private Sphere* (1993).

ROGER S. CLARK, a New Zealander by birth, has taught International Law and Criminal Law at Rutgers Law School, Camden, New Jersey, since 1972 where he is currently a Board of Governors Professor. He is a graduate of Victoria University of Wellington, in New Zealand and of Columbia University School of Law. Between 1987 and 1990, he was a member of the former U.N. Committee on Crime Prevention and Control. In 1995-96, he represented the Government of Samoa in the International Court of Justice in the Advisory Proceedings on the Legality of the Threat or Use of Nuclear Weapons. He also represented Samoa at the Preparatory Committee on the Establishment of an International Criminal Court and at the United Nations Diplomatic Conference of Plenipotentiaries in Rome in June/July 1998 when the Statute of the Court was finalized.

SHANTHI DAIRIAM is the founder and director of the International Women's Rights Action Watch—Asia Pacific, which is a collaborative non-governmental regional programme aimed at facilitating the implementation of the UN Convention on the Elimination of All Forms of Discrimination against Women. She has been an activist for around twenty years promoting women's rights through law and policy reform and creating scholarships to bring about the domestic application of international human rights norms for the achievement of women's rights. Areas of special interest and experience are mainstreaming women's interests into national development plans, reproductive rights, and violence against women.

YAEL DANIELI is a clinical psychologist (Ph.D., New York University) in private practice in New York City; traumatologist, victimologist; co-founder and Director, Group Project for Holocaust Survivors and their Children; Co-founder, past-President and United Nations Representative of the International Society for Traumatic Stress Studies; former UN Representative, World Federation for Mental Health. Integrates treatment, care, worldwide multidisciplinary study, extensive publishing, teaching/training, expert consulting, and advocacy for the rights of victims/ survivors of crime and abuse of power. Additional degrees in music and philosophy. Editor, *International Responses to Traumatic Stress* and *International Handbook of Multigenerational Legacies of Trauma*.

JULIA TAVARES DE ALVAREZ has been an Ambassador, Alternate Permanent Representative of the Dominican Republic to the United Nations since 1978. She was a member of the Committee that drafted the International Plan of Action on Ageing and chaired the Working Group responsible for drafting the United Nations Principles for Older Persons. She introduced the resolution proclaiming October 1st the International Day of Older Persons and the "Proclamation on Ageing" which, inter alia, called for the launching of the International Year of Older Persons in 1999. In 1989 she received a testimonial from the United Nations "in grateful recognition of dedicated service in support of the United Nations Programme on Ageing."

LEANDRO DESPOUY is a specialist in Public International Law, with wide experience in Human Rights and Humanitarian Law. He was Director of Human

Rights in the Ministry of Foreign Affairs of Argentina during President Alfonsin's Government (1983-1989), in which he held the rank of Ambassador. For twelve years, he was Expert in the UN Sub-Committee of Human Rights, over which he presided in 1987 and in which he was Special Rapporteur of various subjects, among them "The Protection of Human Rights during State of Siege or Exception" (E/CN.4Sub.2/1997/19) and the "Report of Human Rights and Disabled Persons," Publications United Nations Series of Studies Number G. During 1993/1994 he was Assistant to the Representative of the Secretary General of the United Nations and OAS in Haiti.

CLARENCE J. DIAS is the President of the International Center for Law in Development, which is a Third World NGO concerned with human rights in the development process. He holds doctoral degrees in law from Bombay University and Cornell University and has taught at Boston College of Law School and at the Department of Law of the University of Bombay. He has practiced law before the High Court of Bombay and has considerable public interest experience. He has published extensively and his books include *Industrial Hazards in a Transnational World, Legal Professions in the Third World,* and *The International Context of Rural Poverty in the Third World.*

M. ADAMA DIENG, Senegalese jurist, is Secretary-General of the International Commission of Jurists (ICJ). He has been a consultant for UNESCO, UNITAR, the Agence de Coopération culturelle et technique, the International Committee of the Red Cross, the UN Centre for Human Rights, the South-South Commission, the European Commission, and the African Commission for Human and Peoples' Rights. He is a member of the Board of the International Institute of Human Rights (René-Cassin Institute), Member of the Council of the International Institute of Humanitarian Law and Board Member of International IDEA (Institute for Democracy and Electoral Assistance). He authored many publications on International Human Rights Law and Humanitarian Law.

JULIE DORF is the founding Executive Director of the International Gay & Lesbian Human Rights Commission (IGLHRC), a non-governmental organization based in the United States. IGLHRC's mission is to protect and advance the human rights of all people and communities subject to discrimination or abuse on the basis of sexual orientation, gender identity, and HIV-sero-status through documentation, advocacy, coalition building, public education, and technical assistance.

BRIAN ENGDAHL, Ph.D., is a counseling psychologist at the U.S. Department of Veterans Affairs Medical Center in Minneapolis, Minnesota. He received his Ph.D. in 1980 from the University of Minnesota, Minneapolis, where he is also a clinical associate professor. He has received awards for service to former prisoners of war (POWs) and victims of torture. Clinically, he cares for combat veterans, POWs, and veterans with spinal cord and brain injuries. His research focuses on sleep disturbances, brain function, and the diagnosis of posttraumatic stress disorder among trauma survivors.

MALGORZATA FUSZARA, Professor, Director of the Institute of Applied Social Sciences, University of Warsaw, Director of the Gender Studies Program, member of advisory board of "Signs. Journal of Women in Culture and Society," co-author of draft of legislation "Equal Status Act." She is author of over forty articles, e.g., *Will Abortion Issues Give Birth to Feminism in Poland?, The Law— A Special or Normal State?, Sociology of Law in Poland, Legal Regulation of Abortion in Poland, Does the Law Protect Women in Poland?, The Effects of Divorce in the Opinions of The Divorced, The Activities of Family Courts in Poland, Women's Movements in Poland;* and two books: *Codzienne konflikty i odswietna sprawiedliwosc (Everyday conflicts and festive justice)* and *Rodzina w sadzie (Family in Court).*

HUGO GARCIA GARCILAZO, Argentine, blind since childhood, attorney at law since 1958. He is former Chief of the Social and Legal Service of the Social Welfare Department in Buenos Aires (1965-1975); former Chief of the National Service of Rehabilitation and Training of the Blind, Argentina (1975-1978); coordinator of the National Braille Press and Talking Book (since 1992, still holding that post), Argentina; co-founder and former Secretary-General of the Argentine Federation of Institutions for the Blind (1965-1970); co-founder and former president of the Argentine Association for the Study of Blindness and Visual Impairments (1971-1980); co-founder and Secretary-General of the Argentine Coordinating Body of Institutions Concerning Disability (1987-1989); former Secretary of Disabled People's International and at the same time former Latin America Regional President (1985-1990). UN expert for the Evaluation Meeting on the Mid-term of the UN Decade of Disabled Persons (Sweden, 1987); UN expert in the Meeting on Human Resources Development in the Field of Education for the Disabled Persons (Tallyn, Estonia, 1989).

MICHAEL GRODIN, M.D., FAAP, is Director of the Law, Medicine, and Ethics Program and Professor of Health Law, Philosophy, Medicine and Management in the Boston University Schools of Public Health, Medicine, Management and the College of Arts and Sciences. His books include *The Nazi Doctors and the Nuremberg Code: Human Rights in Human Experimentation, Children as Research Subjects: Science, Ethics and Law* and *Meta Medical Ethics: The Philosophical Foundation of Bioethics.* He is the co-founder of Global Lawyers and Physicians.

HURST HANNUM is Professor of International Law at The Fletcher School of Law and Diplomacy of Tufts University, where he teaches courses in international organizations, international human rights law, and nationalism and ethnicity. From 1980 to 1989, he served as Executive Director of The Procedural Aspects of International Law Institute, in Washington, D.C., and he was a Jennings Randolph Peace Fellow of the United States Institute of Peace in 1989-90. Professor Hannum has served as counsel in cases before the European and Inter-American Commissions on Human Rights and the United Nations; he also has been a member of the boards of several international human rights organizations, including Amnesty International-USA, the International Human Rights Law Group, Survival International-USA, and the International Service for Human Rights.

VINCENT IACOPINO, M.D., Ph.D., a specialist in internal medicine, is Senior Medical Consultant for Physicians for Human Rights (PHR). Dr. Iacopino has represented PHR in medical fact-finding investigations to Thailand, Punjab, Kashmir, Turkey, and South Africa and documented violations of medical neutrality, evidence of torture, extra-judicial executions and other abuses. Dr. Iacopino teaches Health and Human Rights at the University of California, Berkeley School of Public Health. From 1992 to 1997, Dr. Iacopino was Medical Director of Survivors International of Northern California, a non-profit organization providing medical and psychological assistance to survivors of torture from around the world.

MEL JAMES is International Liaison officer at the Law Society of England and Wales and Secretary of its International Human Rights Working Party. She previously worked as Advisor on International Organizations at Amnesty International's Secretariat.

JAMES JARANSON, M.D., M.A., M.P.H., is Director of Medical Services and Research at the Center for Victims of Torture in Minneapolis, Minnesota, and Director of the Cultural Psychiatry Training Program at the University of Minnesota, Medical School, where he holds a faculty appointment in the Department of Psychiatry. He founded the International Mental Health Program in the Psychiatry Department of St. Paul-Ramsey Medical Center (Regions Hospital) in St. Paul, Minnesota, represents North America on the International Council for Torture Victims, Co-Chairs the Section on the Psychological Consequences of Torture and Persecution of the World Psychiatric Association, and is a steering committee member of the Society for the Study of Psychiatry and Culture.

MARIANNE KASTRUP, M.D., Ph.D., is Medical Director of the Rehabilitation Centre for Torture Victims, Copenhagen, Denmark. Clinically, she cares for survivors of torture who have obtained asylum in Denmark. She is a member of the WHO Expert Advisory Board on Mental Health. She is currently a member of the Executive Committee of the World Psychiatric Association and chairs the International Committee to Review the Abuse of Psychiatry. She is Vice-President of the International Federation of Psychiatric Epidemiology and member of the Executive Committee of the European Association of Psychiatrists.

MILOON KOTHARI is Convener of the Housing and Land Rights Committee of the Habitat International Coalition (HIC) and co-ordinator of the HIC global campaigns on housing rights and against forced evictions. Since 1991 he has represented HIC at UN human rights bodies in Geneva. He was the founder and Co-Director of the Centre on Housing Rights and Evictions (COHRE) from 1991 to 1997 and the Joint Convener from 1988 to 1994 of the Indian National Campaign for Housing Rights (NCHR). In his various capacities within HIC, he is working closely with community groups and campaigns on housing rights and forced evictions in India, Palestine, Israel, and the United States to promote the housing and land rights approach and to apply international human rights law in local and national situations.

IAN MARTIN is a Fellow of the Human Rights Centre at the University of Essex, United Kingdom. He was Secretary-General of Amnesty International from 1986 to 1992. Since then he has worked for the United Nations as Director for Human Rights of the United Nations/Organization of American States (UN/OAS) International Civilian Mission in Haiti; as Chief of the UN Human Rights Field Operation in Rwanda; and as Special Adviser to the UN High Commissioner for Human Rights.

IRENE MELUP served as Senior Crime Prevention and Criminal Justice Officer in the UN Crime Prevention and Criminal Justice Programme, responsible for the work on victims of crime and abuse of power. She was involved in the development and adoption of the UN Declaration on victims, and the efforts to promote its application. She is the recipient of several awards, including the von Hentig Prize, from the World Society of Victimology. She is a member of the International Scientific and Professional Advisory Council of the UN crime programme and author of numerous reports.

VITIT MUNTARBHORN is a Professor at the Faculty of Law, Chulalongkorn University, Bangkok. He was formerly Special Rapporteur of the UN Human Rights Commission (on the sale of children) and executive director of Child Rights ASIANET. He has published widely. His publications include Annual Reports for the UN Human Rights Commission (1990-1994); *The Status of Refugees in Asia* (Oxford: Clarendon Press); *Sexual Exploitation of Children* (New York/Geneva/UN); *A Sourcebook for Reporting Under the Convention on the Rights of the Child* (Bangkok: UNICEF/ASIANET).

BACRE WALY NDIAYE is currently Director of the New York Office of the United Nations High Commissioner for Human Rights. From 1992 to 1998, he was Special Rapporteur of the UN Human Rights Commission on extrajudicial, summary, or arbitrary executions. Among his numerous other UN assignments, he has served as a member of the Truth and Justice Commission in Haiti. He received his law degree from the University of Dakar, Senegal. He founded the Senegalese section of Amnesty International, and was Vice President of Amnesty's International Executive Committee. He has published numerous articles in the field of Human Rights Law.

B. G. RAMCHARAN is a Director in the Department of Political Affairs in the United Nations. Prior to this, for twenty-five years he was in legal posts in the UN, including human rights, Office of the Secretary-General, and with peace negotiations in the conflict in the former Yugoslavia. He received his L.L.M. and Ph.D. in Law at the University of London, and is a Barrister-at-Law (Lincoln's Inn) and Attorney-at-Law in his native Guyana. Since 1988, he has been

Adjunct Professor of Human Rights Law at Colombia University in New York. He has published over a dozen books and numerous articles in the field of international law.

MARTA SANTOS PAIS is currently the Director of the Division of Evaluation, Policy and Planning in UNICEF, where she has specific responsibilities for human rights and child rights policy and monitoring issues. A national of Portugal, she is a lawyer whose previous positions included providing legal and human rights advice to several government Ministers as well as to the Portuguese Delegation to the UN General Assembly and other UN high-level meetings. Active in the drafting of the Convention of the Rights of the Child, Ms. Santos Pais was elected in 1991 to be a member and Rapporteur of the UN expert Committee on the Rights of the Child. In this role, she accepted considerable responsibility for the analytical and policy work of the Committee, as well as the preparation of many of its documents. She is the author of several articles and publications in the field of children's rights.

SUSANNAH SIRKIN is Deputy Director of Physicians for Human Rights (PHR). She has held this position since 1987. Ms. Sirkin has organized medical human rights investigations to dozens of countries, including PHR's exhumations of mass graves in the former Yugoslavia and Rwanda for the International Criminal Tribunals. She has authored and edited numerous reports and articles on the medical consequences of human rights violations, physical evidence of human rights abuses, and physician complicity in violations. Previously, Ms. Sirkin was Director of Membership Programs for Amnesty International USA.

ELSA STAMATOPOULOU is Deputy to the Director, New York Office of the UN High Commissioner for Human Rights. She has been with the UN since 1979, seventeen years in the human rights area. Previous positions include as Senior Legal Advisor to the UN Under-Secretary-General for Management and Chief of the New York Office of the UN Centre for Human Rights. Co-founder of Children's Forum 21, Member of the International Advisory Board of the International Training Center of Indigenous Peoples. Specialization includes the rights of indigenous peoples, women, children, human rights education, institution-building and civil society. Law degree, Athens University, masters studies in the administration of justice, Northeastern University, doctoral studies in international law, IUHEI University of Geneva.

MARIA STAVROPOULOU completed her law studies at the Athens Law School and obtained her first LL.M. from the University of London and her second LL.M. from Harvard Law School. Since 1990 she has been working in the field of refugee and human rights law, first as attorney at the Greek Council for Refugees, later at the UN Centre for Human Rights and currently as protection officer with UNHCR in Athens.

MARIA SUAREZ TORO is a Puerto Rican and Costa Rican feminist, teacher, and women's human rights activist. Currently she is a producer of the radio program FIRE: Feminist International Radio Endeavor. For FIRE, she has covered the actions and activities of the international women's movement at every major United Nations Conference of the decade. She was formerly Coordinator of the Human Rights Popular Education Secretariat at the Central American Human Rights Commission. From 1976 to 1988, she taught adult literacy in Honduras, Costa Rica, Nicaragua, and El Salvador and from 1974 to 1982 she was a professor at the University of Costa Rica School of Education. She holds a Masters Degree from The State University of New York at Albany.

LEE SWEPSTON is chief of the Equality and Human Rights Coordination Branch of the International Labour Office. A graduate of the University of North Carolina at Chapel Hill and of Columbia Law School, he is the author of numerous works on human rights, rights of the child and indigenous and tribal peoples.

JANUSZ SYMONIDES is Professor of International Law and International Relations; former Vice-Chancellor of Nicolaus Copernicus University, Torun, Poland (1969-1974); and former Director of the Polish Institute of International Relations, Warsaw, Poland (1980-1987). He was Distinguished Scholar-in-Residence at the Institute of East-West Studies, New York, USA (1987-1989). Since 1989, he is Director of the Division of Human Rights, Democracy and Peace, UNESCO. He has published more than 400 articles and books on human rights, international law, peace and security. He is a member of many scientific, editorial boards and professional associations.

DAVID TOLBERT is Senior Legal Adviser, Registry in the International Criminal Tribunal for the former Yugoslavia. He previously served as Chief, General Legal Division in the United Nations Relief and Works Agency in Vienna, Austria. He has taught international law in the United Kingdom and was a practicing attorney for a number of years in the United States. He received a B.A., *magna cum laude,* from Furman University, a J.D. from the University of North Carolina and an LL.M., *with distinction,* from the University of Nottingham. He has published several articles on the work of the International Tribunal and on International Environmental Law.

HEATHER A. THUYNSMA, B.A. (Hons), although her interests and publications concern political science and strategy, has spearheaded the Johannesburg-based *Institute for Human Rights Education's* (IHRE) innovative educational approach. As Projects Co-ordinator of the IHRE she has created and produced the **RIGHTS** *Radio* audio cassette programme and helped develop the human rights component for South Africa's primary level Life Skills learning programme.

PETER N. THUYNSMA, Ph.D., is presently executive director of the Institute for Human Rights Education in Johannesburg, South Africa. He is listed as a member of the UN High Commissioner for Human Rights (Geneva) *Roster of*

Experts, and is a former professor of African Literature at the University of the Witwatersrand, Johannesburg.

THEO VAN BOVEN is Professor of Law, University of Maastricht, Netherlands; member of the Committee on the Elimination of Racial Discrimination of the United Nations; former Special Rapporteur of the United Nations Sub-Commission on the Right to Restitution, Compensation and Rehabilitation for Victims of Gross Violations of Human Rights and Fundamental Freedoms (1990-1993); former Director of the United Nations Division of Human Rights (1977-1982).

ALWINE A. DE VOS VAN STEENWIJK left a career in diplomacy in 1961 to join Father Joseph Wresinski, founder of the International Movement ATD Fourth World. With him, she attained international recognition for the Movement. She created the Institute for Research and Training in Human Relations, through which Father Joseph initiated a new kind of research on poverty in France and later in Europe and around the world. Today, Ms. de Vos is the President of the International Movement ATD Fourth World.

Index